TANTRA IN BENGAL

TANTRA IN BENGAL

A Study in its Origin, Development and Influence

S.C. BANERJI

MANOHAR
2026

First published 1978
Second revd. and enl. edn. 1992
Reprinted 2026

ISBN 978-81-85425-63-4

Published by
Ajay Kumar Jain *for*
Manohar Publishers & Distributors
4753/23 Ansari Road, Daryaganj
New Delhi 110 002

Printed at
Replika Press Pvt. Ltd.

Contents

PREFACE TO THE FIRST EDITION

Bengal (both West Bengal and Bangladesh taken together) may or may not have been the original home of Tantras, as believed by some scholars. The fact, however, remains that in this region, many Tantras, Hindu and Buddhistic, were written. Tantra permeated the soil of Bengal; it became the warp and woof of the cultural fabric of this province. It influenced the life and literature of the Bengalis very intimately. Its appeal to the mass was so great and pervasive that many folk-songs contained Tāntric elements. Mother Kālī, introduced by Tāntra, is a household word in Bengal.

Aspects of Bengal Tantra have been studied. But, there is not a single book which gives a connected account of its origin, development and impact on Bengali culture. It is to remove this want that the present work has been planned.

We have studied this literature against the social and religious background.

While prolixity has been avoided, care has been taken to see that no important information on the subject is left out.

We have tried to examine the extent to which Bengal Tantra breaks away from the orthodox Brāhmanical religion, but puts judicious curbs on self-indulgence that disfigures many Tāntric rites, and appears to be indecent to cultured people.

Of the appendices, one gives a list of Bengal Tantras hitherto unpublished. In fact, these outnumber the published ones. In one appendix we have collected the names of authors and works, cited in Bengal Tantra. This will show the range and variety of the literature utilised in it.

One may miss insights in this work, into the high philosophy of Tantra as provided by Woodroffe. The author's main object is to give a connected and sustained account of the origin, development and influence of Bengal Tantra. Nevertheless, philosophy of Bengal Tantra has been set forth in chapter IX. The philosophy of Tantra in general has been outlined briefly in chapter I. One may find the author's permissiveness of the *Vāma Mārga* a little excessive. Bhāsa, a renowned pre-Kālīdāsa dramatist, approved the way of the Tāntric devotees. Thus, there was, even in remote antiquity, a marked tendency of approbation of *Vāmācāra* in Tantras. So, our treatment of it does not amount to special pleading for this Tāntric way.

In two appendices, we have set forth the Bengal works, particularly on Smṛti and Vaiṣṇavism, citing Tántras. This will show the extent to which Tantra in general and Bengal Tantra in particular influenced the Bengali culture even in medieval times.

S.C. Banerji

PREFACE TO THE SECOND EDITION

It is heartening to note that the first edition of this work has been sold out in course of a few years.

The scope of this work has been set forth in the Preface to the first edition. Considerable new information regarding some Tāntric texts of Bengal and the influence of Tantra on the cultural life of this province has been incorporated in the new edition. The Glossary and Bibliography have been supplemented .

As regards abbreviations used in the Notes, we do not give a list; because, all these have been explained under Select Bibliography.

The labours of the author will be amply repaid if this work can apprise the readers of the history of Tantra in Bengal, and of the pervasive influence of this Śāstra on the life and literature of this province.

S.C. Banerji
77A, Golf Club Road,
Calcutta–33

New Year's Day,
1398 B.S.

I. Tantra:
General Remarks

Meaning of 'Tantra'

Various meanings of the term have been suggested:

(i) Essence of a thing (Śatapatha Brāhmaṇa).

(ii) A special set of doctrines, practices, mystic syllables, occultism, etc.

(iii) Derived from root *tan*, it means that which spreads or extends knowledge.

(iv) Derived from the above root, it means a Śāstra which dilates upon *Tattvas* and *Mantras*.

(v) Derived from *tanu* (body), it is so called as it saves the body by yogic practices.

(vi) Derived from root *trai* (to save), it means a Śāstra which saves its followers.

(vii) Derived by some from root *tantri* (to explain) or *tatri* (to understand) *Āgama* is divided into three classes—*Tantra, Yāmala* and *Ḍāmara*. These are called respectively *Sāttvika, Rājasika* and *Tāmasika*.

In another way, Tantras have been divided into five *Āmnāyas*. According to some Tantras (e.g. *Śaktisaṃgama*), *Āmnāyas* are six. The word '*Āmnāya*' may be taken to denote a zone of culture.

Again, Tantras are divided into four regional schools, viz. Kerala, Kāśmīra, Gauḍa and Vilāsa. Those of the last class are stated to be current everywhere in India.

According to the *Brahmayāmala*, in accordance with *srota* (current of thought?) Tantras are divided into three classes, viz. *Dakṣiṇa* (with *Sattvaguṇa* as dominant), *Vāma* (with preponderance of *Rajas*) and *Madhyama* (with *Tamas* as dominant).

According to H.P.Sastri 'Tantra' means shortening; it seeks to shorten *mantras* which would otherwise be very long.

Classification of Tantra

Tantra is often used to denote the three classes of works, viz. *Saṃhitā, Āgama* and *Tantra* of the Vaiṣṇavas, Śaivas and Śāktas respectively. *Saṃhitā, Āgama* and *Tantra* mean respectively collection, tradition and a set of doctrines or a book. The terms do not divide the three into watertight compartments. For example the Vaiṣṇava *Padma-saṃhitā* is also called *Padma-tantra*. Again, *Pañcarātra-āgama*, which is a Saivite work, is referred to as *Pañcarātra-saṃhitā*.

Tāntric works are also classified as *Āgama* and *Nigama*. Generally, the contents of these works are represented as dialogues between Śiva and Pārvatī. Those works, in the form of Pārvatī's questions and Śiva's answers are designated as *Āgama*. *Nigama* indicates those works in which this process is reversed.

According to a Tantra, India has been broadly divided into three well-marked regions,[1] viz.,

(i) Viṣṇukrānta : from the Vindhya hill up to Java in the Far East.

(ii) Rathakrānta : from the above hill to the north comprising Nepal and Mahācīna.

(iii) Aśvakrānta or Gajakrānta : from that hill to the west including Persia, Egypt and Rhodesia. In a later edition of the work, it includes the land from the above hill up to Kanyākumārī in the south.

The extent and boundaries of these regions are controversial. According to their origin in the above places, the Tantras are divided into three classes; there is difference of opinion about the places of origin of the particular works. Sixty-four Tantras are believed to belong to each of these classes.[2]

Tantras are popularly divided into two categories, viz. *Sadāgama* and *Asadāgama* i.e. good and bad *Āgamas*. There is a controversy about which of the works are *sat* and which *asat*; generally the work, in which the worship accords with practice or custom is *sat*; the reverse is *asat*.

Tantras are also divided as *āstika* or Vedic and *nāstika* or non-Vedic. In accordance with the predominance of the deity the *Āstika* works are again divided as *Śākta*, *Śaiva*, *Saura*, *Gāṇapatya* and *Vaiṣṇava*. The *Śākta* Tantras are divided into ten classes according to the names of ten Mahāvidyās. Of these, the *Ṣoḍaśītantra* is known as Śrīvidyā.

Srotas, *Piṭha* and *Āmnāya* are three other classes into which the Tantra literature is divided.[3]

Tantras are further divided as Hindu and non-Hindu. The non-Hindu works are those of the Buddhists[4] and the Jainas. Both these belong to the above *Nāstika* class.

A classification of Tantras is based on the mythological ages, e.g. Varāhakalpa, Kālakalpa, etc. A further classification is made in accordance with their origin from the different mouths (and their different positions) of Śiva.

Another mode of classification is into *Kālīkula* and *Śrīkula*. The former attaches the greatest importance to the cult of Kālī. To this school belong the *Mahākālasaṃhitā*, *Jayad-ratha-saṃhita*, *Uttaratantra*, *Śaktisaṃgama-tantra* (Kālīkhaṇḍa). The followers of this school are purely monist. According to them, Śakti and Brahman are identical; Śiva-Śakti is beyond dualism.

According to the latter, Śiva is both the efficient and material cause of the world. The atomic elements, with which the individual souls and the material world are composed, are produced by His Śakti. The followers of this school look upon Śakti as *Vimarśinī* or Śiva's natural vibrating power. Thus, they have a leaning towards the Viśiṣṭādvaita view of Rāmānuja.

A further division of Tantra is into *Kādimata* or *Kālīmata*, *Hādimata* and *Kahādimata*, mentioned in the *Śaktisaṃgama Tantra*. In the first school, the theoretical doctrines use the letter *KA* as their symbol. It was popular in Gauḍa region or Bengal (*Śaktisaṃgama*, Tārākhaṇḍa, Lviii. 81-82, Kālīkhaṇḍa, V.24-26).

The second school is so called as it uses *HA* as the symbol of Śiva (Ibid, Tara, Lviii. 81).

The third school is also called *Tāriṇīmata*.

It is stated that, according to *Kādimata*, *Mahāśakti* is called Tripurā in Kerala, Tāriṇī in Kashmir and Kālī in Gauḍa. According to *Hādimata*, She is called Kāli in Kerala, Tripurā in Kashmir and Tārā in Gauḍa.

Tantras—*Raison d'etre*

The question that naturally arises is—what are the causes that led to the composition of these works when so many Brahmanical *Śāstras* existed? The Vedas and the works which followed them were too abstruse for the common people. The Brahmanical philosophical systems were too recondite for them. The ritualistic works provided for rites and rituals which were too elaborate, and required rigorous discipline and meticulous performance of details. The result was that they failed to satisfy the cravings of the people preoccupied with various worldly matters. The Brahmanical works denied the personal right of important religious performances to Śūdras, particularly to women not only of the Śūdra caste but also of the higher castes.

Thus the need was gradually felt for easier works inculcating doctrines more intelligible to the common man, prescribing less complicated practices and giving freedom of religious performances to Śūdras and women. The result was the formulation of Tantras. These are not deliberately hostile to the Veda, but hold that the precepts and practices, contained in the Veda, are too difficult for our age. In rendering religious practices easier, the Tantras allow a person to follow his natural inclination, e.g. drinking of wine, enjoyment of women etc. The human body has been regarded by these works as a microcosm; these seek to inculcate the belief that whatsoever is in the universe is in the body itself. In other words, what is not in the body does not exist in the universe.[5] These works lay stress on utilising the body as the best means of *sādhanā*. According to them, the body contains the highest power which, if properly utilised, can lead the *sādhaka* to the highest goal; it can enable him to control the universal energy.[6] This Śakti, called *Kulakuṇḍalinī*, is realised by the *Sādhaka* as a serpent coiling in the middle part of the body.

The authors of Tantras may have been prompted to compose these works by a desire to attract the common folk when the latter were embracing the popular religion of Buddhism. The common man was naturally prone to sexual intercourse, fond of wine, meat, etc. So, they were allowed the use of *pañca makāras* and were told that thus they could attain liberation.

Subject-matter of Tantras

The *Vārāhī-tantra* sets forth the contents of the different classes of Tāntric works as follows:

Āgama: sṛṣṭi, pralaya, devapūjā, sādhana, puraścaraṇa, ṣaṭkarma, (māraṇa,uccāṭana, stambhana, vaśīkaraṇa, vidveṣaṇa, śānti).

Yāmala: sṛṣṭi, jyotiṣa, ākhyāna, nityakarma, kramasūtra, varṇabheda, jātibheda, yugadharma.

Tantra: sṛṣṭi, pratisṛṣṭi, tantra-nirṇaya, devatākṛti, tīrtha, āśrama, Brāhmaṇa, prāṇilakṣaṇa, yantra, devotpatti, kalpavṛkṣa, jyotiṣa, purāṇākhāyna, kośa, vrata, śaucāśauca, naraka, haracakra, strīpuruṣalakṣaṇa, rājadharma, dānadharma, yugadharma, vyavahāravidhi, adhyātma-varṇanā, etc.

The subject-matter of a complete Tantric work may be broadly divided as follows:

1. *Jñāna*: knowledge including philosophical and metaphysical doctrines with a monotheistic tendency and sometimes a monistic bias. It contains occultism including a knowledge of the mystic powers of letters, syllables, formulae and figures.

2. *Yoga*: means of controlling the mind, especially for acquiring magic powers.

3. *Kriyā*: containing instructions for making idols and constructing and consecrating temples.

4. *Caryā*: rules about rites, festivals and social duties. The contents of each of the Tantric works cannot be clearly divided into the above classes. These four represent a broad spectrum of the subject-matter of the works of these classes. Regarding worship, Tantra recognises three aspects of the deity worshipped by a devotee, viz. *sthūla* (image), *sūkṣma* (mantra) and *parā* (highest, to be realised by the mind alone).

Broadly speaking, the Tantra literature has two-aspects: one philosophical and spiritual, and the other popular and practical. The latter contains *magic, mantra, mudrā, maṇḍala, nyāsa, cakra, yantra,* etc. Tantra aims at two things, viz. liberation and *Siddhis* (power).

The features, distinguishing Tantras from other religious works in Sanskrit, are briefly as follows:

The assurance of the acquisition of superhuman powers, the realisation of the Supreme Principle within a brief period, emphasis on the worship of the goddess with *makāras* alone as ensuring the desired result, peculiar rites with *mantras*, *bījas* (apparently meaningless mystic syllables), *nyāsas, mudrās, cakras, yantras* and such other things. The basic difference between orthodox religious works and Tantras is that, while the former emphasise renunciation (*tyāga*), the latter allow enjoyment (*bhoga*) as means to the end.

Internal Components of Human Body

Kośas: The body, regarded as a microcosm[7], is believed to have the following within it:

The body consists of five *Kośas* or sheaths. These are: (i) *annamaya* — made of food, (ii) *prāṇamaya* — consisting of vital breath, (iii) *manomaya* — made of mind, (iv) *Vjñānamaya* — consisting of special consciousness, (v) *ānandamaya* — consisting of joy.

Nāḍīs

According to some Tantras, the human body contains three crores and a half, according to others, 72,000 nāḍīs (veins and arteries). Of these, fourteen are the principal ones. Of these fourteen again, the most prominent are *Iḍā*, *Piṅgalā* and *Suṣumṇā*. The last, the longest one, extends from the *mūlādhāra*, stated below, up to Brahmarandhra in the head. Also called *brahmanāḍī* or *mokṣamārga*, it is believed to contain the universe. Through it *Kuṇḍalinī* is supposed to move upward. Iḍā is on the left side of the spinal cord, entwining Suṣumṇā. Its exit is through the left nostril. A symbol of the moon, it is white, and represents the *Amṛta* aspect of Śakti. *Piṅgalā* is on the right side of the spinal cord. Rising from *Mūlādhāra*, its exit is through the right nostril. Also called *Sūrya Nāḍī*, it symbolises the waking condition and leads to violence.

Six Cakras

The body is supposed to contain six *cakras* (circles, nerve-plexus) in it.

These are:

(1) *Mūlādhāra*: Just in the middle of the body. It is triangular in shape with its apex facing downward. It is like a red lotus with four petals. *Kuṇḍalinī* is supposed to coil around it.

(2) *Svādhiṣṭhāna*: above the *mūlādhāra*, but below the navel. It is like a lotus of six petals.

(3) *Maṇipūra*: in the navel. Also called *Nābhicakra*, it is like a golden lotus of ten petals, containing a letter. It is supposed to contain a triangle of the colour of the rising sun. The outer sides of the triangle are represented by three *Svastika* signs.

(4) *Anāhata*: in the region of the heart. Like a deep red lotus of twelve petals; it is the seat of air.

(5) *Viśuddha* or *Bhāratī*: in the throat. Seat of Sarasvatī, it is grey and like a lotus of sixteen petals.

(6) *Ājñā*: in between the eyebrows. Also called *paramakula* or *muktatriveṇī*, it is like a lotus of two petals, white in colour. It is from here that the three *nāḍīs*, *Iḍā* etc., spread out to different directions. It is the seat of mind. *Ājñā* means order; order of *guru* is supposed to reside in it.

Cakra-bheda or Ṣaṭcakrabheda is frequently found in Tantras. Bheda means manifestation or activation; it is necessary for keeping the body fit and the attainment of *siddhis*.

The six *cakras* are identified in some Tantric works (e.g. *Saundaryalahari*, v.9) with the five elements and the mind.

The names and number of *Cakras* differ in different works. A *Śrī cakra* is often mentioned.[8] The *Cakrabheda-tantra* (Deccan College Ms. no.962 of 1884-87) mentions the following five *Cakras* used in Durgāpūjā according to *Kaulagama: Rāja, Mahā, Deva, Vīra, Paśu* (See *Catalogue*, Vol. xvi on Tantra, p.163). In another Ms. (Ibid no. 964 of 1887-91) some other *Cakras* are described as *Akaḍamacakra*. These are *Ṛṇadhana, Śodhana, Rāśi, Nakṣatra* (*Catalogue*, Vol. xvi on Tantra, p. 251). The *Śrīcakra* above, connected with *Śrīvidyā*, is also called *Śrīyantra* or Tripuracakra.

Sahasrāra-Padma

The *Brahmarandhra*, supposed to be at the centre of the head, through which vital breath or life is supposed to exit at death, is fancied to contain a multicoloured lotus of thousand petals (*Sahasrāra-padma*) and to face downward.

HUMAN NATURE

Human nature has been divided into three classes according to the qualities of *Sattva, Rajas* and *Tamas*. It is due to the diversity of human nature that the necessity for a *guru* arises for initiation; the *guru* initiates the disciple with the particular *mantra* suitable to the nature of the latter. On the basis of these qualities, human propensities have been divided into three classes, viz. *paśubhāva*,[9] *vīrabhāva* and *divyabhāva*. A person, with the predominance of *paśubhāva*, is tied with the bonds of kindness, infatuation, fear, shame, hatred, family, conduct, caste, etc. Among such people, there is an excess of the quality of *Rajas* over *Tamas*. Among them, there is forgetfulness, idleness and drowsiness. They lack faith in *mantras* and *guru*; they observe Vedic practices. The Tantras dub such people as worst.

Due to the excess of *Rajas*, those who have *vīrabhāva* do such acts as breed sorrow.

Those, who have *divyabhāva*, have an excess of *Sattva*. Such people have been characterised as best. They are kind, pious, pure, truthful, and have an even attitude towards friends and foes.

There is difference of opinion about the type of people who are greater in number in Kali Age. According to the *Mahānirvāṇa-tantra* (i. 24), people of *vīrabhāva* are of a greater number than the other two types. A verse, quoted in the *Prāṇatoṣiṇī*, holds that, in this Age, there is none having *divya* or *vīrabhāva*. In spite of differences of opinion, there is a consensus that people of *divyabhāva* are rare.

Sādhanā—Pañcatattva

Sādhanā (worship, propitiation) is the means of reaching the goal. There are many ways of *Sādhanā*, viz. pūjā (external and mental), knowledge of *Śāstras*, *japa* (muttering or repeating a *mantra* or the name of a deity) *tapas* (penance) and *mantra* (incantation), etc.

Sādhakas and *Sādhikās* are divided into the following classes according to their physical, mental and moral qualities: (1) *Mṛdu*, (2) *Madhyama*, (3) *Adhimātraka*, and (4) *Adhimātrama*. According to the *Kaula* school of Tantra, the *sādhakas* are of the following classes:

(i) *Prakṛti — Vīrācārins*: engaged in sacrifice and other rituals and resorting to *pañcatattvas*.

(ii) *Madhyama Kaulika*: Like Prakṛti, but their minds are more attracted to meditation, knowledge and concentration.

(iii) *Kaulikottama*: those who go beyond ritualism, and meditate on the Supreme Being.

In the Tāntric way of worship, *pañca-tattvas* or five *makāras* play an important role. These five are *madya* (wine), *māṃsa* (meat), *matsya* (fish), mudrā[10] and *maithuna* (sexual intercourse). The *Sādhaka* of *Vīra* type will enjoy these things in their literal sense, and proceed along the path of *Sādhanā*. Those of the *paśu* class will take coconut-water or milk, etc. instead of *madya*, red radish, red sesamum, the kind of pulse called *masūra* in place of fish, ginger, sesāmum, salt or garlic for meat; *mudrā* in their case will denote rice, barley. etc. Instead of *maithuna*, he will surrender himself, like a child, to the feet of Śakti. To the *sādhaka* of *deva* type, *madya* means maddening realisation of the Supreme Being, obtained by *Yoga*, by which he becomes unconscious of the external world. For him *māṃsa* means that action by which he dedicates all acts to himself identified with Brahman. In his case, *matsya* menas *Sāttvika* knowledge by which he identifies himself with all beings, and himself shares their feelings of pleasure and pain. For him *mudrā* means the giving up of association with all evil things which cause bondage. Such a *sādhaka* means, by *maithuna*, the union of the *Kuṇḍalinī* energy, with the thousand-petalled *cakra* at the centre of the head.

The *Kulārṇava-tantra* gives the following explanation of *pañcatattvas*. *Madya* is the nectar flowing from the union of *Kuṇḍalinī Śakti* with Śiva in the *sahasrāra* in the head. He is an eater of *māṃsa* (flesh) who kills, with the sword of knowledge, the animals of merit and demerit and leads his mind to Supreme Śiva. He eats fish who controls his senses, and places them in his *Ātman*. *Maithuna* means the union of Supreme Śakti and Ātman; Śakti is aroused in a *Kaulika*, but not in a devotee of the *paśu* type. *Maithuna* symbolises the basic unity which underlies the apparent duality of everything.

Some people bitterly criticise Tantras for their advocating the *pañcatattvas*. But, a closer look at the philosophy of Tantras will reveal that they do not encourage immoral practices among the adherents by allowing them to satisfy their animal instincts. These are prescribed as *preya* (favourite articles) leading to the *śreya* (well being); these are means to an end, but not the end itself. The enjoyment of these things, for which there is natural inclination, is supposed to help the *sādhaka* in the realisation of Brahman, full of bliss. A *Sādhaka* is not allowed to indulge in these enjoyments as he likes. After reaching a very high stage of spiritual life, he can take to *pañcatattva* under the vigilant guidance of the *guru*. As a safeguard against levity, alternative articles have been prescribed for those with the preponderance of animal propensities and, as such, lacking in requisite restraint. This *sādhana* is commended for the *sādhakas* of *vīra* type, possessed of self-control.

For progress along the path of *sādhana*, one requires preparation of the body, vital breath and mind. The body is made fit by different postures (*āsana*). For preparing the vital breath, one has to practise *prāṇāyāma*. The mind has to be prepared by *bhāvānā* (contemplation).

Three stages of *sādhana* are *Śuddhi*, *Sthiti* and *Arpaṇa*. At first, the *sādhaka* will have to be pure after removing physical and mental impurities. In the second stage, he will be free from the darkness of delusion and the light of knowledge will dawn on him. In the third and final stage, he will realise identity with the object of meditation.

Snāna, tarpaṇa, sandhyā, pūjā and *homa* — these five are musts for the *sādhaka*.

Kuṇḍalinī-yoga[11]

The fundamental concept of Tāntric *sādhana* is *Kuṇḍalinī-yoga*. The dormant spiritual energy within the human body is called *Kuṇḍalinī*, conceived as a serpent coiling round the *mūlādhāra*.[12] It is also realised by the *Sādhaka* as lustrous like a crore of suns and cool like a crore of moons. By rousing this energy, a person can reach the higher state of human existence. When it is roused, the entire being of a person is flooded with very delicate nectar of music; this music is called the *Kūjana* (singing) of *Kuṇḍalinī*.

Besides the individual *Kuṇḍalinī*, the *Tantras* speak of a *Mahākuṇḍalinī*. The former develops the personal existence. While admitting the relationship of spiritual life with the divine, Tantra says that if a *sādhaka* can get upon *Mahākuṇḍalinī*, then, by transcending the narrow personal state, he can be established in the wide universal state; *Mahākuṇḍalinī* is at the root of the universe.

Pūjā

Tantras ordain that the worshipper must identify himself with the deity he worships.[13] An essential element of *pūjā* is *nyāsa*.[14] The offerings in a *pūjā* may be five to eighteen in number. *Dhyāna* and *japa* are other requisites in *pūjā*. Tantra, however, lays the greatest emphasis on mental worship (*mānasa-pūjā*).[15] In fact, this *pūjā* is regarded as far superior to external *pūjā*. Some Tantras assert that, without *mānasa pūjā*, external *pūjā* is futile. The *Śāktānanda-taraṅgini*[16] holds that the search for god outside, having disregarded god within one's ownself, is like the quest of glass after ignoring the *kaustubha* jewel within one's own hand. Self-surrender (*ātma-samarpaṇa*) is a characteristic of Tāntric *pūjā*. For example, the *Kramadīpikā* ordains.

gandhādibhiḥ saparivāram athārghyamasmai
dattvā vidhāya kusumāñjalim ādareṇa/
stutvā praṇamya śirasā culukodakena
svātmānam arpayatu taccaraṇāravinde//

Then having given offering to Him, along with His family, with sandal-paste, etc., having lovingly given a handful of flowers, eulogised them and saluted Him with the head, offer yourself to His lotus-feet with a *culuka* of water. (*Culuka* means hollowed palm).

Siddhi

Siddhi, to be achieved through *sādhanā*, may be *mantrasiddhi* (success in *mantras*) by which *mantras*, used by a *sādhaka*, produce the desired result; *vāksiddhi* (success in speech) by which words, uttered by a *Sādhaka*, become infallible. After reaching the summit of spiritual life, one can possess the following eight *siddhis*: *aṇimā* (power of assuming a figure of atomic size), *mahimā* (power of increasing size at will), *laghimā* (power of assuming excessive lightness), *garimā* (power of assuming excessive heaviness), *prāpti* (power of obtaining anything at will), *prākāmya* (irresistible will), *īśitva* (superiority over others), *vaśitva* (power of keeping others under control).

There are other lesser *siddhis* too. The greatest *siddhi* is *Mahānirvāṇa* or *mokṣa*; it is, indeed, the highest object to be aimed at in life.

Mantra and Puraścaraṇa

Mantra occupies a very high place in Tantra. God is conceived as *mantra* which again has been mentioned as the surest means of attaining *mokṣa. Mananāt trāyate* it *mantraḥ* — that which saves through contemplation is *mantra*. The *Piṅgalātantra*, quoted in the *Śaradātilaka*, says-

mananaṃ viśva-vijñānaṃ trāṇaṃ saṃsāra-bandhanāt/
yataḥ karoti-saṃsiddhaṃ mantra ityucyate tataḥ//

Mantra is so called as it saves one who has reached *siddhi* from the bondage of rebirth through *manana* which means the knowledge of the universe.

Tantras believe that the lifeless syllables of a *mantra*, being pronounced in contact with *Suṣumnā*, acquire unlimited power. The power of *mantras* is manifold. In some *mantras*, will predominates, in others joy. In some, the creative power is predominant, while in others peace figures prominently

Mantras are constituted by the letters from *A* to *Kṣa*; these *mantras* are called *bīja* (seed). A *bīja-mantra* is obtained by the disciple from his preceptor at the time of initiation; it symbolises the form of the desired deity. Seed is sown on a soil which is cultivated, cleaned and watered. Similarly, the *bīja-mantra* is put into the disciple's heart which is pure, and has been drenched by the water of God's mercy.

The word *Puraścaraṇa* literally means performing before something. According to the *Vāyavīya-saṃhitā*, it means the perfecting of the procedure of *mūlamantra*, because it has to be performed before the acts in which it is to be employed. The *Kulārṇava* (XVII.87) states that it is so called, because, by this rite, the intended deity moves before the worshipper for granting favour to him.

Puraścaraṇa of a *mantra* has the following constituents: *dhyāna, pūjā, japa, homa, tarpaṇa, abhiṣeka* and *brāhmāṇa-bhojana*. In a shorter form, the first three only are performed. *Daśāṅga puraścaraṇa* consists of the following three additional items: *aghamarṣaṇa, sūryārghya, jalpana (Kaulāvalī-nirṇaya*, XV). Several Tantras incidentally deal with *puraścaraṇa*: e.g. *Kulārṇava* (XV. 7-9, 11-12),

Śāradātilaka, (11. 138-140), *Śaktisaṃgama*, Sundarī, III. 155-156, etc. The *Puraścaryārṇava* (VI) deserves special mention in this connexion.

There are different forms of this rite depending on the nature of the devotee concerned, *Divya, Vīra* or *Paśu.*

In some texts, the body of God is called *Mantratanu. Mantrayāna* is the name of Tāntric Buddhism.

As we have seen above, the *bījas* in Tantra are mystic syllables without any meaning. These are believed to have great potency and efficacy. It may be noted that many people of ancient times used to believe in the mystic power of letters or words, which might not have any sense. E.J. Thomas writes (*History of Buddhist Thought*, p. 186) that spells, similar to Hindu and Buddhist types, occur in Old English, Old High German and Keltic.

The letters of the alphabet are also called *Mātṛkās* (sources). *Mantras*, being written in the letters, they are regarded as sacred.

Flesh and blood of the body are also called *mantra* (Rāghavabhaṭṭa on *Śāradātilaka*, v.95-96).

Some works (e.g. *Prāṇatoṣiṇī* IV.1.p.222, *Gāndharva* XXIX.24-25) provide for rites for rousing the consciousness of *mantras.*

Some Tantras (e.g. *Tantrarāja* XXXV.64-66, *Puraścaryārṇava* VI, p. 526) require a devotee to realise that every letter of a *mantra* is the manifestation of the real nature of Śakti, and feel that he is merged in the essence of the object of his spiritual exercise.

The ten ways of purifying *mantras* are *janana, jīvana, tāḍana, bodhana, abhiṣeka, vimalīkaraṇa, āpyāyana, tarpaṇa, dīpana* and *gupta.* (Kṛṣṇānanda's *Tantrasāra).*

One, who attains *mantra-siddhi*, acquires a peculiar brightness of the body and a lasting peaceful state of mind.

Mantra-śikhā is the name of a purificatory flame roused, within the body, during the upward march of *Kuṇḍalinī* (*Puraścayārṇava*, VI).

Rāghavabhaṭṭa on *Śārdātilaka* (ii.III) speaks of the purification of *mantras* with *Prāṇāyāma* according to the *Yonimudrā* process and reciting them for 1008 times.

The *Kulārṇava* (vi) prescribes the process of purifying a *mantra* by reciting its letters in the regular and reverse orders.

Yoga

Tāntric Yoga is mainly twofold — *haṭhayoga* and *samādhiyoga.* The former consists in physical methods by which the way to mind-control is paved. It has the following five external accessories instead of the eight, prescribed in the *Yoga* system of Patañjali.

(i)*Yama*: control of the senses, non-violence, etc.

(ii) *Niyama*: study of Śāstras, meditation on God.

(iii) *Prāṇāyāma*: control of breath.

(iv) *Āsana*: a particular posture.

(v) *Pratyāhāra*: withdrawal of the senses from worldly objects.

Samādhi-yoga[17] is sixfold:

Dhyāna-yoga, Nāda-yoga, Rasānanda-yoga, Layasiddhi-yoga, Bhakti-yoga and *Rājayoga.*

The basic difference between the *yoga* in the *Yogaśāstra* of Patañjali and Tāntric *yoga* is this. In the latter, there is no difference between *Śakti* and *Tattva* so that *Śakti* surmounts all obstacles, and effects the union of the *yogin* with the Supreme *Śiva.* But, Patañjali does not recognise any Supreme Power beyond Prakṛti so that the *Yogin* has no familiarity with any *Śakti* beyond *Prakṛti.*

Maṇḍala, Mudrā, Yantra, Nyāsa

Maṇḍalas or diagrams of various shapes and colours are regarded as indispensable for Tāntric rites. The *Jñānārṇava* (XXIV. 8-10, XXVI. 15-17), which describes several *maṇḍalas,* holds that *maṇḍala* and *cakra* mean the same thing. The *Śāradātilaka* (iii. 113-118, 131-139) and several other Tantras, both Hindu and Buddhist, describe some *maṇḍalas.*

Some of the *maṇḍalas* are *Sarvatobhadra, Caturliṅgatobhadra, Prāsāda-vāstu-maṇḍala, Gṛhavāstu-maṇḍala, Harihara-maṇḍala. Ekaliṅgatobhadra,* etc. According to the Śāradātilaka (iii-106-130), the *Sarvatobhadra* (auspicious on all sides) is common to all kinds of worship.

The word *Maṇḍala* also denotes a gathering of Tāntric devotees who assemble to perform rituals involving *Pañcamakāras.* Some Tantras, e.g. *Kaulāvalī-nirṇaya* (viii) and *Mahānirvāṇa* (viii, 154-156) deal with such *Maṇḍalas.*

The celebrated commentator, Rāghavabhaṭṭa, derives the word *mudrā* (pose of hand or finger) as *mudaṃ rāti dadāti,* that which gives delight.

The *Kulārṇava,* (xvii. 57) derives the word from root *mud* (to give delight) and *drāvay* (causative of *dru,* to melt); the word means that which gives delight to gods and melts their hearts.

It is one of the five *Makāras* regarded as essential for Tāntric worship.

The names, number and description of *mudrās* differ in different works. The number ranges from nine to fifty-eight.

Some of the Tantras, dealing with *mudrās*, are the *Śāradā-tilaka* (xxiii. 106-114), Jñanārṇava (iv. 31-47, 51-56, xv. 46-68, *Jayākhya-saṃhitā* (Paṭala 8), *Kulārṇava* (xvii. 90-93) *Kaulāvalī-nirṇaya* (vii. 5-14), *Mahānirvāṇa* (vi. 77).

Nine *mudrās* are common. According to the *Śāradātilaka*, there are *Āvāhanī, Sthāpanī, Sannidhāpana, Sannirodhanī, Sammukhikaraṇī, Sakalikṛti, Avaguṇṭhana, Dhenu* and *Mahāmudrā.*

Some other *mudrās* are *Śaṃkha, Abhīti, Trikhaṇḍā, Khecarī, Yoni, etc.*

The names of a few *mudrās*, mentioned in the *Nityāṣoḍaśikā*, indicate the purposes for which they were used, e.g. *Sarva-saṃkṣobhakāriṇī, Sarvavidrāvaṇī, Ākarṣiṇī, Sarvavaśakārī, Unmādinī.*

Mudrā is an important subject in Buddhist Tantra also. The *Āryamañjuśrī-mūlakapa* names and defines 108 mudrās.

The term *mudrā*, in some cases, appears to mean yogic posture of the body, e.g. *Khecarī*, Yoni.

Theory of Creation — Śiva and Śakti

The Supreme Brahman is eternal and immutable. He is at once *niṣkala* and *sa-kalā*;[18] *kalā* means Prakṛti. The *Śakti*[19] of Brahman is eternal and inseparable from Him. This *Śakti* is *nirguṇa* (without attributes) and *saguṇa* (with attributes). In her aspect of goddess in the form of consciousness, she manifests the being, and through her as the goddess in the form of bliss (*ānanda*) Brahman manifests Himself.[20] Śakti is immanent in universe like oil in sesamum. From Brahma-Śakti arises *Nāda* from which proceeds *Bindu.* By characterising the goddess as *mūlamantrātmikā* (constituted by the basic mantra) her subtle body is referred to Śiva, wrapped in the web of *Māyā*, and the latent *Śakti* is fancied as the supreme *Bindu*. This *Bindu* is circular, bounded by the circumference of Māyā. At its centre is the place of Brahman, the abode of Prakṛti-Puruṣa. This very *Bindu* is Prakṛti-Puruṣa; it is Śabda-Brahman or Apara-Brahman.[21] From the union of Śiva and Śakti, the goddess becomes inclined (*unmukhī*) to Śiva. Then the web of *Māyā* is rent asunder, and creation proceeds. The relationship of Śiva and Śakti is controversial. On this, the following statement of the *Kulārṇava-tantra* may be noted:

advaitaṃ kecidicchanti dvaitamicchanti cāpare/
mama tattvaṃ na jānāti dvaitādvaita-vivarjitam// (i. 110)

'Some desire non-duality, while others want duality. Man knows not my actual state which is free from duality and non-duality.'

Śabda-Brahman manifests itself in three Śaktis, viz. *Jñāna* (knowledge), *Icchā* (desire) and *Kriyā* (action). The goddess is described as *icchāśakti-jñānaśakti-kriyāśakti-svarūpiṇī*. The following terms are used to convey the completeness of Śiva:

svatantratā (independnce), *nityatā* (eternality), *nitya-tṛptatā* (quality of being eternally contented), *sarvajñatā* (omniscience).

From Paramaśiva arises Śambhu, from Śambhu *Sadāśiva*, from Sadāśiva Īśāna and with their own *Śaktis* arise Rudra, Viṣṇu and Śiva. Without these *Śaktis*, Rudra, etc. have no power.[22]

In the *Mahānirvāṇa-tantra*, Śiva has been addressed as Śambhu, Sadāśiva, Śaṃkara, Maheśvara, etc. All these are but names of the different conditions, qualities or manifestations of the single Śiva.

Śakti is at once of the form of *Māyā* and *Mūlaprakṛti*. Through the power of this *Māyā*, Brahman conceals His own form, and appears in different forms. *Mūlaprakṛti* is unmanifested. In the manifest state, she resides in the universe consisting of various names and forms. Śiva-Śakti dwell in the *mūlādhāra* and *Kuṇḍalinī* within the human body. In all processes, Śabda-Brahman resides in the form of *Kuṇḍalinī*, and is manifested as *akṣaras* (letters).

The order of creation in Tantra is as follows:

Mūlaprakṛti=Śakti (resorting to Śive)
- Mahat
  - Ahaṃkāra (Vaikārika or Sāttvika)
  - Taijasa or Rājasika Ahaṃkāra
  - Tāmasika or Ahaṃkāra of beings
    - Pañca Tanmātra (*Śabda, sparśa, rūpa, rasa, gandha*)
      - Pañca Mahābhūta (*Kṣiti, ap, tejas, marut,vyoman*)

Śakti is variously termed as *Māyā, Mahāmāyā, Devī, Prakṛti*, etc. She is both *Vidyā* and *Avidyā*. As *Avidyā*, she causes bondage, and as *Vidyā* she puts an end to rebirths, and gives liberation. She is called *Ādyā Śakti* (the primeval energy) as she is supposed to have existed before creation. As the manifestation of *Cit* in Prakṛti, she is called the Denoting Power (*vācaka-śakti*). Being in the form of *Cit*, she is also the Denoted Power (*vācya-śakti*). *Ātman* is to be conceived as Devī. So, Devī or Śakti is only a manifestation of Śiva in the form of mother.[23] It is She who is Ambikā and Lalitā.

As Parabrahma, Devī is beyond form and quality. She has been conceived in three ways; 1. supreme form; she is beyond knowledge.[24] 2. subtle body constituted by *mantra*; this formless aspect is beyond meditation. 3. the gross body which is easily comprehensible.[25]

As Mahādevī, Śakti exists in different forms, e.g. Sarasvatī, Lakṣmī, Durgā, Annapūrṇā, etc. As Satī, Umā, Pārvatī, etc. She is the consort of Śiva. As Satī, she manifested herself before Śiva, prior to Dakṣayajña, as ten Mahāvidyās. When Satī renounced her body, Śiva carried the corpse. With his disc Viṣṇu cut the body to 51 pieces which dropped at different places which were called *Mahāpīṭhasthānas*. At each of these places, Devī, along with her Bhairava, is worshipped.

Infinite are the forms of Śakti. She resides in all the animate and inanimate objects of the universe. But, in reality, she is one. As the single moon, reflected in the waves, appears to be many, so the single Śakti has various manifestations.

Śakti always resorts to Śiva. Her first manifestation is with the emanation of the universe. Before this, Śakti in dormant in Śiva. This dormancy or latent character of the existence of Parama Śiva, in an attributeless state, is generally known as Śūnya in Śaiva Āgamas (*Śūnyarūpaṃ śivaṃ sākṣāt*). This state is beyond comprehension. It is so called as it is beyond all definitions or knowledge.

Ten Mahāvidyās

In Tantra, Śakti is also called Vidyā or Mahāvidyā. The same Śakti has been conceived in ten aspects. Hence they are collectively called Das'a Mahāvidyā. The names vary in different works.

In *Cāmuṇḍā* and *Muṇḍamālā-tantras*, the names are as follows, Kālī, Tārā, Ṣoḍaśī, Bhuvaneśvari, Bhairavī, Chinnamastā, Dhūmāvatī, Vagalā, Mātaṅgī, Kamalā.

The *Mālinīvijaya* gives the following list: Kālī, Nīlā, Mahādurgā, Tvaritā, Chinnamastakā, Vāgvādinī, Annapūrṇā, Pratyaṅgirā, Kāmākhyā, Vāsalī, Bālā, Mātaṅgī, Śaila vāsinī. It is curious that the number here is 13.

In some Tantras (e.g. *Niruttara* i-6-8), the Mahāvidyās are divided into two groups; those belonging to *Kālīkula* and those belonging to *Śrīkula.*

To the former belong Kālī, Tārā, Chinnamastā, Bhuvanā, Mahiṣamardinī, Tripuṭā, Tvaritā, Durgā, Vidyā and Pratyaṅgirā. To the latter belong Sundarī, Bhairavī, Bālā, Vagalā, Kamalā, Dhūmāvatī, Mātaṅgī, Svapnavatī, Madhumatī and Mahāvidyā. The total number is twenty.

Ācāra

According to Tantra, there are *sādhana* and *upāsana* of different kinds. These varieties are seven according to some works, nine according to others. In the *Kulārṇava-tantra* (Chap.ii) are mentioned the following ways:

i) Vedācāra, ii) Vaiṣṇavācāra, iii) Śaivācāra iv) Dakṣiṇācāra, v) Vāmācāra, vi) Siddhāntācāra, vii) Kaulācāra.

Each succeeding one is higher than the preceding way. In *Vedācāra*, there is preponderance of Vedic rituals. In the second *ācāra*, the *sādhaka* overcomes blind faith, and has unflinching faith in the saving power of Brahman. It is the way of devotion.

In the third one, there is entrance into the way of knowledge. In it, there is a combination of *bhakti* and *śakti* with faith in the mind of the *śādhaka*; the *sādhaka* endeavours to acquire *śakti*. In the fourth way, the *sādhaka* becomes capable of meditating upon the three Śaktis of *kriyā, icchā* and *jñāna* of Brahman, and acquires fitness for the worship of three, viz. Brahmā, Viṣṇu and Maheśvara. The fifth way is so called, according to some, because, in it, stress is laid on *Vāmā* (woman) as an essential element of *Sādhana*. Others, however, think that the word is *Vāma* (left) as distinguished from *dakṣiṇa* (right) in *Dakṣiṇācāra*. The *sādhaka* proceeds from *pravṛtti* (inclination) to *nivṛtti* (cessation of desire). Some take *Vāmā* to mean a crooked way resorted to secretly. In this *ācāra*, the *sādhaka* breaks the bonds of delusion, shame, etc. with which a person of *paśubhāva* is tied. The way to the attainment of Śivahood, found in this *ācāra*, is completed in the sixth. Now he gets the opportunity, with the help of *guru*, to reach *Kaulācāra*.[26] In this state, he becomes liberated in life (*jīvanmukta*) and, acquiring the knowledge of Brahman, reaches the state of Paramahaṃsa; this, indeed, is the highest goal of Tāntric *Sādhana*.

In some Tāntric texts, *Ācāras* are divided into two broad classes, *Aghora* and *Yoga*.The former is so called as it is followed by Aghorins, a sect of the Śaivas.

Guru, Śiṣya-Dīkṣā, Abhiṣeka

Some Tantras (e.g. *Nirvāṇatantra*) mention four classes of *gurus*, viz. *guru, paramaguru, parāparaguru* and *parameṣṭhi-guru*. According to some works (e.g. *Nīlatantra* V.73), Goddess Śakti is *parāparaguru* and Śiva *parāmeṣṭhi-guru*. One's preceptor is one's *guru* and his *guru's* preceptor is his *paramaguru*.

Some works (e.g. *Nīlatantra* V. 65, 66) classify *gurus* as *Divyaugha* (divine), *Siddhhaugha* (sages) and *Mānavaugha* (human). In another way, *gurus* are divided into two classes (e.g. V. 64, 71), viz. *Tārāguru* and *Devaguru*. It is stated (e.g. *Nīlatantra* V. 70) that the names of male *gurus* should end in — *ānanda* (e.g. Brahmānanda) or- *nātha* (e.g. Matsyendranātha) and those of female *gurus* in — *ambā* (e.g. Jayāmbā).

Tantras believe that none can take to the Tāntric way of life and worship without initiation by a *guru* of certain qualities.[27] He will, at first, assume the vitality of the *paramaguru* in his own body, and then cause it to enter into that of the disciple. The *guru* will decide the suitability of the particular *mantra* for a particular disciple. Initiation by a woman is especially effective; eight times more potent is the initiation by one's mother. It is interesting to note that one is forbidden to receive *mantra* from one's father. The husband is debarred from initiating his wife.

In some Tantras (e.g. *Nīlatantra* V. 68) the Tāntric *guru* is regarded as superior even to one's father.

Initiation of a special type is called *Abhiṣeka*, which consists in sprinkling holy water on the neophyte while reciting *mantras* to propitiate different deities, especially for warding off evil spirits.

Abhiṣekas of different types are applicable to disciples in different stages of spiritual life. These are as follows:

(i) *Śāktābhiṣeka*: for the disciple who has just begun *sādhanā*. In it, the *guru* reveals the nature of Śakti and a wonderful new energy is infused into the disciple.

(ii) *Pūrṇābhiṣeka*: for the disciple who has acquired fitness by means of *puraścaraṇa* etc. Real *sādhanā* begins in it. For this kind of *Abhiṣeka* one has to undergo severe ordeals;[28] it is believed to confer divinity on the devotee.

(iii) *Kramadīkṣābhiṣeka*:

(iv) *Sāmrajyābhiṣeka*:

(v) *Mahāsāmrājyābhiṣeka*:

(vi) *Yogadīkṣābhiṣeka*:

(vii) *Pūrṇadīkṣābhiṣeka*:

(viii) *Mahāpūrṇadīkṣābhiṣeka*: in it the *sādhaka* reaches the fulfilment of spiritual aspiration. He then performs his own *śrāddha*, offers *pūrṇāhuti* with the sacred thread and *śikhā* (tuft of hair on the head). In this stage, the relation of *guru-śiṣya* ceases. The *sādhaka* himself gradually realises the *so'ham* (I am that) state, attains liberation in life and is called *Paramahaṃsa*. In fact, the realisation of the identity of *Jīva* and Brahman is the highest goal of Tāntric initiation.

According to some, *Dīkṣā* is twofold, viz.

(i) *Vahirdīkṣā*: consists of *pūjā*, *homa* and other external rites. By it the *sāttvika* feeling is aroused.

(ii) *Antardīkṣā*: it helps the awakening of the *Kuṇḍalinī* energy.

According to others, *Dīkṣā* is threefold, viz.

(i) *Śāmbhavī*: in it the mind is purified.

(ii) *Śāktī*: in it the spiritual energy is aroused.

(iii) *Māntrī*: it arouses the power of *mantra* and gods.

According to the *Viśvasāra-tantra*, *dīkṣā* is fourfold, viz. *Kriyāvatī Kalāvatī*, *Varṇamayī* and *Vedhamayī* (see *Prāṇatoṣiṇī* II.4, p.118). The *Kulārṇava* (XIV) states seven modes of *dīkṣā*, viz. *Kriyā*, *Varṇa*, *Kalā*, *Sparśa*, *Vāk*, *Dṛk*, *Mānasa*. According to the *Rudrayāmala*, it is of three kinds, viz. *Āṇavī*, *Śāktī* and *Śāmbhavī* (See *Prāṇatoṣiṇī*, II.4). The other forms are *Krama*, *Pañcāyatana*, *Ekamantra*, *etc*. *Āṇavī dīkṣā* is divided in the *Ṣaḍanvaya-mahāratna* into ten sub-varieties.

In another way, *dīkṣa* is twofold, *Kriyā* and *Jñāna*. Of these, *Kriyā* is manifold. In accordance with the propensities and capacity of the devotees concerned, *dīkṣā* is of infinite varieties. According to Abhinavagupta, *dīkṣā anantavibhedabhāk*. The object of *dīkṣā* is to guide the person concerned along the way to salvation by removing the *malas* (dirty substance) which are:

Āṇava: it gives rise to the narrow *jīva-hood* of Śiva; unless it is removed the realisation of the identity of *Śakti* is not possible.

Buddhigata: by its removal the acquisition of real knowledge is possible.

Māyīya: the root of the knowledge of *viṣaya* and *viṣayī;* the cause of *ahaṃkāra*. Unless it is removed, salvation is unattainable.

Ways to Liberation

The Tāntric work, *Pārānanda-sūtra*[29] ordains three paths for the attainment of the goal. These are:

(i) *Daksiṇa*: prescribed in the Veda, Smṛti and Purāṇa.

(ii) *Vāma*: declared in the Veda and *Āgamas*.

(iii) *Uttara*: shown by the word of the Veda and the *guru* who is *jīvanmukta*.

Vāma is of two kinds:

(i) *Madhyama*: in it all the five *makāras* are resorted to.

(ii) *Uttama*: in it only *madya, maithuna* and *mudrā* are used.

Some Tantras, however, add a few more paths. For example, the *Kulārṇava* (ii. 7-8) provides as many as six; these are *Vaiṣṇava, Śaiva, Dakṣiṇa, Vāma, Siddhānta, Kaula*; each succeeding is superior to the preceding one. The *Kulārṇava* (ii. 6-7) ordains five *āmnāyas* or paths to *mokṣa*. These are East, West, North, South and Ūrdhva. The *Paraśurāma-kalpasūtra* (i. 2) has the same thing to say.

The Attainment of Liberation

The *Kulārṇava* holds (I. 105-107) that liberation is not possible by the study of the Veda and other *Śāstras* nor by resorting to *āśramas* (stages of life). *Mukti* is possible by correct knowledge alone. This knowledge is to be acquired from one's *guru*. It further states (I. 111-12) that egoism leads to bondage, and that the words 'nothing is mine' lead to liberation.

Tantra recognises *jīvanmukti* (Liberation in life) which consists, as the *Pārānanda* holds (p.9, Sutras 3-8), in visualising the deity worshipped. A person, liberated while alive, is not affected by *Karman*, meritorious or sinful.

TANTRA VIS-A-VIS ANCIENT INDIAN CULTURE

Śākta Works and Tantra

The Tantras and Śākta works are, to a great extent, similar. But, a line of demarcation is drawn by some between the two. According to

P. V. Kaṇe, the Śāktas look upon Devī as Supreme, but Tantras (including Buddhist and Jaina works) are not confined to Devī or Śakti alone. The latter may be agnostic, Vedāntic or Sāṅkhyaite in outlook.

Veda and Tantra

Some are of the opinion that Tāntric religion is opposed to the Vedic.[30] The great Śaṃkarācārya, in his commentary on the *Brahmasūtras*, condemns Tantra as running counter to the Veda. We shall briefly deal with this matter.

The *Rudrayāmala* (ch. xvii) includes the Supreme Goddess in the Atharvavedic pantheon. The *Kulārṇava-tantra* states (II. 10. 85, 140-41) that Kulaśāstra is based on the Veda. It has been pointed out that Śakti of Tantra has its precursor in the goddess of the Devīsūkta. There is, however, no unanimity on this point. Those, who want to prove the antiquity of Tantra, hold that the germ of many Tāntric matters is found in the Veda. The *Ṛgveda* refers to Śakti of God. The word Śakti is found several times in the *Ṛgveda* both in the singular and plural. There is, however, no provision for the worship of Śakti as a separate creative principle. Protection, courage and bounty, etc., are associated with Śakti. In *Ṛgveda*, X. 125 Vāk is a goddess associated with all gods; she is the principle of all energy. As Śakti is associated with Śiva in later literature, so females of gods are mentioned in the *Ṛgveda*; e.g. Indrāṇī and Varuṇānī are the consorts respectively of Indra and Varuṇa.

Some scholars point out the Vedic *Mahāvrata* rite as an instance. It is intended to strengthen, at the winter solstice, the sun so that it may resume its vigour, and make the earth fruitful. In an older form of the ritual, sexual union as a fertility rite is permitted. The magic and *abhicāra*, etc., contained in the *Atharvaveda*, are supposed to be the precursors of such matters in Tantra.

Some find Tāntric elements in the concept of Mahānagnī (the Great Naked Woman) in this Veda. The genital organ of her is stated (AV.IV.1.36) to have been sprinkled by the As'vins. It was, perhaps, part of a feritility rite.

In the *Ṛgveda Khila*, which is perhaps a later addition, we meet with Mahānagnī who is told that 'he', not being satisfied, is roaring (V. 22.6, AV.XX.136.5 with variants). There is a reference (A.V.xx.136.6 *RV. Khila*-V.22.9) to Mahānagnī running after Mahānagna, her male partner, and the male enjoying the female (AV.XX.136.11=*RV. Khila* V.22.9).

Mahānagnī may symbolise the altar for Vedic sacrifice, which is described as a young woman supervising the ritual (RV.X.114.3).[31]

That Tantra does not militate against Vedic tradition can be proved in many ways. Śiva and Śakti, the pivot of Tāntric philosophy, occur in many texts of the Vedic literature. For example, in the *Haṃsopaniṣad*, we find *Sadāśivaḥ śaktyātmā*. In the *Śvetāśvatara*, the Supreme Energy of God is stated to be heard in many ways (*Parāsya śaktir-vividhaiva śrūyate*). This Energy, from which emerge the three deities Brahmā, Viṣṇu and Maheśvara, presiding respectively over Creation, Preservation and Destruction, is *Ādyā Śakti* of Tantra. So, it is stated, in the *Rāmapūrvatāpanī Upaniṣad, Śaktayastisra eva ca.* (Three indeed are the *Śaktis*).

The *Varāhapurāṇa* says: *prayojanavaśāc-chaktir-ekaiva trividhā bhavet* (The single *Śakti*, according to necessity, becomes threefold). The *Gaurīsaṃhitā* declares.

Jñānam icchā tathā kriyā gaurī brāhmī tu vaiṣṇavī/
tridhā śaktiḥ sthitā yatra tatparaṃ jyotir-omiti//

The supremacy of the female energy is aptly expressed in the following lines of the *Kubjikā-tantra*:

brahmāṇī kurute sṛṣṭiṃ na tu brahma kadācana/
vaiṣṇavī kurute rakṣāṃ na tu viṣṇuh kadācana//

The consort of Brahman performs creation, not Brahma; the wife of Viṣṇu gives protection, not Viṣṇu; (similarly the wife of Rudra devours, not Rudra).

Śaṃkarācārya, a vigorous exponent of the Brāhmanical religion, says in his *Ānandalaharī*:

śivaḥ śaktyā yukto yadi bhavati śaktaḥ prabhavitun/
naced evaṃ devo na khalu kuśalaḥ spanditum api//

Śiva, united with Śakti, may assume power; otherwise, in this way, the god is not able even to throb.

The paramount power of Śakti is recognised also in various Upaniṣads, e.g. *Tripurātāpanī, Tripuropaniṣat, Devyupaniṣat,* etc. The *Tripuropaniṣad* mentions even worship with five *Makāras*.

So, we cannot brand Tantra as *veda-vāhya.*

It should, however, be noted that these Upaniṣads are regarded by some as apocryphal, and of much later origin.

The *Kenopaniṣad*, which is genuine, illustrates, through legend of Umā-Haimavatī, the supreme power of Umā, corresponding to Tāntric Śakti.

The *Īśopaniṣad* has been interpreted by some, notably the late Pañcānan Tarkaratna of Bhāṭpārā, W. Bengal, from the Śākta standpoint.

In some Brāhmaṇas (e.g. Śatapatha, V. 1.2.9, *Aitareya*, III.1.5, etc.), drinking appears to have been in vogue in sacrifices.

The Vedic sacrifices of *Vājapeya* and *Sautrāmaṇi* appear to foreshadow the Tāntric *Cakra*. In *Vājapeya* (drink of strength) not only *Somarasa* but also ordinary *Surā* used to be drunk. In *Sautrāmaṇi*, *Surā*, instead of *Soma*, was offered to deities.

The Tāntric attitude is noticeable in the idea that, in the performance of a sacrifice, the persons present become Brāhmaṇas, and caste-distinction is not observed.

The mystic syllables *Phaṭ*, *Huṃ*, etc. used in such Vedic texts as *Taittirīya Āraṇyaka* iv.27, remind one of Tāntric *Bījas*.

The Vedic ritual of purifying the body by reciting *mantras* and touching the different limbs, supposed to be occupied by god (*Aitareya Āraṇyaka*, iii.2) reminds one of Tāntric *Nyāsa*.

Those, who advocate the high antiquity of Tantra, call it the fifth Veda, and think that its authority is not less than that of the Veda.[32] Some are of the opinion that the subject-matter of Tantra is nothing but Vedic rites applicable in practical life; the relation of Veda to Tantra is like that of a tree to its branches. Another analogy is that Tantra exists in Veda even as fragrance rests in flowers. Tantra has not given up Vedic rites, the former has only simplified the latter, and made them easier. For example, Tantra, too, recognises the *homa* of the Vedic sacrifice, but unlike the Veda, it does not attach much importance to the external aspect of it. Tantra emphasises self-surrender which is the inner significance of *homa*.

As we have seen above, there are anticipations of the Tāntric conception of the human body in the *Atharvaveda*. In fact, Tantra is sometimes called *upaveda* of the *Atharvaveda*.[33] It should however, be noted that there is no evidence of any direct connexion between this Veda and Tantra.

Kullūkabhaṭṭa, the noted Bengali commentator of the *Manusmṛti*, divides *Śruti* (i.e. revealed literature) into two kinds viz. Vaidika and Tāntrika.

In the interpretation of certain Vedic texts, e.g. *Ṛgveda* i.164.45,[34] the *māntrikas* have declared four stages of speech, viz. *Parā*, *Paśyantī*, *Madhyamā* and *Vaikharī*; the fourth kind of speech is attributed to human beings.

This division is found in Tantra too. In this respect, Tantra may have influenced the Vedic interpreters.

Tantra and Purāṇa[35]

Many of the Purāṇas were influenced by Tantra to a great extent; this influence is most marked in the *Bhāgavata-purāṇa*.

In Xi.3.47, 49 this Purāṇa ordains the worship of Viṣṇu according to Tāntric rules. In Xi.11.37, Xii.11.2, etc., this Purāṇa refers to Tāntric cults of Viṣṇu, Tāntric *dīkṣā* and some Tāntric methods.

Again, the Tāntric form of worship, abounding in *mantra* and *kavaca*, is similar to that occurring in the Purāṇas. There is, however, a vital difference between the Tāntric and Purāṇic methods. The Tāntric worshipper identifies himself with the deity worshipped by him. But, the follower of the Purāṇa does not do so; he is always conscious of the fact that he is finite with limited capacity, whereas God is infinite with unlimited power. The general attitude of the Purāṇas to Tantra is voiced by the *Devībhāgavata* (xi.1.25); it states that as much of Tantra as is not opposed to the Veda is authoritative; whatever is opposed to the Veda is to be abjured. This work refers to the immanence of the Goddess (iii.6).

From the sixth or seventh century onward, Purāṇa began to adopt Tāntric forms of worship. Tāntric *mantra, nyāsa, mudrā, maṇḍala*, etc. infiltrated into Purāṇas and through them into Smṛti.

The *Agnipurāṇa* (chaps 27.81-87, 304) states many Tāntric *mantras* and rites. It provides (cccXII.24) that the worship of Viṣṇu should be in three ways, Vedic, Tāntric and Mixed; the second is for Śūdras alone. The *Kālikā-purāṇa* devotes considerable space to *mantra, mudrā* and *āsana*, etc. The *Brahmāṇḍapurāṇa* contains *Lalitāsahasranāma* which is clearly Tāntric. The *Devīmāhātmya* or *Durgā-Saptaśati*, popularly called *Caṇḍī*, a part of the *Mārkaṇḍeya-purāṇa*, is a glorification of Śakti.

Brāhmaṇa, Upaniṣad and Tantra[36]

Winternitz and B. L. Mukherji think (in Woodroffe, *Shakti and Shāktas*) that there are anticipations of Tāntric occultism in the Brāhmaṇas. The latter holds that allusions to sexual union are prominent in both the classes of works. According to the *Śatapatha Brāhmaṇa* (viii.4.4.11), the woman's place is on the left. Winternitz thinks this to be an anticipation of Tāntric *vāmācāra*.

Kāli, the prominent Tāntric goddess, appears, probably for the first time, in the *Muṇḍakopaniṣad* (i.2.4) belonging to the *Atharvaveda*.

Elements of Tantra, particularly Śakti as the principle of energy, are found in some Upaniṣads. The *Kenopaniṣad* depicts Umā Haimavatī (daughter of Himālaya) as omnipotent. In the *Śvetāśvatara*, it is said that the *Brahmavādins*, through meditation and Yoga, saw *Śakti* as identical with God and hidden by its own attributes or by the three *guṇas*. It speaks (vi.8) also of Brahman as possessed of the highest Śakti in various forms. The *Nārāyaṇopaniṣad* (2.1) contains an invocation of Durgā.

Rāghavabhaṭṭa, on the *Śāradātilaka*, observes that Tantra cult is based on Śruti, as attested by the Upaniṣads *Rāmapūrvottara-tāpanīya* and *Nṛsiṃhottara-tāpanīya*. Bhāskararāya, in his *Setubandha* commentary on the *Vāmakeśvaratantra*, refers to certain Upaniṣads as dealing exhaustively with devotion to *Mahātripura-sundarī*. It explains *catvāri īm* (*Ṛgveda* V. 47.4) as referring to *Kādividyā*.[37] The *Śāktopaniṣad* contains such Tāntric words as Tripurā, Tripurātāpanī, Devī etc. The *Bahvṛcopaniṣad* refers to *Parā Śakti* and *Kādi Vidyās*. According to P. V. Kane, these minor Upaniṣads were composed deliberately to bolster up Tāntric authority in the society where Tantras were generally accorded an inferior position.

Some Tantras cite the authority of Upaniṣads in certain matters. For example, the *Kulārṇava-tantra* quotes the *Śvetāśvatara Upaniṣad* (VI. 23) about the importance of *guru*, as stated before.

The resemblance of the basic principles of Tantra with many of the Upaniṣadic doctrines is clear. For example, the idea of *saguṇa* and *nirguṇa* Brahman of the Upaniṣads occurs in many verses of the second chapter of the *Mahānirvāṇa-tantra*. The *saguṇa* Brahman of the Upaniṣad is God whose aspects are Creator, Preserver and Destroyer. A similar idea has been expressed in several verses of the above Tantra.

Tantra and Smṛti[38]

Though the entire Tāntric system has not been categorically condemned in Smṛti, yet aspects of this system have been denounced. Aparārka on the *Yājñavalkya-smṛti*, i.7, thinks that Manu (xii. 95-96) refers to the scriptures of the Śaivas i.e. Tantras, by the words *Vedavāhya Śāstras*. Manu, xi. 63, however, clearly decries *abhicāra*; it is a prominent topic of Tantra. *Abhicāra* has been treated as an *Upapātaka* or minor sin. Magic rites, designed to harm enemies, have been regarded as sins in such early works as *Āpastamba-dharmasūtra* (i.9. 26-27), Baudhāyana (ii.1.2.16), *Gautama* (25.7), *Manu-smṛti* (ix. 290) and *Yājñavalkya-smṛti* (ii. 289). Wine is regarded as an indispensable article for Tāntric *sādhanā*, but drinking of *surā* has been denounced in Dharmaśāstra as causing *mahāpātaka* or grave sin particularly on the part of Brāhmaṇas. In connexion with *Durgotsava* of the *Tāmasika* type, wine is prescribed as an article to be offered to the goddess. Certain authorities, however, provide that it should be avoided. The Purāṇas forbid the offer of wine by *dvijas*, particularly Brāhmaṇas. The *Brahma-purāṇa* prohibits wine in the Kali Age on the part of *dvijas* (*kalau varjyaṃ dvijātibhiḥ*). The *Kālikāpurāṇa* declares that a Brāhmaṇa, offering wine, becomes degraded (*brāhmṇyād eva hīyate*).

The popularity and spread of Tāntricism induced some Purāṇas to absorb certain Tāntric rites and customs. Partly through Purāṇas and partly under the compelling social conditions, the Smṛti digests had to recognise Tāntric practices. The general attitude of Smṛti writers to Tantra appears to have been one of acquiescense, and even acceptance, insofar as Tāntric rites did not run counter to Vedic authority and the established Brahmanical rites and customs based on the Veda.

Tantra and Vedānta[39]

According to Tantra, *Kuṇḍalinī* is the inner spiritual power lying dormant within the human body. By *Sādhanā* man can reach that stage when the human is transformed into the divine. It is then that *Jīva* becomes Śiva. The Upaniṣad, too, prescribes the means by which the individual soul (*jīvātman*) can be transformed into the Supreme soul (*paramātman*). The fundamental difference in approach between Upaniṣad and Tantra is that according to the former, the means of reaching the goal is *bhāvanā* (contemplation, meditation), and according to the latter, mere *bhāvanā* is not enough; it must be accompanied by *kriyā* (action). The Tantra prescribes physical efforts along with mental or spiritual power. Vedānta accepts the eternal Śivahood of *jīva*, but Tantra holds that *Śivahood* can be attained by practices of special kinds.

In many respects, Tantra is similar to the Upaniṣads. Like the latter, it believes that creation is but the sport (*līlā*) of the Supreme Puruṣa. At the time of creation, *Puruṣa* and *Prakṛti* appear simultaneously, and they resort to the Supreme Puruṣa. At the time of dissolution, they are again merged into Brahman or Īśvara.

Like Upaniṣads, Tantra is non-dualistic.[40]

Tantra and Sāṃkhya

There is an impression among some that Tāntric religion is based on Sāṃkhya philosophy. Both the systems use the terms Puruṣa and Prakṛti; this, perhaps, has led to the above idea. But, there is a gulf of difference between the two concepts as used in the two systems. Unlike the Tāntric Śiva, the Puruṣa of Sāṃkhya is not the Universal soul; he is not the indivisible, infinite and eternal Brahman. According to Sāṃkhya, Puruṣas are many and vary with individuals. He no doubt stays with Prakṛti, but is himself inactive; he has no power to create anything. In the presence of Puruṣa, Prakṛti carries on its creative activity at which Puruṣa is the passive onlooker. *Śakti* or *Parā Prakṛti* of Tantra is different from the *Mūlaprakṛti* of Sāṃkhya. The former is the divine energy of the Supreme Lord—*parāsya Śaktir vividhaiva śrūyate* —by this, Upaniṣad has indicated it as the supreme energy of Brahman.

According to Sāṃkhya, Prakṛti, consisting of the three qualities of *Sattva, Rajas* and *Tamas*, is the source of the material world. Due to its close nearness to Puruṣa, creation proceeds in the order of *Mahat*, etc. At the time of dissolution, all the created objects are merged into the eternal Prakṛti. According to Tantra, however, both Puruṣa and Prakṛti emanate from the Supreme Being who is *niṣkala*. *Prakṛti* is the creative energy of Brahman. Brahman, possessed of this energy, is called *Sakala*. *Sakala* Brahman is Puruṣa and his energy is called Prakṛti: these two are not absolutely distinct entities. Creation is not possible without the union of Puruṣa (Śiva) and Prakṛti (*Śakti*).

Sāṃkhya philosophy has a leaning towards dualism. But, according to Tantra, Puruṣa and Prakṛti are but the manifestations of the one infinite eternal Brahman. The ultimate goal of Tāntric *sādhanā* is communion with the attributeless (*nirguṇa*) *niṣkala* Para Brahman.

A basic distinction between Sāṃkhya and Tantra is this. According to the former, the existence of God has not been established.[41] But, Tāntric religion is founded on theism. The efficient cause of creation, according to Sāṃkhya, is the union of Prakṛti and Puruṣa, the latter being inactive. Due to union with *Puruṣa*, the equilibrium of Prakṛti, constituted of the three aforesaid qualities, is disturbed. Thus, *Prakṛti* becomes ready to create. But, in Tantra, creation is the sport (*līlā*) of Brahman possessed of attributes (*saguṇa*). Brahman is not distinct from His Prakṛti. So, Prakṛti, though having three qualities, is not *jaḍā* (unconscious). She is conscious, and, resorting to her, *Saguṇa* Brahman (=Īśvara) manifests Himself in the divine objects of the world.

The *Śāradātilaka* clearly reveals the influence of the Sāṃkhya system. It enumerates 36 *tattvas* including those of the Sāṃkhya system. It should be noted that, like Sāṃkhya, Tantra regards discriminative knowledge (*viveka*) as essential for reaching the goal.

It should be noted that theistic Sāṃkhya supplied the basis for the early Pāñcaratra, Pāśupata and some other popular religious systems.

Tantra, Buddhism and Jainism

Hindu Tantra is opposed to the basic principle of Buddhism that non-violence is the highest religion. It thinks that this principle is meaningless: because, without violence of some sort or other life cannot exist. The food, that is essential for life, is *jīva*. Animal slaughter is directly perceived. But, when we gather fruits from a tree, we commit violence to it. When we drink cow's milk, we deprive the calf of it; thus, it is a kind of violence. In this way we find that violence is indispensable for our existence.

A comparison of Hindu Tantra with the Buddhist fundamental reveals fundamental similarities in some respects and differences in others. Gods of the Hindu pantheon are not generally recognised in Buddhism. Buddhist Tantra is silent about Śakti and Śāktism, the corner-stone of the philosophical edifice of Hindu Tantra. Instead of Śiva and Devi (*Śakti*), the male and female principles of Hindu Tantra, the Buddhists have *Upāya* and *Prajñā*, the latter having the same characteristics as the former but in a reverse process. Buddhists advocate *Śūnyatā* (nihilism) not recognised by Hindus. As regards the goal and the means to its attainment, both have remarkable similarities. The importance of *mantra, guru, maṇḍala*, etc. is recognised in both the systems.

The cult of *Śakti* and Tāntrism of the Hindus are much older than the earliest extant Tāntric works of the Buddhists. Some scholars hold that the description of Tārā in such works as the *Tārārahasya* of Brahmānanda and the *Tantrasāra* of *Kṛṣṇānanda* is Buddhistic in origin.[42] It is believed by some that Nāgārjuna, the celebrated Buddhist scholar of the 7th century, introduced the worship of Mahācīnatārā in India. It is claimed that names of Hindu deities, ending in or beginning with Vajra, owe their origin to Buddhist Tantra. Some believe that the Hindu goddesses Mahācīnatārā, Chinnamastā, Kālī, etc. were originally Buddhistic. It may be noted that Buddhist Tantra recognised such Purāṇic deities as Gaṇeśa and Sarasvatī.

Buddhist Tantra does not emphasise the cult of Mother Goddess with as much zeal as is found in Hindu Tantra. Nevertheless, it recognises Her. The reason is, perhaps, that the cult was too popular to be ignored.

From the arguments and counter-arguments about the mutual relationship of Hindu and Buddhist Tantras, we can conclude that, though the former had an independent origin, it absorbed certain elements of the latter. The latter also, perhaps, borrowed certain matters from the former.

The above facts lead to the conclusion that Hindu Tantra could not have been modelled on Buddhist Tantra, as is supposed by some scholars. It has been pointed out elsewhere that none of the three famous Chinese travellers refers to the study of Buddhist Tantra in India. Again, excepting perhaps the *Guhyasamājatantra* and *Mañjuśrīmūlkalpa*, there is hardly any Buddhist Tantra dating back to a period earlier than 650 A.D.; but there is evidence of the prevalence of Tāntric practices in India long before 600 A.D.

The *Rudrayāmala* (17-119-25) states that the Buddha taught Vaśiṣṭha the *Kaula* way of Tantra. This is pointed out by some as an evidence that the Hindu Tantra was derived from the Buddhists. This is, however, rejected by others, notably P. V. Kane, as unfounded.

Some miraculous powers like transformation of a dragon into an insect, crossing rivers on foot, etc., attributed to the Buddha in some works (e.g. *Mahāpadāna Sutta*), remind one of Siddhis in Tantra. It is, however, believed by many that such powers were attributed to him by later writers.

Some literary evidences are pointed out to show that the Buddha came under the influence of Tāntric ideas. For instance, in the *Majjhima Nikāya* (ed. Mitra, p. 315), the Buddha is stated to have remained at a cemetery, using bones as his pillow. This is dismissed by some as an interpolation. Others do not find any Tāntric practice in it. The same work (I. 79) states the views of some *Śramaṇas* that sexual enjoyment with young female ascetics is a means to salvation. The *Kathāvatthu* (*Majjhima*, PTS, I. p. 305) mentions sexual union as a way to salvation.

These practices are inconsistent with the essence of Buddhism which advocates cessation of desire (*taṇhā=tṛṣṇā*) as the goal of *Sādhanā*. These were probably later fabrications or intruded into Hindu Tāntric ideas with the conversion of Hindus who imbibed ideas of

Hindu Tantra.

The use of skulls as begging bowls by the monks (e.g. *Cullavagga*, XXIII. 1-2) was, perhaps, introduced by the practice of the above converts.

The belief in the use of charms and spells for benevolent and malevolent purposes, as reflected in some Buddhist works (e.g. *Cullavagga* V-10-2), is clearly Tāntric.

The injunctions for the preservation of the body and disciplining the mind, found in some Buddhist works, appears to point to Tāntric influence.

The importance, attached in Jaina works (e.g. *Mudrāvicāra, Mudrāvidhi*) to *Mudrā*, the Jaina rules for physical and psychological discipline, the Jaina *Mātṛkas Vidyādharī, Yoginīs*, etc., the belief in magical rites and potency of *mantras*, the attribution of miraculous powers to Mahāvīra, etc. appear to betray Tāntric influence on Jainism. But, the extreme austerity of Jainism and ascetic morality, inculcated in it, made it less vulnerable to Tāntric infiltration than Buddhism.

Tantra and Vaiṣṇavism

We have seen that there was a distinct class of Vaiṣṇava Tantras. So, the influence of Tantra on Vaiṣṇavism, as on other religious faiths of India, is obvious. According to the Vaiṣṇavas, Kṛṣṇa and Rādhā are the two Supreme Realities, or the two manifestations of one Supreme Reality. It is believed by many modern scholars that Kṛṣṇa-Rādhā is only another form of Śiva-Śakti of Tantra. Rādhā is characterised as the *Hlādinī Śakti* of Kṛṣṇa. Śiva-Śakti of Tantra may have inspired the moulding of Kṛṣṇa-Rādhā or both Tantra and Vaiṣṇavism may have been indebted to a common popular source for their respective ideas. Nevertheless, the similarity between the two faiths is too striking to be explained away.

The Pañcarātra works of Vaiṣṇavas reveal a very close relation with Śākta Tantras in some respects. For example, in the latter, the all-pervading Ādyā Śakti has been designated as 'Yoni' (source) of everything. Likewise, in the *Ahirbudhnya=saṃhitā* (59.7), *Śakti*, in the form of Lakṣmī, has been called 'Yoni'. Like Tantra, the *Ahirbudhnya* (51. 54-61) designates Śakti as Tārā as well as 'Hrīm'. The same work, like Tantra, holds (10.55) that Lakṣmī, as the Supreme Energy (*Parā Śakti*), resides in *Mūlādhāra*. Like Tantra again, the Pañcarātra works provide for *Nyāsas* as a means of *Sādhanā*, and regard letters of the alphabet as *Mātṛkās*.

Tantra regards the body as the abode of God. In the different *cakras* and *padmas*, supposed to be within the body, *Śaktidhāma* (abode of Śakti) and *Śivadhāma* (abode of Śiva) are conceived. In certain Vaiṣṇava Saṃhitās, too, Mathurā, Vṛndāvana, etc. are regarded as the abodes of God. In some Purāṇas,[43] *Gokula* has been described as God's abode in the shape of a thousand-petalled lotus. According to Tantra, this lotus is called *Sahasrāra-padma* which is supposed to be within the head. The description of Viṣṇu and his Śakti, Lakṣmī, and of their abode, contained in the *Brahma-saṃhitā*, a highly authoritative work in Bengal Vaiṣṇavism, is Tāntric in character. Rūpa Gosvāmin, a famous scholar-devotee of Bengal, holds[44] that Rādhā is the essence of *Mahāśakti* glorified in Tantra. Both Jīva Gosvāmin, another celebrity in Bengal Vaiṣṇavism, and Kṛṣṇadāsa, a famous biographer of Caitanya, have quoted a verse about Rādhā from the *Bṛhad-gautamīya* Tantra.[45] In his commentary on the *Brahma-saṃhitā*, Jīva Gosvāmin has cited a verse on Rādhā from the *Sammohana-tantra*. A scholar has attempted to establish Rādhā as the *Mūlā ādyā prakṛti śakti*.[46] The works like *Rādhā-tantra*, popular among the Vaiṣṇavas of Bengal, are believed by many modern scholars to be fabrications. Without going into the authenticity of such works, we can say that Tantras acquired such an exalted position in the society that Vaiṣṇavas had to write Tantras on their own cult in order to attract popular support.

The *Bhāgavata-purāṇa*, the most authoritative work of the Vaiṣṇavas, recognises[47] the authority of Tantra in matters concerning worship, initiation, etc. In his comment on a passage[48] of the *Bhāgavata*, Śrīdhara Svāmin refers to the authority of the Veda and Tantra for both *bhukti* (enjoyment) and *mukti* (liberation).

The influence of Tantra on Vaiṣṇavism was, however, not a one-way traffic. Vaiṣṇavism, in its turn, exercised considerable influence on Tantra. In certain original Tantras, Caitanya has been mentioned. The portions, mentioning Caitanya, may not have been written by Bengali authors, but on their authors the influence of Caitanya is obvious. The *Īśāna-saṃhitā*, known to be a part of the *Kulārṇava*, asserts the divinity of Caitanya. In the *Gūḍhāvatāra* portion, stated to be a part of the *Viśvasāra* or *Viśvasāroddhāra*, Caitanya is described as an incarnation of Viṣṇu. In the *Ūrdhvāmnāya saṃhitā*, Caitanya replaces the Buddha, as an *avatāra* of Viṣṇu. Some portions of the *Brahmayāmala* and *Kṛṣṇayāmala* are called Caitanya-kalpa.

Tantra, Music and Dance

The influence of Tantra on the musical works is marked. For example, the *Saṃgīta-ratnākara* of Śārṅgadeva mentions *Cakras, Nāḍis* etc. within the human body like Tantra. The concept of *Nāda*, occurring in the Sanskrit works on music, has a close parallel to that occurring in Tantra. According to Tantra, *Nāda* is of two kinds, viz. struck or with vibration (*āhata*) and unstruck or without vibration (*anāhata*); the former leads to pleasure, and the latter is heard by the Yogin who has been able to withdraw his senses, from the external objects, into himself. The conception of *Vāyu* within the body, supposed in the musical lore to produce *Nāda* in conjunction with fire, is also similar to that found in Tantra.

Like Tantra, musicologists believe (e.g. *Saṃgīta-ratnākara,* I.2.149) that the gradual ascent of *Kuṇḍalinī* through the various *Cakras,* up to *Sahasrāra* within the head, is the highest fulfilment of *Sādhanā.* In the manner of Tantra, some musical works (e.g. *Saṃgītaratnākara.* I.2) recognise several sheaths (*Kośa*) in the body, e.g. *Annamaya, Manomaya.* The same work reveals (I.2.140 f.f.) the belief that the soul, residing in certain petals of *Anāhata Cakra*, desires success in song, etc. The soul, resorting to certain petals of *Viśuddhicakra* and in *Lalanā,* also ensures success. Resting in *brahmarandhra*, it is satiated with nectar, and produces songs of a high quality. As in Tāntric rites, Mudrā (position of hands and fingers) is an essential element, so also in dance, various *Mudrās* were used. The *Nāṭyaśāstra* of Bharata (C. earlier than 4th or 5th century A.D.) is the earliest extant work on dance. It is not certain whether, in the conception and use of *Mudrās*, Tantra influenced the former or vice versa. Though Tāntric ideas were, perhaps, contemporaneous with the *Atharvaveda*, yet no Tāntric work is known to have been composed or compiled before the fifth or sixth century A.D. So, there is no chronological difficulty in Bharata's influence on Tantra in this respect.

In Tantra, Śiva-Śakti is the pivot round which everything revolves. In works on music also Śiva is generally held in high esteem. Śārṅgadeva starts writing his work with salutation to Śiva. From Śiva *Grāma*, *Varṇa* etc. are supposed to emanate.

Rāgas, on which music rests, are associated with Śiva and Pārvatī. One *Rāga* is declared to have emerged from each of the mouths of Śiva and one *Rāga* from the mouth of Pārvatī. The *Vīṇātantra*, belonging to *Yāmala*, deals, among other things, with music. Of the 32 *Yāmala*

Tantras, some deal with *Gāndharva* or the art of music. The *Trotala-tantra*, and *Kuṇḍīśvara-tantra*, belonging to *Yāmala*, deal with instrumental music.

Besides the above, we find some Sanskrit works referring to certain results obtained by *Abhicāra*, produced by classical music. Such rites, supposed to cause harm to the enemy, are prominent in Tantra.

Tantra, Art and Architecture

Here we shall see how Tantra influenced sculpture,[49] painting and architecture. The relation of Tantra and music has already been discussed.

On the sculptural delineation at Khajuraho (850-1050 A.D.), Konarak (13th cent.), Ellora (8th cent.) Tantric influence is discernible. In this connexion, the Hoysaleśvara temple (12th cent.) of Mysore, the temple-walls of Middle and West India also deserve mention. Nudity, various methods of sexual union, etc. are some of the features of the sculpture of these places. Depiction of sex-act at Sānchi, Amarāvatī and Mathurā, the delineation of a naked couple in an erotic posture in the Liṅgarāja temple (11th cent.), of Bhuvaneswar and some images at various places[50] reveal Tāntric ideas.

Erotic designs, presumably derived from Tantra, are found in some terracotta figures also. For instance, a terracotta couple, found at Chandra Ketugaḍ (2nd cent. A.D.) resembles the aforesaid figure in the *Liṅgarāja* temple. Some seals also appear to reveal Tāntric influence. The Rupar seal (3rd cent. A.D.), for example, depicts copulation.

Various modes of sex act are delineated in some sculptures in caves and temples of various places, e.g. Kārlā, Badāmi (old Vātāpi), etc. A pillar sculpture from south India (17th cent.) represents a devotee worshipping the vulva of the Great Goddess.

Depiction of *mithunas* is common on some doors and at the entrance of some monuments. A divine couple in sexual intercourse is represented in a wooden bracket panel from a temple car (South India, 18th cent.).

Some scholars wonder why such erotic motifs should be in temples and other places. Various reasons for this have been suggested. Some think that *maithuna* being an essential item of *pañcamakāras*, indispensable for *Tāntric Sādhanā*, it was delineated at sacred spots.

Some suggest that such depictions were designed to pander to the carnal propensities of the rich people who constructed the temples.

Others suppose that such erotic representations were intended to attract the common people who are fond of such gross things of life.

Some think that a superstitious belief underlies such sculptures. Nobody disturbs a couple in sexual union. So, gods would not destroy or damage temples, representing men and women engaged in sexual intercourse, with such devastating calamities as thunder, earth-quake, etc.

There is another ingenious suggestion that these were designed to test the mental strength of those who were about to enter spiritual life.

One more suggestion is that as *maithuna* causes child-birth, so its representation at holy places will ensure the fertility of the land.

Another feature in the sculptural designs is the representation of *Mudrās* which constitute one of the five essential *makāras* in Tāntric Sādhanā. Some of these *Mudrās* are *Bhūmispars'a*, *Dharmacakra*, *Varada* and *Abhaya*, mostly associated with the Buddha.

The influence of Tantra is probable on some images, e.g. Ardhanārīśvara representing Śiva and Umā corresponding to Puruṣa and Prakṛti or Liṅga and Yoni.

Some of the sculptures, inspired by Tantra, are absolutely free-from eroticism; e.g. Ārya Tāra of Nālandā (c.7th cent. A.D.), Vajrasattva of Nālandā (c.10th cent.), Heruka of Sārnāth (c.10 cent.) etc. These are all Buddhistic.[51]

Some figures in bronze (e.g. Buddhist destroyer of death, united with his female partner—Tibet, 18th cent.), wood (e.g. South Indian Icon of the Divine Vulva stained with the coloured powders used to worship it), Yoginī with serpentine energy emerging from her vulva (South India, C. 1800 A.D.), demonstrate Tāntric influence.

Tantra influenced the domain of painting too.[52] Some manuscripts contain Tāntric paintings. There are such paintings on paper and cloth also.

The *Āryā-mañjuśrī-mūlakalpa* contains a section on *Paṭavidhāna* (Picture-drawing). It may be noted that the Bengali artists, known as *Paṭuyās*, of whom those of Kalighat in Calcutta are the most well-known, still pursue the art-tradition set forth in the above works.

Tantra included architecture also within the ambit of its influence. In this respect, Orissan architecture deserves special mention. Two major styles of temple-architecture of this province are *Rekha* and *Bhadra*, the former fancied as male and the latter as female. These two, being united, are conceived as bridegroom and bride whose garments are tied together.[53]

The Haṃseśvarī temple (completed 1814 A.D.) at Bansberia, Hooghly (West Bengal) is a unique example of temple-architecture inspired by Tantra.

The interior is like the six *Cakras* through which *Kuṇḍalinī*, in the form of goddess Haṃseśvarī, goes upward. Besides the three well-known Tāntric nerves, *Iḍā, Piṅgalā* and *Suṣumnā*, two more, called *Vajrākhya* and *Citriṇī* are also indicated by ladders.

The aforesaid goddess is seated on a lotus resting on a stem emerging from the navel of Śiva lying on a *Trikoṇa Yantra*. She has a human head in her lower left hand and *Abhayamudrā* in her upper right hand, in the other hands are a sword and a conch.

The very name *Haṃseśvarī* is Tāntric. *Haṃ* is a *Bīja* and *Sa* stands for Śakti. The two are locked (*kīlaka*) together; this locking is believed to lead to the highest goal.

From the foregoing account it seems that a twofold motive was, perhaps, responsible for Tāntric representations in art and architecture; one religious and the other secular. Regarding the latter, visual expression of the passionate feelings of the artist, sculptor or architect or the gratification of the lustful propensities of the people might have motivated their work.

Tantra and Inscriptions

The extreme popularity of Tantra naturally influenced inscriptions also. For example, the Gangadhar Stone Inscription of Viśvavarman of 480 Mālava era (= 424 A.D.) refers to *Mātṛs* (Mother Goddesses) and Tantra.

Homeland of Tantra—Was Tantra of Foreign Origin?

The place of origin of Tantra is difficult to locate. Nothing definite has as yet been known. All that we can do is to put forward conjectures. It is believed by some that Tantras of *Āgama* type originated in Kashmir. What is known as Tantra may have originated in Bengal, a view shared, among others, by Winternitz. In this connexion, it may be noted that a number of manuscripts of the *Āgamas*, written in Kashmir (Śāradā) script, are found in Kashmir. Those of Tantras, in Bengali script, exist in large numbers in various collections in Bengal.[54] The works of the Saṃhitā class are generally supposed to have originated in different parts of India, particularly Bengal and Deccan. It is significant that, in Kāmākhyā (Assam), a stronghold of Tantra, Śāktism is known to have been preached by the Bengali Śākta Kṛṣṇarāma Nyāyavāgīśa.[55] His influence on the religious life of Assam induced the Ahom king, Rudrasiṃha, to become his disciple. In the remote Hiṃlāj, in Baluchistan, the Bengali Brahmānanda and his disciple, Jñānānanda, preached Tāntric philosophy and Sādhanā. The Tāntric way of *Sādhanā* in Nepal reveals the influence of Bengal.[56] The dissemination of Tāntricism in China and Tibet is believed by some to have taken place through Buddhism propagated from Bengal. The supporters of Bengal origin also point out that all the three kinds of fish for use in sacrifice, mentioned in the *Mahānirvāna-tantra*, (vi. 7.3.) are found in plenty and widely consumed in Bengal. This fact appears to bear out the Bengal origin of this famous work. They find corroboration of their theory in an apocryphal verse[57] stating that, appearing in Gauḍa, this Śāstra developed in Mithilā, rested at some places in Mahārāṣṭra and was destroyed in Gurjara. The noted Bengal work *Prāṇatoṣiṇī* quotes the *Varadā-tantra* (x) stated to contain a description of some sounds of the Nāgara alphabet. From it we learn that the sound 'h' preceding 'y' is pronounced as 'jh'. Again 'h' preceding 'v' is pronounced as 'bh'. Initial 'y' is pronounced like 'j'. These sounds occur in dialects of Bengal, and, in some cases, in East Bengal. The colophon to the *Mahākaulajñāna-vinirṇaya* mentions Candradvīpa in East Bengal from where it appeared.

Arthur Avalon (Woodroffe) is not inclined to accept the theory, put forward by a few scholars, that the fundamental principles of Tantra were imported into India from China. The pro-China theorists point out, *inter alia*, that the *Rudrayāmala*, a well-known Tantra, mentions China; Vasiṣṭha is said to have gone there where the Buddha (Buddhist doctrine) was established.[58] The words TĀ-RĀ, RU-D-RA, TAN-T-RA, used in Tantra, are supposed to be loan-words from the Chinese language. Another ingenious, though not very convincing, argument is that the flower, called *javā*, which is considered to be very appropriate for the worship of Śakti, is called Chinese rose. There is a work called *Mahācīnācāra-tantra*. It is true that Tāntric doctrines and rites were widely prevalent for a long time in the region called Mahācīna.

Mahācīna is identified with Arabia felix by some, with China by others. The pro-China theorists give some other arguments too. The mystic syllables *hrīṃ, krīṃ*, etc., which are indispensable in the Tāntric rites, show the preponderance of the nasal sound. So, the above Tāntric syllables may have come from China (Vide *Mātṛkābheda-tantra*, Paṭala

12). The diagrams remind us of the pictorial writing in an age when letters did not yet originate. Chinese alphabet is a sort of pictorial writing. May be that the diagrams were borrowed from China. A mode of *Tāntric Sādhanā* is called *cīnācāra*. According to the *Tārā-tantra, cīnācāra* came from Mahācīna. *Cīnācāra* is mentioned in some other Tantras too; e.g. *Śaktisaṃgama*, Sundarī, I. 188ff, *Puraściaryārṇava*, I, *Merutantra*, etc. There is considerable divergence of opinions about the location of Mahācīna.

P.C. Bagchi points out that the female energies (Yoginīs), mentioned in Brahmanical Tantras, include Lāmā; this word is Tibetan, and denotes Devī or Śakti. He further says that Ḍākinī, Hākinī, Śākinī, Lākinī, etc., are also exotic.

The *Sammoha-tantra* mentions the Tāntric culture of foreign lands like Bāhlīka, Kirāta, Bhoṭa, Cīna, Mahācīna, Pārasika, Airāka, Kamboja, Hūṇa, Yavana, Gandhāra and Nepāla. P. C. Bagchi seems to be right in deducing, from this fact, that these countries also had some esoteric modes of *Sādhanā* which were known in India to be similar in character to Indian Tāntric practices.

According to the *Pag Sam Jon Zan*, Buddhist Tantra originated in Uḍḍiyāna. The location of Uḍḍiyāna (also spelt as Oḍḍiyāna, Oḍiyāna, Odṛyāna) is highly controversial. While some identify it with Udyāna in the Swat Valley, others would place it in Kashgarh. Haraprasād Śāstrī, followed by others, places it in Orissa. It is considered by some to have been a part of Bengal.

Some scholars believe that the conception of Śakti and her worship is unIndian. The introduction of the Śakti cult, as a main theme, makes them feel that Tantra is exotic.

While foreign elements in Indian Tantras cannot be ruled out, these, if any, have been mixed up in such a way that it is difficult, if not impossible, to sort them out.

H.P. Śāstrī thought, on the basis of a verse in the *Kubjikāmata-tantra*, that Tantra came to India from outside.[59] According to others, this verse does not prove anything conclusively; it might simply hint at the prevalence of Tantra in India from earlier times. Arthur Avalon is of the opinion that Tantra was imported to India from Chaldea or Śakadvīpa. There is a Tibetan tradition that Asaṅga, the noted Buddhist philosopher of the fourth or fifth century A.D. introduced Tantric principles and practices in India. P.V. Kane does not attach importance to this tradition which is mainly based on the *History of Buddhism* by

Tāranātha (b.1573 or 1575) who wrote over one thousand years after Asaṅga. Some have tried to establish the foreign origin of Tantra on the ground that the exalted position of the *guru* in it has nothing comparable in the Vedic and Purāṇic religions. Others, however, reject this argument by pointing out the high place of honour accorded to *guru* in the *Nirukta* (II.4), the *Śvetāśvatara Upaniṣad* (vi. 18.23), the *Liṅga-Purāṇa*, *Devībhāgavata*, etc. After an examination of the diverse views on the question, P.V. Kane concludes that a few mystic practices like *kulācāra* and *vāmācāra* might have originated abroad and have been brought to India, but there is no positive evidence of the Tāntric system as a whole arising outside. On the contrary, he thinks that Tāntric doctrines migrated to other places, notably China and Tibet, from India.

Against the view that Tantra was brought to India from China or Tibet, it may be pointed out that, whereas many Sanskrit Tantras were translated into Chinese and Tibetan, there is no evidence of any Tāntric work of these places having been translated into Sanskrit.

India, as indeed all other ancient lands with an advanced civilisation, never lived in isolation.

The pottery, unearthed among the relics of Indus Valley civilisation (c. 3000 B.C.), appears to indicate links with Sumeria and Mesopotamia.

The theory of the influence of Babylon on Indian astronomy has been postulated by some scholars. The *Baveru Jātaka* testifies to contacts between the two countries.

The discovery of Sanskrit manuscripts, both Brahmanical and Buddhist, as well as of some images in various parts of Central Asia are unmistakable evidences of Indian influence in that region. Buddhism was the most powerful factor in the dissemination of Indian culture in that area.

Besides Indian colonial expansion and establishment of Indian kingdoms in some countries of the Far East, there were brisk cultural exchanges.

With China, India's contact dates back to centuries before Fa-hien set foot (401 A.D.) on the Indian soil. The Chinese looked upon India not only as the holy land of the Buddha's birth, but also as a country with immense possibility of trade and commerce. The words *Cīna-karpūru* (a kind of camphor), *Cīna-Karkaṭikā* (a kind of gourd), *Cīnaja* (steel), *Cīnapiṣṭa* (a kind of lead), *Cīnamaya* (an article made of red lead), *Cīnāṃśuka* and *Cīnasicaya*, both denoting cloth, *Cīnarājaputra* (a kind of fruit-tree), etc. leave no doubt about Sino-Indian contacts.

We have already seen that, on some grounds, Indian Tantra is supposed by some to have been borrowed from China.

It is interesting to note that the Chinese Taoist concept of *Yang* (Male principle) and *Yin* (Female principle), underlying everything, appears to correspond to the Tāntric concept of Śiva and Śakti. The acquisition of supernatural power by a devotee in China is like the achievement of *Siddhi* in Tantra. Among other things, this school advocates the utility of the following for long life and immortality in the mortal world; respiratory exercise, desciplined sexual intercourse; regulated diet. These prescriptions are found in Tantra too.

Some scholars find, in the celebrated Tārādevī of Tantra, close similarity with Astarte or Ashtaroth, the famous Mother Goddess of Western Asia.

There was brisk commercial and cultural contact between Tibet and India. The *Jayadratha-yāmala* refers to the practices of Lāmās (*Lāmāvarga*). It mentions 24 Lāmās; the list includes Lāmā, Śakinī. The term Lākinī, found in Tantra, is derived from Tibetan Lha-Kṣa which stands for a class of sorcerers and witches. In the *Hevajra-tantra*, the Lāmās are referred to in association with Ḍākinīs.

Besides the above facts, the *Sammoha-tantra* refers, *inter alia*, to China and Tibet as centres of Tāntric culture.

It is, perhaps, significant that Jālandhara, one of the early *Śākta Pīṭhas*, is situated on a highway connecting India with Tibet.

There are evidences galore that India had cultural and commercial relations of give and take with Greece, Rome and Egypt.

It should be noted that, according to the *Sammoha-tantra*, goddess *Nīlasarasvatī* was born in a land included in Mongolia. In this connexion, we should bear in mind that one of the ethnic elements of the Indian population was Mongolian.

The cult of Mother Goddess was important in the ancient religious systems of many other countries. In those lands, there were beliefs and practices similar, in many respects, to those of the Tāntric religion.[60] For instance, we may cite the galli of the Syrian Mother Goddess, Astarte of Hierapolis, the Eleusian and Phrygian mysteries, the Dinonysian rites, the Marian secrets, etc. Esoteric forms of worship, resembling Tāntric rites to some extent, prevailed in Phrygia, Syria, Lydia, Cappadocia, Pontus and Galatia; in these regions, the cult of Mother Goddess was popular.

Indiscriminate sexual intercourse was a part of a Greek festival in honour of goddesses Demeter and Persephone. The rituals, connected with the union of Cybele and Attis, Aphrodite and Adonis, Ishtar and Tammuz, Demetes and Zeus, were marked by sex-rites.

We have it on Frazer's authority[61] that the Mother Goddess was worshipped, under different names, by many peoples of West Asia.

Hogarth testifies[62] to the wide prevalence of the worship of Mother Goddess in Asia Minor and around the Mediterranean.

R. P. Chanda draws our attention to the similarity between the Śakti cult and the worship of the female deity in Asia Minor, Syria, Egypt and other Mediterranean countries. Analogous sex-practices are also to be noted.

Antiquity of Tantra

The number of extant Tantras is quite large. It can be presumed that centuries elapsed before the Tantra literature grew into a huge bulk. But, the origin of this literature is shrouded in obscurity.

The earliest Nepalese manuscripts of Tantras appear to have been written between the seventh and ninth centuries A.D. The *Mahābhārata* contains no reference to Tantra, although *Itihāsa* and *Purāṇa* are mentioned. Tantra is conspicuous by absence in the accounts of the famous Chinese travellers, Fa-hien (fourth century A.D.), Hiuen Tsang (seventh century) and I-tsing (seventh century A.D.). No Buddhist Tantra appears to have existed before 650 A.D. The first clear reference to this literature appears to occur in the *Bhāgavata-purāṇa* (c.800 A.D. or earlier) perhaps clearly refers to Tantra for the first time. These reasons led scholars like Winternitz to conclude that Tantra literature did not probably originate earlier than the fifth or sixth century A.D. In this connexion, it should be added that the *Devī-purāṇa*, a Bengal work probably originating about the seventh century A.D., shows profound influence of Tantra.[63]

Some scholars[64] think that female terracotta figures, discovered among the ruins of the Indus Valley civilisation, testify to the prevalence of Tantrism in the pre-Vedic period.

Some[65] hold that, in the *Devīsūkta* (x. 125) of the *Ṛgveda*, there are covert references to Durgādevī, who represents the earlier form of Śakti or Kālī, the principal goddess of Tantra. They also try to prove that there are other elements of Tantra in the *Ṛgveda*. For example, the *Rātri-sūkta* (x. 127) clearly refers to *Devī Durgā*. This theory is rejected by the opponents. Others, however, regard this Sūkta as a supplement (*khila*) interpolated into the *Ṛgveda* at a later time. It is further claimed that the magic and malevolent spells (*abhicāra*) of the *Atharvaveda* are the precursors of later Tāntric rites.[66] Some are of the opinion that Tāntric ideas originated from the *Saubhāgyakāṇḍa* of this Veda. The existence of Tantra, in very remote antiquity, is sought to be established with reference to certain Upaniṣads.

There is a view that Tantra originated among the Buddhists. It is argued that the Buddha, in order to popularise his teachings among all classes of people, introduced the Tāntric ways. It is believed that all extant Buddhist Tantras originated from Mahāyāna Buddhism. The Mother Goddesses, Kālī, Tārā, etc. are supposed to have been originally Buddhist in conception.

In considering the antiquity of Tantra we have to think of Tāntric ideas, Tāntric practices and Tāntric literature. Tāntric ideas and practices are generally supposed to hark back to time immemorial. Primitive people, even before the dawn of civilisation, resorted to some practices which were the result of the natural propensities. The Tāntric *Yantra, mudrā* and the mystic *Bījas*, etc. appear to indicate pictorial writings, use of finger pose as symbols of language and monosyllabic language of the primitive people. The black acts of Tantra, generally known as *abhicāra*, also appear to indicate the naive beliefs and crude practices of the primitive age.

With the passage of time, the ideas were cystallised and the crude and vulgar practices were retained. Tāntric literature is of a much later growth. As in the case of literature in general, the long development and evolution of a language gives rise to literature; so also, in the case of Tantra, the natural human instincts found expression in human actions, which were followed by systematic works on Tantra literature. The primitive practices evolved into Buddhist Tantra at a certain time and at a certain palce, and into Hindu Tantra at a different time and place. As pointed out by Winternitz (*History of Indian Literature*, I), we find in Tantra an admixture of crude ideas and sublime philosophy, profound philosophical thought side by side with wild superstition and confused occultism. On the one hand, we find an impeccable code of morality side by side with wild orgies testifying to reprehensible immoral practices. All this shows later refinement introduced into primitive crudities.

The two hymns to Durgā in the *Mahābhārata* by Yudhiṣṭhira (Virāṭa, ch. 6) and by Arjuna (Bhīṣma, ch. 23) are supposed by some to indicate Tāntric influence. But, these are regarded by other scholars as spurious and discarded in the critical edition of Poona. Another argument in support of the great antiquity of Tantra is that, in the *Mārkaṇḍeya* and *Liṅga Purāṇas*, the influence of Tantra is indubitable. There is mention of Tantra in the following Purāṇas: *Varāha, Padma, Skanda, Brahma,* etc. Śaṃkara (c. eighth-ninth century) has accepted the authority of Tantra in his *Ānandalaharī* and *Śāktāmoda.* The six *Cakras* of Tantra have been mentioned by him in his *Śārīraka-bhāṣya.* Bāṇabhaṭṭa (seventh century) and Bhavabhūti (eighth century) mention the term Kāpālika, and refer to Tāntric views. The prevalence of Tāntric and Śākta worship in the contemporary society can be presumed from Bāṇa's works. While dealing with Pātañjala philosophy, Mādhavācārya (fourteenth century) has quoted many lines from Tantra in his *Sarvadars'anasaṃgraha.* It is rather curious that even the heterodox philosophical systems of Bauddhas, Jains and Cārvākas have been dealt with in this work, but there is no mention of Tantra in it. This tends to indicate aversion of the orthodox section of the society to the break-away Tantra Śāstra.

It was pointed out by the late Yoges Vidyānidhi that the names Brāhmī and Devanāgarī, as applied to Indian alphabet, bear the impress of Tantra. He thinks that the name Brahmā has been derived from *Brāhmī,* one of the eight *mātṛkās* in Tantra. He further believes that, in very early times, there was the practice of worshipping painted symbols of the goddess. One such symbol was *devanāgara* or the abode of the deity. From this Devanāgarī script was so called.

Those who are inclined to assume a very late origin of Tantra and to deny its authority, put forward several arguments the chief of which are as follows:

(i) Unlike ancient Dharmaśāstra, Tantra does not exercise authority all over India. The influence of non-Aryan aborigines, led to its origin in Bengal where alone its authority has been recognised.

(ii) Among the Māhāyāna Buddhists, the worship of deities Tārā, Vajrayoginī, etc., and *mantra, bīja* and *japa*, etc., are in vogue. Similar practices are found among the followers of Tantra also. So, it seems likely that Tantra arose from Māhāyāna Buddhism.

(iii) From the practice of the worship of Śakti, ghosts, serpents, trees, etc., current among the aborigines, it seems that such practices crept into Tantra under their influence.

(iv) Tantra, as a Śāstra, does not find a place in the famous Sanskrit lexicon *Nāmaliṅgānuśāsana*, generally known as *Amarakoṣa*.

(v) According to the *Sūtasaṃhitā* (Mukti-khaṇḍa) the customs of Pañcarātra, etc., will be beneficial to those who have strayed away from the Vedic ways of life. This clearly indicates that Tantra arose long long after the Veda, at a period when Vedic authority lost much of its hold over the society, probably due to the spread of Buddhism.

(vi) According to the *Śāmba-purāṇa* the people, drifting away from the Vedic way of life, and averse to Vedic expiatory rites, will resort to Tantra for gradulally entering into the Vedic way.

(vii) In the *Meru-tantra*, the following couplet occurs:

phiraṅgabhāṣayā mantrasteṣāṃ saṃsādhanād bhuvi/
iṃrejā navaṣaṭpañca laṇḍrajāścāpi bhāvinaḥ//

The occurrence, in it, of the words *Phiraṅga* (one born out of the union of an Englishman), married to an Indian, *iṃreja* (Englishman), *laṇḍra* (London), etc., indicates that it was not composed earlier than at least the eighteenth century.

The *Nāṭyaśāstra*, which in its present form is generally supposed to have originated about the fourth or fifth century A.D., does not mention *Nāḍi*, *Cakra* or *Nāda* arising from them. This fact tends to prove that either Tantra did not arise before the *Nāṭyaśāstra* or this literature had not yet established its authority.

There are counter-arguments also. For example, in the *Yaśastilaka-campū* (Āśvāsa V), Bhāsa is stated to have said the following about *Vāmācāra* — one should drink *surā* and put on grotesque dress which attracts the mind of the people. *Vāmācāra* is a well-known Tantric way of life, and Bhāsa is placed by some in the fifth century B.C. At any rate, he appears to have flourished long before Kālidāsa (c. 5th century A.D.) who refers to him in the drama *Mālavikāgnimitra*. In the *Lalitavistara* (Chap. X) of about the first century A.D. the Buddha is stated to have learnt from *Viśvāmitra* 46 letters including *aṃ, aḥ* and *kṣa*. These three are treated as separate letters in *Tantra* alone. From this fact the pre-Buddha origin of Tantra can be inferred. In the above work, the word *mātṛkā* occurs only in Tantra. The same work mentions *Nigama* which appears to be a designation of *Tantra* in this context. Among the relics of Indus Valley Civilisation, there are terracotta figures of *mātṛkās* and male figures sitting in a Yogic posture. Some scholars think that, even in those pre-Vedic times, Durgā as Mother of the universe and Śiva as Father were worshipped. This is a germ of later *Tantra*. It is not correct to say that Tāntric authority was not established outside Bengal. Like the Bengalis, the inhabitants of the upper classes in other parts of India are divided into three major sects—Śaiva, Śākta and Vaiṣṇava. The *mantras* of all these sects are Tantric. If similarity alone between Mahāyāna Buddhism and Tantra is regarded as indicating the latter having been derived from the former, then, on the same ground, the former may be supposd to have been influenced by the latter. A few basic differences between the two render it impossible for Buddhism to give rise to Tantra. Buddhism teaches action without desire for its fruit, but Tantra ordains action with an object in view. Tantra prescribes different ways of *sādhanā* in accordance with the different temperaments and capabilities of the persons concerned. But in Buddhism, there is not much consideration for differences in the mental or intellectual make-up of individuals. Buddhism categorically forbids violence like animal-sacrifice; Tantra allows the sacrifice of animals.

It is not clear what is meant by the reference to aborigines. Of the non-Aryan races, India was inhabited by Drāviḍas, Oḍras, Pauṇḍrikas, etc. They were residents of the south. To believe that Bengali scholars produced Tantra under their influence is to deny the genius which characterised Bengal writers through ages. Other classes of aborigines, viz. Sāntāl, Gāro, Koch, etc., inhabited the hilly regions of Assam. The Bengalis have always distinguished themselves for intellectual independence. For example, while the rest of India implicitly recognised the authority of the *Mitākṣarā* in the laws of inheritance and succession, Bengal formulated her own laws in the *Dāyabhāga*. In literature, they created a new literary style called *Gauḍī rīti*. In music, she contributed a distinct *Rāga* called *Gauḍa*. To say that Bengali intellectuals borrowed Tantra from the above aborigines is an outrage towards their capacity and a denial of historical truth. Śakti has been worshipped in different forms and under various appellations in different parts of India. For example, Kāmākhyā in Kāmarūpa, Guhyeśvarī in Nepal, Vindhyavāsinī in the Vindhya region, Jvālāmukhi in Jalandhara, sixty-four Yoginīs and Annapūrṇā, in Varanasi etc. So, the Śakti-worship of Tantra is very late, and originated in Bengal—this view cannot be wholly accepted.

Durgā-worship, influenced by Tantra, is in vogue not only in Bengal. As *Durgāpūjā* or *Navarātravrata*, it is current in other places too.

There is an image of Manasā Devī even on the far-off Govardhana hill. So, it cannot be asserted that serpent-worship has been in vogue in Bengal alone.

The *Yoginī-tantra* is mentioned by Raghunandana in his *Aṣṭāviṃśati-tattva* and by Kṛṣṇānanda in his *Tantrasāra*. These writers belong to the sixteenth century. So, it is wrong to think that the above Tantra could not have been composed before the last three centuries. The work refers to the Koch King Viśvasiṃha (middle of 16th cent.). Some Tāntric works, like the aforesaid *Meru-tantra*, may have been composed very late. There is nothing to prove the late origin of Tantra as a class of literature.

Those, who attribute high antiquity to Tantra, push it back to prehistoric times. B. Foote claims to have found phalli among the neolithic remains in the Deccan.[67] Shāma Śāstrī is of the opinion that the symbols, found on some old coins, dating back to periods earlier than even the sixth or seventh century A.D., are nothing but Tantric hieroglyphics[68] which, according to him, are the precursors of the Devanāgarī alphabet. He thinks that some Tāntric works may be of later origin, but they represent a much older tradition.[69] Thus, the Tāntric Upaniṣads like the *Tripuropaniṣad*, containing Tāntric mystic syllables, contain a tradition of remote ages.[70]

From the above arguments for and against the high antiquity of Tantra we can conclude that, in the matter of the origin of this class of literature, we must guard against the two extremes of a stupendously ancient period and a ludicrously modern epoch. May be that Tantric ideas originated even in Vedic times or earlier but systematic works were not, perhaps, composed earlier than the fifth century A.D.

In the welter of arguments for and against the antiquity of Tantras, some light is clearly visible. The Gaṅgādhara Stone Inscription of Viśvavarman (424 A.D.) mentions *Mātṛs* or Mother Goddesses and Tantra. The mention of *Ḍākinīs* in association of the temple of the Mothers proves that P. C. Bagchi is wrong in his assumption about their late entry into Indian conception. The *Bṛhat-saṃhitā* (57.56) of Varāhamihira (c. 475-550 A.D.) mentions the groups of *Mātṛs*. The *Viṣṇu-purāṇa*, one of the earliest of the existing *Purāṇas*, speaks of Viṣṇu endowed with Śakti. It also mentions several names of Durgā, and states that if she is worshipped with wine, flesh, etc., she fulfils all desires of the devotee. In the *Kādambarī* of Bāṇabhaṭṭa (first half of the seventh century), there is a description of a temple of Caṇḍikā. It mentions the lion mount, the killing of Mahiṣāsura, the offering of heads of animals, doctrines of Pāśupatas, etc. The *Mātṛs* and *Yantras* (diagrams) are also mentioned. The *Harṣacarita* of the same author refers to magic circles and human sacrifice, *Siddhis*, etc. The *Mālatīmādhava* of Bhavabhūti (c. eighth century) mentions human sacrifice to Cāmuṇḍā, Kāpālika, etc. It also refers to supernatural powers acquired by *mantras*.

The Hilsa image of Tārā, dating back to Devapāla's time (c. 812-850) bears a Tāntric formula containing the mention of Tārā, who, therefore, cannot be regarded as very late.

Whatever the date of origin of Tantra might have been, it appears, from epigraphical and literary evidences, that Tāntric practices were established well before the sixth century A.D. In the case of the *Ṛgveda*, centuries elapsed between the origin of the *mantras* and their compilation into *Saṃhitā*. Similarly a long time might intervene between the origin of Tāntric ideas and practices and their codification in treatises. There is enough of evidence to prove that Tantra reached the acme of popularity during the period between the seventh and twelfth century A.D.

Science in Tantra[71]

The matters, dealt with in Tantra, are supposed by many to be speculative nonsense entirely divorced from the realities of life. Those, who have approached Tantra with a scientific bent of mind, have found in it much that is true scientifically.

Seeing and hearing from afar, medical treatment from a great distance — these are some *Siddhis* (success, power) stated in Tantra to be attainable through *sādhanā*. It seems that the above *Siddhis* could accomplish what can be done now-a-days by means of television, radio and teletherapy, etc. The great power of concentration and will force is recognised by those who study psychology.

In Tantra, each deity has some colour or other. The Buddhas, in the posture of *Dhyāna*, are represented as having a colour. In respect of creation, the Buddhist Tantra has the theory of nihilism (*Śūnyavāda*). From this as well as from their knowledge of colours, some presume that the Tantra writers were conscious of the light and its diffusion in the primordial state of the material world. What is now called cosmic ray was, perhaps, not unknown to them.

The monosyllabic *bījamantras* of Tantra have inner significance. For example, *laṃ* and *vaṃ* stand for earth and water respectively of the five elements (*pañcabhūta*).

Tantra and Āyurveda

These two branches of learning exercised influence on each other. Portions of some Tāntric works deal with *Āyurveda*. For example, the *Kālītantra* devotes chapter II to etiology of diseases. Chapter xii prescribes medicines for diseases.

One Bhāvamiśra of Akbar's court (16th. cent.) is known to have written a *Tāntrika-cikitsā*.

The science of Āyurveda appears to have developed on two lines, Vedic and Tāntric. The latter, believed by some to have prevailed in pre-Āryan times, proceeds along two ways, one applying chemicals particularly, and the other poison.

It is significant that the Āyurvedic work, attibuted to Agniveśa, is entitled Agniveśa-tantra. The last part of the *Suśruta-saṃhitā* is called Uttara-tantra. Surgery is called Śalyatantra.

There is difference of opinion regarding both the number and names of the Tantric works. The *Nityāṣoḍaśikārṇava* (i.22) gives the number as millions. According to orthodox scholars, whose opinions are referred to by A. Avalon, it is a lac or more. In some Tantras, the number is stated to be 64.[72]

Tantras of Yāmala class are eight; the names differ in different sources.

According to the *Sammoha Tantra*, Cīna has 100 main Tantras and 7 subsidiary ones, Draviḍa possesses 20 principal and 25 secondary works, Kerala has 60 chief works and as many as 500 subsidiary ones. The Āgamas number 18 according to the *Niḥśvāsa-tattva-saṃhitā*. From the *Meru-tantra* (i.21) we learn that Śiva composed 108 Tantras.

The *Siddhānta Āgamas* of South India number 28; however, opinions differ as to their number and extent.

The number of *Pañcarātra Āgamas* is generally said to be 108. But, actually their number is over 200.[73]

Works on Tantra[74]

Besides those published, there is still a considerable number of works in manuscripts in different collections of India and in some foreign institutions. We shall note below only the principal titles which are very widely known.

Principal works on the *Āgamaśāstra* of Kashmir:

(i) Mālinīvijaya, (ii) Svacchanda, (iii) Vijñānabhairava, (iv) Ucchuṣmabhairava, (v) Ānandabhairava, (vi) Mṛgendra, (vii) Mātaṅga, (viii) Netra, (ix) Naiśvāsa, (x). Svāyambhuva, (xi) Rudrayāmala.

The main works of the *Pratyabhijñā* literature, closely related to Āgama, are:

(i) *Śivadṛṣṭi* of Somānanda (ninth century), (ii) *Pratyabhijñākārika* of Utpala (ninth century), (iii) *Mālinivījayottaravārtika* of Abhinavagupta (tenth-eleventh century), (iv) *Pratyabhijñā-vimarśinī* of Abhinavagupta, (v) *Tantrāloka* of Abhinava, (vi-vii) *Tantrasāra* and *Paramārthasāra* of Abhinavagupta, (viii) *Pratyabhijñāhṛdaya* of Kṣemarāja, disciple of Abhinava.

Main works of the Saṃhitā class:

(i) Ahirbudhnya, (ii) Īśvara, (iii) Pauṣkara, (iv) Parama, (v) Sāttvata, (vi) Bṛhadbrahma, (vii) Jñānāmṛtasāra, (viii) Jayākhya.

Noteworthy among Tantras are:

(i) *Mahānirvāṇa*, (ii) *Śāradātilaka* of Lakṣmaṇadeśikācārya, disciple of Utpala (ninth century), (iii) *Kulacūḍāmaṇi*, (iv) *Tantrarāja*, (v) *Kālivilāsa*, (vi) *Jñānārṇava*, (vii) *Prāṇatoṣiṇī* of Rāmatoṣaṇa, (viii)*Varivasyārahasya* of Bhāskararāya (eighteeth century), (ix) *Kulārṇava* (c. tenth century), (x) *Prapañcasāra* of Śaṃkarācārya, (xi) *Rudrayāmala.*

The *Saundarya-laharī* is a famous Tāntric work attributed to Śaṃkarācārya.

The *Vārāhī-tantra* mentions fifty-four Tantras. Besides original Tantras, there are many digests, commentaries, lexicons, etc., e.g. *Tantrasāra* of the Bengali Kṛṣṇānanda (sixteenth century), *Tantrābhidhāna, Mantrakośa*, etc.

Of the Buddhist Tantras, famous are *Ārya-mañjuśrīmūlakalpa* (variously assigned to dates between the fourth and ninth centuries A.D.), *Hevajratantra* (c. eighth century A.D.), *Prajñopāya-viniścaya-siddhi* of *Anaṅgavajra* (c. seventh to eighth century). *Jñānasiddhi* of Indrabhūti, disciple of Anaṅgavajra.

Important Vaiṣṇava Tantras are the *Gautamīya*, *Kramadīpikā* of Keśava. The *Agni-purāṇa* (39. 1-7) names twenty-five Vaiṣṇava Tantras; these are but the twenty-five Pañcarātra Saṃhitās including the Saṃhitās mentioned above.

Women in Tantra

Women occupy a very high position in Tantra. They are allowed equal freedom with men in Tāntric rites. A woman, associated with a man for Tāntric worship or for *maithuna*, is called Śakti, Prakṛti or Latā. She can be one's own wife, the wife of another person or even a courtesan. *Maithuna*, one of the five *makāras*, is not possbile without a woman. The mother is stated to be the most worthy person to be one's *guru*. The worship of virgin girls is regarded as a must in *dīkṣā* and *puraścaraṇa*.

Bhakti in Tantra

The following nine modes of *Viṣṇu-bhakti* are stated in the *Bhāgavata-purāṇa* (vii. 5-23-24): *śravaṇa* (hearing), *kīrtana* (reciting names,) *smaraṇa* (remembering), *padasevā* (shampooing the feet), *arcanā* (worship), *vandanā* (salutation), *dāsya* (service), *sakhya* (friendship), *ātma-nivedana* (self-surrender).

Some Tantras also recognise nine forms of *bhakti*. For example, the *Rudrayāmala* (XXVII. 103-104) mentions nine ways with *manana* (reflection) for *śravaṇa*, *dhyāna* (meditation) for *sakhya*. This work leaves out the word *Viṣṇu*, mentioned in *Bhāgavata*.

The *Pārānanda-sūtra* (pp 6-7, *Sūtras* 35, 38-59) declares—*bhoga-svargāpavarga-kāṃkṣiṇām bhaktireva ekaḥ panthāḥ*; *bhakti* is the sole means for those who desire enjoyment, heaven and salvation.

Yuganaddha

The word literally means bound or tied (*naddha*) to a yoke (*yuga*). The idea is that the male and the female are united like a pair of bulls tied to the yoke. It is a symbol pointing to the unique harmony and inter-relation of masculinity and feminity, of blunt truth and symbolic truth of intellect and humanity.

It represents the union of the Male and Female Principles. In Buddhist Tāntric philosophy, it is the non-dual state of unity of Śūnyatā (Vacuity) and *Karuṇā* (compassion).[75]

Guenther, in his book, *Yuganaddha*, tries, on the basis of Buddhist Tantras, to show that the Buddhist Tāntrics view life as a whole. They do not permit excessive indulgence of passions nor do they teach total abstention or escape from life. They advocate complete reconciliation to the facts of life. The Tāntric accent on the sexual aspect is a corrective against the one-sided intellectualism and rationalism of philosophy which cannot tackle the problems of daily life.

Value of Tantra

Tantra liberalised the rites and rituals by reducing the rigour of Brāhmaṇical practices. It ensured greater freedom of religious performances to women and Śūdras; the rigid caste discrimination of the Brāhmanical system was rejected. It laid greater emphasis on *kriyā* or practices of certain kinds as means to progress on the way to salvation. Mere contemplation or meditation was not regarded as enough by Tantra. It prescribed means of healing diseases, causing mischief to enemies and of acquiring worldly happiness. Tantra also taught *Siddhis* or means of acquiring supernatural power whereby many worldly things could be achieved.

These are the reasons which made Tantra popular among the mass of people. Its popularity was so deep and wide that it left its imprint on the Purāṇas[76] and Smṛti digests which played a vital role in the religious and social life of India. The Brāhmanical religious practices were deeply tinged with Tāntric colour. The mystic syllables, *maṇḍalas* (circles), *yantras* (diagrams) and *mudrās* (postures of hands) were incorporated into the traditional modes of worship as indispensable elements. It appears that Tantra began to wield its influence on Purāṇas from the eighth century onward. In several Smṛti digests, there are many references to Tantras, and quotations of Tāntric verses, *mantras*, etc. According to the *Kulārṇava-tanttra* there was predominance of *Śruti* (=Veda), *Smṛti* and *Purāṇa* respectively in the Ages called *Satya*, *Tretā* and *Dvāpara*; in the present *Kali* Age Tantra predominates. The predominance of Tantra in Kali has been stated also in the *Mahānirvāṇa-tantra* (i.28).

The influence of Tantra is most marked on Buddhism. The deep influence on this religion led to the rise of Buddhist *Sahajiyā* cult which, in its turn, was responsible for the growth of Vaiṣṇava *Sahajiyā* cult. As stated above, the Jainas, too, had their Tantra.

The basic unity of the apparently different popular cults like *Baud-dha Sahajiyā* and *Vaiṣṇava Sahajiyā*, etc., is that all of them aim at the attainment of Supreme bliss caused by *Sādhanā* performed by man and woman in conjunction. According to these faiths, two separate currents combine to give rise to one principle, the *advaya-tattva*, which is complete bliss. This is *mithuna-tattva*, *yāmala-tattva* or *yugala-tattva*, the *yuganaddha-tattva* of the Buddhists. This *advaya-tattva*, according to Tantra, is pure bliss caused by the union of two currents represented by Śiva and Śakti. This state of supreme bliss is attainable by Tāntric Sādhanā which consists in Yogic practices. According to the Bauddha Sahajiyās, too, Yogic practices are necessary to reach the goal which they call *Mahāsukha*. But, in place of Yoga, the Vaiṣṇavas substituted love (*prema*).

Tantra is valuable in other respects too. Some Tāntric works mention rivers, lakes, hills, forests, *pīṭhasthānas*, etc. Thus, their geographical importance is undoubted.

Some Tantras mention names of *gurus*. Of them, the gurus of the *Mānavaugha* category (e.g. *Nīlatantra* V.65, 66; *Śyāmārahasya* iii. 241-44; *Mahāvidyātantra*, *Tārākhaṇḍa* 164-169, *Nityotsava*, *Ullāsas* iii, V appear to have been people of flesh and blood. Moreover, they represent different traditions. The *Pārānanda-sūtra* mentions the names of six Tantric teachers, and cites three.

Articles of food and drink, recommended for offering to the deities, appear to reflect the food-habits of the people.

Some Tantras reveal the ethical outlook of the people and their moral ideas. Thus, they throw light on the ways of life of the people in the periods concerned.

Some Tantras, particularly those related to Kashmir Śaivism, contain highly philosophical ideas. They have some value for the history of Indian philosophy.

Biographical or autobiographical information about the authors is very meagre in Sanskrit works. Happily for us, some Tāntric works, both original and commentaries, contain information about their authors, their dates and patrons, etc. In this connexion, mention may be made of Rāghavabhaṭṭa, author of a gloss on the *Śāradātilaka*, *Śāktapramoda* of king Rājanandana, *Tantrapradīpa* of Gadādhara, *Mantrapradīpa* of Harapati, *Prāṇatoṣinī* of Rāmatoṣaṇa, *Sarvānanda-taraṅgiṇī* of Śivanātha, *Ṣaṭcakranirūpaṇa* of Nandarāma and *Tārābhakti-sudhārṇava* of Narasiṃha Ṭhakkura.

From the point of view of history of Sanskrit literature, Tantra is valuable. Some Tantras refer to such works as are lost. Again, a particular Tantra, mentioning a work,[77] about which we know nothing, throws some light on the relative chronology of the two.

We know of at least one Tantra, entitled *Vidyārṇava* (Calcutta Asiatic Soc. Cat., VIII, Serial No. 6206), which is important for political history. It gives an account of the foundation of the town of Vijaynagar, which is different from all accounts found in several modern works on Vijaynagar.

The work is stated to have been composed at the request of a King of Vijaynagar, the posthumous son of Prauḍhadeva. The author states that, after the death of Prauḍhadeva, he acted as regent according to the wishes of the people. As regent, he is stated to have built the town of Vijaynagar resembling the mystic *Śrīcakra.*

The unnamed patron of the author is supposed by Gopinath Kaviraj, probably on the testimony of a MS. of the above work at Varanasi Sanskrit College (*Brahmasūtra-Acyutagranthamālā*, Varanasi, Intro., p. 54).

The historicity of the above account is doubted by some scholars (Calcatta Asiatic Soc. Cat. VIII. pt.2, Intro., p.XXV).

In the above work, there is a list of teachers of the school of Śaṃkarācārya beginning with this great exponent of *Advaitavāda* and ending with the author himself who claims to have belonged to this school. This list, which is corroborated by a list occurring in the *Kramottama* (Calcutta Asiatic Soc. MS. Cat., VIII, Serial No. 6351-2), contians some names which are otherwise unknown.

Some Tantras, which are lost, exist only in Tibetan and Chinese translations. But for these translations, we would have been quite ignorant of a vast portion of the Tantric literature.

From at least one Tantra, viz. *Bṛhad-gautamīya Tantra*,[78] we learn of the different regions of India, in which Tāntric religion developed, and Tantras were composed. It states that the Tāntric preceptors of the West (perhaps Kashmir) are the best, those of the South medium and those of Gauḍa and Kāmarūpa are inferior, and the preceptors of Kaliṅga are the worst.

Śākta sect—A General View

The worshippers of Śakti as the highest divinity are called *Śākta.*

Like Tāntric works in general, Śākta śāstra declares that the principal aim of a Śākta should be to realise his identity with *Yantra, Mantra, Guru* and *Devī.*

Like the followers of Tantra, the Śāktas also developed some practices which appear to be immoral to an impartial observer. For example, the *Kaulāvalīnirṇaya* declares that all women, excepting the preceptor's wife and the wife of a Śākta of the Vīra type, are fit for sexual intercourse. It allows (viii. 223-225) even incestuous sexual union.

A popular Śākta superstition is that jackals (Śivā) are Śakti incarnate.

Śāktavidyās (*mantras*) are divided into three classes, viz. *Kādi* (*KA. 1, LA, HA, LA, HRIM*) *Hādi* (*HA, SA, KA, HA, LA, HRĪM*) and *Sādi* (*SA, KA, HA, LA, HRĪM*).[79]

Śāktas are broadly divided into two classes, *Kālīkula* and *Srīkula*'. Again, they are divided into three schoolds, viz. *Kādi, Hādi* and *Kahādi*.[80]

Śāktism reached a high degree of development in Bengal. The Śākta Tantras of this region regard Śakti as the pivot round which the entire Śākta philosophy revolves.

Śakti is both manifest (*Vyakta*) and unmanifest (*avyakta*). Everything from the principle of *Mahat* to the minutest atom is her creation. The main object of a *Śākta* is the realisation of the identity of Śiva and Jīva.[81]

The idea of Śakti as the Supreme Power, perhaps, owes its origin to the matriarchal or mother superior system which prevailed in ancient India, and is found even now among some tribes. In this connection, it may be stated that, in the *Manu-smṛti* (ii.145) the mother is regarded as superior even to a thousand fathers in point of honour. It may be mentioned that, in Vedic *mantras* relating to marriage, the newly married woman is exhorted by the husband to be a *samrājñī* (Empress) in the household.

India was not the only country where matriarchy was firmly rooted over a wide area. Frazer thinks[82] that it was widespread throughout Asia Minor. He points out that mother superiority lingered on in Egypt down to the Roman times (4th-5th cent.).

Ehrenfels thinks (*Mother Right in India*) that female domination in Indian society was wider and deeper than in any other country of the world.

In course of time, Śākta philosophy became subtle and complex. It recognises the 36 *Tattvas* which are as follows. Śiva, Śākti, Sadāśiva, Īśvara, Vidyā, Māyā, Avidyā, Kalā, Rāga, Kāla, Niyati, Jīva, Prakṛti, Manas, Buddhi, Ahaṃkāra, Pañca-tanmātra, Pañca-bhūta, Daśendriya.

In the philosophy, Śiva is the Supreme principle. Though he is non-dualistic (*Advaita*), yet he is coupled with inherent Śakti. Śakti is the manifestation of Śiva as the rays are of the sun, the burning power of fire and the effulgence of a jewel.

Jīva is nothing but a part of Śiva, but covered by *kañcukas* (cover of Māyā etc.) and *mala* (literally dirt: i.e. impurity causing rebirth and suffering).

Śakti resides in the body as *kuṇḍalinī* (a coiling serpent). *Śākta-sādhanā* aims at the redemption of *Jīva* from suffering and establishing him in everlasting bliss and consciousness.

Supreme Siva resides in the *Sahasrāra* lotus within head.

Kuṇḍalinī, being awakened, rises from the *mūlādhāra* at the base moves upward, penetrates the *Cakras* and finally reaches *Sahasrāra*, abode of Śiva, and is united with Him. This union results in perfect and inexpressible bliss the experience of which is the *summum bonum* of the aspirant's spiritual life.

This philosophy advocates *Pariṇāma-vāda* according to which the unmanifest Śakti Herself is evolved as the manifest objects. This is also called *Satkāryavāda*, i.e. the doctrine of the effect inhering the cause as the sprout pre-exists in the seed.

According to Vedānta philosophy, the world is unconscious illusion (*Māyā*), created by the conscious Brahman. According to Tāntric philosophy, *Māyā* of the conscious Brahman is also conscious as there is identity of the Śaktimān (possessor of Śakti) and His Śakti.

The doctrine of *Śakti-pariṇāmavāda* is also called *Ābhāsavāda*; it is the manifestation of objects by the conscious principle which itself remains unaffected.

An aspirant, endowed with *Divyabhāva*, which is stated as the best (*sarva-bhāvottama*), does not require an image nor any external rite. He is absorbed in *Antaryāga*. For him, *pañcamakāra* does not mean gross substances, but their spiritual forms, as indicated earlier.

A *Sādhaka* of *Vīrabhāva* has to perform external rites; he resorts to *pañcamakāras* in their gross forms. If necessary, he has to perform the six Tāntric black rites of *Māraṇa, Uccāṭana*, etc. He has to face severe tests. He practises *sādhanā* in a cemetery or other lonely spots. He is called *vīra* (hero) as he has to be strong, fearless and self-restrained.

The worship of Śakti, also called Tripurā, Tripurasundarī or Mahātripurasundarī, who is identified with *Parā Saṃvit* (Supreme Consciousness) which again is conceived as Brahman, who is beyond the 36 *Tattvas*; it is twofold; *Antaryāga* stated above and *Bahiryāga* involving external rites.

The Goddess is worshipped in three forms, *Sthūla*, *Sūkṣma* and *Parā*. In the first form, she has anthropomorphic features, and is accessible to the eyes and hands of those who have *mantrasiddhi*.

The second one, consisting in *mantra*, is comprehended by the ears and speech of the holy persons.

The third form is comprehended by the mind of holy devotees. In external worship, differnt symbols of the Goddess are worshipped. Of these, the *Śrīyantra* or *Śrīcakra* is the best.

Śakti-sādhanā aims at the elevation of man from animality to a spiritual height through the restrained enjoyment of worldly pleasures and not by their denial. Irrespective of caste or sex, everybody has a right to practise this *sādhanā* while living the worldly life and not renouncing it.

Protestantism in Tantra

It is interesting to note that at least one Tantra raised a voice of protest against the conventional Tāntric practices.

A fragmentary *Pārānanda-mata* or *Pārānanda-matasaṃgraha*[83] forbids *nyāsa* and animal sacrifice which are generally regarded as essential for Śakti-worship.

Tantra Beyond India

Though the place of origin of Tantra is not known with certainty, we find its influence far beyond India. We have seen, in connexion with the classification of Tantra, that many other neighbouring countries reveal their familiarity with Tantras. China and Tibet deserve special mention is this connexion. It should be noted that some Sanskrit Tantras are preserved only in Chinese and Tibetan versions, the original works being lost. We have evidences of these two countries having been visited by Tāntric philosophers and scholars from ancient India. How deep Tāntric influence was in Tibet can be understood from the life of the famous votary of Tantra, Milarepa[84] (born 1052 A.D.). We are informed of the severe ordeals he had to pass through before the achievement of the highest result of Tāntric *Sādhanā*. We come to learn that his preceptor was Mārpā whose preceptor was Nāropā.[85] We know of at least four Tantras, viz. *Śiraścheda*, *Vināśikha*, *Sammoha* and *Nayottara*, introduced into Kambuja (Cambodia) about 800 A.D. Mongolia and Japan are some of the other regions where Tantra was introduced. Of the Tāntric work, *Gaṇapati-tattva*, an old Javanese text only is available.

Among the nearest neighbours of India, Nepal appears to have been very much influenced by Indian Tantra. The Durbar library of Nepal preserves the *Niḥśvāsa-tattva-saṃhitā*, written in the Gupta script of the eighth century A.D. The original work may date back to the sixth or seventh century.

The same library preserves a manuscript of the *Jayadrathayāmala*. In this connexion, it may be noted that the *Caryāpadas*, dating back to about thousand years ago and regarded as the earliest Bengali work, which are deeply imbued with Tantrism, were discovered in Nepal.

Buddhism was not the only medium through which Tantra migrated outside India. Through Brahmanical media also some Tantras found their way beyond this country. Nearly 1200 years ago, during the reign of Jayavarman II, the Brahmanical Tantras, *Śiraścheda* (i.e. *Jayadratha-Yāmala*), *Nayottara, Vinayaśila* (acc. to some, supplement to *Jayadratha-Yāmala*) and *Sammoha*, all included in *Śivāgama*, were taken to Cambodia.

From Chinese accounts we learn that the worship of several Mother Goddesses, e.g. Mahākālī, Mahiṣamardiṇī, etc. was introduced in Asiatic countries beyond India.

Tantra and Timaeus[86]

Tantra contains certain striking similarities with the Timee (*Timaeus*) of Plato (428-348 B.C.).

Among the vessels, Plato speaks of two conduits existing on both sides of the vertebral column. These, like the Tāntric Iḍā and Piṅgalā on two sides of the Suṣumnā, seem to be fanciful things and not anatomic realities.

Again Plato conceives the earth as a cube, fire as a triangular pyramid, air as octahedral and water as icosahedral. In Tantra, these are represented by *maṇḍalas* (diagrams) which are square, triangle, two equilateral triangles, one upon the other, crescent moon; either is represented by a circle.[87]

The above parallelism might be accidental coincidence. The possibility of the one country influencing the other cannot, however, be absolutely ruled out. It should be borne in mind that cultural contact between India and Greece dates back to a period earlier than the invasion of Alexander (327-26 B.C.).

Tantra and the Jews

The Jewish doctrine of *Kabbalah* has many similarities with Tāntric ideas. Like Tantra, the adherents of this doctrine believe in the power of letters, magic, amulets, the unity of microcosm and macrocosm, etc. These ideas were in vogue in Egypt about the ninth century, and from there migrated to Europe. There are evidences of Indo-Egyptian contacts from long before the above date. So, in all probability the *Kabbalah* was influenced by Tantra via Egypt.

Tantra and Christianity

C. Eliot points out[88] some parallelisms between Tāntric and Christian rituals. He has drawn our attention to the fact that, even in the Anglican Church, an indispensable part of the ceremony of baptism is sprinkling with water; this practice is similar to Tāntric *Abhiṣeka*. The cross of the Christians resembles the *nyāsa* of Tantra as Woodroffe points out.[89] Baptism includes a formula which is similar to Tāntric *mantras*. It is supposed that baptism ensures life in heaven but, the unbaptised have a dubious future. Similarly, Tantra believes in the attainment of the spiritual end through physical means. In the Roman Church, the rite includes exorcism and the use of salt, oil and lights. This is very much like similar practices in Tantra. The bread and wine, offered in an Eucharistic sacrifice, are regarded as the flesh and blood of Christ. The Christians eat this bread and drink the wine. In Tāntric rites, meat and wine are essential.

Though the suggestion of parallelism is ingenious, yet no plausible case of borrowing on either side can be made out. The parallelisms are superficial, and appear to be accidental.

Degeneration and Denunciation

Orthodox Hindus deprecate Tāntric practices. In his *Tantravārtika*, Kumārilabhaṭṭa (c. eighth century A.D.) clearly brands Tantra as outside the pale of Vedic religion. The principal reason of this aversion towards Tantra is that it voiced a protest against the rigours of Brāhmanical religious practices. Again, Tantra allowed greater freedom in religious matters to women and Śūdras who were denied many privileges enjoyed by men of upper classes. Another reason of the anti-Tantra attitude is probably that, contrary to the orthodox religion, it prescribes rites calculated to do harm to others and even destroy them. The Mīmāṃsā definition of *dharma* is *codanālakṣaṇóratho dharmaḥ*. It has been explained as that which, based on Vedic authority, is designed to produce well-being. This outlook on *dharma* naturally led to contempt towards Tantra. Kullūka says — *vedapramāṇkaṃ śreyaḥ sādhanaṃ dharmaḥ.* As some Tāntric practices are deliberately designed to do harm to others, Tantra was looked down upon.

It should be noted that a time came when people cared more for the Tāntric practices than for the philosophical and spiritual aspects of Tantra literature. The result was moral degeneration. Tantra prescribed easier modes of *sādhanā*. In doing so, it allowed the satisfaction of natural human propensities as means of progress in the path to liberation. Human nature being what it is, this attitude of Tantra gave human beings a licence for self-indulgence. In fact, some late Tantras themselves appear to encourage the satisfaction of carnal instincts. The *Kaulāvalī-nirṇaya* (iv. 15 ff.) openly declares that, for Śāktas, there is no greater happiness than sexual enjoyment; by resorting to this practice alone one can attain *Siddhi.* The Tantra allows free sexual intercourse with the wives of others, excepting the *guru*, and of a *Śākta* who has acquired the status of Vīra. The *Kālivilāsa-tantra* permits indiscriminate sexual intercourse on the part of a Śākta. The drinking of wine is also stated to lead to enjoyment and liberation.

The degenerated Tāntric religion gave rise to such sects as *Kartābhajā* in Bengal. *Guruvāda*, according to which the human *guru* was regarded as an incarnation of Śiva, went to such an extreme that a newly married girl had to allow herself to be enjoyed by the *guru* before her first meeting with the husband.

In the wake of the renaissance in the 19th century, as a result of the impact of western education, and the dawning of enlightenment, the rationally disposed people vehemently denounced Tāntric practices. Western stalwarts like Wilson, Monier Williams, Hopkins, etc. also looked down upon Tantras as debased and barbarous. Barth detested a left-handed Śākta as a 'hypocrite and a superstitious debauchee'.

The famous litterateur, Bankim Chattopadhyay, found only lust and liquour in the Tāntric religion.

From an impartial observation it can be said that the Tantras doubtlessly contain highly philosophical matters. But, in actual practice, degeneration set in. With the Śāstric support, the baser instincts of the Tāntric devotees came into full play, and they became extroverts. While such degeneration is, of course, detestable the criticism, levelled against Tantra as a Śastra is not wholly fair. It is not the fault of the

Ganges if its water is used for washing unclean things. Similarly, if some people use Tantras as a means of satisfying animal passions, the Tantra literature in general cannot be categorically denounced.

Some highly intellectual men of India and even of the west not only admired Tantra, but also took to the Tāntric way of life. Sibchandra Vidyārṇava (1860-1913) was a prominent Bengali who mastered the Tāntric philosophy. Justice Woodroffe (1865-1936) became his disciple, and made original contributions to Tāntric philosophy.

Despite the deprecatory attitude of the orthodox Brāhmins towards Tantra, we have seen how this Śāstra influenced almost all the cultural aspects of Indian society. Most of the Hindu Tantras were written by the Brahmins.

Literary Value of Bengal Tantra

Though the Tantras are mainly concerned with rites and rituals and philosophy, yet gems of poetry flash here and there. We quote some verses with their translation.

madhye tu tāṃ mahādevīṃ sūryakoṭi-samaprabhavām/
chinnamastāṃ kare vāme dhārayantīṃ svamastakam//
prasāritamukhīṃ bhīmāṃ lelihānāgra-jihvikām/
pibantīṃ raudhirīṃ dhārāṃ nijakaṇṭha-vinirgatām//

Tantrasāra (Kṛṣṇananda)

[(I salute) that great goddess, Chinnamastā, who, the terrible one, has effulgence like that of a crore of suns, holds her own head in her left hand, extends her face with the licking tip of her tongue, drinking the stream of blood flowing out of her own throat.]

An excellent realistic description of the fierce Chinna-mastā, couched in apposite words.

pāpa-śūla-vinirbhinnaṃ siktaṃ viṣaya-sarpiṣā/
rāga-dveṣānalaiḥ pakvaṃ mṛtyur-aśnāti mānavam//

Śāktānanda-taraṅgiṇī (I)

[Death devours man who is pierced by the spear of sin, wetted by the clarified butter of objects of senses, and cooked by the fire of attachment and animosity.]

NOTES

1. According to the *Śaktimaṅgalatantra,* it is supposed that these regions were named after the vehicles used to traverse them. *Viṣṇu,*

ratha and *aśva* mean respectively sea-going vessel, chariot and horse; *gaja* denotes elephant.

2. See *Tāntric Texts* Vol. I, ed. A. Avalon, Introduction, pp. ii-iv. The *Saundarya-laharī*, attributed by some to Śaṃkarācārya, refers to 64 Tantras. On the number of Tantras, see D.N. Bose, *Tantras — their philosophy* etc., *Saundarya-laharī* (trs., pp. 117-20), P.C. Bagchi, *Studies in Tantras*, p. 5; Abhinavagupta, *Tantrāloka* (i. 18); *Nityāṣḍaśīkārṇava* (part of *Vāmakeśvaratantra*) I. 13-22; *Kaulāvalīnīrṇaya* (I.2-14).
3. Vide P.C. Bagchi, *Studies in Tantras*, p. 3.
4. Buddhist Tantras are generally divided according to the three broad divisions of later Buddhism, viz. Vajrayāna, Sahajayāna and Kālacakrayāna. There are sectarian divisions of Jaina Tantra too.
5. cf. *brahmpadme pṛthivyāṃ tu vartante mānuṣādayaḥ/evaṃ cakre sarvadehe bhuvanāni caturdaśa/pratidehaṃ pareśāni brahmāṇḍaṃ nātra saṃśayaḥ//* *Nirvāṇa-tantra*. (In the earth, the *Brahma-padma*, human beings etc. exist. Thus in the *Cakras* in the entire body fourteen worlds (reside). O Supreme Goddess, every body is a cosmos (Lit. the egg of Brahma). There is no doubt about it.
6. cf. *brahmāṇḍe ye guṇāḥ santi te tiṣṭhanti kalevare.*
7. In the *Atharvaveda*, perhaps for the first time, the body has been stated as having eight *Cakras*, nine doors; it is imagined as containing a golden cell, the heaven covered with lustre.
   cf. *aṣṭācakrā navadvārā devānāṃ purayodhyā tasyāṃ hiraṇmayaḥ kośaḥ svargo jyotiṣāvṛtaḥ//* x.2 .
8. See Woodroffe, *Śakti and Śākta* (3rd. ed.), p. 399.
9. The word 'paśu' is derived from the root *paś* (to bind).
10. It generally denotes various hand-poses used in religious rites; e.g. *Kūrmamudrā, Matsyamudrā*, etc. In the *Yoginītantra* (Chap. vi.), it appears to stand for corns like barley which can be chewed.
11. Gop Kṛṣṇa, in his *Biological Basis of Religion and Genius*, discussed the scientific basis of *Kuṇḍalinī*. Also see introduction by Weizsacker.
12. *Sārdha-trivalayākārā, svayaṃbyu-liṅga-veṣṭitā*. *Sarparājñī* (serpent-queen) of the *Ṛgveda* seems to be the precusor of it.
13. cf. For instance, *deva eva yajed devaṃ nādevo devamarcayet/ Gandharva-tantra.*
14. See Glossary.

15. cf. *akṛtvā mānasaṃ yāgaṃ na kuryād vahirarcanam/ antaḥpūjāṃ vinā devi vāhyapūjā vṛthā bhavet/ Sanatkumāra-tantra.*
Without doing mental sacrifice, do not perform external worship. O Goddess, without internal worship external worship becomes futile.
Sarvāsu vāhyapūjāsu antaḥpūjā vidhīyate/Bhūtaśuddhitantra.
In all external forms of worship, internal worship is prescribed.
manasāpi mahādevyai naivedyaṃ dīyate yadi/ yo naro bhakti-saṃyukto dīrghāyuḥ sa sukhī bhavet/ Gandharva-tantra.
The man who, with devotion, offers eatables to the Great goddess even mentally, becomes long-lived and happy.
16. Ullāsa vi.
17. For details, see Woodroffe : *Introduction to Tantraśāstra*, 1952, (pp. 134-35).
18. Vide *Śāradātilaka*, Chap. (i) and *Śāktānandataraṅgiṇī*, Chap. i.
19. The word occurs, for the first time, perhaps in the *Ṛgveda*, Book VII- Vāsvi su te jaritre astu sāktiḥ.
20. See *Kubjikātantra*, Paṭala i.
21. Vide *Śāradātilaka*, Chap. i.
22. See *Kubjikātantra*, Chap. i.
23. cf. *saccidānandarūpāṃ brahmaivāhaṃ sphuratprabham Yoginītantra*, I, Chap. x.
I am none but Brahman in the form of *Sat* (Existent), *Cit*., (Conciousness) and *Ānanda* (Bliss, Joy), One whose lustre shrines.
24. cf. *mātasvat-paramarūpaṃ tanna jānāti kaścana Śāktānanda-taraṅgiṇi*, Chap. iii.
O Mother, nobody knows your Supreme Form.
25. cf. *amūrtau cit sthiro na śyāt tato mūrtiṃ vicintayet/*
Consciousness does not become fixed on the formless; so contemplate an image.
26. The ignorant critics denounced the followers of this *ācāra* in the following manner:
antaḥśāktā vahiḥ śaivāḥ sabhāyāṃ vaiṣṇavā matāḥ/
nānārupadharāḥ kaulā vicaranti mahītale//
The Kaulas roam the earth asssuming many guises — they are inwardly *Śāktas*, outwardly *Śaivas*, and regarded as Vaiṣṇavas in the assembly.
27. On the qualifications of a *guru*, see *Tantrasāra*, Chap. i.

28. About its many varieties and sub-varieties, see G. Kaviraj, *Tāntric Sādhanā O Sidhānta*, I, pp.149 ff.
The significance of *dīkṣā* is stated in the following verse:
dīyate jñānasadbhāvaḥ kṣīyate paśuvāsanā/
dānakṣapaṇasaṃyuktā dikṣā teneha kīrtitā//
By it one is given knowledge and one's animality is destroyed.
29. GOS ed., pp. 1-3,13.
30. Also see section on Brāhmaṇa, Upaniṣad and Tantra.
31. See S.A. Dange, Sex in Stone and the Vedic Mithuna, *ABORI, Diamond Jubilee* Vol., pp. 546ff., 350.
32. Vide A. Avalon : *Principles of Tantra*, p. 41.
33. cf. *ātharvaṇaṃ copaveda-stantrarūpaḥ sa eva hi/ Śukranītisāra* iv. 3.39.
34. *Catvāri vak parimitā padāni manuṣya vadanti.*
35. R.C. Hazra, *Studies in Puranic Records*, etc. Chap. V.
36. Also see *Tantra and Vedānta.*
37. Tāntric *Vidyā* is divided into three groups, *Kādi, Hādi* and *Sādi.*
38. See P.V. Kane, *History of Dharmaśāstra*, Vol. V.
39. Also see section on *Brāhmaṇa, Upaniṣad* and *Tantra.*
40. In some later Tantras, dualism is recognised; e.g. *Mṛgendra-tantra*, ii.11.
41. *Īśvarāsiddheḥ* — Sāṃkhyasūtra, i.92.
42. See B. Bhattacharya, *Sādhanamālā*, Intro.
43. e.g. *Padma-purāṇa*, Pātāla (ed. K.N. Bhaktivinoda), Ch. 38.
44. *Ujjavala-nīlamaṇi*, section on Rādhā.
45. See Jīva's *Laghubhāgavatāmṛta* and his commentary on the Brahmasaṃhitā as well as Kṛṣṇadāsa's *Caitanya-caritāmṛta*, Ādi, Ch. iv. The verse is —
devī kṛṣṇamayī proktā rādhikā parā devatā/
sarva-lakṣmīmayī sarvakānitḥ sammohinī parā//
Goddess Rādhikā, made of Kṛṣṇa, possessed of all grace, all lustre, the Supreme enchanter, is said to be the supreme Divinity.
46. See S.B. Das Gupta, *Śrīrādhār Kramavikāś*, p. 332.
47. cf., for instance, *Bhāgavata*, xi, 3.47; 5.28, 31 etc.
48. *Ubhābhyāṃ veda-tantrābhyāṃ mahyantūbhaya-siddhaye.*
49. See D. Desai, *Erotic Sculpture of India.*
50. See Cunningham, *Archeological Survey Report*, IX.
51. See *Tantrayāna Art.*
52. See *Tantrayāna Art*; Rawlinson, *Tantra;* Nawab, *Jain Paintings*, Vol. I.

53. See N.K. Bose, *Canons of Orissan Architecture*, pp. 92, 154.
54. See Prajnanananda, *Bhāratīya saṃgīter Itihās*, (in Bengali) I, pp.300ff.
55. According to some, it is the Hinduised form of Ka-me-kha, the name of a goddess worshipped by the Khāsi tribe in the form of *Yoni* (female organ). See N.N. Bhattacharyya, *History of the Tāntric Religion*, p. 103.
56. See *Vāṅglār Sādhanā* by Kṣitimohan Sen, pp. 47-48.
57. *gauḍe prakāśitā vidyā maithilaiḥ prabalīkṛtā/*
kvacit kvacin mahārāṣṭre gurjare pralayaṃ gatā//
Vide R.C. Chanda, *Indo-Aryan Races*, p. 153 f.n.
58. cf. *vaśiṣṭho brahmaputro' pi cirakālaṃ susādhānam/*
jagāma cīnabhumau ca yatra buddhah pratiṣṭitaḥ//
(Even Vasiṣṭha, son of Brahman, attained good penance for a long time in the land of China where the Buddha is established.)
59. *gaccha tvaṃ bhārate varṣe adhikārāya sarvataḥ/*
pīṭhopapīṭhekṣetresmin kuru sṛṣṭimanekadhā//
(You go to India for all-round possession. In this land, perform creation in many ways in *Pīṭhas* and sub-*pīṭhas*.
60. Vide N.N. Bhattacharyya, *History of the Tāntric Religion*, pp. 87ff.
61. See *Adonis Attis Osiris*, pp.34-35.
62. *Ency. of Rel. and Ethics.*, I.
63. See R.C. Hazra, The Devī-Purāṇa, *Indian Antiquary*, V. 1942-43.
64. R.D. Banerji, *Pre-historic Ancient and Hindu India.*
65. On this question, see Yādaveśvar Tarkaratna, Tantrer Prācīnatva, *Sāhitya-saṃhitā* (Journal), Āśvina, 1317 B.S.
66. The *Nṛsiṃha-tāpanīyopaniṣad*, belonging to the *Atharvaveda*, is like a Tantra. Śaṃkarācārya wrote a commentary on it.
67. Vide Foote, *Collection of Indian Prehistoric and Proto-historic Antiquities*, Madras, 1916; K.R. Subramanian, *Origin of Śaivism and its History in Tamil Land*, Madras, 1929; P.T.S. Iyengar, *Stone age in India*, Madras University.
68. *JASB*, IV, p.628.
69. *Ind. Ant.*, 1906, pp.277ff.
70. *Ibid.*, 1906, pp. 274-76.
71. See B. Bhattacharya, *Scientific Background of the Buddhist Tantras*, *IHQ*, xxxii, No. 2, 3.
For the scientific basis of the *Kuṇḍalinī-yoga* of Tantra, see G. Krishna, *Biological basis of Religion and Genius* and its introduction by Weizsacker.

72. See *Śabdakalpadruma* under Tantra.
73. See Schrader's list.
74. Works of Bengal will be dealt with separately.
75. *Sādhanamālā*, II, p. 505.
76. For Tāntric influence on Purāṇas, see R.C. Hazra, *Studies in Purāṇic Records*, etc., p. 260. According to some, the Devīmāhātmya of the *Mārkaṇḍeya-purāṇa* is only an epitome of Tāntric physiology and cosmogony. Vide *Pāñckaḍi Vandyopādhyāyer Racanāvalī*, II, p. 298.
77. For influence of Tantra in the Far East, see P.C. Bagchi, *Studies in Tantras*; R.C. Majumder, *Inscriptions of Kambuja and JRAS*, 1950. Also see S.C. Banerji, *Sanskrit Beyond India.*
78. See P.C. Bagchi, *Op. Cit.*, pp. 17-18; *The Age of Imperial Kanauj*, p. 321.
79. See Classification of Tantras.
80. *Ibid.*
81. This idea accords well with Śrī Aurobindo's following line " we are sons of God and must be even as He.

    His human portion, we must divine." In Vedānta philosophy also, the realisation of the identity of *jīvātmā* and *paramātmā* is the highest knowledge. In the famous oft-quoted line *Śṛṇvantu viśve amṛtasya putrāḥ*, the last two words are taken by some to denote human' beings who are regarded as the progeny of the Immortal One. Religion, according to a scholar, is the progressive realisation of the divinity in man.
82. *Adonis, Attis, Osiris*, pp. 394-95.
83. Calcutta Asiatic Society MS. No. 8476, Serial No. 5982 published in the Society's Journal, 1939, with a short summary of the contents in English.
84. See *The Life of Milarapa*, trs. from Tibetan into English by L.P. Lhalungpa.
85. "Of Indian, saint of the new esoteric order and King of Translators" *Ibid.*, p. 43. Naropa was, perhaps the Tibetan name or designation of the Indian saint concerned.
86. On this topic, see Filliozat, *Classical Doctrine of Indian Medicine*, pp. 234-35.
87. Vide A. Avalon, *Tantric Texts*, Vol. III.
88. *Hinduism and Buddhism*, II, p. 275.
89. *Principles of Tantra*, pp. Lxxi-Lxxvi.

II. Geographical Account of Bengal

The subject of the present work is the contribution of Bengal to Tantra literature. So, before taking up the subject of study, it is necessary to define the geographical limits of Bengal through the ages. Bengal today is a truncated province. One should not think that Bengal had always its present boundaries. We shall deal with not only the political confines of this region, but also with its cultural boundaries; the culture of a place transcends its narrower political limits.

The *Aitareya Brāhmaṇa* (vii 17-18) contains the earliest reference to *Puṇḍra*; a portion of ancient Bengal was called Puṇḍravardhana-bhukti. The *Aitareya Āraṇyaka*, for the first time, mentions the tribe called Vaṅga. The Āryāvarta of *Baudhāyana Dharmasūtra* does not appear to have comprised the region known as Vaṅgadeśa. Manu's Brahmāvarta (ii 17) or Madhyadeśa (ii 21) did not include this portion of India. But, Manu's Āryāvarta (ii 22) appears to have comprised it.

It is not possible to determine precisely when Bengal was Aryanised. This much, however, is certain that there was an interval of centuries between the settlement of the Aryans in north-western India and their conquest of Bengal which was inhabited by non-Aryan tribes. R. C. Majumdar infers that this region came under the control of the Aryans in the period between the sixth and the fourth century B.C. That Bengal had been beyond the pale of Aryan civilisation in ancient times is proved, *inter alia*, by a verse[1] which ordains that a person visiting this land as also Aṅga, Kaliṅga, Saurāṣṭra and Magadha except for pilgrimage, is degraded requiring sacrament of refinement again. This verse has been current from very early times, though the exact time of its origin is unknown.

Greek and Latin sources are of special importance in determining the geography of ancient Bengal. From their accounts we learn that the major part of the present-day Bengal was known as Gangaridae. According to Ptolemy, it extended from the river Suvarṇarekhā or Hooghly up to the Padmā. Pliny's testimony is that Puṇḍravardhana was the capital of Gangaridae which, broadly speaking, comprised Vaṅga, Suhma and the stretch of the land called Puṇḍra. The other places, included in ancient Bengal, were known as Samataṭa, Harikela, Karṇasuvarṇa, Gauḍa, Varendra and Rāḍha.

The present West Bengal comprised Suhma, Rāḍha and Karṇasuvarṇa. Most of the modern Midnapore district was known as Suhma. The famous Tāmralipta (=modern Tamluk) was included in it. Rāḍha extended over the eastern portion of the above district and the district of Burdwan. Probably the river, Dāmodara, was the dividing line between north and south Rāḍha. Broadly speaking, the district of Mursidabad was called Karṇasuvarṇa.

The present East Bengal (=Bangladesh) included Vaṅga,[2] Samataṭa and Harikela. In course of time, the land to the east of the Brahmaputra, comprising northwest Mymensing, Comilla, Tripura, Noakhali and, perhaps, even Chittagong, came to be included within Bengal. 'Vaṅgāladeśa'[3] used to denote the whole of East Bengal. The stretch of land to the south of Kamrup or Assam, the south-east of Karṇasuvarṇa and to the east of Tāmralipta was known as Samataṭa. According to some, the modern district of Faridpur in Bangladesh was named Samataṭa. Others, however, take it to stand for modern Dacca district. Some scholars are of the opinion that the present district of Twenty-four Parganas (North and South taken together) near the sea and the districts of Khulna and Bakharganj were comprised in Samataṭa. Harikela used to denote the region in the eastern boundary of Vaṅgadeśa. The north Bengal of to-day was constituted by Puṇḍra (or, Pauṇḍra or Pauṇḍra-vardhana), Varendra(ī) and Gauḍa. The modern districts of Malda, Rangpur, Dinajpur, Rajshahi etc., and a part of Bogra were known as Puṇḍra. Varendra and Gauḍa, though constituents of Puṇḍravardhana, were also knwon as distinct entities by virtue of their superior culture and material resources. Varendra was constituted by the present Rajshahi Division and a part of Pabna district. A part of modern Malda district was called Gauḍa. Through centuries it had been regarded as a principal city of Bengal. For long it was known as Lakṣmaṇāvatī which, perhaps, originated from king Lakṣmaṇasena.

In the cultural history of Bengal, Bāgḍi and Bālavalabhi are well known. Bāgḍi is, perhaps, a corrupt form of Vyāghrataṭī which, according to historians, stood for the entire delta from the Ganges to the Brahmaputra. Modern Calcutta appears to have been a part of it. Bālavalabhi was, according to some, the name of a place in Nadīyā district, while others take it as the ancient name of Southern or Eastern Bengal.

In the twelfth century, Vaṅga generally used to refer to East Bengal. Later on it came to stand for the entire province. It was, perhaps, the Muslims who, for the first time, used the word 'Vengala'[4] to denote the land in between the Ganges and the Brahmaputra, i.e. the fairly long stretch of land from Gaḍi in Bihar up to Chittagong. Gradually this name came to include also Bihar and Orissa which passed under Muslim rule.

In the beginning of the British rule, the entire land under East India Company, from the Vindhya Hill up to the Himālaya, from the Punjab to the estuary of the Ganges and the Brahmaputra constituted Bengal Presidency. The gradually conquered territories of Assam, Arakan and Pegu, etc., also came to be included in Bengal.

NOTES

1. *aṅga-vaṅga-kaliṅgeṣu saurāṣṭra-magadheṣu ca/ tīrthayātrāṃ vinā gacchan punaḥ saṃskāram arhati//*
2. For the significance of this word and its geographical limits, *see* B.C. Law, The Vaṅgas (*Indian Culture*, I).
3. The word *Vaṅgāla* has been variously derived from *vaṅgapāla* — *Vaṅga-āla* : *āla* or *āli* denotes the boundary of a field. The existence of many *ālis* in this region is supposed to have given rise to this name. Sukumar Sen holds that the name *Vaṅgāla* originated in the early part of the Muslim conquest of Bengal. According to him, the process of evolution of the name Bengal is as follows:
   French Vaṅgālah — Portuguese Bengala — English Bengal. See *Itihāsa (Bengali* Journal), ix 1, pp. 17-20; R. Banerji, The Vaṅgālas, *Indian Culture*, ii.
4. According to some, the Venetian traveller, Marco Polo, used (1298 A.D.) the word 'Vengala' for the first time. The fact seems to be that the Nesari plates (805 A.D.) mention Dharma (Dharmapāla) as the King of '*Vaṅgāla*' and the Tirumalai Inscription (1025 A.D.) refer to Govindacandra of 'Vaṅgāla-deśa'.

III. Historical Background

The political and social conditions of a place go a long way in influencing the literary activities and religious practices of the people living there. So, before dealing with the contribution of Bengal to Tantra, we shall attempt a rapid survey of the political and social background against which Tantra arose in the province and was nurtured.

The materials for the reconstruction of the history of ancient Bengal are extremely scanty. From the Buddhist and Jaina works as well as from numismatic evidence it appears that, towards the middle of the sixth century B.C. independent principalities were established in Vaṅga and Rāḍha. Though sufficient evidence is not available for about the following two hundred years, yet it appears that the land was divided into some small States. In the first quarter of the fourth century B.C., a powerful State arose out of the union of lower and western Bengal; it was the Gangaridae of the Greeks.

According to tradition, it was a part of the Empire of Asoka. At the time of the Kushanas, the major part of it used to be ruled over by three agents. In course of time, these rulers shook off allegiance to the Kushanas, and became independent. Then followed a period of confusion and turmoil.

Siṃhavarman and his son Candravarman, mentioned in the Susunia Hill inscription (near Bankura), were probably rulers of Bengal when the Guptas came to power (319-20 A.D.). From the Allahabad Stone Pillar inscription, we learn that Samataṭa was a part of the kingdom of Samudragupta. Epigraphical evidence points to the inclusion also of North Bengal within the Gupta empire.

During the decline or disappearance of Gupta sway, Bengal appears to have been ruled over by independent rulers of whom Gopacandra, Dharmāditya and Samācāradeva are mentioned in copperplate grants.

Towards the middle of the sixth century A.D., Gauḍa gradually became a powerful State which attained its zenith under King Śaśāṅka. In course of time, it grew to be an empire extending up to Kānyakubja in the west and Ganjam (Orissa) in the south. For a short period, Śaśāṅka was deposed by Bhāskaravarmā, king of Kāmarūpa. But, Śaśāṅka retrieved his position after Bhaskara's death in 650 A.D.

After Śaśāṅka, Bengal became a target of incursions by neighbouring States which were probably attracted by the fabulous wealth[1] of this region. In the eighth century, the then ruler of Bengal lost his life in a defensive battle for the friendly State of Magadha attacked by Yaśovarman, king of Kānyakubja. In the same century, another ruler of Bengal was slain by Lalitāditya, king of Kashmir. These are the factors which gave rise to chaos and confusion in Bengal.

After a long period of anarchy, the people of Bengal elected one, Gopāla, as their king. He founded the Pāla dynasty. The conditions, in which he was installed, are described in inscriptions and in the history of the Tibetan Tāranātha. The domain of Dharmapāla, successor of Gopāla, is stated to have extended from Kedar in the Himālaya up to Gokarṇa in Bombay.

Devapāla, son of Dharmapāla, after successfully repulsing the inroads of Gurjaras, Rāṣṭrakūṭas and Kambujas, established his sway from the Himālaya down to the Vindhya. Kāmarūpa, too, acknowledged his suzerainty. There is evidence of his contacts with royal powers beyond India too. From the Nālandā copperplate grant we learn that Devapāla made a gift of five villages for the benefit of the monastery founded there by Bālaputra, king of Suvarṇadvipa.[2]

Devapāla was succeeded by Vigrahapāla who in turn was succeeded by Nārāyaṇapāla after whom the Pāla empire was attacked by the hill tribe, called Kamboja, which was repulsed by the next king Mahīpāla. At the time of Mahīpāla's accession, East Bengal was under the rule of the Candras and the Kambojas lingered on in the western and northern Bengal. Mahīpāla conquered not only east Bengal, but also annexed Tīrabhukti and the whole of Magadha. Towads the end of his rule, the Cedi King, Gāṅgeyadeva, attacked his territory and conquered Tīrabhukti. The Tamil king, Rājendracola, advanced through Orissa, and vanquished Mahīpāla in 1023 A.D.

Mahīpāla was succeeded by Nayapāla whose son and successor Vigrahapāla III was succeeded by Mahīpāla II whose weakness led to the revolt of the Kaivartas in north Bengal under the leadership of Divyoka. The king was slain, and Divyoka held north Bengal under his sway for sometime. His successor, Bhīma, was defeated by Rāmapāla who was the last noted Pāla king. The kings, who followed him, were weak and caused the decline and fall of the Pāla kingdom. Towards the end of the eleventh century, when the Pāla dynasty was on the wane, the Varman dynasty was founded in east Bengal. Harivarmadeva was the most celebrated ruler of this race. Probably, in the first half of the twelfth century, Vijayasena of the Sena dynasty dealt the death-blow to this dynasty.

Taking advantage of the decline of the Pāla regime, Vijayasena assumed power and founded the Sena dynasty in 1095 or 1125 A.D. His son and successor, Ballālasena, instead of trying to expand the kingdom, devoted himself to social reforms and literary activities. Ballāla's son, Lakṣmaṇasena, with his capital at Nudiya, annexed Mithilā and Gayā to the kingdom of Bengal. He was famous alike for heroism and patronage of learning.

In 1197 A.D. Bakhtiyar Khilji, General of Kutbuddin, launched a surprise attack on the capital. The aged king fled to East Bengal where, even after his death, his descendants ruled independently for sometime.

Towards the close of Lakṣmaṇa's reign, Madhumathanadeva carved out an independent State on the eastern bank of the river Meghnā. In the first half of the thirteenth century, the kings of Deva dynasty ruled over that small State. The State of Paṭṭikera (within the modern district of Comilla), too, was perhaps, under their domination.

There were a few small States in Bengal no doubt. But, after the dethronement of Lakṣmaṇa, the sun of Hindu glory set for ever in the region. After usurping the throne Bakhtiyar struck heavy blows at the vital spots like Gauḍa, Varendra, etc. Ere long the whole of Bengal accepted his overlordship. But, Bakhtiyar paid a heavy penalty for what he grabbed by unfair means. He was slain by one Āli Mardān.

Anarchy ensued. During the period of sixty years, from 1227 to 1287, fifteen rulers in succession occupied the throne of Bengal. Of them, ten belonged to the Mamluk race which ruled over Delhi.

One, Tughral Khan, with the intention of establishing supreme suzerainty in Bengal, revolted against Giyasuddin Balban, the then Sultan of Delhi. The Sultan drove him off, and placed his own son, Bugrā Khan, on the coveted throne of Bengal.

The Mamluk rule in Bengal was supplanted by the Tughlak; Sultan Muhammad Tughlak annexed this State to his empire.

The Tughlak regime gave way to the Iliyas Shahi rule. At this time, an Arabian traveller visited Bengal. He has left us a dependable economic account of this province.

The fickle fortune of Bengal resorted to a Hindu ruler for a brief spell. He was Gaṇeśa whose son was popularly known as Jitmal, Jaymal, Yadu or Yadusena. Yadu embraced Islam, reverted to Hinduism and again became a Muslim. After his father's death, he occupied the throne of Bengal under the name of Jalaluddin. He probably died in 1431 A.D. Then the second series of Iliyas Shahi rulers came to power.

Towards the close of the fifteenth century, the royal fortune passed over to the Husain Shahi dynasty. It fell to the Afghans who ruled up to the last quarter of the sixteenth century.

The Afghan regime was supplanted by Mughal rule. Under the Mughals, their governors were virutally the rulers of Bengal. In the sixteenth century, the Portuguese visited Bengal for commercial purposes. Gradually, other European traders, viz. English, French and Dutch, were attracted to Bengal.

In the middle of the eighteenth century, Ālivardi Khan declared himself as the Nawab of Bengal, Bihar and Orissa. During his rule, Bengal was overrun by the Mārāṭhās. Their onslaught was popularly known as the menace of Bargis. The Nawab died in 1756.

He was succeeded by his daughter's son Sirājuddaulā. Under the doting care of his maternal grandfather, Sirāj became passionate, haughty and self-willed. He had no capacity for bearing the heavy burden of a kingdom. In the battle of Plassey, in 1757 A.D., due to the treacherous machinations of his General, Mir Jāfar, he was defeated by Lord Clive. While on the run, Sirāj was slain by Miran, son of Mir Jāfar.

Thus, the rod of the balance of the English trader turned into the sceptre of the ruler. Gradually the whole of India came under the imperial sway of the British.

We have seen the changing political canvas of Bengal through centuries. The society was also not static. We shall see the dynamism of Bengal in the spheres of manners, customs, religious practices, etc.

Bengal may or may not have developed a distinct culture before the advent of the Aryans. But, in the *Manusmṛti*,[3] we find that Vaṅga was an integral part of the land inhabited by the Aryans. Vaṅga is included among the famous *janapadas* mentioned in the *Rāmāyaṇa*. In the *Mahābhārata*,[4] the bank of the river Karatoyā and Gaṅgāsāgarasaṃgama,[5] both in Bengal, are mentioned as holy places.

Even after the Aryanisation of Bengal, non-Aryan influence did not fully disappear in this region. Even to-day certain religious rites and Bengali vocables bear testimony to the fact that Bengal was the abode of non-Aryans. The Brāhmanical religion pervaded this region no doubt. In Bengal, we find evidence of the fact that the Aryans attracted within their fold non-Aryans whose customs and rites they partly absorbed into their own and whom they initiated into their way of life. Indeed, this tendency of the followers of the Brāhmanical religion lent viability to it through ages. In Bengal, the tribes Vaṅga, Suhma, Śabara, Puṇḍra, etc., came to be treated as Kṣatriyas. As a result of the spread of the Aryan influence in Bengal, the Brahmins began to multiply. There is historical evidence of the existence of a very large number of Brahmins here in the fifth and sixth centuries A.D. and even earlier.

In course of time, the admixture of the principal castes led to the rise of the mixed ones called Karaṇa, Ambaṣṭha, etc.; it perhaps occurred towards the close of Hindu rule. In the *Bṛhāddharma-purāṇa* (c. thirteenth century), as many as forty-one non-Brahmin castes are designated as Śūdra. The *Brahma-vaivarta-purāṇa*, too, dating back to c. 7th or 8th Cent. A.D. in its original form and to about the 16th Cent. in its present form, presents almost a similar social picture. These two Purāṇas presumably represent the social condition of Bengal. The members of the main and mixed castes began to pursue fixed vocations. Gradually, do's and don'ts developed with regard to dining and drinking by the members of the higher and lower castes.

From the work of Bhavadeva Bhaṭṭa (c. eleventh-twelfth century) it seems that inter-caste dining and drinking had not yet been so severely condemned as in later times. It appears that, even as a result of eating rice from a Caṇḍala, a Brāhmaṇa did not lose his caste; expiatory rites, performed by him, were supposed to absolve him of sin. It is interesting to note that, contrary to the usual practice obtaining in other parts of Bengal, the Brahmins of this region used to eat fish and meat with impunity. Bhavadeva Bhaṭṭa, a great Smṛti writer of the pre-Raghunandana period, defends this practice. Bhavadeva, however, condemns the drinking of *surā* on the part of all.

Presumably due to their Buddhistic persuasion, the Pālas did not pay much attention to social reforms. There was a Brāhmanical revival with the advent of the Senas. Ballāla introduced Kulinism the main purpose of which was the creation of a class of Brahmins possessed of learning, modesty, good conduct, etc. But, it seems, even worthless Brahmins basking in the sunshine of royal favour, enjoyed the exalted status of Kulins. The evils of this system did not take long to manifest themselves. The worthless Kulins, vaunting their social status, were much in demand as bridegrooms. The result was polygamy, and the consequent neglect and ill-treatment of the wives by Kulins. From the

Ballāla-carita it appears that a caste might be raised by the king to higher status or lowered to an inferior one.

From the *Kulajis* (genealogical works), whose testimony is not free from doubt, we learn that Ādiśūra, king of Gauḍa, brought five *Sāgnika*[6] Brahmins from Kānyakujba in order to resuscitate Vedic rites in Bengal. Gradually, they settled in Rāḍha and Varendra. Since the time of Ballāla, they are said to have been divided into two groups, Rāḍhī and Vārendra respectively.

In the wake of the invasion by the Turks, the Hindu society suffered reverses to a great extent. The invaders, besides demolishing temples and shrines, forcibly converted many Hindus to Islam. Their conversion, perhaps, had a fillip in the repression of the lower classes by the higher ones. The economic factor was also probably responsible to some extent. Many a conservative Hindu fled to Nepal, Kashmir, etc., in order to save their religion, honour and even life.

After the firm establishment of Muslim rule, some wise people set about saving the shattered Hindu culture. During the period between thirteenth and sixteenth century, many Smṛti digests were composed to regulate the society. A noteworthy feature of this period is that some Muslim rulers extended their generous patronage to the cultivation of Sanskrit and Bengali literatures.

A varied picture is presented also by the religious scene of Bengal. We are in the dark about the religious condition before and immediately after the Aryanisation of Bengal. Considerable influence of Jainism in the second century B.C. is attested by the mention of the three sects of Tāmraliptika, Koṭivarṣīya and Puṇḍravardhanīya in the Jaina *Kalpasūtra*. A Pāhārpur copperplate grant testifies to the existence, in that region, of a Jain monastery in the fourth century A.D. or earlier. Hiuen Tsang, (630 A.D.) too, speaks of many Digambar Jains in the then Bengal.

Epigraphical and sculptural evidences bear out the considerable spread of Brāhmanism in Bengal. The society of this age reveals great influence of the Purāṇic religion and the Vaiṣṇava and Śaiva ways of worship.

The religious condition in the period between the end of the Gupta rule and the rise of the Pālas is not very clear.

From the mention of the Vāmācārī sect in Rāḍha and Varendra, found in the *Devī-purāṇa* (c. seventh-eighth century), it seems that, in those times, Śakti-worship widely prevailed in Bengal. It should not be presumed that the Pālas introduced Buddhism in Bengal for the first time. It is true that their patronage helped the development and expansion of this religion. That Buddhism was an established religion in this region at the time of Aśoka is cetain. From stone inscriptions we learn that Bengal was one of the principal centres of Buddhism in the third century A.D. In the fifth century, Fa-hien saw twenty-two Buddhist monasteries in Tāmralipta. Hiuen Tsang attests deep influence of this religion in the seventh century. In this century, Śīlabhadra, a scion of the royal family of Samataṭa, achieved great fame among the contemporary Buddhists, and became the supreme head of Nālandā University. Under the Pālas, the Bengalis did not rest content by merely embracing Buddhism. They avidly studied Buddhist scriptures, and composed Buddhist works, especially Tantras. Their fame passed far beyond the confines of India. At the invitation of the king of Tibet, Atīśa Dīpaṃkara (980-1053 A.D.), the famous Buddhist scholar, went there in order to reform Tibetan Buddhism. Countless Buddhist images of this period, many *Vihāras* and volumes of Buddhist works, composed by Bengali authors, bear eloquent testimony to the wide prevalence of Buddhism in the Bengal of that age.

This province-wide diffusion of Buddhism gradually gave rise to the Buddhist Sahajiyā cult which, like flood-water, reached every nook and corner of this region. The *Caryāpadas*, the earliest specimens of Bengali language and literature, are the creation of Siddhācāryas, initiated to this religion. It should not be supposed, however, that there was a holiday of the Brāhmanical religion in this period. There are many references, in the copperplate grants of the Pālas, to Brahmins versed in the Veda, Vedāṅga, Mīmāṃsā, etc., and conversant with Vedic rites and rituals. Nārāyaṇapāla is known to have established a temple in honour of Śiva.

Numerous Sanskrit works, images of Hindu deities, inscriptions and coins, etc., are mute witnesses to the revival of the Brāhmanical religion during the post-Pāla period under the Senas of Vaiṣṇavite and Śaivite persuasions.

After the overthrow of the Senas, Hinduism suffered to a great extent. But, this religion of immearsurable vitality did not disappear even after the onslaughts of hostile people and unfavourable conditions. The age-old Hindu religion assumed a new garb, and was revitalised by Caitanya and Caitanyaism. This great preacher and reformer brought home to the people the utter hollowness of rigid rites and customs without self-purification and love of humanity. He made bold to declare that even a devout Caṇḍāla, devoted to God, is the best of *dvijas*. The flood of devotion-cum-love, let loose by Caitanya, swept the soil of Bengal, and this vast land was filled with reverberations of *Saṃkīrtana* and rapturous rapport seized all classes of people, high and low. Even the acute logician was turned into an emotional devotee.

It was at this juncture that, due to influence of the Sahajiyā cult, in its dual grab of Vaiṣṇava and Bauddha, gripped the imagination of the people. The rigours of Brahmanical ritualism yielded place to the easier Tāntric practices. Tāntricism became so popular that Raghunandana, the famous social reformer and maker of many Smṛti digests, set the seal of his recognition on Tāntrika *dīkṣā*. This period saw the advent of the erudite Kṛṣṇānanda Āgamavāgiśa who wrote the essentials of Tantra and, thus, paved the way for the spread and practice of Tāntricism.

NOTES

1. Kalhaṇa has mentioned, in the *Rājataraṅgiṇī*, the prosperity of the citizens of Pauṇḍravardhana.
2. Comprising modern Sumatra, Java, Borneo and Bali.
3. According to P.V. Kane, it assumed the present form in the period between 200 B.C. and 200 A.D.
4. According to Winternitz, the *Mahābhārata* perhaps assumed its present form about the fourth century A.D. and the *Rāmāyaṇa* had its present form a century or two earlier.
5. Also mentioned as a sacred place in the *Matsya-purāṇa* (22.11), *Viṣṇudharmasūtra* (85/28), *Padma-purāṇa* (1.39.4) and in the *Tīrthaprakāśa* portion of the *Vīramitrodaya*.
6. Those who preserve the fire at which their initiation to Vedic studies is performed, and subsequently perform rites with it.

IV. Tāntric Texts of Bengal

We have seen the pervasive influence of Tantra on the social and religious life of Bengal. It is, therefore, natural that some Bengali scholars, among whom there were a few *Sādhakas*, engaged themselves in the writing of Tāntric works. These works can be broadly divided into two groups, Buddhist and Hindu. The early works of the former class are earlier than the earliest extant works of the latter. With regard to Buddhsit Tantras of Bengal, it should be observed that many of them exist only in their Tibetan and Chinese versions, the original Sanskrit works being lost to all intents and purposes. The earliest extant Hindu Tantra dates back to the fourteenth century A.D.

A noteworthy feature of Hindu Tantra of Bengal is that it belongs to *Kālīkula*, while most of the Tantras of the other regions of India belong to *Śrīkula*.

The followers of *Kālīkula* have a monistic outlook. They believe in the identity of Śakti and Brahman in its threefold aspect of *Sat* (that which exists), *Cit* (consciousness) and *Ānanda* (bliss). According to them, Śakti is not a separate entity as the *Māyā-vivarta* of Brahman. They think that the Śiva-Śakti concept is beyond dualism, it can be realised through experience.

The followers of *Śrīkula* recognise the above threefold aspect of Śiva, and consider Śakti as Vimarśinī or Śiva's natural vibrating power.

Another charcteristic of the Bengal school of Tantra is that it concerns itself more with the *Karma Kāṇḍa* of Tantra than with *Jñānakāṇḍa*. In other words, Bengal Tantra is ritualistic while Kashmirian Tantra is more philosophical and metaphysical. A study of the Tantras of Bengal reveals that many are shortcuts or epitomes as the *Tantrasāra* of Kṛṣṇānanda, and a larger number of works are of the nature of priestly manuals designed to facilitate the performance of Tāntric rites.

It is not known where Tāntric works began to be composed in Bengal. Hindu Tantra of this province appears to have originated about the eighth century A.D. Tāntric studies continued here down to the 19th century. Even in the early years of the present century Tāntric manuals were written.

Hindu Tantra of Bengal breaks fresh ground in some respects, as our account of the Mahānirvāṇa will reveal.

Buddhist Tantra—Kaulajñāna-nirṇaya

Buddhist Tantra of Bengal appears to have originated as early as the first half of the seventh century A.D. As we shall see, many of the Buddhist Tantras of Bengal are lost, their translations only being preserved in Tibetan and Chinese. Of the extant Buddhist Sanskrit Tāntric works, the earliest one dates back to the earlier half of the tenth century.

There are some marked differences between Hindu and Buddhist Tantras. The latter does not recognise Śakti or Śaktism. Like the Hindus, the Buddhists also recognise one male principle and one female underlying everything. Instead of Śiva-Śakti of Hindu Tantra, Bauddha Tantra recognises Upāya-Prajñā to which the same function of Śiva-Śakti is attributed, but in a reverse order.

The Buddhists advocate the idea of *Śūnyatā* according to which one should not fix one's mind even on higher objects like deities. One must learn to live in a state of void in which there is neither space nor time.

Buddhist Tantra teaches the *mantra Oṃ maṇipadme Huṃ*, not found in Hindu Tantra. *Maṇipadma* means 'jewel in the lotus' or 'male within the female organ', the state of completeness, energy infusing wisdom. *Huṃ* is the sound of power that forces the *mantra* into realisation. This energy is symbolised by an implement known as *Vajra*, a word occurring only in Buddhist Tantra.

Some Hindu Tantras try to show that they are based on the Veda and quote Vedic *mantras*. But, Buddhist Tantras generally do not look upon the Veda as authoritative. A few works, using some Vedic *mantras*, may have done so as a result of Brāhmanical intrusion.

While Hindu Tantra recognises Śakti and some other deities as real, some Buddhist Tantras, (e.g. *Sādhanamālā*), look upon gods as mere conceptual entities existing only in the mind of the worshippers.

Hindu Tantra makes much of *Kuṇḍalinī*, supposed to reside in *mūlādhāra* whence it rises through *Suṣumnā* up to the thousand-petalled lotus in the head. Buddhism rejects sensuous imagery. Buddhist Tantra, however, recognises the inner 'god' ascending the spinal column. It is represented in art by such female figures as red Ḍākinī.

Buddhist Tantra attaches little importance to the lowest lotus within the body, and is inclined to exclude that behind the genitals.

This Tantra recognises a set of energy-fields within the body. The set is located in five circles within a flat disc. Of these, four are at the four directons, the fifth being at the centre. In each of these, there is a figure of the Buddha of a symbolic colour.

He meditates in sexual union with his wisdom, along with subsidiary figures. Wisdom is conceived as a female. This union is sometimes symbolised by a blue Buddha calmly seated in the sexual embrace of pure white wisdom. The entire process may also be symbolised in sets of *yantras* in which shades and colours, rather than human figures, are the medium.

Some features are, however, common to both the Hindu and Buddhist Tantras. Both have two aspects, one philosophical and the popular, the latter including magic, exorcism, etc.

Many Hindu Tantras are dialogues between Śiva and Pārvatī or Skanda or Bhairava, Buddhist Tantra often professes to quote the Buddha.

The emphasis on *Guruvāda* is common to both. The qualifications of *guru* and *śisya* are mostly similar.

The importance, attached to *mantra*, is similar in both. *Maṇḍala* and *mudrā* play a prominent role in both the types.

Nyāsa is an important practice to Hindus as well as Buddhists. The accessories of *yoga*, called *prāṇāyāma*, *dhyāna*, etc., are by and large common to both.

Both recognise nerve-cycles (*cakras*) within the body. Hindu Tantra recognise six *Cakras* the penetration of which by *Kuṇḍalinī* till it reaches *Sahasrāra* is regarded as the highest goal of *sādhanā*. Buddhist Tantra recognises three *cakras* corresponding to the three bodies of the Buddha, viz. *Dharma*, *Sambhoga* and *Rūpa* or *Nirmāṇa*. Corresponding to *Sahasrāra*, the Buddhists speak of *Uṣṇīṣa kamala* which symbolises the Buddha's *Vajrakāya* or *Sahajakāya*.

Corresponding to *Iḍā* and *Piṅgalā* with *Suṣumnā* in between, mentioned in non-Buddhist Tantra, Buddhist Tantra speaks of two nerves, one on each side of the spinal cord; in between them is the one known as *Sahaja* or *Avadhūtī*.

As stated before, the Buddhist works do not recognise *Kuṇḍalinī*. Instead, they mention a Female Energy having the force of fire and residing in the *Nirmāṇacakra* near the navel. It is known as *Caṇḍālī* which, being activated, ignites *Dharma-* and *Sambhoga-cakras*. Its upward march terminates in union with the *Uṣṇīṣa-kamala*, and like *Kuṇḍalinī* comes back to its original position. In both types of Tantra *Siddhi* is a subject of discussion.

The common topics, dealt with in Buddhist Tantra are: *Nature of kula*, *Upāya* (male principle) and *Prājñā* (female principle), Creation and Dissolution, *Bindu*, *Kalā*, *Mokṣa* or *Nirvāṇa*, *Siddhi*, *Yoga*, *Sahaja-tattva*.

Some Buddhist Tantras deify prominent personages of Buddhism.

Gaṇeśa, Sarasvatī and some other deities of the Brahmanical pantheon have got into Buddhism. Buddhist Tārā is different from her namesake in Hindu Tantra where she figures as a Vidyā or Śakti.

The Mahāyāna Buddhism, in order to have a wide popular appeal, absorbed popular cults and rituals. Thus, it was considerably influenced by Tāntrism.

A type of Mahāyānic works is called *Dhāraṇī* (between 4th and 8th centuries A.D.) or protective spells. These are Tāntric in character.

The *Prajñāpāramitās* emphasise the cult of the Female Principle.

The *Bodhisattvabhūmi*, besides mentioning many spells, deals with the significance of mystic syllables.

As regards *Pañcamakāra*, these were so common and popular that, despite the Buddha's unequivocal prohibition of adultery and the strict code of moral conduct, enforced in the Buddhist *Saṅgha*, Buddhist Tantra could not ignore it. Works like the *Prajñopāya-viniścaya-siddhi* go to the extent of prescribing indiscriminate sexual intercourse.[1] Sex relations even with one's mother and sister are recommended in Tāntric works like *Guhyasamāja*.

The concept of *Yuganaddha* or *Samarasa*, god and goddess in union, a form by which the Buddha and Bodhisattvas are represented, shows the extent of the influence of general Tāntric way of life on Buddhist Tantra.

First of all, we take up the Buddhist Tantras. Of the extant Buddhist Tāntric works in Sanskrit, the most well-known, perhaps, is the *Kaulajñāna-nirṇaya*. In the work itself, we find the remark *macchaghnapādāvatārita*, i.e. revealed by Matsyendranātha who is identified by some with Lui Pā and is credited with some pieces in the *Caryāgīti*.[2] From this it seems that it was composed or compiled by some follower or followers of the school of Matsyendranātha. According to tradition, Matsyendra, also called Macchendra, Macchenda or Macchindra, Macchaghna, was the founder of the Kaula school. He is believed to have lived, in the earlier half of the tenth century, at Candradvīpa (=modern Sandvīp) in the Noākhāli district of Bānglādesh.

The work is divided into 24 sections (*paṭalas*). The principal subjects, dealt with in it, are meaning of 'Kula', practices prescribed by a *Kaula* (one versed in *Kula*), the principle called *Akulavīra*, relation of Śiva-Śakti, *Bindu, Nāda, Kalā, Mokṣa*, mode of worship, meditation, the principle of *Sahaja*, means of acquiring powers by which one can kill others and enjoy long life, denunciation of the prevailing Śāstric rites and the importance of *Yoga*, knowledge of *tīrthas*, characteristics of Ḍākinī and Yoginī.

A few of the topics, dealt with in it, will be briefly dwelt on below.

Nature of Kula

That state is called *Kula* in which the mind and sight unite, the independence of the senses is lost, man's own power becomes at one with Jīva and the sight is merged in the visual objects.[3] Such an exposition of the term is rare in Hindu Tantras where the terms *Kula, Kulācāra, Kulaśāstra*, etc., are frequently used. According to this school of thought, *Kula* and *Śakti* are identical. In fact, this meaning of *Kula* is intended in the term *Kulakuṇḍalinī* used in Tantra. In the *Kaulajñāna-nirṇaya, Kula* and *Akula* are synonymous.[4]

Śiva-Śakti

Śakti is merged in Śiva, the latter in *Kriyā* (action). Through will or desire *Kriyā* loses itself in *Jñāna* (knowledge). The will-power is merged in Supreme Śiva[5] into whom the phenomenal world is dissolved. *Icchā, Jñāna* and *Kriyā* — these three aspects of Śakti have been recognised. In it (xvii. 8,9a) Śiva and Śakti are stated to be inseparable like fire and smoke or tree and its shade. Śiva has been conceived as symbolised (*liṅgātmaka*) in a fourfold manner—*Siddhiliṅga, Mānasaliṅga, Manoliṅga* and *Dehaliṅga*.

Creation and Dissolution

Parama Śiva is merged in Śakti. Creation proceeds from the varied external manifestations of Śakti. When these manifestations are inward, dissolution occurs. While describing this Yogic mode, it is stated that there are seven lower regions and seven upper. *Kālāgni* or the Śakti, called Rudra, resides in *Mūlādhāra*. Creation lasts so long as it is in the lower regions. Dissolution starts when it proceeds upwards.

Bindu, Nāda, Kalā

Bindu is the name of the creative energy of Supreme Śiva who is inseparably associated with Supreme Śakti. From *Bindu* arises *Nāda* from which creation starts. *Bindu* is threefold; in it lie the germs of *mātā* (knower), *māna* (knowledge) and *meya* (object of knowledge). These three forces of Nāda, known as *Kalā* or *Kāmakalā*, are also collectively called *Tripurasundarī*.

Mokṣa (Liberation)

The stay of *Kula* or *Śakti* in the lower region is *bhukti* or *bhoga* (enjoyment, suffering) while its presence in the upper region constitutes *mukti* or liberation[6] which is attainable by means of the proper knowledge of 'Haṃsa'. Haṃsa or Śiva is immanent, the cause of the universe and the giver of suffering and liberation. With the knowledge of Haṃsa, mind is possessed of a superhuman state in which it passes beyond sin and merit. By perceiving, within the body, Śiva of the *Dehaliṅga* type, mentioned above, and by acquiring the knowledge of his movement in the world man attains Śivahood, becomes himself liberated and liberates others.[7]

Siddhi or mystic mental power, as a means to liberation, has been discussed in the work. Some of the principal *Siddhis*, attainable by special *mantras*, are

(i) *Nigrahānugraha* — punishment and favour.
(ii) *Kramaṇa* — power of getting into another body.
(iii) *Haraṇa* — stealing, carrying off.
(iv) *Pratimājalpaṇa* — making an image speak.
(v) *Ghaṭapāṣāṇa-sphoṭana* — causing cracks in pitchers and stones.

These are collectively called *Pāśastobha*. The other *Siddhis* are

(i) *Māraṇa* — killing.
(ii) *Uccāṭana* — causing expulsion or mental agitation of the enemy.
(iii) *Stambhana* — rendering the efforts of the enemy abortive or causing paralysis to his body.
(iv) *Mohana* — causing delusion or bewildermemt in the enemy.
(v) *Śāntika* — appeasement of hostile deities.
(vi) *Pauṣṭika* — increasing physical vigour.
(vii) *Ākṛṣti* — attracting others.
(viii) *Vaśa* — controlling others.

The following powers and qualities are stated to be acquired by *Yoga*:

Popularity, freedom from disease, poetical ability, eloquence, hearing from afar, levitation, union with Yoginīs, warding off physical infirmity, great speed, assuming many forms, causing motionlessness of the army, etc.

A peculiar practice, advocated for removing physical infirmity and ensuring long life, is this. By *haṭhayoga* one has to extend the tongue so as to drink the nectar exuded from the thousand-petalled lotus (*sahasrārapadma*). This process is stated to be capable of even leading to immortality.

Mode of Worship

The worship of symbols, made of stone, earth or metal, has been prohibited. The worship of *Mānasaliṅga*, within the body, alone is ordained as a means of *Siddhi*. This *pūjā* is to be done by mental flowers and resin. Non-violence, control of the senses, kindness, absence of anger, meditation, knowledge, etc., constitute mental flowers. *Siddhi* and *Mokṣa* cannot be attained by the mode of worship prevailing among the people. Equanimity is to be practised by an aspirant after giving up passion, anger, pride and greed. There is no truth in the Śāstras, current among the people, so that modes of worship, prescribed in these works, are to be abjured. In this work, greater stress has been laid on meditation than on external worship.

Sahaja

A circle within the body is called *Sahaja*. It is also called *Vajra*, and can be reached by means of *Vajrayoga*. When it is reached, the body becomes firm like thunder and free from decrepitude. In this condition, the mind, too, acquires equanimity. The *Sahajiyā* cult plays a prominent role in the *Dohās* attributed to *Siddhācāryas*.

A comparison of the *Kaulajñāna-nirṇaya* with Hindu and Buddhist Tantras reveals its greater connexion with the latter than the former. The term 'Vajra', used in it, is virtually absent in Hindu Tantra, whereas it has been frequently used in the Buddhist Tantra. The *Siddhis*, called *Śāntika* and *Pauṣṭika*, mentioned in the *Kaulajñāna*, are not generally mentioned in Hindu Tantra, but occur in the Buddhist works.

Other Works of Matsyendranātha

Besides the above work, ten other Tāntric works are associated with Matsyendra and his school. These are

(i) Akulavīratantra, (ii) Akulāgamatantra, (iii) Kulānandatantra, (iv) Gorakṣaśataka, (v) Gorakṣabhujaṅga, (vi) Gorakṣa-sahasranāmastotra, (vii) Gorakṣasaṃhitā, (viii) Jñānakārīkā, (ix) Nityāhnika-tilaka, (x) Śrīkāmākhyā-guhyasiddhi.

Dohās

The Buddhist *Siddhācāryas*, who resorted to the modes of *Sahajasiddhi*, are credited with *Dohās*, compiled in the *Caryāgīti*, referred to earlier. From the Tibetan *Tanjur* we learn that some of these *Siddhācāryas* wrote Tāntric works in Sanskrit. To Kukkuripāda are attributed six works at least three of which appear to have dealt with Mahāmāyā.[8] Ten works on *Vajrayāna* are associated with the name of Śabari who is, perhaps, identical with Śabarīśvara. To Śabrīśvara are ascribed a few works on *Sādhanā* relating to Vajrayoginī. Lui Pā, whose identity with the aforesaid Matsyendra is not free from doubt, is known to have written four works on *Vajrayāna* including the *Abhisamayavibhaṅga*. The *Vāyutattva-bhāvanopadeśa* appears to have been written by Gorakṣa who may have been identical with Gorakṣanātha. To Jālandharipāda, who was perhaps the preceptor of Gopīcānd, are ascribed four Vajrayāna works of which one is the *Śuddhivajra-pradīpa*, a commentary on Saroruhavajra's *Hevajra-sādhana*. Ten Vajrayāna works are mentioned as written by Virūpa. In the Tibetan language are preserved four *Vajrayāna* works associated with the name of Tilopā or Tailikapāda. About 25 Tāntric works[9] are ascribed to Saraha or Sarahapāda (=Rāhulabhadra).

OTHER BUDDHIST TANTRAS

Śīlabhadra

From the Tibetan *Tanjur* and Lāmā Tāranātha's history of Tibet, we learn about quite a number of other Buddhist Tantras by Bengali authors. Their Sanskrit originals are lost, and are preserved only in Tibetan versions and, in a very few cases, in Chinese. The *Tanjur* preserves translation of *Āryabuddha-bhūmi-vyākhyāna* of Śīlabhadra. Hiuen-Tsang testifies to his authorship of many works of which Chinese translation alone is available. Śīlabhadra appears to have been born in a Brahmin royal family of Samataṭa in Bengal. Initiated to

Buddhism at Nālandā, he was the principal *Ācārya* and the head of that Mahāvihāra when Hiuen-Tsang visited it. The inmates of the *Saṅgha* gave him the honorific title 'Saddharmanidhi'. The above Chinese traveller is stated to have studied *Yogaśāstra* under him. Śīlabhadra passed away about 654 A.D.

Śāntarakṣita

Another prominent figure among the Buddhist authors of Bengal is Śāntarakṣita who was at one time the principal Ācārya at Nālandā. He is known to have established a temple in Tibet in 749 A.D. According to S. C. Vidyābhūṣaṇa, he was a scion of the royal family of Jāhor which is held by Benoytosh Bhattacarya to have been the Tibetan form of Sābhār, a well-known place in East Bengal (Bāṅglādesh). According to Sarat Das, he was a resident of Gauḍa-Vaṅga. Born at Jāhor in 705 A.D., he died in Tibet in 762 A.D.

Besides the philosophical works, entitled *Tattva-saṃgraha* and *Tattva-siddhi*, he appears to have written several works mainly on Buddhist Tantra. These are available only in Tibetan translation.

Kumāravajra

According to Tibetan tradition, the Bengali Buddhist Kumāravajra, a contemporary of the Bengal King Mahīpāla and Nayapāla (c. end of tenth century and first half of the eleventh century), wrote the Tāntric work entitled *Cakrasambara-maṇḍala-vidhi-tattvāvatāra*.

Divākaracandra

According to the *Tanjur*, Divākaracandra was a Bengali, a contemporary of king Nayapāla (c. first half of the eleventh century), and a disciple of Maitrīpā. The above Tibetan work contains translation of some Buddhist Tāntric works including the *Herukasādhana*.

Jetāri

Jetāri, a resident of Varendra and preceptor of the famous Atīśa Dīpaṅkara, was a scholar at Vikramaśīla Vihāra at the time of king Mahīpāla. He appears to have written, besides three works on logic, eleven works on *Vajrayāna-sādhanā* which are preserved only in Tibetan rendering. According to Tāranātha, Jetāri was the author of one hundred works.

Atīśa

The brightest star in the galaxy of Buddhist writers of Bengal is Atīśa Dīpaṅkara.[10] He is known to have been born in the royal family of Gauḍa at Vikramaṇipura or Vikramapura[11] in 980 A.D. or 982 according to some. Son of Kalyāṇa Śrī and Prabhāvatī, he was named Candragarbha. His preceptor, Śilarakṣita of Odantapuri Vihāra, by whom he was initiated to Buddhism at the age of 19, conferred on him the title of *Dīpaṅkara Śrījñana*. In course of time, he became a monk, and having studied long under Candrakīrti in Survarṇadvīpa, travelled in Ceylon and went to Magadha. At the invitation of king Mahīpāla I, he took over as the principal Ācārya of Vikramaśīla Vihāra. Subsequently, at the request of the then king of Tibet, he went (1042) to Tibet and effected the reformation of Buddhism there. He died there in 1053 or 1054 A.D. During his thirteen-year stay in Tibet, he is stated to have penned about 200 works of which many exist only in Tibetan versions in the *Tanjur*. Most of these woks deal with *Vajrayāna-sādhanā*.

Ratnākaraśānti

Ratnākaraśānti, who was probably identical with Śānti to whom two Bengali songs are attributed,[12] was born sometime in the tenth century. He is known to have written several Buddhist Tāntric works, besides two on Buddhist logic.

Abhayākaragupta

Abhayākaragupta appears to have been born in the latter half of eleventh century in a Kṣatriya family of Bengal. According to some, he was an Oriyā or a native of Bihar. According to the *Tanjur*, he worte about 20 works on *Vajrayāna*. Of these, at least four are available in original Sanskrit. Besides original works, he wrote a commentary, called *Āmnāyamañjarī*, on the Tantra called *Śrīsampuṭa-tantrarāja*. Another commentary by him is on the *Buddhakapālātantra*. The *Vajrāvalināma Maṇḍalopāyikā* is also attributed to him.

Prajñāvarman

Prajñāvarman, an Ācārya of the Kāpaṭyavihāra of Bengal, probably flourished sometime under the Pālas. Of the several works, written by him, two, viz. *Viśeṣastava-ṭīkā* and *Devātiśaya-ṭīkā* are Tāntric.

Minor Buddhist Writers

Besides the above writers on Buddhist Tantra, there are a few others who are supposed to have been Bengali and about whom no more dependable information is available than traditional accounts. The information, that can be gathered about them, is given below:

Names of authors in Devanāgarī alphabetical order

Author	Work	Personal history
Kumāracandra	*Ratnāvalī* comm. on *Kṛṣṇayamāri-tantra.* Also comm. on *Śrīvajra-bhairava-tantra-pañjikā* and another Tantra.(Only Tibetan versions available).	An *Avadhūta* of Vikramapuri Vihāra.
Nāgabodhi	13 Tāntric works including *Yamāri-siddha-cakra-sādhana, Āryanīlām-baradhara-vajrapāṇi-sādhana.* (Available only in Tibetan translation).	A resident of Śivasera in Vaṅgāla-deśa. He is said to have been a disciple of Nāgārjuna and to have hailed from Uḍḍiyāna.
Putali or Puttali	*Bodhicitta-vāyu-caraṇa-bhāvanopāya* (Only Tibetan rendering).	Said to have been a Śūdra of Bengal, and one of the 84 *Mahā Siddhas.*
Bodhibhadra	*Rahasyānanda-tilaka, Samādhisambhāra-parivarta, Bodhisattva-sambara-vidhi Yoga-lakṣaṇa-satya, Bodhisattva-sambara-viṃśati-pañjikā, Kāla-cakra-gaṇita-mukhādeśa,* etc. (Only Tibetan versions).	Of Somapuri Vihara. May be same as Bodhibhadra of Vikramaśila, men-tioned by Taranatha, No direct evidence of his belonging to Bengal.

Author	Work	Personal history
Mokṣākaragupta	?	Ācārya of Jagaddala Vihāra.
Śubhākara	?	Preceptor of Śākya Śrībhadra, Ācārya of Jagaddala Vihāra.

HINDU TANTRA

Parivrājakācārya

Mahāmahopādhyāya Parivrājakācārya is the earliest known Bengal writer on Hindu Tantra. We know practically nothing about his personal history; even his real name has been forgotten. A manuscript of his *Kāmyayantroddhāra*,[13] the only Tāntric work known to have been written by him, is dated 1297 Śaka (=1375 A.D.). In the absence of other evidences, this date may be taken as the lower terminus of his lifetime. This work describes the diagrams used in Tāntric rites.

Sarvānanda

Sarvānanda[14] (born c. 1400 A.D.) is a prominent figure among the Tāntric *Sādhakas* of Bengal. A resident of village Mehār in the district of Tripurā under Bānglādesh, he was the first *Sādhaka* of the famous *Śaktipīṭha* of Mehār. Vāsudeva, grandfather of Sarvānanda and a devotee of Mother Goddess, is said to have hailed from village Purvasthali in Burdwan district of West Bengal. Sarvānanda's father was Sambhunātha. According to tradition, Sarvānanda was originally illiterate. By the grace of the goddess, who was pleased with his *Śavasādhana*, he is said to have achieved *Siddhi* in 1425 A.D.[15] and was endowed with supreme knowledge (*parāvidyā*). As he visualised all the different forms of the goddess, he is said to have earned the sobriquet *Sarvavidyā*. His descendants have many disciples. M.M. Annadā Tarkacūḍāmaṇi is said to have belonged to this family. Even now a great festival is held at Mehār on the anniversary of Sarvānanda's acquisition of *Siddhi*. His son, Śivanātha, appears to have written his biography in the work entitled *Sarvānanda-taraṅgiṇī*.[16] From it we learn that Sarvānanda was born at Mehār when it was under the rule of a king (Zamindar) having the cognomen Dāsa. It is said that, owing to maltreatment by the ruler of the place, Sarvānanda left Mehār, and wandering at many places at last settled in the forest of Vijayātalā on northern boundary of village Senhāṭi in the district of Jessore (now partly in Bangladesh) partly in West Bengal.

It was here that he married Gaurī Devī, daughter of Candracūḍa Tarkālaṅkāra, Court Pandit of the ruler of Jessore.

Sarvānanda had two sons, Śivanātha and Śivānanda. At Senhāṭi he wrote the *Sarvollāsa.*

Later in life he went to Varanasi where he spent the rest of his life. Here he faced much antagonism from Śaiva Daṇḍi-svāmins who hated Sarvānanda's *Pañcatattva-sādhana.* Ultimately he settled at Sāradā Maṭh, established by Śaṃkarācarya. After a few years, he is said to have gone to Badarikāśrama (Badrinath) in Uttarpradesh.

The work, *Sarvollāsa,*[17] is associated with his name. The *Navāhna-pūjā-paddhati* in the Raghunātha temple of Kashmir and the *Tripurārcana-dīpikā* appear to have been composed by Vāsudeva or Sarvānanda.[18]

The *Sarvollāsa* is a compilation dealing with Tāntric *Sādhana* in general and *Vīrasādhana* in particular. As D. C. Bhattacharya writes in the introduction, only the two introductory verses and the chapter-headings are from the pen of the compiler. To these we may add the chapter colophons. The entire work is a collection of verses from different Tantras. From the *Ullāsa-nirṇaya* (determination of subjects under different chapters), it appears that the original work contained 64 chapters. But, the available manuscripts end in chapter 63. It is significant that, while the subjects under 63 chapters have been mentioned, no subject is stated under chapter 64; it is only stated that the work is completed in the sixty-fourth chapter (*catuḥṣaṣṭau samāptaśca*). The tradition goes that the last chapter contained the *mantra* by which the compiler attained *Siddhi.* So, it was kept back from the public. It is said that the last chapter had been taken away by himself when he renounced worldly life in order to settle as an *Avadhūta* at Vārāṇasī.

The topics under different chapters are briefly as follows:

(1) Characteristics of Prakṛti, Nigama, Āgama; origin of Yāmala, *Śāstra,* practice of *Śāstra* in different ages, construction of images, origin of Veda.
(2) Enumeration of 64 Tantras.
(3) Creation, Śyāmāstotra by Mahākāla, Sundarīstotra, Tārāstotra.
(4) Creation — a different account.
(5) Determination of creation in another manner.
(6) Account of *laya.*
(7) Discussion on *Bhāva.*
(8) Threefold *bhāvācāras,* characteristics and worship of a *Kumārī* (virgin girl).

(9) Characteristics of *bhāva*, etc., cause of *kaula-jñāna, paśvācāra*, speaking ill of *guru*.
(10) Characteristics of *guru, dhyāna* of *guru*.
(11) Same continued, 13 characteristics, *Śānta*, etc.
(12) Vaiṣṇava *ācāra*, prohibition of Śakti worship by Paśus.
(13) *Iṣṭabhakti*, characteristics of *Sādhakas, Sāttvikī, Rājasī* and *Tāmasī pūjās*.
(14) Animal sacrifice.
(15) *Śaiva ācāra, aṣṭāṅga yoga.*
(16) Characteristics of *Vibhāva, Paśu, anukalpa of 5 Makāras, vibhāva Vīra, pañcatattva-pramāṇa, tilaka-pramāṇa.*
(17) On *Yantra.*
(18) *Śākta ācāra, vīra-lakṣaṇa, vīrācāra, paśu-vīra- lakṣaṇa.*
(19) *Śādhaka, Cakra.*
(20) *Śrīcakra, Cakreśvara, cakra-praveśa.*
(21) *Śrīcakra* continued.
(22) *Śrīpatra, pañcatattva* and its result.
(23) On *ādya-tattva.*
(24) Kinds of *dravya, Śakti-śudhi.*
(25) On *madya.*
(26) *Dhyāna* of *Ānanda Bhairava, Ānanda Bhiravī, dravyaśodhana.*
(27) On *māṃsa, matsya, mudrā.*
(28) Śakti.
(29) Śakti-śuddhi.
(30) On *Saṃvidā*, mantra for drinking.
(31) *Pātrādhāra* of *Sādhaka* in Śrīcakra.
(32) *Śrīcakra-sādhaka-pātra-sthāpana.*
(33) *Vaṭukabali.*
(34) Result of *aṅganyāsa*, etc., *prāṇāyāma; tarpaṇa.*
(35) *Pātra-svīkāra.*
(36) *Pāna-niyama, navamapātra-lakṣaṇa, guru, dhyāna, Prāṇāyāma, Japa.*
(37) *Bāhya pūjā.*
(38) *Pātre madhudāna.*
(39) *Krīḍā.*
(40) *Maithuna.*
(41) *Pañcamānanda.*
(42) *Ānandārthi-sādhaka.*
(43) *Daivānanda.*

(44) *Maithuna, Yonistotra, Śrīcakra-pādodaka-māhātmya.*
(45) *Ānanda-stotra.*
(46) *Abhiṣeka.*
(47) *Dakṣiṇācāra-vīra.*
(48) *Vāmācāra.*
(49) *Puṣpa-śodhana-mantra.*
(50) *Kula-lakṣaṇa.*
(51) *Maithuna-lakṣaṇa.*
(52) *Śakti-Jñāna, Vāmāpūjā-lakṣaṇa.*
(53) *Siddhāntācāra.*
(54) *Maithunānanda, caturvidha-bhuktyānanda.*
(55) *Pūrṇānanda.*
(56) *Śaktyānanda.*
(57) *Śakti-māhātmya.*
(58) *Haṃsa-bīja-māhātmya.*
(59) *Dhyāna-traya-māhātmya.*
(60) *Divyācāra.*
(61) *Kulācāra.*
(62) *Prakṛti.*
(63) *Brahmajñāna.*

Kṛṣṇānanda (Āgamavāgīśa Bhaṭṭacārya)

A native of Navadvipa, he was undoubtedly the brightest luminary in the firmament of Bengal Tantra. He was, indeed, one of the triumvirate that built up the massive cultural edifice of medieval Bengal, the other two having been Raghunandana, the great Smṛti writer, and Raghunātha, the master of Navya-nyāya of the Bengal school. Had there been no other Tantra writer in Bengal, this province might be justifiably proud of Kṛṣṇānanda alone. He is generally supposed to have been a contemporary of Caitanya, the renowned religious reformer of Bengal. Some scholars are of the opinion that Kṛṣṇānanda flourished a little later than Caitanya. According to D. C. Bhattacharya,[19] he was born round about 1500 A.D. From the evidence, contained in *Kulajis*, whose testimony is not universally accepted, the aforesaid scholar concludes that Kṛṣṇānanda was the seventh lineal descendant of a certain sage who was a Vārendra Brāhmaṇa with the family title of Ojhā. Bhattacharya holds[20] that Rāmatoṣaṇa, author of the Prāṇatoṣiṇī, was the seventh lineal descendant of Kṛṣṇānanda.

Kṛṣṇānanda's father was Maheśvara and teacher Vāsudeva Sārvabhauma who was also his spiritual preceptor.

The *Tantrasāra*[21], compiled by Kṛṣṇānanda probably about 1580 A.D.,[22] is a renowned treatise. The most noteworthy feature of the work is that it contains the essence of the Tantra works of all the sects, viz. Śaiva, Śākta, Vaiṣṇava, Saura, Gāṇapatya, etc. This accounts for its wide popularity. A comparison of the manuscripts, some of which are fairly old, with the vulgate text reveals that the original text has undergone many changes.[23] No attempt has as yet been made to reconstitute the text in the original or near-original form. The oldest manuscript, available so far, is dated Śaka 1554(=1632 A.D.).

The Vaṅgavāsī edition of the work contains three chapters followed by some matters under the heading *Atha Prakaraṇam*. This portion is followed by certain matters concluded by the remark *iti tantrasāraḥ samāptaḥ*. After this there are certain *mantras*, hymns, procedural matters, etc.

This massive digest deals with all the important topics of Tantra, e.g. *dīkṣā*, modes of worship, *homa*, *kulācāra*, *Yantra*, *maṇḍala*, *cakra*, etc. It contains also hymns addressed to several deities. It quotes passages from Tāntric works,[24] both original and digests; of these works, some are known merely by name. Kṛṣṇānanda is credited with the conception, for the first time, of the Kālī image current in Bengal. He is also believed to have introduced the worship of this goddess in this province. Manuscripts of this work are written in several scripts besides Bengali; this fact attests its recognition far beyond the confines of Bengal.

Of the topics, dealt with in it, the noteworthy ones are briefly described below. According to the *Tantrārṇava*, quoted by Kṛṣṇānanda, the derivative meaning of the term 'guru' is as follows: ga ensures *siddhi*, *u* indicates Śambhu and *ra* removes sin. So *guru* is one who is Śiva himself and destroys sin; he is the greatest of all. Alternatively, *ga* indicates knowledge and giver of prosperity, *u* confers Śivahood and *ra* burns off sin. So, *guru* is one who is the dispenser of knowledge, prosperity and the state of Śiva, and removes sin. Another meaning, suggested in it, is this: *gu* stands for darkness and *ru* is destroyer of darkness. So, guru is one who dispels darkness; here darkness is, of course, the darkness of delusion, ignorance. A *guru* has the following characteristics: calm, highborn, polite, having a pure dress, of pure conduct, of established reputation, dexterous, possessed of a salutary motive, belonging to an *āśrama*, i.e. one of the four stages of life, given to meditation, versed in Tantra and *mantra*, capable of rewarding and punishing the disciple. He deserves greater respect than one's father.[25] Doomed to perdition is one who looks upon *guru* as a human being. The following physical and mental features are condemned in a *guru*; afflicted with leucoderma or leprosy, having bad nails, discoloured teeth, deformity having a limb more or less than usual, garrulous, gluttonous, effeminate, sonless, uncouth, wicked, devoid of the prescribed rites and duties.

A disciple should have the following qualities: calm, polite, respectful, of pure conduct, self-restrained, etc.

Those, who are devoid of right conduct, foolish, irreverent, attached to objects of sense or adulterous, are not worthy of *mantras*.

Tāntric *dīkṣā* is looked upon as indispensable. It is stated that one, not initiated to Tantra, is doomed to hell and that *japa, pūjā*, etc., performed by him, become futile. One has to receive *mantra* from the *guru*. If one learns it from some work, without the help of the *guru*, he will have no deliverance even after thousand *Manvantaras*.

The etymological meaning of the word 'mantra' has been given as follows — *mananāt trāyate yasmāt tasmān mantraḥ prakīrtitaḥ; mantra* is that by meditating on which one is liberated. Women and Śūdras are debarred from certain mantras, e.g. *gāyatrī, oṃkāra* and *lakṣmīmantra* (Śrī).

Besides Tāntric meditation, worship, etc., the work reflects popular beliefs and superstitions. There are also rites and customs calculated to ensure worldly happiness and security against evil forces. Kṛṣṇānanda deals, *inter alia*, with *vaśīkaraṇa* (method of controlling others), *vidveṣaṇa* (causing enmity), *uccāṭana* (ruining an enemy), *abhicāra* (employment of magic spells for malevolent purposes), *adarśana* (art of remaining invisible), etc. Some of these are briefly described below.

For *vaśīkaraṇa*, one has to meditate upon goddess Cāmuṇḍā, and to repeat the following *mantra* for a lakh times. Then *homa* is to be perfomed with ten thousand Palāśa flowers.

Cāmuṇḍe jaya cāmuṇḍe mohaya vaśamānaya amukaṃ svāhā.

Cāmuṇḍā has been described as having huge teeth, fierce look and four hands. In her right hands there are a *khaṭvāṅga* (a staff with a skull at the top) and *khaḍga* (sword). In her left hands, there are a *pāśa* (noose) and *naramuṇḍa* (a human head). She has dark complexion and tawny hair. Clad in tiger-skin, she is seated on a corpse. She lives in dense darkness.

In order to create enmity between two persons, their names are to be written with a mixture of the dung of buffaloes and horses and cows' urine. Several other methods are prescribed for this purpose. The names of the intended persons are to be written, with the blood of a buffalo and a horse, on a piece of cloth obtained at a cremation ground. The names of the persons intended are to be written in a circle (*cakra*) with six angles (*koṇa*). The following *mantra* should also be written there:

oṃ namo mahābhairavāya śmaśānavāsine amukāmukayor vidveṣaṃ kuru kuru huṃ phaṭ/

With the following *mantra* one has to perform *homa* with *neem* leaves and *kaṭutaila* in fire kindled with *Khadira* wood and in fire from the cremation ground. *Homa* for ten thousand times is to be performed with sesamum, *javā* flowers and *ātapa* rice. The *mantra* is this:

oṃ namo bhagavati śmaśānakālike amukaṃ vīdveṣaya vidveṣaya hana hana paca paca matha matha huṃ phaṭ svāhā/

The form of Kālī, to be meditated upon in this connexion, is as follows:

Possessed of complexion like the colour of *indranīla* (sapphire), blue like the sky, extremely fierce, defeating gods and demons, three-eyed, crying very loudly, decked with all ornaments, holding a human skull and a small sword, standing on the moon and the sun, surrounded by corpses and Bhairava, residing in a cremation ground, granting all success.

Besides offering various flowers, goats are to be sacrificed. After worshipping the deity, one should keep the *homa-bhasma* consecrated by *mantra*. The persons, on whom the ashes are thrown, will incur enmity.

To ensure the expulsion of a person from his native place, the following procedure is necessary. One has to write the *mantra 'oṃ namaḥ kākatuṇḍi'*, along with the name of the enemy, on a neem leaf, with a pen made of a crow's wing and the mixture of the dung of buffaloes and horses. After performing worship on that leaf, homa should be done with the wood of a crow's nest from a neem tree. In the *homa* are also to be used *narataila*[26] or *trikaṭu*[27] and the wood of the plant *dhustura* mixed with the oil of white mustard. It is to be performed in the fire of a burning ghat. Then goddess Dhavalāmukhī is to be worshipped with five articles (*pañcopacāra*). Finally the worshipper, with his mind absorbed in *dhyāna*, should throw the ashes on the enemy's house. The description of the goddess is as follows:

Grey complexion, three eyes, emaciated, crescent moon on forehead, matted locks on head, wearing tiger skin, garland of bones in one hand, knife in the other, sunken eyes, fierce teeth and belly like the nether region.

The rite of *abhicāra* is briefly as follows. A goat is to be procured after worshipping, with *khaḍgamantra*, the sword addressing it with the following mantra — *oṃ viruddhe rūpiṇī caṇḍike vairiṇam amukaṃ dehi dehi svāhā*. The enemy is to be present in the form of the above goat which is to be addressed by the name of the enemy and told 'You indeed are that person'. After tying its face with a threefold piece of red thread, the life of the enemy is to be infused into it by *mantra*, and flowers are to be showered on its head reciting this *mantra* — *ayaṃ sa vairī yo dveṣṭi tamimaṃ paśurūpiṇaṃ vināśaya mahādevi spheṃ spheṃ khādaya khādaya*. Then one has to recite *balimantra*, worship the *bali*, consecrate it with the *mantra āṃ hūṃ phaṭ*, etc., and then sacrifice it. The blood and the head of the goat are to be offered to goddess Durgā with the *mantra—etad rudhiraṃ durgāyai namaḥ*. In conclusion, *homa* is to be performed with the flesh of the eight limbs of the goat.

The procedure for ensuring invisibility is as follows. In a Śiva temple, five lights are to be kindled with human oil and placed on five human skulls. The wicks of the lights are to be made of *ākanda, śālmali, kārpāsa, padmasūtra* and *paṭṭasūtra*. Collyrium of five kinds is to be made with the flames of these five lights. The mixture of the different kinds of collyrium is to be applied on the eyes after reciting for 1008 times the following *mantra—oṃ hūṃ phaṭ kālī mahākālī māṃsa-śoṇitaṃ khādaya khādaya devimā paśyatu mānuṣeti hūṃ phaṭ svāhā*. By so doing one becomes invisible even to gods.

Kṛṣṇānanda says that *homa* does not produce the full fruit without *Kumāri-pūjā* (worship of a virgin girl). Girls of the age-range of one to sixteen years are virgins. In each year of her age, a girl has a distinct appellation. For example, in the first year she is called *Sandhyā*, a two-year old girl is designated as *Sarasvatī*, and so on. On *mahāpārvaṇs* (days of certain great festivals), particularly on the *Mahānavamī tithi* (i.e. the day on which the *Navamī Pūjā* of Durgā is performed), *Kumārī-pūjā* is a must.

The *Tantrasāra* does not deal with *Durgāpūjā* as a distinct topic. It, however, incidentally lays down Durgā-mantra, Mahiṣamardinī-mantra, Durgā-śatanāma, Durgā-kavaca, Durgā-yantra, etc., and states the special efficacy of *Kumārī-pūjā* on the Mahānavamī day. From these the influence of Tantra on *Durgāpūjā* is obvious.

Besides descriptions of *maṇḍala, mudrā, japa, homa*, etc., there are some portions in Tantra, which are eminently readable and testify to the literary excellences, even poetic gifts, of the writers. In hymns to gods and goddesses, and the description of their imaginary forms we find soaring flights of imagination, graceful words, sonorous metres and the deft use of figures of speech. Parts of such hymns, compiled in the *Tantrasāra*, are quoted below:

Hymn to Gaṇeśa

kṛtāṅgarāgaṃ navakuṅkumena mattālimālāṃ madapaṅka-lagnām/
nivārayantaṃ nijakarṇatālaiḥ ko vismaret putram anaṅgaśatroḥ//
aṅke sthitāyā nijavallabhāyā mukhāmbujālokana-lolanetram/
smerānanābjaṃ madavaibhavena ruddhaṃ bhaje viśvavimohanaṃ taṃ//
hiraṇyavarṇaṃ jagadīśitāraṃ kaviṃ purāṇaṃ ravimaṇḍalastham/
gajānanaṃ yaṃ pravadanti santastatkālayogais tamahaṃ prapadye//

To Viṣṇu

samudrakāñcī sariduttarīyā vasundharā merukirīṭabhārā/
dantāgrato yena samuddhṛtā bhūstamādikolaṃ śaraṇaṃ prapadye//
śaṅkhaṃ sucakraṃ sugadaṃ sarojaṃ dorbhir dadhānaṃ garuḍādhirūḍham/
śrīvatsa-cihnaṃ jagadādimūlaṃ tamālanīlaṃ hṛdi viṣṇumīḍe//
kṣīrāmbudhau śeṣaviśeṣatalpe śayānamantaḥ smita-śobhi-vaktram/
utphulla-netrāmbujam ambudābham ādyaṃ śrutīnāmasakṛt smarāmi//

To Gopāla

navīna-nīrada-śyāmaṃ nīlendīvaralocanam/
vallavī-nandanaṃ vande kṛṣṇāṃ gopālarūpiṇam//
sphurad-varha-dalodbaddha-nīlakuñcita-mūrdhajam/
kadamba-kusumodbaddha-vanamālā-vibhūṣitam//
gaṇḍa-maṇḍala-saṃsargi-calat-kāñcana-kuṇḍalam/
sthūla-muktāphalodāra-hāra-dyotita-vakṣasam//
hemāṅgada-tulākoṭi kirīṭojjvala-vigraham/
manda-māruta-saṃkṣobha-valgitāmbara-sañcayam//

The various forms of Kālī, described by Kṛṣṇānanda, are Dakṣiṇā Kālī, Guhya Kālī, Bhadra Kālī, Śmaśāna Kālī, Mahā Kālī. These forms are briefly described below.

To Kṛṣṇānanda is ascribed also a commentary, called *Śrītattva-bodhinī*.

Dakṣiṇākālikā

Dishevelled hair, garland of human heads, face with long or projecting teeth (*dantura*), four arms, lower left hand holding a human head just severed, upper left hand holding a sword, lower right hand posed as giving a boon, the upper right hand posed as granting freedom from fear, deep dark complexion, naked, two corpses of arrows as ornaments in the two ears, girdle of hands of corpses, three eyes radiant like the morning sun, standing on the chest of Mahādeva (Śiva) lying like a corpse, surrounded by jackals, fierce face, yellow blood flowing from the lip-ends.

Another description is as follows:

Four arms, dark, garland of human heads, two right hands holding a sword and two blue lotuses, two left hands holding a *kartṛkā* (small sword) and a human skull, garland of human heads on the head and neck, necklace of serpents on the chest, wearing a piece of black cloth, tiger-skin round the loins, left foot on the chest of a corpse and right foot on the back of a lion, represented as licking a corpse.

Guhyakālī

Deep black like a mass of clouds, wearing a black cloth, lolling tongue, sunken eyes, smiling face, fierce teeth, necklace of serpents, crescent moon on the forehead, one tuft of matted locks rubbing the sky, licking a corpse, sacred thread made of serpents, lying on a bed of serpents, garland of fify human heads, serpent Ananta with a thousand hoods on her head, surrounded by serpent-hoods, two hands with the serpents Takṣaka and Ananta as bangles on the left and the right respectively, girdle of serpents, Śiva as a boy on the left side, two corpses as ornaments in the two ears, pleased face, decked with nine gems, served by sages like Nārada, terrible on account of loud laughter.

Bhadrakālī

Emaciated through hunger, sunken eyes, face ink-dark, dishevelled hair, crying and saying 'I am not satisfied, I shall make this entire world a single morsel', two hands holding two nooses like the flames of burning fire, teeth resembling black berries.

Śmaśānakālī

Dark like a mountain of collyrium, living in a cremation ground, red eyes, dishevelled hair, fierce with flesh dried up, tawny eyes, left hand holding a vessel filled with wine and meat, right hand holding a human head just severed, smiling face, chewing raw meat, decked with various ornaments, naked, intoxicated with wine.

We have already stated that the *Tantrasāra* cites the authority of many Tantras and Tantra-writers. Of the editions of the work, none,[28] excepting the Vaṅgavāsī edition, cites either Pūrṇānanda or any of his works. As we shall see, Pūrṇānanda was a great Tāntric *Sādhaka* of Bengal having several Tantra works to his credit. The Vaṅgavāsī edition mentions[29] Pūrṇānanda and his *Śrītattva-cintāmaṇi*. As a matter of fact, this mention is not a part of the text of the *Tantrasāra*; it is only a marginal note in one of the codices used in preparing the edition.

Amṛtānanda Bhairava and Rāmānanda Tīrtha prepared revised versions of the *Tantrasāra*. The latter was a court-Paṇḍit of Kṛṣṇacandra, king of Nadiya, in the eighteenth century. Of the *Tantrasāra* of Rāmānanda, there is a complete manuscript in ten chapters in Asiatic Society, Calcutta. It should be stated that exactly the portion of the *Śrītattvacintāmaṇi*, stated above to be quoted in the Vaṅgavāsī edition of Kṛṣṇānanda's *Tantrasāra*, occurs at page 93 of the aforesaid work of Rāmānanda existing in Asiatic Society.

Brahmānanda Giri

Brahmānanda Giri, disciple of Tripurānanda, and spiritual guide of Pūrṇānanda, flourished probably in the early or middle part of the sixteenth century.

Two Tāntric works, associated with his name, are *Śāktānanda-taraṅgiṇī* and *Tārārahasya*.

The *Śāktānanda-taraṅginī*[30] consists of eighteen chapters called *Ullāsas*.

The first chapter deals exhaustively with the development of the foetus in the mother's womb. In the embryonic stage, a creature has memory of its previous birth and yearns after salvation. Everything is, however, forgotten with birth. The author speaks of happiness and sorrow in accordance with past action. The physical frame and life are said to be ephemeral. Nescience (*avidyā*) has been mentioned as the cause of the bondage of rebirth. The cause of release is meditation on Mahāmāyā in the form of *Vidyā* (true knowledge). In this chapter, we find also an account of the condition after death. The body has been regarded as a microcosm.

The second chapter lays down the rules and the good effects of *dīkṣā* (initiation), the time of initiation, characteristics and glory of the spiritual preceptor (*guru*). It deals also with the *Saṁskāra* (refinement) of *mantra*.

The third chapter deals with the metaphysical subject of the two-fold Brahman—*saguṇa* (with attributes) and *nirguṇa* (attributeless). For the steadiness of the mind of the worshipper, an image of the attri-buteless Brahman is conceived. It dwells on the great merit of *dhyānayoga* (meditation). The worshipper has been advised to identify himself with the object of his worship. Both *bhukti* (enjoyment) and *mukti* (liberation) are said to be obtainable through the meditation on Śakti.

The fourth chapter is devoted to daily duties—morning duty, washing face, bath, prayer. It again brings in *guru* who plays a great part in the spiritual life of a Tāntric devotee. In this chapter, we have *dhyāna* and *stuti* (eulogy) of the *guru*. This chapter describes the six circles (*cakra*) within the human body and the mode of *yoga* to be performed in them.

Chapter five deals with various kinds of seats, e.g. those made of *Kuśa* grass, and the different sitting postures like *Padmāsana* along with results accruing from them.

The following chapter lays down rules regarding *antaryāga*.

Chapter seven sets forth the procedural details about the worship of Śakti—purification of the place, sitting on a seat, manner of arranging the material for *Pūjā*, placing of *Śāntikuṇḍa*, purification of the seat, removal of *bhūtas* or ghosts (*bhūtāpasāraṇa*), purification of *bhūtas* or elements of the body (*bhūtaśuddhi*), various *nyāsas*, *prāṇāyāma*, meditation, mental worship, invocation (*āvāhana*), worship of the deity, self-surrender, salutation and *visarjana* (bidding farewell, immersion).

In the eighth chapter, we find rules about rosaries for *japa*, *karamālā* (palm-rosary), number of rosaries of jewels, etc., suitable for particular rites, determination of the material of the rosary suitable for a particular deity, purification of rosaries, consecration of rosaries, determination of letters of the alphabet.

In the ninth chapter, we have rules regarding *japa*, description of the heart, eyes, etc., of *mantras*, determination of *brahmarandhra*, etc., as six sites of *mantra*, called *sakala*, *niṣkala*, *sūkṣma*, *sakala-niṣkala*, *kalābhinna*, *kalātīta*. The author deals also with the consciousness of *mantras* and the materials suitable for the beads to be used in *japa*.

The tenth chapter seeks to determine the different kinds of *mantras*, viz. *setu*, *mahāsetu* and *kullukā*, in accordance with the different deities.

Chapter eleven deals with the different kinds of *mantra* for *mukhaśodhana* (purification of the mouth) applicable in the cases of different deities.

The next chapter deals with the important Tantra rite called *Puraścaraṇa*. It consists of the five devotional acts of *japa, homa, tarpaṇa, abhiṣeka* and feeding of Brāhmaṇas. Incidentally, it speaks of the number and mode of application of *japa*, etc. The results accruing from the above five acts are reduced by 9/10 in each succeeding act; e.g. *homa* produces 1/10th effect of *japa, tarpaṇa* 1/10th of *homa* and so on. One, who is unable to perform any of these five acts, has to perform twice the usual *japa*. In this chapter are also laid down special rules for *puraścaraṇa* on the occasion of lunar and solar eclipses.

Chapter fourteen enumerates the substances (*upacāra*) necessary for eighteen, sixteen, ten and five kinds of offerings to gods. It deals also with flowers permitted and prohibited for the worship of different deities, and lays down rules for the offering of the *upacāras*.

In chapter fifteen, we have rules about *kulācāra* and offerings to jackals. It contains the *nitya-saṁketa-stava*. We have also the declaration that particular kinds of *japa* expiate the sin arising from various acts of omission and commission. Finally, we have expiatory measures in the event of the destruction of the talisman (*kavaca*) held by a person.

The next chapter speaks of persons with whom association is prohibited. It contains expiatory rules in the event of the destruction of an established *yantra*, as well as of the spoiling of a *yantra* at the time of worship.

The following chapter gives rules for the construction of *maṇḍapa* and *kuṇḍa*.

The last chapter lays down rules regarding *kuśaṇḍikā* and *homa*.

This work quotes over one hundred works on Smṛti, Tantra, Purāṇa, etc., thus indicating the vast range of the study of the author.

The *Tārārahasya*,[31] complete in four *Paṭalas* (sections), deals with the rites and customs relating to the worship of goddess Tārā and her various images. It contains also rules and regulations regarding initiation appropriate for Tārā worship. The main topics of this work are:

creation, morning duties, bath, daily prayer, *mantra* and *gāyatrī* relating to Ekajaṭā, Ugratārā and Nīlasarasvatī, Śivaliṅga-pūjā, *antaryāga*, *yantras* relating to threefold Tārā mentioned above, *mahā-śaṃkhādi-mālā* and *saṃskāra* thereof, *homa*, *prāyaścitta* for *mantra-vismaraṇa*, *saṃskāra* for *pañcatattvas*, *pātrabandhanādi-rahasya*, *Tārā-pūjā-prayoga*, *trividha-ṣoḍhā-prakaraṇa*, *yoga-prakaraṇa*.

Pūrṇānanda Giri[32]

Brahmānanda's disciple, Pūrṇānanda, was known as Paramahaṃsa Parivrājaka. He had also the title of Yati. A native of village Kāṭihāli, under Netrakoṇā Subdivision of Mymensingh district in Bāṅglādesh, he was a Brāhmaṇa of Kasyapa gotra of the Rādhīya class. From his descendants we learn that he was son of Purandara, a devotee of Śakti, and Aparṇā. His real name was Jagadānanda. Pūrṇānanda was the name given by his preceptor. He was born in Śaka year 1423 (=1501 A.D.). He is famed to have been a devotee of a very high order. Until recently his descendants were held in high esteem in Bengal, particularly East Bengal.

Among his Bengali disciples, the most celebrated was Kṛṣṇānanda, author of the *Tantrasāra*.

Pūrṇānanda's seventh ancestor is said to have migrated, due to Muslim oppression, from Baranagar in Mursidabad district to the aforesaid village.

He is said to have gone to Kāmākhyā (Assam) where he achieved *Siddhi* by preaching Vīrācāra.

As a disciple of Brahmānanda in Mursidabad, he was invited by the then king of Kashmir to mediate in disputes between the Śaivas and Śāktas in that region. He went there, and succeeded in bringing about rapprochement between the two sects.

In his later life, he is said to have gone to the Himalayas, and settled there.

The following are the works of Pūrṇānanda:

(i) *Śyāmārahasya*[33] — in sixteen chapters it describes the practices for the Kālī-worshipper. It is the most celebrated of his works. The important topics, dealt with by him, are as follows: *mantroddhāra*, morning duties, bath, daily prayer, *tarpaṇa*, *nyāsa*, etc., *pūjāvidhi*, *stava* and *kavaca*, *puraścaraṇa*, various *dhyānas* and *mantras* relating to Kālī, Śmaśāna-kālī, etc., *Kulācāra*, *Kuṇḍagolodbhava svayambhu-*

kusuma-grahaṇādividhi, dūtiyāga, Śivābali, mantra-siddhi, Kāmyaprayoga, mahiṣa-mardinī-pūjā, vīra-sādhana, Kālīstava and *Kavaca.*

(ii) *Śāktakrama* (1571) — in seven chapters (*ullāsa*), it deals with Śākta practices, etc. Composed in Śaka 1493 (=1571 A.D.)

(iii) *Śrītattva-cintāmaṇi* (1577)[34]

(iv) *Tattvānanda-taraṅgiṇi* — it deals with the well-known Tāntric topics, *bījoddhāra, mantroddhāra*, etc.

(v) *Ṣaṭkarmollāsa* — it deals mainly with the six magic rites of Tantra, *āsana* (postures) and *kuṇḍa* (receptacle of sacrifical fire).

He is said to have written the following works also: *Yogacintāmaṇi, Yogavilāsa, Kālikakārakūṭa, Bhūtaśuddhi, Sarasvatītantra.*

In the Bengali encyclopaedia, *Viśvakoṣa*, the following additional titles are attributed to Pūrṇānanda:

Kakārādi-kālī-sahasra-nāma, Kālikārahasya, Gadyavallarī, Ṣaṭcakrabheda or *Ṣaṭcakrakrama, Subhagodara-darpaṇa.*[35]

He is stated also to have commented upon the *Ṣaṭcakra-dīpikā* of Brahmānanda. He is further credited with the authorship of the *Kālikādi-sahasra-nāma-stutiratna-ṭīkā* and *Vāmakeśvara-tantre Mahātripurasundarī-mantra-nāma-sahasra.*

The *Śrītattva-cintāmaṇi*[36] of Pūrṇānanda is an extensive metrical work on Tantra. It consists of 26 chapters called *Prakāśas*. The sixth chapter, called *Ṣaṭcakra-nirūpaṇa*, was so well known that it used to be regarded as a separate work; many manuscripts of this chapter are found at different places.

The author states the name of his *guru* as Paramahaṃsa Parivrājaka Brahmānanda. The date of composition is given as 1499 Śaka (=1577 A.D.). The topics, dealt with in it, are as follows:

Brahma-svarūpa, Tattva-jñāna-pratibandha-karaṇa, Śabda-brahma-svarūpa, Tattva-jñāna-svarūpa, Dīkṣā, Mantra-śabdārtha, Mantrāṇāṃ daśa-saṃskārāḥ, Vāstuyāga, Maṇḍapa-nirmāṇa, Ṣaṭcakra-nirūpaṇa, Kuṇḍa, Homa, Mantrabheda, Śakti, Ṣoḍaśīvidyā, Prātaḥkṛtya, Snāna-krama, Antaryāga, creation, Śrīcakra-svarūpa, Mudrā-svarūpa, Yantra-nirmāṇa, Saparyākrama, Tripurasundarī-stotra, Puraścaraṇa, Prāyaścitta, Jñāna-dūtiyāga, Tripurasundarī-vidyājīvana-prāptyupāya, Devatā-stava-pāṭha, Śrimahātripurasundarī-stotra, Mahāyantra-saṃskāra.

Some of the interesting matters are briefly stated below.

The author holds that the *summum bonum* is not possible without the body: so the body must be preserved before embarking on action (i. 8). The causes of loss of longevity are as follows:

> acceptance of gifts from those who are averse to the duties of their caste and stage of life, lust for others' wives, greed for others' money, non-study of Vedas and other Śāstras, deception of *Guru*, indulgence of the senses (i. 26-27).

Association of the good people and discrimination are like two eyes without which a man is blind (i. 30). The root of sorrow is attachment to the world; detachment is conducive to happiness (i. 32), as it leads to *divya-jñāna* (divine knowledge) and to the destruction of sin. Or, it is so called as, through it, the preceptor imparts the knowledge of God and *mantras*. Or, it is so called as it generates a divine feeling in this world full of illusion, and as it wears out action and leads to the acquisition of the fruits of the four ends of life (ii. 1-3).

Dīkṣā is threefold:

(i) Śāmbhavī (ii. 16-17). In it there is no motive on the part of either the preceptor or the disciple: it leads to the manifestation of Śivahood in the disciple in whom the requisite Śakti has appeared.

Or

> In it the disciple is roused to a peculiar awareness merely at the sight of the *guru* or at his touch or speech alone.

(ii) Śākteyī (ii. 14-15) In it, the disciple is initiated simply by the power seen in him; in it the usual formalities are absent. Others hold that it is that kind of *dīkṣā* in which there is knowledge.

(iii) Māntrī (ii. 10-13) In it, a man perceives the desired deity according to the way of *mantra*. Then the preceptor teaches the disciple. Or, it is given by the *guru* according to Śāstra, by the way of yoga, by means of *mantra, pūjā* and *dhyāna*. In it are used *kuṇḍa, maṇḍala*, etc. It is called *kriyāvatī* (consisting of rites). According to others, it is so called because of the teaching of *mantra*. This *dīkṣā* is stated to be suitable for all castes and to Śāktas as well as Vaiṣṇavas.

Salvation cannot be obtained by those who look upon their homes and forests as equal, give up shame and remain naked; because even asses, etc., act like this. By merely remaining unaffected by cold, heat, wind and looking upon eatables and uneatables as equal, salvation is not possible; because, even boars act in this way. It will not do if one merely lives on the banks of holy rivers from birth till death, because even frogs and fish live in such places. For the highest goal, what is really necessary is direct knowledge of reality (*sākṣāt tattva-jñāna*).[37]

The author states the views according to which *mukti* consists in the avoidance of infinite misery (*ananta-duhkha-viraha*)[38] or the destruction of thirst or hankering (*tṛṣṇā-nāśa*).[39] In his own opinion, *mokṣa* consists in the merger of the individual soul into the Supreme Soul (*paramātman*) which is of the form of a mass of bliss and is imperishable.[40]

Jñāna, which alone is the cause of salvation, is twofold—arising out of discrimination (*viveka*) and arising out of scriptures (*āgama*).[41] While *Śabda-brahman* is knowable by the latter, *Paraṃ Brahman* can be realised by the former.

Dīkṣā (initiation) has been stated to be conducive to the attainment of the four ends of life. The derivative meaning of *dīkṣā* is as follows: it is so called as it gives divine knowledge (*divya jñāna*) and destroys sin (*pāpa-saṃkṣaya*). *Di* of *divya* and *kṣa* of *kṣaya* appear to be supposed as constituting the word.

Considerable space has been devoted to the merits and demerits of *guru* and *śiṣya*, the manner of service to the former by the latter, the evil effects resulting from the disrespect and deception of *guru*.

Ablution is stated to be of two kinds—*bāhya* (external) and *ābhyantara* (internal). The latter consists in mental bath with the *mūla-mantra* preceded by *prāṇāyāma*. Such a bath is said to yield the result of visiting a crore of holy places.

Chapter sixteen is devoted to *antaryāga* (internal sacrifice). Fifteen *bhāva-puṣpas* (flowers in the forms of *bhāvas* or feelings) are enumerated for internal worship which is praised as the best. These are:

> absence of illusion, pridelessness, passionlessness, absence of conceit, absence of delusion, want of arrogance, absence of jealousy, absence of agitation, want of malice, greedlessness, restraint of the senses, kindness, forgiveness, knowledge and non-violence which is the best flower.

This chapter contains also the order of creation. Supreme Brahman —subtle, eternal and not perceptible to senses—was originally all alone. The watery portion having receded, desire of creation arose. After destruction was created a big bubble so that it might contain the worlds. That egg-like thing was to become twofold.

Ātman has been stated to be fourfold—*ātman*, *antarātman*, *paramātman* and *jñānātman*. According to Pūrṇānanda, the distinction between *jīvātman* (individual soul) and *paramātman* (Supreme Soul) is only apparent. An analogy is used to show the oneness of the soul. The sky is actually one; but it looks differently in different pitchers in which diversity is caused by the difference in the potter's wheels with which these are made. So, the one soul appears as different in different individuals.

Antarātman is so called as the soul pervades the mobile and immobile objects inwardly. From *paramātman* proceeds creation in the following order: the five gross elements called sky, wind, fire, water, earth.

That, by which all is always known to be equal, is called *Jñānātman*; it is the witness of all beings (xvi. 115-117).

The derivative meaning of the term 'yantra' is as follows: it is formed by the combination of the roots *yam* and *trai*; it restrains all sins (*yamayatyakhilaṃ pāpam*), and protects the *sādhaka* from great fear through worship and meditation (xvii. 2). *Yantra* is the body of the goddess, *mantra* being her knowledge (*jñāna*). Hers is not ordinary knowledge; it is *akhaṇḍita* or eternal.

The goddess has a threefold body, viz. *bhautika* (constituted by elements), *manomaya* (made of mind) and *jñānamaya* (consisting in knowledge). *Mudrā* is the first kind of body, *yantra* the second and *mantra* the third. The *jñānamaya* body is said to be superior to others, because it is eternal and imperishable.

Mudrā is so called because it delights the *ātman* and melts it which is tranquil and full of bliss.[42]

The author gives details about the construction and worship of *Śrīcakra* which should be worshipped for the acquisition of prosperity, beautiful appearance, fame, sons, good health, etc. It is called *Cakrarāja* (king of *cakras*). The work takes its name from this *Cakra* which is thus looked upon as very important by the author. It should be noted that this *Cakra* is not included among the usual *Cakras* of Tantra.

The other additional *Cakras*, described by him, are nine divided into three classes:

(i) Sṛṣṭi-cakra (representing creation) *Trailokya-mohana, Sarvasva-paripūraka, Sarva-saṃkṣobhaṇa.*

(ii) Sthiti-cakra (representing preservation) *Sarva-saubhāgya-dāyaka, Sarvārtha-sādhaka, Sarva-rakṣākara.*

(iii) Saṃhāra (destruction) *Sarva-roga-hara, Sarva-siddhi-prada, Sarvānandamaya.*

The presiding deities of these *Cakras* are respectively Tripura, Tripureśvarī, Sundarī, Tripura-vāsinī, Tripurāśrī, Tripuramālinī, Tripurasiddhā, Tripurāmbikā, Mahātripurabhairavī.

Japa is threefold according to our author, viz:

(i) *Nigada* — with the movements of the tongue and lips.

(ii) *Upāṃśu* — with the movement of the tongue alone.

(iii) *Mānasa* — mentally thinking of the letters of a *mantra*.

These three kinds are called respectively *adhama* (worst), *madhyama* (medium) and *uttama* (best).

As regards the offer of wine to the goddess, the views of our author are as follows. He says that the pleasing (*tarpaṇa*) of the goddess is possible with three kinds of wine, viz. that distilled from honey, that fermented from rice and that made from molasses. A Brāhmaṇa should offer cow's milk, a Kṣatriya cow's milk and wine, a Vaiśya honey and a Śūdra flower-juice, etc. A Brāhmaṇa is clearly forbidden to offer wine to the great goddess (xviii, 574). A Brāhmaṇa, following *Vāmācāra*, is forbidden even to take meat and wine (xviii. 574). The author further provides that, wherever wine is ordained, a Brāhmaṇa should offer, as substitutes, cocoanut water in a vessel made of bell-metal and honey in a copper vessel. According to the *Jñānārṇava*, the things to be offered by the four castes in order are milk, ghee, honey and *maireya*.[43] (xviii. 578).

The author gives an elaborate procedure of *Puraścaraṇa*.[44] It is so important that, without it, a *mantra* is as futile as a body devoid of life.

Chapter xxi opens with the expiation of sin arising from such offences as murder of a Brāhmaṇa. The means of atonement is the worship of the *Cakra*,[45] of all colours (?)[46] and beautified with camphor-dust, in accordance with *Kulācāra*. By so doing for three months one is redeemed from grave sins even incurred in other births. Then the author dwells on the result obtained by the worship with different kinds of flowers (*puṣpa*).[47] Sins are stated to be washed off by worship with *Javā* flowers, white lotuses, flowers called *bandhūka, mallikā, campaka*, etc. Also efficacious is worship with *dūrvā* grass, leaves of *aśvattha, bel*, etc. Neither Śākta worship nor Śaiva worship is possible without *bel* leaves. The following flowers are called *Śākta* or especially suitable for the worship of Śakti:

Kinds of lotus called *ambhoja, utpala, bandujīva, vijaya, punnāga, nāga, jāti, kunda, kuraṇṭha, campaka, javā, yūthī, ramā, pāṭala, aśoka, hayāri, kubja, madana, mandāra, droṇa, aparājitā*.

Great merit is stated to accrue from the use of pearls and various gems and jewels, e.g. *prabāla, marakata, padmarāga, hīraka, nīlakānta, gomeda, vaidūrya*, etc.

Stale flowers are generally prohibited; but this does not apply to *padma* and *campaka.* Buds of all flowers, excepting the above two, are prohibited.

Certain flowers are condemned in certain seasons. For example, *śephālikā* and *kahlāra* are not to be used except in autumn. Some flowers are to be used with their stems, while others without them. For example, *bakula* and *aśoka* should be without stems; *nāgakesara* and *javā* should have stems.

Some flowers are specially recommended on certain days of the week. For instance, red lotus, water lily, *tagara, kahlāra* (white lotus) and lotuses in general are especially recommended respectively on the days commencing with Sunday.

The articles, to be offered in worship, on seven days beginning with Sunday are as follows in order—*pāyasa*, milk, banana, butter, sugar and ghee.[48]

Different results are stated to accrue from worship of the goddess at different places. viz. hill-top, forest, seashore, *akṣadrumapīṭha*, cremation ground and garden of areca-nuts. Different effects are produced by worship of the goddess at midnight at different places. viz. cremation ground, Caṇḍikā-temple, lonely forest.

Then the author lays down the ways and means of acquiring the following powers: *vetāla-siddhi, tirodhāna-siddhi, māyā-siddhi, kāmarūpa-siddhi* and *trikālajñatva-siddhi.* For example, by worshipping the *Cakra*, imagined among the spokes of the six receptacles, with white sandal paste, musk, etc; one can know the past, present and future. By fixing prayers on the third eye of the goddess one can acquire the art of remaining invisible.

The author then deals with the worship of Cupid in spring. The chapter is concluded by rules for the worship of the goddess in the *pūrṇimā tithis* of twelve months starting with Śrāvaṇa.

Chapter xxii is devoted to the sacrifice called *Jñānadūti*. The goddess has four aspects, viz. Hastinī, Śaṃkhinī, Citriṇī and Padminī. Hastinī is identified with Vaikharī, Śaṃkhinī with Madhyamā, Citriṇī with Paśyantī and Padmini with Parā.[49]

In order to ensure learning in a man in future, within three days of his birth, a particular *mantra* should be written on his tongue with honey and white *dūrvā* grasses or a golden pencil.

Chapter xxiii opens with the means of making *Tripurasundarī-vidyā* effective. Incidentally are related some magical practices, both black and white.[50] The following are included in white magic: power of being murder-proof, dear to the king, being like Cupid, destroying the effect of poison at sight, attracting goddess of prosperity, flying, becoming free from decrepitude and death, destroying all sins and of acquiring various *siddhis*, viz. *Khaḍga. Vetāla, Guṭikāñjana, Pudukāñjana, Manaḥsiddhi, Mahāvīraṇa*, etc.

In black magic are included *vaśīkaraṇa, mahā-kṣobhakaraṇa, māraṇa, vidveṣaṇa, uccāṭana, stambhana, mahāhāni-karaṇa, śatru-nāśa.*

Chapter xxiv begins with the rules regarding the recitation of hymns to gods and goddesses. It is interesting to note that, while mental worship has been repeatedly stated as better than external worship, in the case of hymns audible recitation has been stated to be better than mental recitation.[51]

The topic of *bali-dāna* has been dealt with in considerable detail. The following animals are commended: Kinds of deer called *Camara, Kṛṣṇasāra*, fish, sheep, boar, buffalo, monkey and rhinoceros. Goats seem to be the best of all. Six kinds of goats are mentioned in this connexion, viz. white, black, red, tawny, variegated and pale white (*pāṇḍara*). The first two are best, the last two medium and the tawny and brindled ones worst.

A white goat with a black tail, a black goat with a white tail are to be avoided. Also to be avoided are the deformed animals. Female animals are excluded for the purpose of *bali.*

For *bali* birds of all colours and of good look are commended.

Satisfaction of divine beings from such offerings is stated to last for varying periods. The offerings, mentioned in this connexion, include, besides those mentioned above, human beings, tortoise, *godhikā* (a kind of lizard). *Vānara* of the previous list is excluded. The period of satisfaction, derived from human offerings, is stated to be the longest.

The 25th chapter contains the *Sahasranāma-stotra* of Mahātripura-sundarī.

The concluding chapter lays down rules about *mahāyantra-saṃskāra*,[52] *mudrā-māhātmya*, establishment of deities, consecration of shrines, praise of *cakra*, condemnation of deceitful economy[53] (*vitta-śāṭhya*), warning against the deception of preceptors and gods, etc.

Pūrṇānanda's work is important in more ways than one. Its historical importance is that he names his *guru*, and states the date of composition. As a Tāntric compilation, its merit lies in the fact that it is not a mere compilation. A considerable portion of it is the author's own composition. The work, unlike several other Tantras of Bengal, is not confined to mere Kālī-worship or rites and rituals; it contains much that is philosophical or metaphysical. The style is lucid and the presentation methodical. The author's poetic ability flashes here and there. The following verses may be quoted to show his metrical skill and command over language:

daśaśatadala-padma-prollasat pūrṇacandre
himaruci-rucirāṅgo haṃsapīṭhāntarasthaḥ/
abhaya-vara-karābjo yogapūrṇo dvinetraḥ
kula-kamala-vilāsī pātu māṃ devadevaḥ//

(Opening verse.)

hṛdaya-kamalamadhye prollasat-karṇikāntaḥ
pramudita-śiva-śayyā — saṃsthitā kāpi mūrtiḥ/
suravara-hara-mauli-smera-muktā-pradhāna-
pravilasita-padābjā pātu māṃ mohakūpāt// (i. 6)

na pītaṃ nāpītaṃ nahi parimitaṃ nāparimitaṃ
na raktaṃ nāraktaṃ nahi dhavalitaṃ nādhavalitam/
nirākāraṃ nityaṃ triguṇa-virahitaṃ divyamajaḍaṃ
tamātmānaṃ vande parama-sukha-santāna-nilayam// (1.7).

The *Śyāmārahasya* comprises nineteen chapters. The highlights of its contents are: *Kulaguru*, characteristics of *Kuṇḍalinī*, *Antaryāga*, *Viṣayapuṣpa*, *Gurukrama*, *stavas*, *stotras* and *kavacas*, *Kulācāra*, *Samayācāra*, *mantraśuddhi* without *Puraścaraṇa*, *Cīnakrama*, *Śavasādhana*, stages of *Śakti-sādhanā*, special *japa*, *Siddhi*, *Ṣaṭkarma*, *prāyaścitta* for incest including sexual intercourse with one's mother.

In ii. 22, worship with *viṣayapuṣpa* has been praised. Verses ii. 24-26 state the flowers as follows. *Amāyā*, *Anahaṃkāra*, *Aśabda*, *Apada*, *Amoha*, *Adambha*, the threefold causes of these, viz. the qualities of *Sattva*, *Rajas and Tamas*, *Amātsarya*, *Alobha*, *Ahiṃsā*, *Indriyanigraha*, *Dayā*, *Kṣamā*, *Jñāna*.

Under *gurukrama*, the *gurus* of the *Mānavaugha* category may have been historical personages. The author calls them *Kalīkālagurus*. It may be noted that, though some other Tantras mention both male and female *gurus*, this work mentions male ones' only.

KUṆḌALINĪ

DAKṢIṆA-KĀLIKĀ YANTRA

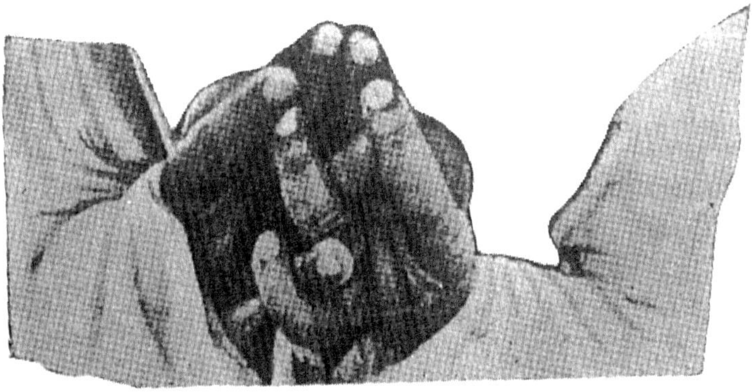

YONĪ-MUDRĀ

SARVATOBHADRA MAṆḌALA

The work refers to over sixty Tantras besides referring to others as 'tantrāntare', 'anyatra'.

It mentions the following authorities: Padmapādācārya (under iii. 78) and Rāghavabhaṭṭa (under iii. 165).

Śaṃkara

Another Tantra writer of Bengal is Śaṃkara with the qualifying epithet Gauḍīya. His real name was probably Śaṃkara Āgamācārya. He appears to have composed several Tāntric works. From the date of a manuscript[54] of his work, *Tārārahasyavṛtti*[55] (or, *vṛttikā*) (Lakṣmaṇa Saṃvat 511=1630 A.D.), he appears to have flourished in the period between the latter half of the sixteenth century and the middle of the seventeenth. In the colophon, he is described as son of Kamalākara and grandson of Lambodara.

Written in 15 chapters, the *Tārārahasyavṛtti* deals with such Tāntric matters as *dīkṣā, puraścaraṇa* in a general way, and specially with practices relating to the worship of Tārā. It is probably identical with the *Tārārahasyavṛttikā* mentioned in Nṛsiṃha Ṭhakkura's *Tārābhakti-sudhākara*, p. 141.

Besides the aforesaid *Tārārahasyavṛtti*, the following works are associated with the name of Śaṃkara:

Śivārcana-mahāratna, Śaivaratna, Kulamūlā-vatāra, Kramastava.

Several other Tantra works are attributed to Śaṃkara without the qualifying epithet Gauḍīya; his identity with Gauḍīya Śaṃkara is not free from doubt.

Raghunātha Tarkavāgīśa Bhaṭṭācārya

Raghunātha Tarkavāgīśa Bhaṭṭacārya gives, at the end of his work, an autobiographical account. From this we learn that he was a scion of the renowned family of the Bengali Śākta devotee, Sarvānanda[56] (attainment of *Siddhi* in 1425, 1426 or 1437 A.D.). The genealogy is this Sarvānanda → Balabhadra, → Kāśīnātha and (younger brother) Avanībhūṣaṇa → Śivarāma → Raghunātha. The editor gives the name of Raghunātha's native village as Napāḍā which, he states, is the name of one of the villages of this name in Susang Parganā of the district of Mymensing in Bangladesh. Raghunātha refers (1. 34) to the *Tantrasāra*,[57] obviously of Kṛṣṇānanda, and, at times, refers to the views of this eminent, Tantra writer of Bengal. So, the former must be later than the latter. The author gives the date of composition of his work as *graha-viyat ṣaṭ-candra* which comes to 1609 Śaka=1687 A.D.

The *Āgama-tattva-vilāsa* (flash of the principles of *Āgama*), a huge work in five lengthy chapters, is admittedly a digest setting forth the essence of a large number of works, Vedic, Purāṇic, Tāntric, astronomical and Smṛti-śāstra. The compiler himself states that he has drawn upon 160 *vidhi-śākṣī* (authoritative in rules) works which are Tantras, besides works on various other branches of knowledge.

The highlights of the chapters are as follows:

(i) Contents of the chapters, *varṇa, bīja*, nature of attributeless Puruṣa and Śakti, order of creation from Sadāśiva to human beings, nature of *Kuṇḍalini, Dīkṣā, Guru, Śiṣya, Mantra, Nāḍī, Cakra, Mahāvidyā, Maṇḍala, Mālā, Bali, Aśauca, Pūjā.*

(ii) Daily duties, *Nyāsa, Prāṇāyāma, Mānasa-pūjā*, materials for *Pūjā, Āsana*, flowers permissible and prohibited for *Pūjā*, 32 kinds of offences, rules about *Vādyayantra*, kinds of *Pūjā, Ṣaṭkarma, Yoga, Śānti, Japa, Mudrā, Puraścaraṇa*, rules to be observed on the occasion of an eclipse, *Śavasādhana*, various other *Siddhis, Kulācāra, Kula-vṛkṣa, Pīṭhasthāna, Bhāvas, Antaryāga, Kumārī-pūjā, Dūtiyāga, Mālya* and Brāhmaṇa, *Pañcamakāra, Yantra, Homa, Abhiṣeka.*

(iii) Sections on Gaṇeśa, Sūrya, Viṣṇu, Rāma, Kṛṣṇa, Lakṣmī, Sarasvatī. Under each section, the *dhyāna, mantra* and *Pūjā-paddhati* of the deity concerned have been laid down.

(iv) Sections on Bhuvanesvarī, Nakṣatra-vidyā, Pracaṇḍa-caṇḍikā, Tripura-bhairavī, Vagalāmukhī, Mātaṅgī, Dhūmāvatī.

The nature of treatment is like that of the previous chapter. The chapter on *Nakṣatra-vidyā* deals with *Tārā-vidyā*, the story of Sarasvatī's assuming the Nīlā form, the existence of both Nīlā and Śuklā Sarasvatī, identity of Viṣṇu and Śiva.

The fifth and the last chapter contains mainly *Stavas* (hymns) and *Kavacas* (protective verses, i.e. such verses as are supposed to protect the reciter) invoking a number of deities, male and female. In this chapter, we also find the following topics: *Yoga, Nāḍi, Ṣaṭcakra, Karmayoga*, eulogy of *Āgama*, genealogy of the author, date of composition.

The work is at best a painstaking and laborious compilation, at worst a digest on hackneyed Tāntric topics produced in the conventional manner. The only redeeming feature is that the compiler occasionally discusses divergent views, and gives his own conclusion. The hymns to various deities are in pedestrian verses which are lacking in the melody and variety of metres the commonest of which is the trite *Śloka*. One misses in them the sublime dignity, the sonorous language and the pleasant swing and music of the hymns of Vālmīki and Śaṃkarācārya. There is no philosophy in it. The *Āgama-tattva-vilāsa* admirably fulfils the object of the author who frankly states, at the outset, that he has compiled the essence extracted from various treatises. Though lacking in literary value, it has some importance in the history of Tantra literature as it mentions as many as 160 Tāntric works. Besides preserving the titles of so many works at one place, it helps us, to some extent, in determining the relative chronology of the works mentioned. The *Āgama-tattva-vilāsa*, being dated, furnishes the *terminus ad quem* of the dates of the works mentioned. It must be admitted that those, who are particular about the punctilious perform-ance of Tāntric rites with meticulous attention to details, will find this work helpful.

The *Rādhā-tantra*,[58] of unknown authorship and date, may have been of Bengal provenance. Most of its manuscripts are in Bengali script and are available in Bengal. It is mentioned in the *Śyāmāsaparyā-vidhi* of the Bengal author *Kāśinātha Tarkālaṃkāra*. The *Śaktiratnākara* of Rājakiśora cites the authority of the *Rādhā-tantra*. The date of the *Śaktiratnākara*, however, is not known.

In the *Rādhā-tantra*, Kṛṣṇa has been represented as a worshipper of Śakti. In fact, the life of Kṛṣṇa symbolises the worship of Śakti. The thesis of the work is that Kṛṣṇa's *Siddhi* consists in his union with Rādhā.

The nineteenth century saw a spurt in Tāntric activities of Bengal. The atmosphere of this province was surcharged with Tāntric ideas which found free and wide expression in the Bengali poems, Bāul songs and Śākta devotional songs. The teachings of Rāmakṛṣṇa and the liberal preachings of his follower, Vivekānanda, the Tāntric writings of Niveditā and the rational interpretation of Hinduism by Rāmmohan may have been indirectly responsible for doing away with the conventional rigours of religious practices and for paving the way for simpler and easier ways of fulfilling the religious aspirations of the people. The impact of Western ideas, in the wake of British domination, served also to open a new intellectual horizon among the Bengalis.

Haragovinda Rāya

Towards the close of the first quarter of the nineteenth century,[59] a huge Tantra was compiled in Bengal. The compiler was Haragovinda Rāya,[60] Zamindar of Pargaṇā Palāś under Sylhet, now in Bangladesh.

The work, entitled *Pañcama-veda-sāra-nirṇaya*, is divided into six sections (*Kāṇḍa*) called respectively *Sṛṣṭi, Dīkṣā, Karma, Jñāna, Sādhana* and *Yoga*. Each section is divided into sub-sections (*paṭala*) the number of which is respectively 24, 64, 13, 25, 22, 27. The work is a digest.[61] It deals chiefly with the worship of *Dakṣiṇā Kālikā* and *Kula* rites. It contains Tāntric rites, but not Tāntric philosophy.

Amara Maitra

In the second quarter of the nineteenth century, Amara Maitra, a Vārendra Brāhmaṇa, son of Vāsudeva, composed or compiled three Tantras on Tāntric *Sādhana* and *Yoga*. These are as follows:[62]

(i) *Jñanadīpikā* (1753 Śaka=1831 A.D.). In 23 chapters called *Prakāśas*.

(ii) *Amarasaṃgraha* (1765 Śaka =1843 A.D.) Complete in 18 sections called *Pādas*. The topics, dealt with in it, are *jaganmithyātva, tattvabodha, viveka, layayoga, navacakra, piṇḍajñāna, yoga-rahasya, ṣaṭcakra-yoga, pañcāmara-yoga, haṭhayoga, mudrā, dhāraṇā, rājayoga, jñānayoga, brahma-mantra-sādhana, sannyāsayoga, kāśīyoga, kālajñāna, vipralakṣaṇa, sāṃkhayayoga.*

(iii) *Āmarīsaṃhitā* (Śaka 1768=1846 A.D.) In four chapters, called *Upadeśas*, each of which is subdivided into several sections. The topics, dealt with in it, are: *sāṃkhyayoga, mantrayoga, nāḍikā-lakṣmaṇa, āsana, pratyāhāra, prāṇāyāma, dhyāna, dhāraṇā* and other rules of *haṭhayoga*, procedure of *pūjā*.

Durgārāma

A *Karpūra-stotra-ṭīka*, by Durgārāma Siddhāntavāgīśa, was published in Calcutta in 1891 with the text and Bengali translation by Gurunātha Vidyānidhi. The text, with commentary by Kṛṣṇanātha Nyāyapañcānana, was published in Calcutta in 1899.

Mahānirvāṇa-tantra

The *Mahānirvāṇa-tantra*,[63] a popular work in Bengal, is believed by some scholars to have been written in this province. Unfortunately, it does not state the name of its author or compiler. Nor does it afford sufficient evidence about its provenance. None of the arguments, put forward to prove its origin in Bengal, is conclusive. It is to be distinguished from the *Nirvāṇa-tantra* in which Rādhā is glorified as the consort of Viṣṇu.

Some scholars think that the present work, with a leaning to Vedāntic elements, had an older version which, as the word 'nirvāṇa' in the title appears to indicate, was in use among the Buddhists. In their opinion, it perhaps underwent a revision with Vedāntic ideas interpolated and pure Tāntric ritualism modified so as to boost its appeal to the Brahmanical intelligentsia.

Its date cannot be determined with certainty. That it is not very old seems to be indicated by one fact. Many Tantras have been cited in the works on Bengal Smṛti. But, even Govindānanda and Raghunandana, the last great figures in this field, who flourished in the sixteenth century, do not mention the *Mahānirvāṇa*. It should also be observed that none of the early well-known Tantras of Bengal, which cite a lot of Tantras, mentions the *Mahānirvāṇa*.

Some suspect that it was fabricated partly or entirely by Hariharānandanātha, preceptor of the great social reformer, Rām Mohan Roy (1772(?)-1833 A.D.) in order to bolster up his reformist views. This suspicion gains ground from the fact that the first edition of the work was published by the Ādi Brāhma Samāj, founded by Rām Mohan. The scarcity of manusripts of the work, which is not usual in the case of other well-known Tantras, seems to lend countenance to the theory of fabrication.[64] In this connexion, it may be pointed out that this work states *Brahma-dīkṣā* as the best form of initiation. *Brahma-dīkṣā*, not occurring in the earlier Tantras of Bengal, seems to hint at the fact that it was designed to propagate the doctrine of the *Brāhma Samāj*. In support of the theory of its Bengali origin, it is pointed out that this Tantra mentions (vi. 7) three species of fish, viz. *Śāla, Pāṭhīna* and *Rohita*, as best. These particular kinds of fish are said to be found in Bengal. Farquhar, in his *Outline of Religious Literature*, thinks that it is not earlier than the eighteenth century.

Whatever its place of origin might have been, about its popularity in Bengal there is no doubt. So, it is worthwhile to give the highlights of its contents. A work of the Āgama class, it consists of fourteen chapters (*Ullāsas*) which are named respectively as follows:

jīvanistāropāya-praśna (question about the liberation of creatures),
brahmopāsanakrama (procedure of meditation on Brahman),

parabrahmopadeśa (instructions about Supreme Brahman),

paraprakṛti-sādhanopakrama (procedure of meditation on Supreme Prakṛti),

mantroddhāra-kalaśa-sthāpana-tattva-saṃskāra (rescue of *mantra*, placing of the pitcher and purification of *Tattvas*),

śrīcakra-sthapāna-homacakrānuṣṭhāna (placing of *śrīcakra* and the performance of *homacakra*),

stotra-kavaca-kulatattva-lakṣaṇa (description of hymns, protecting spells, *kula* principles),

varṇāśramācāra-dharma (customs and duties of castes and stages of life),

kuśaṇḍikā-daśavidha-saṃskāra-vidhi (rules regarding *kuśaṇḍikā* and ten sacraments),

vṛddhiśrāddhādi-mṛtakriyā-pūrṇābhiṣeka (matters relating to *vṛddhiśrāddha* and other obsequial rites, *Pūrṇābhiṣeka*),

svaparāniṣṭa-janaka-pāpa-prāyaścitta (expiation of sin causing harm to oneself and others),

vyavahāra (secular law),

vāstu-grahayāga-jalāśayādi-pratiṣṭhā-devagṛha-dānādi-sarva-deva-pratiṣṭha (matters relating to *vāstu, grahayāga,* consecration of tanks, etc., temples, gifts and consecration of all gods).

Śiva-liṅga-sthāpana-caturvidhā-vadhūta-vivaraṇa (establishment of *Śivaliṅgas*, description of four kinds of Avadhūtas).

It states Brahman as the highest divine principle, and uses Upaniṣadic expressions to describe Him. He is Śakti who is conceived as Mother. Prakṛti, Pārvatī, Umā, Durgā, Kālī, Lakṣmī, Rādhā are but different designations of the *Jaganmātā* (world-mother). In her reside Brahman, the Creator, Viṣṇu, the Preserver, Śiva (Mahākāla), the Destroyer, along with their respective Śaktis. As she devours the latter, she is Ādyā Kālikā who is also the Mother of Mahākāla. She is Mahāyoginī, and is the Creator, Preserver and Destroyer of the world. Every woman is her incarnation.

The Supreme Being is one, without a second and beyond the three qualities. He is *Sat, Cit , Ananda*. The worshippers of Brahman do not require any other means to acquire salvation.

The work also advocates Śākta monotheism holding Durgā as the highest *Prakṛti* known also by the names of Mahāvidyās, and equated with Lakṣmī, Sarasvatī and Śakti. According to this Tantra, Śakti is, on the one hand, the Supreme Prakṛti of Brahman, and, on the other, is everything from the *Mahatattva* to the atom; in short, all that is dynamic and static. She is of infinite forms as Tārini, Durgā and the various Vidyās.

The *Tattvas* of Sāṃkhya philosophy, viz. *Prakṛti, Mahat, Ahaṃkāra*, etc., and some Vedic *mantras* have also been incorporated in it.

It declares (ii. 31) that, in the Kali Age, the Vedas, Purāṇas and other Śāstras have hardly any use.

The five essentials, called *Pañca-tattva* or *Pannñcamakāra*[65] are as follows:

(i) *Madya*—intoxicating drink which causes joy, helps one forget deep sorrow and serves as a medicine.

(ii) *Māṃsa*—meat which gives vigour, energy and increases intelligence.

(iii) *Matsya*—fish which is delicious and increases the generative power.

(iv) *Mudrā*—delicacies made of parched foodstuff; these, which grow on earth, constitute the root of the life of the three worlds.

(v) *Maithuna*—sexual union which affords intense pleasure, is the origin of all creatures and is the root of the world which is without beginning or end.

The above five are allowed only to the circle (*cakra*) of the initiated and are purified by sacred rites and formulae. In such a circle, each man has his Śakti to his left.[66] No caste-distinction is necessary. But, evil-minded and faithless persons cannot be admitted to the circle.

The Tantra warns against the abuse of the five essentials. Drinking beyond limit makes one unfit to be a devotee. Woman should only smell wine. In Kālī Age, a man should enjoy only his wife as Śakti. One, unable to control the senses, should use sweet substances like milk, honey, etc., as substitutes for *madya*. Instead of sexual intercourse, such a person should worship the lotus feet of the goddess.

A hero (*Vīra*), possessing secret powers and fit to be a *Sādhaka*, is allowed in a 'circle' to take to a Śakti who is not his wife. She can be made his 'wife' by a rite specially prescribed for the purpose. For a man, possessed of *divyabhāva* or the highest state, who has overcome all earthly temptations, symbolical acts are prescribed in place of the above essentials.

The *Kaula* mode has been declared (Ch. iv) as the best in Kali Age. Great importance is attached to the following:

(i) *Mantra*—incantation.

(ii) *Bīja*—mystic syllables like *hrīm, aim*, etc.

(iii) *Yantra*—mystic diagrams.

(iv) *Mudrā*—particular position of fingers and movement of hands.

(v)*Nyāsa*—placing the finger-tips and the palm of the right-hand on various parts of the body to the accompaniment of certain *mantras*.

By the above means, the Sādhaka is supposed to make the Devī favourably disposed towards himself. The last one is believed to impart Devī's life to the body of the devotee.

The ultimate goal of *Sādhana* is *Mokṣa* or liberation from the bondage of rebirths and consequent release from sufferings. This state can be reached by communion with the godhead in *Mahānirvāṇa* or 'great extinction'. The perfect *Sādhaka* is a *Kula*. He visualises Brahman in everything and everything in Brahman. He may or may not perform the requisite Tāntric rites. But, he will attain *jīvanmukti* (liberation while alive).

Mokṣa is attainable only through Tantra in the Kālī Age. Veda, Smṛti, Purāṇa, etc, were meant for ages long gone by.

In meditation (*dhyāna*) on the Devī, the devotee makes offerings in the following way. At first, he offers his heart-lotus as her throne, the nectar exuding from the petals of this lotus as water for washing her feet, his mind as a gift of honour, the restlessness of his senses and of his thought as dance, selflessness and passionlessness, etc., as flowers. Then he offers, in large quantities, the first four *Makāras* and the nectar of *strīpuṣpa* (woman flower) and the water used for washing the Śakti.

Behind all the various gifts and outward *pūjā*, there is the inner calm in which the devotee looks upon Mother as the inmost soul and light.[67]

Besides rites and rituals, the Tantra contains many ethical principles[68] which, however, in essentials, resemble the Brahmanical Smṛtis like those of Manu and Yājñavalkya. Besides duties of castes and stages of life, the duties of the king and his officers, etc. have also been laid down. The four Brāhmanical castes are recognised, but a fifth, called *Sāmānya*, has been postulated. It originated from the intermixture of the four castes. It alllows caste-restriction in marriage, dining and other social matters. But, no such restriction is applicable in the case of Tāntric devotees. Instead of the four usual stages of life (*āśrama*), recognised in Brāhmanical Śāstra, the Tantra says that only two, *gārhasthya* (householdership) and *bhaikṣuka* (asceticism), are suited to Kālī Age. Some of the important duties, taught in the Tantra, are as follows:

(1) A householder should never inflict physical punishment on his wife, but should cherish her like his mother.

(2) Even if he is about to die of hunger, he should never take food before feeding his parents, dependents and guests.

(3) A man should engage his son in household duties up to his twentieth year, but after that should look upon him as his equal.

(4) One should cherish one's daugher and educate her (*śikṣaṇīyā*) with great care till her marriage.

(5) Lust and anger must be abjured by all means.

Chapter IX enumerates and describes the ten sacraments (*saṃskāras*) from impregnation to marriage substantially in the manner of the Brāhmanical scriptures. Of the eight forms of marriage, recognised in the orthodox Brāhmanical works, Brāhma appears to be the only form recognised in the *Mahānirvāṇa*. It is regarded as so important that one is debarred from taking another wife in the Brāhma form without the consent of the first wife married according to this form.[69] The wife, married in this form, is *patnī* in the real sense of the term; she is the *gṛheśvarī* (mistress of the house).[70]

Another kind of marriage, recognised in it for Śāktas, is *Śaiva-vivāha*. It is of two kinds—one for a limited period according to the rules of the *Cakra*, stated above; the other till death. It is brought about by the fellow Śāktas, at the time of Cakra rituals, according to the mutual desire of a man and a woman. Having obtained their permission, one should repeat *mantra*, salute the Supreme Kālī for 108 times. Then the man asks the woman to choose him as her husband. Thereupon, the woman, having chosen him with sandalpaste, flower and *ātapa* rice, will place her hand on that of the man. Next, the leader of the *Cakra* will utter a *mantra* praying to Kālī for protecting the couple and sprinkle over them honey or *arghya* water for twelve times. Simultaneously, other members of the *Cakra* will utter *Svasti*.[71] Then the leader will instruct the husband and the woman, bowed before him, to act as promised.

The text clearly states that, in such a marriage, there is no restriction of age and caste.[72] The only restrictive injunction is that one should marry a woman who is without husband (*bhartṛhīnā*) and is not a *sapiṇḍā*.[73] In Brahmanical scriptures even a *sagotrā*, that is a woman having the same *gotra* as that of the man intending to mary her, is debarred. This restriction appears to have been waived in this Tantra. The eligibility of a *bhartṛhīnā* woman appears to indicate that even a widow was allowed for the purpose.

In the first kind of *Śaiva-vivāha*, the husband, desirous of issue, should meet his wife after her monthly impurity, and leave her with the expiry of the *Cakra-period*.[74] The child, born out of *Śaiva-vivāha* in the regular order,[75] should be regarded as having the caste of its mother. In the reverse order,[76] the child will be looked upon as having a *sāmānya jāti* or mixed caste. The son, born of such a union, is debarred from offering *piṇḍa* to the ancestors.

The *Mahānirvāṇa* forbids the *Śaiva-vivāha* of a girl of good family if such a marriage is arranged by her father out of anger or avarice. The father of an only daughter is not allowed to give his daughter in such a marriage.

Chapter X deals with the disposal of the dead, *Vṛddhiśrāddha*[77] and other kinds of *śrāddha*, *aśauca*, gifts, etc. The contents of this chapter, relating to these subjects, substantially agree with the prescriptions of Brāhmanical Smṛti works. Finally, it deals with the Tāntric rite called *Pūrṇābhiṣeka*.

Chapter XI deals with sin, expiatory rites and punishment inflicted by the king on those who transgress the rules of conduct.

The next chapter treats of civil and criminal law which, in essentials, agree with the codes of Manu and Yājñavalkya. A departure is found in the law relating to a woman married in accordance with the Śaiva rite, stated before. The son of such a woman is debarred from inheriting the property of her deceased husband if there is a child of his wife married according to the Brāhma rite or if his *pitṛ-sapiṇḍa* or *mātṛsapiṇḍa* exists. A woman, married according to Śaiva rite, and her sons are entitled only to maintenance from the successor of the deceased in proportion to the property left by the latter. Such a woman does not inherit the property of her father or mother. The property of a dead person, whose Śaivī wife and her children have predeceased him, devolves upon the following persons, each preceding being preferable to the succeeding one: *Samānodaka*, *Ācārya* (preceptor) and king. The successor will offer *piṇḍa*[78] till his death in memory of the person whose property he inherits. But, the son of a Śaiva wife is debarred from the right of offering *piṇḍa*.

Incidentally, the rules regarding adoption of a son have also been dealt with in this chapter.

Chapter XIII deals with Mahākālī, establishment of images of deities, tanks, etc., *vāstuyāga, grahayāga*, consecration of temples, mounts of gods, etc.

The topics, dealt with in the last chapter, are — mode and result of the establishment of immovable Śiva-liṅga, the rites consequent upon the break of worship of such a Śiva-liṅga, rules regarding the giving up of broken images of deities, means to salvation, knowledge and action, indispensability of knowledge for salvation, characteristics of four kinds of Avadhūtas. In this chapter, *Kaula-dharma* has been praised very highly. It has been spoken of as the best of all religions. Great merit is said to follow the adoration of a *Kula* saint.

The usual Tāntric topics of *Dīkṣā, Nyāsa, Puraścaraṇa, Mantra,* etc. have been death with.

Consideration for women is a noteworthy feature of this work. It ordains (*Ullāsa* viii) that a daughter also should be brought up and educated carefully.

There are flashes of literary skill as in the following description of the Ādyā image of the Supreme Śakti:

meghāṅgīṃ śaśiśekharāṃ trinayanāṃ raktāmbaraṃ vibhratīm pāṇibhyām-abhayaṃ varaṃ ca vikasad raktāravindasthitām/

nṛtyantaṃ purato nipīya madhuraṃ mādhvīka-madyaṃ mahākālaṃ vīkṣya vikāsitānanavarām ādyāṃ bhaja kālikām//

The Goddess has a complexion like the colour of cloud. She is moon-crested, three-eyed, wearing a red cloth. She is granting freedom from fear and a boon with her two hands. She is on a red lotus in bloom. She is smiling at the sight of Mahākāla (Śiva) who, having drunk wine, is dancing in front of her.

Composed in the stately Śārdūlavikrīḍita metre, the verse conjures up a vision of the Goddess in a vivid form. The pictorial effect of the words and occasional alliterations are noteworthy.

Time was when a keen controversy raged among Sanskrit scholars and social leaders as to whether or not the rites and worship performed in accordance with the *Mahānirvāṇa-tantra*, would be valid. There were stalwarts both for and against the above work. For an idea of such controversial issues, the reader may look up the *Guru-tantra, Saṃśaya-nirāsa*, pp. 1-11, 30, 31.

The *Prāṇatoṣiṇī*[79] is a well-known huge Tāntric digest produced in the nineteenth century. It was compiled by Rāmatoṣaṇa Vidyālaṅkāra, great grandson of the famous Kṛṣṇānanda, author of the celebrated

Tantrasāra. It was written in 1743 Śaka (=1821 A.D.) with the patronage of Prāṇakṛṣṇa Viśvāsa.[80] The work has been so named with the initial portion of 'Prāṇakṛṣṇa' and the concluding portion of 'Rāmatoṣaṇa'. Son of Rāmahari, Prāṇakṛṣṇa was a patron of learning and landlord of Khardah, a suburb of Calcutta in the 24-Parganās district of West Bengal. He lived from 1764 to 1834-1836 A.D. The works *Bhasmakaumudī* and *Viṣṇukaumudī* are associated with his name. To him are attributed also the *Ratnāvalī* (*Cikitsā-saṃgraha*), *Vaiṣṇavāmṛta, Vijñakaumudī* (?). Besides these, works on Āyurveda and Smṛti, too, are attributed to him. In the Introductory portion of the *Prāṇatoṣiṇī*, he is stated to have got the *Prāṇakṛṣṇa-kriyāmbudhi* compiled by many scholars who consulted many works on Jyotiṣa. To his inspiration is attributed also the compilation, called *Prāṇakṛṣṇa-śabdāmbudhi*. It seems that the works were composed by Paṇḍits at his inspiration.

The work has been conceived as a creeper (*vratatī* or *latā*). The compiler says that it excels *Kalpadruma, Cintāmaṇi* and *Kāmadhenu*. The first yields whatever is desired by a person, the second gives whatever is thought of, and the last one bestows the intended object. But, this work always gives the fruit as soon as it is seen (*dṛṣṭaiva yacchati phalaṃ bhuvi sarvadeyam*).

It opens with the genealogy of Prāṇakṛṣṇa, the author's patron. Then the compiler mentions a number of Tantras by consulting which he prepared this digest.

The work is divided into seven sections callecd Kāṇḍas. These are named in order as follows: *sargādyakāṇḍasya ādimaḥ pariccheda, aṅkurapariccheda, śākhāpariccheda, praśākhā nāma viccheda, pallavarūpeṣupariccheda, stabaka-rūpartupariccheda, koraka-viccheda*. Each *Kāṇḍa* consists of several sub-sections.

It deals in detail with all the Tāntric topics. A few interesting matters are stated below. On the authority of the *Matsyasūkta*, it is laid down that a man, without a wife, has no future; all his actions become futile. A wifeless man should avoid the worship of deities and great sacrifices. As a car, with a single wheel, and a bird, with one wing, are useless, so an unmarried man is unworthy of all acts. On the same authority, a man is asked to resort to *Saṃnyāsa* as an alternative to *Gārhasthya*, but not the third stage or the life of a forest-dweller.

Elsewhere the first state is stated to be unsuitable in Kālī Age. For a Brāhmaṇa, the Brāhmaṇa wife is *dharmapatnī* (wife for religious purposes) and a wife of any other caste is *kāmapatnī* (wife of pleasure). This is contrary to the Brahmanical Smṛti which categorically prohibits the marriage of a girl of an unequal caste. It is not clear whether or not the wife of an unequal caste can be the *dharmapatī* in the case of Kṣatriyas and Vaiśyas.

From the trend of the discussion, which of the eight *Smārta* forms of marriage is approved is not clear. It is, however, obvious that the Brāhma form is regarded as the best.[81]

It is interesting to note that, though citing the authority of the *Mahānirvāṇa* at several places, the work does not appear to approve of Śaivavivāha, prescribed in the latter.

On the authority of the *Kulārṇava*, the derivative meanings of the words *guru, nātha* and *ācārya* are given as follows:

guhyāgamārtha-tattvā-nusandhānād bodhanādapi/
rudrādi-deva-rūpatvād gurur-ityabhidhīyate//

[*Guru* is so called as he seeks and imparts the knowledge of the meaning of the secret Āgamas and the principles laid down therein; and as he assumes the forms of divine beings Rudra, etc. It is interesting to note that 'gu' of *guhya* and '*ru*' of Rudra constitute the word '*guru*'].

sthagitajñāna-cihnatvāt śrīnāthaḥ kathitaḥ/

[*Nātha* is so called as he is the embodiment of esoteric knowledge].

svayamācarate śiṣyānā-cāre sthāpayatyapi/
ācinoti hi śāstrārthānā-cāryas-tena kathyate//
carācara-samāsannam-adhyāpayati yaḥ svayam/
yamādi-yogasiddhatvādā-cārya iti kathyate//

[*Ācārya* is so called as he himself practises good conduct, and makes disciples practise the same, gathers the meanings of Śāstras, himself teaches matters relating to the movable and immovable objects, and as he has attained success in the Yogic practices called *Yama*, etc.]

The seven *ācāras*, dealt with in the work, are —

(i) Related to *paśubhāva—vedācāra, vaiṣṇavācāra, śaivācāra, dakṣiṇācāra.*

(ii) Relating to *Divya* and *Vīra—vāma, siddhānta, kaula.* In the above order of *ācāras*, each succeeding is better than the preceding one. Thus *Kaula* is the *ācāra* par excellence.

The various forms of Kālī, mentioned in it, are Daksiṇakālikā, Guhyakālī, Śmaśanakālī.

On the authority of the *Kulārṇava*, the etymological meanings of *Matsya* and *Māṃsa* are given as follows:

Matsya — it puts an end to *Māyā* and impurities, etc., determines the path to salvation, removes eightfold misery, etc.

Māṃsa — it produces welfare, gives the pleasure of right knowledge; it is the favourite of all gods.

Of the different kinds of wine, mentioned in the work, two main classes are discernible, viz. *madya* and *surā*.

panasa (made from jackfruits),
drākṣā (made from grapes),
mādhūka (made from *madhūka*[82] tree or flower),
kharjūra (made from dates),
tāla (made from palm fruits),
aikṣava (made from sugarcanes),
madhūttha (fermented from honey),
sīdhu (distilleld from molasses, rum),
mādhvīka,[83]
marieya (?),
nārikelaja (distilled from cocoanuts).

These eleven kinds of *Madya* are said to be conducive to *bhukti* (enjoyment) and *mukti* (liberation).

The following three are called *surā*:

Gauḍī (distilled from molasses), *Mādhvī* (fermented from honey) and *Paiṣṭī* (fermented from rice). These three are said to be the best as these lead to all kinds of success.

In this connexion, it may be noted that all the three kinds of *surā* have been categorically condemned, particularly for Brāhmaṇas, in the Smṛti literature. The drinking of such wines taints a Brāhmaṇa with the gravest sin the expiation for which is nothing short of death.

The *pañca-tattvas* for Vaiṣṇavas are *guru-tattva, mantra-tattva, manas-tattva, deva-tattva, dhyāna-tattva.*

The work lays down procedures for attaining the ability to interpret the cries of various creatures, terrestrial and aerial. Of the former, we have chameleon, mouse, cat, jackal, frogs, lizard, cow, deer, sheep, goat, tiger, elephant, lion, boar, etc. In the latter class are crow, khañjana, peacock, crane, sparrow, parrot, pigeon, cock, partridge. Some aquatic birds and insects are also mentioned in this connexion.

Among the means of controlling others are mentioned *Vaśīkaraṇa, Adarśana*, etc.

Among the rites for causing harm to others, the most noteworthy are *stambhana, uccāṭana, māraṇa, śatrūtsādana, vidveṣaṇa*. Rites for counteracting the above are also described.

Certain spells and rites are prescribed for effecting the following:
victory in disputes, preventing theft, freedom from disease, removal of thirst, loss of sleep, appetite.

As a panacea is prescribed the following recipé:
ghee is to be stirred and in it the root of *nala* (lotus stalk) is to be crushed.

Then one should drink it with a *mantra*. For preventing the loss of semen one should smear the root of the navel with the pulverised root of the *Eraṇḍa* plant. Also to be applied is the bile of the *Rohita* fish. For this also there is an incantation.

The work devotes some space to the glory of the names of Viṣṇu, and enumerates His hundred and eight names in a hymn quoted from the *Nāradapañcarātra*.

The wrok describes *Durgotsava* in detail. *Śabarotsava* on the *Daśamī* day, prescribed in the Smṛti digests of Bengal dealing with *Durgāpūjā*, is conspicuous by its absence in this work.

An important topic in this work is the duties laid down for the twelve months from Āśvina to Bhādra.

A few other important matters, discussed in the *Prāṇatoṣiṇī*, will be dealt with under Aspects of Bengal Tantra which will follow.

Caitanyaism and Tantra

It is interesting to note that, in certain Tantras, Caitanya is mentioned. Though these works or portions thereof containing references to Caitanya, may not have been composed by Bengali authors, yet the influence of Caitanya on their authors is undoubted. In the *Īśāna-saṃhitā*, stated to be included in the *Kulārṇava-tantra*, attempts have been made to establish the divinity of Caitanya. In the *Gūḍhāvatāra*, stated to be a part of the *Viśvasāra-tantra* or *Vīśvasāroddhāra*, Caitanya has been described as an incarnation of Viṣṇu. In the *Ūrdhvāmnāya-saṃhitā*, Caitanya, instead of the Buddha, is mentioned among the incarnations of Viṣṇu. Some portions of the Tantras *Brahmayāmala* and *Kṛṣṇayāmala* are called *Caitanyakalpa*.

It is rather strange that, despite the age-old sectarian hostility between the Śāktas and Vaiṣṇavas, the above Tantras, should accord such an exalted position to Caitanya. The avowedly Vaiṣṇava Tantras may do so. But, in other Tantras, this phenomenon can be explained by assuming that these were composed or compiled in Bengal, and naturally the authors or compilers could not escape the compelling influence of Vaiṣṇavaism, as preached by Caitanya. Indeed, Caitanyaism flooded the religious life of Bengal and *gaurapāramayavāda* (doctrine which holds Caitanya to be Supreme Being) was an accepted creed. In this connexion, it is interesting to note that some devotional singers of Bengal, notably Rāmprasād, attempted to syncretise Viṣṇuism and Śāktism.[84] Vṛndāvana was another stronghold of Vaiṣṇavaism. The religious leaders of that region also held Caitanya in high esteem. The above Tantras, or at least some of them, might have been influenced by the post-Caitanya Vaiṣṇava leaders of that region.

Minor Works

A few minor works, composed by Bengali writers, have also been published. Most of these are manuals on procedural matters relating to various Tāntric rites, particularly Kālī worship. Among the authors of such works, Harakumāra Tagore (1798-1858) of the well-known Tagore family of Pathuriaghat, Calcutta, figures prominently. One of his works is entitled *Hara-tattva-dīdhiti* (1881). In it, he describes various matters relating to Hindu rites and customs, and copiously cites Tantras.

Another work of his is styled *Puraścaraṇa-bodhinī* (1895). The subtitle, *Puraścaraṇa-paddhati*, speaks of the contents of the work. It comprises eight chapters (*ullāsas*). *Puraścaraṇa* is a well-known Tāntric rite. The author describes, on the authority of 'Tantrādi-śāstra', various matters relating to this rite. In the beginning, the author states the names of some of his ancestors. He states his object in composing this work though there is an excellent section on this topic in the ocean-like treatise, called *Tantrasāra*, written by Kṛṣṇānanda. He says that he has cited additional authorities so that his novel work may give delight to the hearts of wise people.

From the concluding verse, we learn that the work was composed *śara-śruti-saritpati-kṣiti-mite śāke*, i.e. in Śaka 1745=1823 A.D.

The main topics, dealt with in the work, are: Definition of *puraścaraṇa, puraścaraṇa* whether obligatory or optional, effect of the rite, appropriate time and place, duties in connexion with it, *Saṃkalpa, Kūrma-cakra, Āsana, Japa, Varṇamālā-nirūpaṇa*, post-*japa* duties. *Tarpaṇa, Abhiṣeka, Brāhmaṇa-bhojana, Pañcavādya, Kumārī-pūjā*, procedure of *puraścaraṇa*, miscellaneous *puraścaraṇas*.

The same author composed a work, entitled *Śilā-cakrārtha-bodhinī*. In it Tāntric works, along with Purāṇas and other works, are cited. It comprises ten chapters (*ullāsa*). It deals with the origin, and various kinds of *Śālagrāma-śilās* or stones which are worshipped as symbols of Nārāyaṇa. The author states the place where such stones are available and discusses the good and bad features of them. Among the bad features, there are some which render them unfit for worship. It is interesting to find that the stones are variosuly named in accordance with particular features. Some of the names are Sudarśana, Lakṣmīnārāyaṇa, Pītāmbara, Nṛsiṃha, Vāmana, Dadhivāmana. Some of the stones have various names containing the word Rāma, e.g. Paraśurāma, Dāśarathi-rāma, Kauśalyānandana-rāma, Rāmacandra, Vīrarāma, Sītārāma, etc. Some stones have the various names of Kṛṣṇa, e.g. Bālakṛṣṇa, Gopāla, Vaṃśīgopāla, Kaṃsamardana, etc. Some names hint at various aspects of Viṣṇu, e.g. Vainateya, Garuḍadhvaja, Madhusūdana, etc. A kind of stone is named Vaikuṇṭha, the abode of Viṣṇu.

The stones have been classified in accordance with the number of *cakras* (circular marks) contained in them. These are divided into thirteen classes, the number of *cakras* ranging from one to twelve. A stone of the thirteenth class contains *bahucakras; bahu* obviously means more than twelve. One particular kind in this class is designated as *Bahurūpin* (having many forms). It is described as *bahucakram* (having many cakras), *bahudvāram* (having many openings), *bahurekham* (having many lines), *bahūdaram* (having many interior hollows).

It is interesting to note that certain stones are named after the various designations of Śiva, e.g. Sadyojāta, Īśāna, Sadāśiva, Tryambaka, Dhūrjaṭi, etc. The worship of such stones is stated to be pleasing to Śiva.

Some stones are named after Śakti, e.g. Śrīvidyā, Mahākālī, Gaurī. Their worship is said to please goddess Bhavānī. A few kinds of stones are named after Gaṇeśa, Ravi, Candra and Grahas.

A stone, which grows at Dvārakā, is said to be as holy as a crore of holy places. One is stated to be free from all sins, accumulated for one year, at the sight of such a stone but once.

On the authority of the *Garuḍa-purāṇa*, the provenance of *Śālagrāmas* is determined as follows:

The holy place, called Cakranadī, situated in the land intervening between the northern bank of the Gaṇḍakī and south of the Himālaya. The mountain, with golden summit, is to the north of this place. Its extent is twelve *yojanas*.

According to the *Meru-tantra*, it is as follows:

At Gaṇḍakī, the land covering ten yojanas to the south of the Himālaya, there is a holy place called *Cakra-tīrtha*.

The familiar topic of *puraścaraṇa* engages the attention of Mihirkiran Bhattacharya. In the *Puraścaraṇa-ratnākara*, he has compiled various texts, mainly Tāntric, in his discussion of the different matters relating to *puraścaraṇa*. The work is divided into two parts of which the principal contents are as follows:

Part I: Meaning of the term, characteristics of *puraścaraṇa*, necessity of it, determination of the number of *Japa, Homa, Tarpaṇa*, etc. in it, prohibition of *puraścaraṇa* for the uninitiated person, appropriate time, appropriate place, *Bhūmi-nirṇaya, Bhūmi-parigraha, Aṅkurāropaṇa, Kūrmacakra, Āsana, Diknirṇaya, Bhakṣyābhakṣya*, practices at the time of *puraścaraṇa*, commencement, *Saṃkalpa*, appropriate time for *Japa* and *Pūjā*, commencement of *Japa*, procedure of *Japa*, making of garlands, practices permitted and prohibited in connexion with *mālā-japa*, dedication of *Japa*, praise of *Japa*, post-*japa* duties, *tarpaṇa, Abhiṣeka*, feeding of Brāhmaṇas, necessity of *Puraścaraṇa*.

Part II: *Guru-puraścaraṇa, Mahā-puraścaraṇa, Pañcāṅga-puraścaraṇa, Brahma-puraścaraṇa*, miscellaneous *Puraścaraṇas, Grahaṇa-puraścaraṇa*, duties in the absence of *mantrasiddhi* after *puraścaraṇa*, procedure of *mālā-saṃskāra*, procedure of *Kumārī-pūjā, Bṛhathoma*, means of rapid success.

The *Rahasya-pūjā-paddhati*, compiled by Jñānendranātha or Jñānānanda Tīrthanātha, son of Jaganmohana Tarkālaṅkāra, deals with the procedure of *Rahasya-pūjā* which means worship with *pañca-makāras*. The main topics of the work are: *Viśeṣapūjā, Vijayā-śodhana, Vijayā-dhyāna, mantra* of *saṃvidā*,[85] *sudhā-ghaṭa-sthāpana, dravya-śodhana, dhyāna* and *pūjā* of Ānandabhairava and Ānandabhairavī, purification of *māṃsa, matsya, mudrā, Śakti, Kula* flowers, *śripātra-sthāpana, tarpaṇa*, purification of *tattvas*,[86] *bindu, bali, cakrānuṣṭhāna*.

Jaganmohana Tarkālaṅkara compiled a *Nityapūjā-paddhati* according to Tantra; it was enlarged by his son Jñānendranātha. The same author compiled the work, entitled *Sanātana-dharmā-nuṣṭhāna*, the first volume of which deals with the procedure of tenfold saṃskāra in accordance with Tantra and the second with the procedural matters relating to *śrāddha* in conformity with Tāntric practices.

The *Guru-tantra* appears, from the colophon to the archetype, to have been composed by one Rāmaśaṅkara who may have been a Bengali. The date of its composition is given as Śaka 1416 (=1494 A.D.). This short tract seeks to lay down the means whereby one can attain *mantra-siddhi.* As the title indicates, it emphasises the role of a *guru* who is regarded as superior to all Śāstras, *tapas, Śiva, japa*, etc.

The *Kālyarcana-candrikā*, compiled by Nīlakamala Lāhiḍi, gives an exhaustive account of the procedure of Kālī-worship. Incidentally it dwells upon places and time suitable for worship, the various kinds of *pūjā — nitya, naimittika, kāmya, sāttvika, rājasika, tāmasika, mānasī, antaryāgātmikā, bāhyā, siddha-pīṭhas, bhāvas, ācāras*, various images and symbols of Kālī, *puraścaraṇa, kumārīpūjā, Śivābali*, etc. It brings out the great importance of *guru*, and describes Kuṇḍalinī, Ṣaṭcakra-bheda, morning duties, etc. The work cites a number of Tantras. In the beginning of the work, the author traces his genealogy from Nārāyaṇa, stated to have been one of the five Brāhmaṇas brought from Kānyakubja by Ādiśūra, ruler of Bengal. The author's father's name is given as Kālīmohana. One of his ancestors is named as Vallabhācārya who is said to have been called Maṇḍana Miśra and to have married Līlāvatī, daughter of Udayanācarya. The original home of his ancestors is mentioned as village Kakaiḍ in the district of Rajshahi (now in Bangladesh). One of his ancestors is reported to have migrated to a place called Kacuyā in Rajshahi. Another ancestor of the author is stated to have migrated to Rangpur (in Bangladesh).

The author appears to have been appointed an assistant to Śivanātha, minister of the then ruler (*dharāpati*) who was perhaps a local Chief, and grandfather of the author. The name of the author's *guru* appears as Harinātha.

The date of composition of the work is given as Śaka 1784 (=1862 A.D.). The date of printing is stated as Śaka 1801 (=1879 A.D.).

Unpublished Tāntric Works

We have dealt with Bengal Tantra available in print. Those still unpublished far outnumber the published ones. We have set forth the names, along with references, of such unpublished Tāntric works as appear to have been composed or compiled by Bengalis. The list is not exhaustive. Tantra manuscripts in a very large number are available in different collections and libraries of West Bengal and Bangladesh. The principal institutions, where Tantra manuscripts are deposited, are Asiatic Society, Sanskrit College, Vaṅgīya Sāhitya Pariṣat, Saṃskṛita Sāhitya Pariṣat and Calcutta University—all in Calcutta. The Navadvīpa Sādhāraṇa Granthāgāra at Navadvīpa, Nadiya, in West Bengal, has a good collection of Tantras. Noteworthy manuscript libraries in Bangladesh are in Dacca University and Varendra Research Society, Rajshahi.

The unpublished Tāntric manuscripts, whose titles have been collected by us in an appendix to this work, show little or no originality. Many of them deal with the procedure of worshipping the deities of the Mahāvidyā group, particularly Kālī. Some are merely epitomes of other works. A few works deal with initiation, *puraścaraṇa, maṇḍalas* and their application in *Durgāpūjā, Yantras, Mudrās, Cakras, Ṣaṭkarma*, various Tāntric *mantras*. Quite a few manuscripts are commentaries on such well-known works as *Ānandalaharī, Karpūrādi-stava, Mahimanaḥ-stotra, Svarūpākhya-stotra, Sundarī-rahasya, Guru-pādukā-stotra, Gautamīya-tantra*, etc. Two manuscripts dwell on the origin of sound and the significance of letters starting from 'A'. At least one work, entitled *Vaśakārya-manjari*, deals with the rites designed to keep others under control. Vaiṣṇavite persuasion is manifest in the *Lalitā-rahasya* in which the author seeks to establish the predominance of Kṛṣṇa. An interesting fact about the unpublished manuscripts is that some non-Brahmins appear to have composed a few works. For instance, the *Tantracandrikā* (Calcutta Asiatic Soc. Ms. Cat., VIII, serial no. 6274) is associated with the name of Rāmagati Sena. Kṛṣṇānanda author of the *Āgama-candrikā*, was a Kāyastha of Pūrvasthalī in West Bengal. He is known to have[87] written eighteen works.[88] This work is referred to as his own in the concluding verse of the fifth canto of his *Kamalodaya* (VSP. Cat., p.xxvi).

From the incomplete manuscript that exists, it appears to have dealt with *dikṣā* and worship of Kālī, Tārā, Śrīvidyā, Bhuvaneśvarī, Bhairavī, Chinnamastā and Lakṣmī.

One Nandarāma Tarkavāgisa appears to be the author of a commentary on the *Ṣaṭcakranirūpaṇa* in which he refers to Harivallabha Ray as his patron. To him are attributed a number of small tracts on Tantra and philosophy. He probably flourished in the first half of the 18th century.[89]

From the biographical account, contained in the *Sundarīrahasya Vṛtti*,[90] we learn that the author, Ratnanābha Āgamācārya, a Vārendra Brahmin of Maitreya denomination, was son of Nārāyaṇa and grandson of Mukunda, and disciple of Gopīnātha, disciple of Hayagrīva.

A *Sundarīrahasya Vṛtti* is referred to in Yadunātha Cakravartin's *Mantraratnākara*.[91]

The author of the *Mantraratnākara* describes himself as a native of Gauḍa (Bengal) and son of Vidyābhūṣaṇa Bhattācārya . It consists of four *paṭalas* (chapters) and of ten *Taraṅgas* (sections) and deals with conventional Tāntric matters including *antaryāga, yoga, Śānti*, worship of Ṣoḍaśī, Śrī-vidyā, etc.

The manuscript[92] is dated Śaka 1774 (=1852 A.D.).

A work, entitled *Śyāmāsantoṣaṇa-stotra* appears to be by Kāśīnātha Tarkapañcānana (MS. No.3540, Serial no. 6661 of Calcutta Asiatic Soc. Cat., VIII) who was probably a Professor at Calcutta Sanskrit College.

The date of the work is given (Fol.104b) as *rasa-śara-muni-candra* (Śaka) which appears to be 1756 Śaka=1834 A.D.

It appears to be complete in four chapters, and deals with the greatness and worship of the goddess.

A *Tantradīpikā*[93] appears to be by Gopāla Pañcānana who speaks of himself as son of Harinātha and grandson of Āgamavāgīśa who appears to be Kṛṣṇānanda, author of the *Tantrasāra*. This Gopāla is probably identical with Gopāla Nyāyapancānana to whom are attributed several Smṛti digests the titles of which end in-*nirṇaya*.[94]

We have already described the contents of the two big digests which are still unpublished. These are the *Pañcama-veda-sāra-nirṇaya* and the *Āmarī-saṃhitā*.

NOTES

1. On sex-union as a means of *Sādhanā* in Buddhist Tantra, see *Prajñopāya*, V.25, *Jñānasiddhi*, I. 80-82, *Guhyasamāja*.
2. On the work and Matsyendra, see *Kaulajñāna-nirṇaya*, ed. P.C. Bagchi, Introduction.
3. cf. *yatra dṛṣṭir manastatra bhūtendriyam apudgalaḥ/*
   svaśaktir jīvabhūtāni dṛṣṭirlakṣyair layaṃ gatā//
   — (iii. 26, 3a)
4. xii. 6.

5. cf.*śivamadhye gatā śaktiḥ kriyāmadhyasthitaḥ śivaḥ/*
jñānamadhye kriyā līnā kriyā līyati icchayā//
icchāśaktir layaṃ yāti yatra tejaḥ paraḥ śivaḥ/
— (ii. 6, 7a)
(Śakti has got into Śiva, Śiva is in the midst of action, action is merged in knowledge, action and will coalesce. Will-force is lost where Supreme Śiva is aglow with lustre or is aflame with the fire of energy.)
6. *adhaḥsthā saṃsthitā bhuktiḥ ūrdhvaṃ muktirvarānane*, ii.. 9a.
7. xvii. 27a.
8. One is found in *Sādhanamālā*, ii, 466-68.
9. Two in Sanskrit are published in *Sādhanamālā*, i. 79 and *Sādhanasamuccaya*, i. 76.
10. For his life and works, see A. Chattopadhyaya, *Atīśa* and *Tibet*, Calcutta. For controversy about his date etc., Devesh Das in Bengali daily *Ānanda Bāzār Patrikā* of 13.9.81. Also see the Bengali weekly *Desh* of 27.2.82 (p. 9), 24. 4.82 (p. 3), 8.5.82, p. 3, 15.5.82, p. 3, 10.7.82, p.6, 17.7.82, p. 5.
11. According to some, he was a native of Bihar. But, in his works, called *Bodhimārga-pradīpa-pañjikā-nama* and *Ekavīra-sādhana-nāma*, both preserved in the Tibetan *Tanjur*, he is stated as a Bengali. Some think that he was born at Sāhar, (Village Sābhār in Bangladesh).
12. See *Bauddha gān o dohā* by H.P. Sastri, Preface, p. 28.
13. See list of unpublished Tantras (*Infra*).
14. For his biography, see *Sarvānanda-taraṅgiṇī* (in Sanskrit) attributed to Śivanātha, son of Sarvānanda; *Sarvānanda* (in Bengali) by A.C. Mukherji and *Ṭhākur Sarvānanda* (in Bengali) by N.K. Chakravarti; *Mātṛgāthā* (in Bengali) by Sitaramdas Omkarnath; *Devayāna* (Bengali monthly), Vol. vii, No. 4 (article by Dinesh Bhattacharya).
15. Acc. to D.C. Bhattacharya (Introduction to *Sarvollāsa*, p. 29, it should be 1426 or 1437 A.D.)
16. Several editions printed since 1882.
17. Ed. R.M. Chakravarti, with Foreward, Preface and Introduction by G. Kaviraj, R.M. Chakravarti and D.C. Bhattacharya, Comilla (Bāṅglādesh), 1941.
18. Vide the Tantra Volume of *Cat. of MSS in Asiatic Society*, Calcutta, Preface by C. Chakravarti.

19. Vide *P.K. Gode Comm. Vol.*, p. 32.
20. *Ibid.*, p. 27.
21. Of its several editions, the following may be noted:
    (i) Ed. P. Tarkaratna, with comm. and Beng. translation, Calcutta, 1927.
    (ii) Ed. R. Chattopadhyaya, with Bengali trans. by Candrakumāra, Calcutta, 1282 B.S.
    (iii) Eḍ. S.C. Mukhopādhyaya, *Vasumatī*, Calcutta, 1334 B.S. It is called *Bṛhat-tantrasāra.*
22. See D.C. Bhattacharya in *P.K. Gode Commemoration Volume*, p. 32.
23. On the text-problem, see D.C. Bhattacharya, *op. cit.*
24. For lists, see T. Aufrecht, *Oxford Catalogue* (1859), p. 95; P.K. Gode in *Journal of G. Jha Res. Inst.*, Vol. I, pp. 177-84; D.C. Bhattacharya, *P.K. Gode Comm. Vol.*, pp. 30-31.
25. In support of this idea, the following line from the *Manusmṛti* (ii. 146) has been quoted — *Utpādaka-brahma-dātror garīyān brahmanaḥ pitā. Brahmada* means *ācārya* who performs the *Upanayana* rite of the pupil, and initiates him to Vedic study. In Tantra, *brahmana* has been used to denote one who gives Tāntric *dīkṣā* to the disciple. The immediately preceding verse of Manu (ii. 145) says — *ācāryāṇāṃ śataṃ pitā gauraveṇātirichate.* Kullūka reconciles the two apparently conficting texts as follows: *ācārya* in ii. 145 is one who has taught the pupil only *Gāyatri mantra.*
26. Oil prepared from the fat of human body.
27. The three spices, viz. black pepper, long pepper and dry ginger.
28. D.C. Bhattacharya informs us that reference to Pūrṇānanda and quotations from his work could not be traced by him in any of the manuscripts examined by him. Vide *P.K. Gode Commemoration Volume*, p. 31.
29. Pages 155 and 488-89.
30. Ed. P. Sastri (with Bengali translation), 1349 B.S.; R. Chattopadhyay, *Vividha-tantra-saṃgraha*, Calcutta, 1881-86.
31. Ed. J. Vidyāsāgra, Calcutta, 1896.
32. See Woodroffe, *Serpent Power*, Preface; *Śaktisaṃgama Tantra*, Kālīkhaṇḍa, ed. B. Bhattacharya, Preface, Padmanath Sarasvati, *Prabandhāṣṭaka* (In Bengali), pp. 96-109; Bengali journal 'Ārati' 1314 B.S., Vaiśakh.

33. Ed. P.C. Pal, etc., Calcutta, 1948 Vikrama Saṃvat; Jīvānanda, Calcutta, 1896; P.K. Shastri, Calcutta, 1313 B.s.; R.M. Chatterji, Calcutta; S. Tirthanatha, with Bengali trs., Calcutta, 1389 B.S.
34. Details will follow. The *Ṣaṭcakranirūpaṇa* is a part of it.
35. In *Sāhityika Varṣapañjī*, 1383 (Calcutta), p. 45, the following works are also attributed to him. *Vāmakeśvara-tantra, Śāktānanda-taraṅgīnī.*
36. Critically ed. by B.M. Sāṃkhyatīrtha and C. Bhattacharya, with Introduction by P.C. Bagchi, Calcutta 1936; Tantrik Texts Series No. 2.
37. i. 47-51.
38. i. 63.
39. i. 63.
40. *ānanda-ghana-sandoha-paramātmani cāvyaye/*
jīvātma-nilayo mokṣa iti me vastuto matiḥ//
— i. 64.
41. i. 67. the word *āgama* is derived thus:
āgataḥ śiva-vaktrebhyaḥ (come from the mouth of Śiva), *gataśca girijā-mukhe (gone to the mouth of Pārvatī), mataśca vāsudevena* (approved by Vāsudeva).
42. *ātmānaṃ modayaty-eṣā śāntānandamayaṃ dravam/*
janayatyeva sā yasmān mudrā bhūtamayaṃ vapuḥ//
— xvii. 12
43. It is thus defined by Mādhavācārya quoted in the *Śabda-kalpadruma:*
sīdhur-ikṣurasaiḥ pakvair-apakvair-āsavo mataḥ/
maireyaṃ dhātakī-puṣpaṃ guḍa-dhānāmla-sahitam//
Sīdhu (a kind of drink) is prepared with boiled sugarcane-juice, *āsava* (a class of drinks) with unboiled (sugarcane-juice), *maireya* (a type of drink) consists in *Dhātakī* flower (*Woodfordia fruticosa*) mixed with powdered grain (usually rice or barley) and sour substances.
44. It is thus defined in the *Haṃsa-maheśvara-tantra*:
japa-homau tarpaṇam ca seko brāhmaṇa-bhojanam/
pañcāṅgopāsanaṃ loke puraścaraṇaṃ ucyate//
Japa (muttering or repetition of a *mantra*), *homa* (oblation to fire), *tarpaṇa* (libation of water), *seka* (sprinkling of water or bath), *brāhmaṇs-bhoiana* (feeding of Brāhmaṇas), this fivefold act is called *puraścaraṇa* among the people.

45. Which *Cakra* is meant is not clear.
46. *Samasta-raśmi-saṃyuta/*
47. The derivative meaning of the word is given in the *Prāṇatoṣiṇī* as follows on the authority of the *Kulārṇava*:
puṇya-saṃvardhanāccāpi pāpaugha-parihārataḥ/
puṣkalārthapradānācca puṣpaṃ ityabhidhīyate//
— (p. 232)
Puṣpa is so called as it increases merit, removes a mass of sin and gives sufficient *artha* (desired objects or money).
48. The number of articles stated is six instead of seven.
49. For *Vaikharī*, etc. cf.
mūlādhārāt prathamam udito yastu tāraḥ parākhyaḥ
paścāt paśyantyatha hṛdayago buddhiyuṅ madhyamākhyaḥ/
vaktre vaikharyatha rurudiṣorasya jantoḥ suṣumṇā
baddhas tasmād bhavati parama prerito varṇasaṃghaḥ//
— *Alaṃkāra-kaustubha*
The loud sound, called *Parā*, that at first arises from the *Mūlsdhāra* (see Glossary), afterwards becomes *Paśyantī* in the heart, (and), united with intellect, it is called *Madhyamā*. In the mouth it is *Vaikharī*. Then, confined in the *Suṣumṇā* (see Glossary), of a person willing to cry, it becomes a number of letters induced by the Supreme Being.
50. For an account of such rites, see Chapter on Magic and Marvel.
51. *na mānasaṃ bhavet stotraṃ vācikaṃ tu praśasyate/*
xxiv.1
52. A mystical diagram used as an amulet.
53. Spending on rites and sacrificial fees less than what is permitted by one's pecuniary circumstances.
54. Belonging to Durbar Library of Nepal.
55. Pub. Savitā Memorial Series, Varendra Res. Museum, Rajshahi, Bangladesh, 1961.
56. For details, see the present author's *Tantra in Bengal*, 1st ed., p.74.
57. There is a work of this title also by Abhinavagupta.
58. Ed. K. Mukhopadhyaya, Calcutta, 1383 B.S.
59. Between 1741 and 1745 Śaka = 1819-23 A.D.
60. For details about him and his work, see C. Chakrabarti in *Vaṅgīya Sāhitya Pariṣat Patrikā*, 59, pp. 68-72.
61. cf. Statement of the author at the commencement —
tantrāṇyanekāni vicārya...sāraṃ samuddhṛtya/

karotyayaṃ-pañcamaveda-sāra-nirṇayam//
Having considered many Tantras (and) gathered their essence this (author) writes the *Pañcamaveda-sāranirṇaya.*

62. For details, see C. Chakravarti in *Vaṅgīya Sāhitya Pariṣat Patrikā*, 58, iii-iv. Vide *V.S.P.* MSS No. 1825, 1835, 1867.
63. Ed. i. Ādi Brāhma Samāj, Calcutta, 1876.
    ii. Vaṅgavāsī, Calcutta, 1296 B.S. (with Beng. translation).
    iii. Madras, 1929 (with Comm.)
    iv. Woodroffe, 1953 (3rd ed.).
    Other editions were also published in Calcutta. Prose Eng. translation by M.N. Dutta, Calcutta, 1900, by A. Avalon (with Intro. and Comm.) under the title *Tantra of the Great Liberation*, London, 1913.
64. On this question, see Introduction and Preface to the edition and translation of the *Mahānirvāṇa* by A. Avalon, Calcutta, 1913; Madras, 1928; and *Gurutantra*; *Saṃśaya-nirāsa*, pp. 3-11.
65. For details, see text vi. 1 ff.
66. This practice was, perhaps, the origin of *Vāmācarā.*
67. Vide text, v. 156.
68. See Chap. viii. 5.
69. cf. *tadanujñāṃ vinā brāhma-vivāhaṃ nācaret punaḥ*
    — ix. 265.
70. cf. *brāhmodvāhena yā grāhyā saiva patnī gṛheśvarī*
    — ix. 265.
71. An expression wishing welfare.
72. ix. 278.
73. *Ibid.* For meaning of *Sapiṇḍa*, see P.V. Kane, *History of Dharmaśāstra*, II.
74. ix. 279.
75. *Anuloma* — father having a caste higher than that of the mother.
76. *Pratiloma* — father having a caste lower than that of the mother.
77. To be performed before each sacrament and before the foundation of a house, garden, etc.
78. A rice-ball offered in *Śrāddha.*
79. *Editio Princeps*, 1823 (vide *Friend of India*, Vol. 3, pp. 611-13). There were other editions, too, e.g. Calcutta, 1266 B.S.; *Vasumatī* ed. Calcutta, 1335 B.S.
80. On his life, see *Sāhityika Varṣapañjī*, 1383 B.S., p. 45.

81. cf. *brāhmo vivāho vihito doṣahīnaḥ savarṇayā/ brāhmodvāhena yā grāhā saiva patnī gṛheśvarī//*
— Page 93, Calcutta ed., 1266 B.S.
82. *Madhuka longifolia.*
83. It may mean — spirit distilled from flowers of the *madhūka* tree or from grapes. In either case, it appears to be a repetition of *madhūka* above.
84. See last chapter.
85. It means hemp. Hemp may denote what is called in Bengali *gāñjā, bhāṅg, siddhi.*
86. The following 36 *tattvas* are accepted in Tantra: Śiva, Śakti, Sadāśiva, Īśvara, *Vidyā* (Avidyā) Kālī, *Māyā, Kāla, Niyati, Śuddhavidyā, Rāga,* Puruṣa (Jīva), Prakṛti, *Ahaṃkāra, Buddhi, Manas,* five sensory organs, five motor organs, five *tanmātras*, five *bhūtas.*
87. See *Calcutta Asiatic Soc. Cat.*, VIII, 6209.
88. *Ibid.*, p. xxxv.
89. *Ibid.*, p. xxxvi.
90. *Ibid.*, 6350.
91. *Ibid.*, 6192.
92. For life and works of Kāśīnātha, see *Sāhitya Pariṣat Patrikā,* Calcutta, Vol. 45, pp. 222-231, Vol. 46, p. 80.
93. Calcutta Asiatic Soc. Cat., VIII, Serial No. 6230.
94. See S.C. Banerji in *New Indian Antiquary*, VII, Nos. 5 and 6, 1944.

V. Principal Topics of Bengal Tantra

We have briefly described the contents of the Tantras produced in Bengal. We propose here to deal with the important topics so as to bring to a bold relief the views of Bengal writers on the same. The topics, to be taken up here, are as follows: *Guru-Śiṣya, Dīkṣā, Pañcatattva, Mantra, Puraścaraṇa, Japamālā, Siddhi, Pūjā, Balidāna Antaryāga, Śaiva-vivāha*, recognised subjects of study, *Deha-tattva, Śavasādhana, Yoginī-sādhana, Bhāvas, Cakras, Yoga*, position of women and Śūdras, curbs on self-indulgence, Bengal Tantra vis-à-vis Dharmasāstra.

Guru-Śiṣya[1]

All the works are unanimous in according the most exalted place to the *guru*. His position is much higher than that of even one's father. In Tāntric rites, a person should seek the help of his *guru*; such rites performed by one's *Purohita* become futile. He is to be considered as Śiva or Para Brahman incarnate. In order to be a *guru*, a person has to acquire many qualities of the head and the heart.

One's father or brother cannot be one's *guru*. The husband cannot be the *guru* of his wife unless he is *siddha-mantra*.

It is interesting to note that a woman, with requisite qualifications, can be a *guru*. Initiation by a woman, possessed of requisite qualities, is said to be salutary (*śubha*). Eight times more efficacious is *dīkṣā* by one's mother. It appears that a widow, and a woman having no son, cannot be *gurus*. As regards initiation by one's mother, it is said that if she gives her own *mantra* to the son, then the latter can acquire the eight well-known *Siddhis*.[2]

The *Mahānirvāṇa* (x. 200f) provides that a Śākta, Śaiva, Vaiṣṇava, Saura and a Gāṇapata are preferable as *gurus* of people of these sects respectively. But, a *Kaula* is the best *guru* for all.

On the authority of the *Sārasaṃgraha*, cited in the *Sāktānanda-taraṅginī*, the *Prāṇastoṣiṇī* appears to hold that only a *dvija* can be a *guru*.[3]

Gurus are of two kinds—*Dīkṣā-guru* and *Śikṣā-guru*. He is the supreme *guru* from whom is learnt the *mahāmantra*. According to an authority, cited in the *Prāṇatoṣiṇī*, *gurus* are sixfold, viz. *preraka, sūcaka, vācaka, darśaka, śikṣaka, bodhaka*. It appears that one can have only one person as *guru*.

Persons of the following kinds are unfit for being *gurus*: afflicted with leucoderma, leprosy, optical diseases, dwarf, possessed of bad nails and teeth, henpecked, having more or less limbs than usual, fraudulent, diseased, extremely greedy, garrulous, accursed, sonless, miserly, addicted to gambling, devoid of prescribed practices, wicked, speaking ill of *guru, jala-rakta vikāra* (?).

A person, endowed with many virtues, can be a *Śiṣya*. He should be quiet, modest, pure, respectful, meritorious, capable of doing many kinds of work, born of a good family, wise, possessed of good character, pious, self-restrained, charitably disposed and given to meditation. He incurs sin by looking upon the *guru* as a human being, by speaking ill of him and by showing disrespect towards him. It is interesting to note that, while implicit obedience to the *guru* is ordained, and the desertion of *guru* is condemned on pain of *prāyaścitta*, the Tantras allow a *Śiṣya* to desert his *guru* who proves to be incompetent or undesirable. On authority, the *Prāṇatoṣiṇī* says that as a bee, desiring honey, goes from one flower to another, so a *Śiṣya*, should go from one *guru* to another[4] in quest of knowledge.

> Persons of the following description are unfit for being disciples: Sinful, cruel, wicked, miserly, mean, devoid of good conduct, hater of *mantra*, speaking ill, foolish, hateful of holy places, devoid of respect for *guru*, having an impure heart, idle, boastful, poor, diseased, irate, addicted to pleasures of sense, jealous, harsh-tongued, possessed of ill-got wealth, having relation with another man's wife, hostile to the learned, pedantic, earning livelihood with great trouble, highly ambitious, condemned by people.

It is interesting to note that the *Mahānirvāṇa* (Ullāsa III) provides for *brahma-dīkṣā* as the highest form of initiation. A member of any sect—*Sākta, Śaiva, Vaiṣṇava, Saura* or *Gāṇapatya* is entitled to it. Members of all castes are eligible. The usual restrictions imposed in connexion with *dīkṣā*, are waived in *brahma-dīkṣā*. So the father can initiate the son, the brother can initiate the brother, the maternal uncle can initiate his nephew (*bhāgineya*), the husband his wife and the maternal grandfather his grandson. One can even, contrary to the usual practice, give one's own *mantra* to the disciple. In short, no *Śāstric* injunctions and prohibitions apply to this form of *dīkṣā*.

Dīkṣā

Tāntric *dīkṣā* (initiation) is unavoidable in a man's life. All the rites, performed by an uninitiate, are supposed to be futile, and such a person is doomed to hell. As a person, not initiated to Vedic studies by *Upanayana*, has no right to the performance of Vedic rites, so one without Tāntric *dīkṣā* is not entitled to the performance of Tāntric rites and rituals. *Dīkṣā* is threefold,[5] viz. *śāmbhavī*, *śākteyī* and *māntrī*.

While mentioning these broad kinds of *dīkṣā*, the *Prāṇatoṣiṇī* quotes several texts in which we find a number of kinds some of which are included in the above three categories.

According to some, *dīkṣā* is threefold, viz. *Āṇavī*, *Śāktī* and *Śāmbhavī*. The first is said to consist in *mantra*, *arcanā* (worship), āsana (sitting postures of particular kinds), *nyāsa*,[6] *dhyāna* and *upacāras* (various articles which are offered).[7] It is subdivided into ten kinds, viz.—

(i) *Smārtī*—in it the disciple remembers the *guru*, living in a foreign land, and is freed from sin.

(ii) *Mānasī*—in it the disciple beholds the *guru* seated in front of himself and is purified mentally.

(iii) *Yaugī*—the *guru*, in the manner laid down in *Yogaśāstra*, enters the body of the disciple and unites his soul with his own body.

(iv) *Cākṣuṣī*—it consists in looking with eyes, filled with compassion, having become sure that 'I am Śiva'.

(v) *Spārśikī*—in it the *guru*, considering himself as Supreme Śiva, touches the *mantra* of the disciple on the head with *Śivahasta*.[8]

(vi) *Vācikī*—in it the *guru*, having considered own mouth as the mouth of the *śiṣya*, affectionately gives, through his mouth the divine *mantra* along with *yantra* and *nyāsa*, etc.

(vii) *Māntrī* or—Māntrikī.[9]

(viii) *Hautrī*—it is done after putting fire in a *Kuṇḍa* or *Sthaṇḍila*.[10]

(ix) *Śāstrī*—it is given to a worthy disciple who is devoted and engaged in the service of *guru* along with Śāstric knowledge.

(x) *Ābhiṣecikā*—in this form, Śiva and His consort are zealously worshipped in a pitcher, and the water of the pitcher is sprinkled over the disciple.

A person receiving them is called *abhiṣikta*. One, reaching the highest stage, is called *pūrṇābhiṣikta*.[11]

The *Viśvasāra-tantra*, quoted in the *Prāṇatoṣiṇī*, mentions four kinds of *dīkṣā*, viz, *kriyāvatī, kalāvatī, varṇamayī* and *bedhamayī*.

The *Prāṇatoṣiṇī* describes *kriyāvatī* and *varṇamayī*. It says that *kalāvatī* is given in the *Tantrasāra* and that *bedhamayī* is obsolete. The author refers the inquisitive reader to the fifth *Paṭala* (chapter) of the *Śāradātilaka*.

On the authority of the *Kāmākhyā-tantra* (Paṭala 32), the *Prāṇatoṣiṇī* speaks of *krama-dīkṣā* without which no *siddhi* is possible in Kālī Age. It appears to consist in the successive worship of Kālī, Tārā and Sundarī.[12] In this form, the disciple is to practise self-restraint on the first day and fast on the second. The *guru* will initiate him on the third day.

Some of the places, condemnend for *dīkṣā* by Kṛṣṇānanda, are as follows: Gayā Bhāskara-kṣetra (Konarak), Viraja, Candra-parvata (Candraśekhara hill), Caṭṭala (Chittagong), Mataṅga, Kanyāśrama. Some take Kanyāśrama to mean Kumārītīrtha in Kānyakubja or Kanauj.

Certain months, *nakṣatras* and *tithis* are declared as auspicious. But, no such consideration is necessary in the period from the *bodhana* (awakening) up to Navamī in the autumnal worship of Durgā. No consideration of auspicious time is necessary in Prayāga, Kāśī, Śri-parvata, Kurukṣetra and other very holy places (*mahātirtha*). The same rule applies if *dīkṣā* takes place on one's birthday, marriage-day, on the day of solar or lunar eclipse. At the command of the *guru, dīkṣā* can take place at any time.

The *Mahānirvāṇa* (Ullāsa iii) prescribes *Brahmadīkṣā* as superior to all other kinds of *dīkṣā*. In it, the *guru* initiates the *śiṣya* to the meditation of Brahman, the Supreme Being. The *Brahma-gāyatrī* is as follows: *parameśvarāya vidmahe, paratattvāya dhīmahi, tanno brahma pracodayāt*.

In connexion with *dīkṣā*, the following practices are held to be reprehensible and disastrous: learning of *mantra* by chance, in hiding, through stratagem, by looking at writing. Proper initiation by a *guru* is insisted upon.

Pañcatattva

The usual five accessories to Tāntric *Sādhana* are recognised in Bengal Tantra.

Surā (wine) is of three kinds, viz. *gauḍī, mādhvī* and *paiṣṭi* distilled respectively from molasses, honey and rice. It is noteworthy that a Brāhmaṇa should never offer wine to the goddess nor drink it.[13] For Brāhmaṇas the substitutes (*anukalpa*) are molasses with ginger (*guḍārdraka*), honey, milk, coconut-water. Even Kṣatriyas and Vaiśyas are not allowed to take any intoxicating drink; they can drink the juice of *makaranda-phala*.[14] Kṛṣṇānanda explains the provision, made by certain authorities, for the compulsory drinking of wine as applicable to only those who belong to the fourth stage of life or *saṃnyāsa* (*tattu caturthāśramipadam*).

The *Mahānirvāṇa* (viii. 170-71) ordains that a householder should offer to goddess *madhura-traya* (i.e. milk, sugar and honey) as substitutes for wine. This seems to imply that the offer of wine is implied only for *Sādhakas* who have renounced the *gārhasthyāśrama*. The same work, however, provides (vi. 193 ff.) that a *gṛhastha sādhaka* should drink only as much wine as can be contained in five drinking vessels. It is stated that if a *Kulasādhaka* indulges in excessive drinking, his *Siddhi* is hampered. Only as much should be drunk as does not cause rolling of the eyes. Drinking beyond the permissible limit is like drinking by a beast. The work further ordains (vi. 193) that a *Kula* woman should not drink wine; for her, the smell of wine amounts to the drinking of it.

The *Prāṇatoṣiṇī* cites many authorities, e.g. *Utpatti-tantra*, *Mātṛkābheda-tantra*, to establish that a Brāhmaṇa incurs no sin by drinking wine; on the contrary, it is his bounden duty in certain Tāntric rites. *Surā* (wine) is said to be conducive to great welfare, physical and spiritual, and the derivative meaning of the term is given as follows: *suratvaṃ bhogamātreṇa surā tena prakīrtitā*. *Surā* is so called as it imparts *suratva* (divinity) to one as soon as it is drunk. The *Prāṇatoṣiṇī* observes that the texts prohibiting the drinking of wine on the part of Brāhmaṇas relate to wine which is not formally sanctified (*asaṃskṛta*) or which is *abhiśapta*[15] (accursed) or not offered in worship. Or, the prohibition may apply to a Brāhmaṇa who has not undergone the rite of *abhiṣeka*.[16] The work quotes the following verse from *Manusmṛti* in support of his contention that no offence is committed by any person by drinking wine:

na māṃsa-bhakṣaṇe doṣo na madye na ca maithune/ v. 56

Wine appears to be divided into two classes, viz. *madya* and *surā*, the former seems to be a simple intoxicant while the latter causes a far greater degree of intoxication. The following couplet mentions eleven kinds of *madya*:

pānasaṃ drākṣa-mādhukaṃ khārjūraṃ tālam aikṣavam/
mahūttaṃ sīdhu-mādhvīkaṃ maireyaṃ nārikelajam//

These are stated to be conducive to enjoyment and salvation (*bhuktimuktikarāṇi*).

The following three are called *surā*:

Gauḍī—fermentation of molasses,
Paiṣṭī—distilled from rice,
Mādhvī—distilled from honey.

The first is conducive to enjoyment, the second leads to all success (*sarva-siddhikarī*) and the third causes salvation.

The work states that the *anukalpa* (substitute) of wine should be offered to goddess only when wine is not available. Thus, it appears that, while the early Bengal Tantras condemn wine for Brāhmaṇas, the latest notable compilation, called *Prāṇatoṣiṇī*, approves it.

As regards *māṃsa*, Bengal Tantra prescribes the meat of certain beasts, birds and aquatic creatures. The derivative meaning of the word *māṃsa* is given below according to the *Prāṇatoṣiṇī* which cites the authority of the *Kulārṇava* in this respect:

māṅgalya-jananād devi saṃvid ānanda-dānād /
sarvadeva-priyatvācca māṃsa ityabhidhīyate //

[*Māṃsa*[17] (meat) is so called, O Goddess as it produces welfare, gives consciousness and bliss and is dear to all gods.]

Meat par excellence (*mahāmāṃsa*), according to the *Tantrasāra* is that of the following: cow, human being, sheep, horse, buffalo, boar, goat and deer. Another authority reads *godhā* (iguana; *gosāp* in Bengali) and *uṣṭra* (camel) in place of human being and boar. Female beasts are prohibited. As regards the meat of human being, the *Prāṇatoṣiṇī* appears to prohibit it.[18] The idea, underlying the prohibition, seems to be that human sacrifice may be obstructed or resisted by others. In another context it is prohibited for *Brāhmaṇas*.[19]

As substitutes for meat are prescribed the following: salt, ginger, oil cake, sesamum, wheat, pulse called *māṣa* and garlic.

So far as fish is concerned, it is divided, in the *Prāṇatoṣiṇī*, into three categories, viz. *uttama* (best), madhyama (medium) and *adhama* (worst). Those of the first class are *Śāla*, *Pāṭhīna* and *Rohita*. To the second class belong the old ones, those devoid of bones, fatty and those having scales. The worst are those which are small. According to the

Mahānirvāṇa, those devoid of bones belong to the second class and those full of bones are the worst. It, however, ordains that even the worst kinds of fish may be offered to the goddess if these are fried very well. The derivative meaning of *matsya* is given as follows in the *Prāṇatoṣiṇī* on the authority of the *Kulārṇava*:

māyā-malādi-śamanān-mokṣa-mārga-nirūpaṇāt /
aṣṭaduḥkhādi-virahān-matsyeti parikīrtitaḥ //

Matsya is so called as it puts a stop to illusion, sin, etc., determines the way to salvation, and causes the cessation of the eightfold misery.

On the authority of the *Kulārṇava* and the *Yāmala*, the *Tantrasāra* divides *mudrā* into two classes, viz.

(i) *Kṛsara*—'a dish consisting of sesamum and grain (mixture of rice and peas with a few spices)' Monier Williams. It is kept in a circular shape, and looks like the orb of the moon and is filled with sugar, etc.

(ii) Fried paddy, etc.—it is so fried that it can be chewed.

The *Mahānirvāṇa* (vi. 9) speaks of three classes of *mudrā*:

(i) *Uttama*—white like the orb of the moon, prepared with Śāli rice or barley or wheat, cooked with ghee, beautiful to look at.

(ii) *Madhyama*—prepared with fried paddy and the like.

(iii) *Adhama*—prepared with other fried grains.

Regarding the fifth *Tattva*, i.e. sexual union, it appears that only a woman, who is initiated, should be resorted to. Such a woman should at first be subjected to *abhiṣeka*. From the *Mahānirvāṇa* (vi. 14 and 20) and other Tantras it appears that one is allowed to use others' wives (*parakīyā śakti*) besides one's own wife. From an authority, cited in the *Prāṇatoṣiṇī*,[20] it appears that one *sādhaka* should take to only one Śakti (woman) who will serve as the fifth *Tattva*.

Mantra

As stated elsewhere, *mantra* plays a very important role in the life and rites of an adherent of Tantra. Care has been taken to ensure the correct pronunciation and precise application of *mantras*. The *Tantrasāra* states several defects which render *mantras* sterile. Some of these defects are *chinna* (torn), *ruddha* (obstructed), *śaktihīna* (devoid of power), etc. A *mantra*, with or without *vāyu-bīja* (*yaṃ*) at the beginning, middle and end, or if it has long vowels thrice, four times or five times, is *chinna*. That mantra, which has two *pṛthivī-bījas* (*laṃ*) at the beginning, middle or end, is called *ruddha*. A *mantra*, devoid of *māyā-bīja* (*hrīṃ*), *tritattva* or *phreṃ*, is *śaktihīna*.

Procedures have been prescribed for removing the defects of *mantras* in order to make them fruitful.

Mantras have been classed as male, female and neuter (*napuṃsaka*). *Mantras* of different classes are stated to be effective in different rites.

In connexion with *mantras*, we should mention *bījas* which are symbolical. Different *bījas* are to be used in different rites and in the worship of various deities. *Bījas* are numerous, and have varying designations. Some of them are *Māyā, Lajjā, Śambhu-vanitā, Vahni, Lakṣmī, Candra Vadhū, Kālī*, etc. The symbolical expressions are *hrīṃ, hlīṃ, śrīṃ, aiṃ, strīṃ*, etc.

It is interesting to note that *mantras* are imagined to possess different limbs like face, ear, etc., and internal organs like the heart. For example, *praṇava* (*oṃkāra*) is regarded as the face of a *mantra*. The vowels are the heart.

Puraścaraṇa

It is an important topic of discussion in Bengal Tantra. We set forth below a brief account of it.

Regarding the derivative meaning of the term, the *Mahānīla-tantra* (Paṭala 26), cited in some works, says — *pūryate caraṇaṃ tasya japa-homādi- tarpaṇaih*. It is so called as, in it, by means of *japa, homa* and *tarpaṇa*, the feet of one's desired deity are filled; 'tasya' in the text means *sveṣṭadevasya*. In some Tantras, e.g., *Yāmala*, it is so-called as it is to be done first of all (*purataḥ*) for the success of *mantras*.

It is stated to consist of five accessories (*aṅga*), viz. *Japa, Homa, Tarpaṇa, Abhiṣeka* (bath), *Brāhmaṇa-bhojana*. *Japa* is threefold,[21] viz. *mānasa, upāṃśu* and *vācika*. In *mānasa-japa*, one has to repeat mentally the syllables of a *mantra* after comprehending its meaning. In *upāṃśu-japa*, the devotee, with his mind concentrated on the deity, slightly moves his tongue and lips and his mutterings are slightly audible. In *vācika-japa*, a *mantra* is audibly repeated. Of these, the first kind is the best, the second medium and the third worst.

The number of *japa, homa, tarpaṇa*, etc., varies in the cases of different deities. For example, *japa* will be for a lac of times in the case of Dakṣiṇakālikā and *homa* will be one-tenth of it. For propitiating Tārā, *japa* will be for four lac times and *homa* one-tenth of it.

The number of *tarpaṇa* is one-tenth of that of *homa* and the number of *abhiṣeka* is one-tenth of that of *tarpaṇa*. In *Gopāla-mantra*, the number of *tarpaṇa* is like that of *homa*. Generally *tarpaṇa* should be performed with water mixed with *aguru, karpūra, madhu, dugdha, ghṛta*, etc. According to the *Gautamīya Tantra*, with water should be mixed *madhu, karpūra* and *ghṛta* or *dugdha* in the cases of Śakti, Viṣṇu and Śiva.

Abhiṣeka is to be performed with water perfumed with *karpūra* and the like.

As regards Brāhmaṇas to be fed, there are injunctions about their suitability. An uninitiated Brāhmaṇa is not suitable. For the followers of *Kulācāra* only Brāhmaṇas, initiated according to the *Kula* rites, should be entertained. As regards their number, it should be one-tenth of the number of *abhiṣekas*.

The accessories are stated to range from one (*ekāṅga*) to eighteen (*aṣṭādaśāṅga*) in accordance with different kinds of devotees. *Vīra puraścaraṇa* consists of seven *aṅgas*, the sixth and seventh being *Śakti-pūjā* and *Kumārī-pūjā* respectively. Sixteen accessories are for the *Kaulikas* and eighteen for the *Aghorins*.

Brāhmaṇa-bhojana is very important, nay, indispensable excepting in connexion with *Mañju-ghoṣa-mantra*. *Homa, tarpaṇa* and *abhiṣeka* can be, in the event of inability, substituted by *japa* twice the number of them. For example, if the number of *homas* be 10,000 that of *japa* will be 20,000. But, there can be no substitute for the feeding of Brāhmaṇas. If there be any lapse in the performance of the rite, amends may be made by fully satisfying a Brāhmaṇa devotee with a sumptuous feast. But, sin is incurred by feeding a Brāhmaṇa who is not initiated and the rite becomes futile.

Without *puraścaraṇa*, success in *mantras* cannot be achieved. It must be done even at the expense of one's all. The *Muṇḍamālā-tantra*, however, provides that, for one in indigent circumstances, mere *japa* serves the purpose of *puraścaraṇa*. Deceitful economy (*vittaśāṭhya*) has been condemned. If a person is himself unable, he should get it done by his *guru* or any other *sādhaka* who may even be a female.

Different periods of time are auspicious for *puraścaraṇa* relating to *mantras* of different deities. For example, the bright half of the month is propitious for Viṣṇu, but *dakṣiṇāyana* is prohibited. Both the bright and dark halves are auspicious for *Śakti-mantra*; *dakṣiṇāyana* is also good. Solar and lunar eclipses are conducive to good effects of *puraścaraṇa*. The months Kārtika, Āśvina, Vaiśākha, Māgha, Agrahāyaṇa, Phālguna and Śrāvaṇa are particularly auspicious. The fortnight in autumn, in which *Śaradīyā pūjā* is performed, is specially commended.

Different places are suitable for different deities in connexion with *puraścaraṇa*. For instance, in connexion with *Viṣṇu-mantra*, Ayodhyā, Mathurā, Māyā, Kāśī, Vadarikāśrama, Gayā, *Gaṇḍakī-tīra*, Dvārakā are auspicious. For *Śaiva-mantra* are commended Kedāra Tryambaka, Kāśī, Kāncī, *Gaṅgā-tīra*, Vaidyanātha, Rāmeśvara. For *Śakti-mantra*, auspicious are Jvālāmukhī, Prayāga, Kāmini, Mālikā, *Sarasvatī-tīra*.

Generally speaking, the following places are auspicious for *puraścaraṇa*: Kṣetratīrtha, forest, garden, temple, river, lake, cottage, lonely spot, house of the *guru*, holy place, cowshed, *Siddha-pīṭha*, a place near young women, confluence of rivers, particularly *Gaṅgā-sāgara-saṅgama*, a place near chaste women and pious people, roots of trees known as *kula-vṛkṣa*.[22] For *Divya-vīras*, particularly effective are cremation ground, empty house, *Muṇḍāsana*,[23] mountain-cave etc.

Particularly effective is *puraścaraṇa* at midnight and midday at the following places: root of the *Vaṭa* tree, forest, cremation ground, empty house, crossing of four roads.

Among the places prohibited are a river which does not flow into a sea, dilapidated temple, root of a decayed tree, stagnant river, ground with hole, cultivated land, barren land, a place full of Mlecchas, wicked people and ferocious animals, a place where the king's men or influential people move about, another's house, etc.

Among the practices prohibited during *puraścaraṇa* are over-eating, garrulity, laziness, excessive sleep or wakefulness, day-sleep, listening to vocal and instrumental music, witnessing dance, eating of betel-leaves, etc., use of unguents, holding unconsecrated flowers, untruth, crookedness, killing of animals, association of heretics and the wicked, touch of dogs, etc., eating food not offered to deities, acceptance of gifts, eating food received from others.

For women there is considerable relaxation of the rules regarding the practices permitted and prohibited. If they are unable to practise *Nyāsa*, etc., according to rules, they can attain success by mere *japa* with devotion.

Guru, the embodiment of Supreme Brahman, plays a prominent role in *puraścaraṇa* as, indeed, in the entire Tāntric system. The rite must be preceded and followed by *guru-pūjā*. The first thing on the day of commencement is the salutation of the *guru* or, in his absence, of his wife or son. If none of them is available, one related to the *guru* is to be pleased with the gift of land, money, clothes, etc. according to one's capacity. If the *guru* is present , he will perform worship, etc. In his absence, his son will do these things. If even the latter is not available, the wife of the *guru* will perform the acts. If she does so, there will be no necessity of *balidāna* and *homa*. In the absence of all of them, a person himself will do the needful. Utterly futile will be all rites performed by any Tāntric *sādhaka* or *purohita* engaged by a person without the permission of his *guru*.

During *puraścaraṇa* one has to worship the deity by day. Those, who have undergone *pūrṇābhiṣeka*, as well as those, who have adopted *vīrabhāva*, worship at night is also prescribed.

Kumārī-pūjā[24] is a must in *puraścaraṇa*; otherwise *pūjā, japa, homa*, etc. become futile. All gods are said to be pleased with *kumārī-pūjā*. A maiden girl is to be entertained in the beginning, middle and at the end of *puraścaraṇa*, with sandal paste, flowers, various dishes, clothes, ornaments, gold, silver, etc. A person is regarded as particularly fortunate if he gets a maiden girl who is initiated or has undergone the Tāntric rite called *abhiṣeka*. A girl, aged seven, eight or nine, is especially commended. The girls, acceptable for the purpose, are those possessed of bright complexion, of high castes having both parents alive and those who have not had sexual intercourse nor have thought of association with a man. The girls, prohibited for the purpose, are of the following descriptions: having dark complexion, long teeth, scanty brow-hairs, more or less limbs than usual, too much hair on body, uncouth appearance, squint-eyed, lame, irate disposition, blind, born of a female slave or maidservant, greedy and wicked.

Like *Kumārī-pūjā, Śakti-pūjā* is also ordained in the beginning, middle and at the end of *puraścaraṇa*. Eight Śaktis, mentioned in the *Kulacūḍāmaṇi*, are: Brāhmaṇī, Kṣatriyā, Vaiśyā, Śūdrā, Veśyā, Nāpitakanyā, Rajakī, Naṭakī. After mentioning these eight women, it states that any family woman, endowed with special accomplishments, may be regarded as a *Śakti*. One authority provides the worship of any *Śakti* in the absence of *Kula-śakti*. A *Śakti*, though younger in age, inferior in caste, should be duly worshipped. A woman, possessed of children, or a widow may be a *Śakti*. If other Śaktis be not available, one should worship one's daughter, younger sister, mother, stepmother or maternal aunt. An initiated *Śakti* is preferable to an uninitiated one; the latter, however, is to be selected in the absence of the former. The *Śakti* is to be worshipped as a goddess; lust towards her is highly reprehensible.

In the case of *japa* for 10,000 times, the fee (*dakṣiṇā*) is one *suvarṇa* and of *japa* for one lac times it is ten *suvarṇas*; one *suvarṇa* is equivalent to 80 *Ratis*. One who can afford should give away his all as fee or half of one's total earnings. The rite is stated to be futile if fee is not paid according to one's capacity.

In the *Puraścaraṇa-ratnākara*, the author describes the means of achieving success quickly. He however, warns the reader that these means should be resorted to under the guidance of one's *guru* or of a person who is a veteran in these practices. These means are as follows:

(1) *Bilva-mūla-sādhana*: The *sādhaka* should go, at the expiry of the first watch of the night of *amāvasyā, caturdaśī, aṣṭamī, pūrṇimā* or *saṃkrānti* or on Tuesday, to the root of a *Bel* tree and perform this *sādhana*.

(2) *Śayyā-sādhana*: At midnight, the *sādhaka* being naked should perform *śayyā-saṃskāra* after causing his own wife or that of another to sit on the bed decked with fragrant flowers. Those, who have elaborately performed *śayyā-sādhana*, can perform *japa, pūjā, puraścaraṇa*, etc., on the bed.

(3) *Muṇḍa-sādhana*: In it, the *sādhaka* is required to sit on *muṇḍas* (heads, rather skulls). As regards the creatures, whose *muṇḍas* are suitable, the *Yoginī-tantra* mentions human being, buffalo, cat; in such a case, one each or three in all are prescribed. As an alternative, three human *muṇḍas* serve the purpose. In case of five *muṇḍas*, one each of the following is necessary: jackal, snake, dog, monkey, human being. An alternative to it is an aggregate of five human *muṇḍas*. In the case of the latter, even a crore may be used. The heads are to be buried and an altar of the prescribed dimensions should be constructed over them.

According to the *Śakti-saṃgama-tantra*, even one *muṇḍa* may serve the purpose.

As regards the human heads, those of Caṇḍālas and the like appear to be best and those of Śūdras worst.

As an alternative to the *trimuṇḍa āsana*, stated above, one may use one head each of human beings, jackal and monkey.

As an alternative to *pañca-muṇḍa*, mentioned above, *sādhakas* appear to prescribe two human heads, one head each of a jackal, a monkey and a snake.

The places, suitable for *muṇḍa-sādhana*, appear to be almost identical with those prescribed for *Śava-sādhana* (q. v.). As regards the kinds of persons, whose heads are suitable, they are almost the same as prescribed for use as corpses in *Śavasādhana* (q. v).

(4) *Śmaśāna-sādhana:* This is suitable in the following periods of time; *aṣṭamī* and *caturdaśī* in both dark and bright fortnights, the former being more suitable, Tuesday night after the expiry of the first watch. A cremation ground, which has not been cleansed and washed, is the best.

If the *sādhaka* is afraid, he may place armed friends and other *sādhakas* a little distance away.

(5) *Śava-sādhana*: Described elsewhere.

Japamālā

Rosaries are used by Tāntric devotees at the time of *Japa*. We find descriptions of the various kinds of rosaries in Bengal Tantra. Rosaries are broadly divided into three classes, viz. *Sthirā, Carā* and *Karamālikā*. These are briefly described below.

Varṇamālā is called *Sthira* or *Akalpitā*. A rosary, made with the letters of the alphabet from *a* to *kṣa*, is called *varṇamālā*. The following source-letters (*mātṛkā-varṇa*), followed by *anusvāra*, are fifty in number: all vowels, short and long, and *AṂ, AḤ*; the five *vargas KA, CA, ṬA, TA, PA*; the four semi-vowels, the three sibilants, sonant aspirate *HA* followed by a second *LA*. After these fifty comes *KṢA* which is called *Meru*.

Each *mātṛkā-varṇa*, with *anusvāra* added to it, has got to be recited or repeated with the *mūla* or *bīja-mantra*. For example, in the *japa* of the *mantra, HRĪṂ*, one has to recite *AṂ HRĪṂ, ĀṂ HRIṂ* and so on. Then *KṢAṂ* should be recited without the *mūlamantra*. After this, one has to recite *HRĪṂ* preceded by each of the *mātṛkā* letters in the reverse order; e.g. *LAṂ HRĪṂ, HAṂ HRIṂ* and so on. Thus, one hundred *japas* are completed. For eight *japas*, the following should precede the *bīja-mantra. AṂ, KAṂ, CAṂ, ṬAṂ, TAṂ, PAṂ, YAṂ, SAṂ*. According to some, the following should precede the *bījamantra*: *AḤ, ṄAṂ, ÑAṂ, NAṂ, ṆAṂ, MAṂ, VAṂ, LAṂ*. In the opinion of others, the following eight, followed by Anusvāra, should precede the *bīja-mantra* in eight japas: *Ṛ, Ṛ, Ḷ, Ḹ, L, L, Ṛ, Ṝ*.

Another kind of *varṇamālā* is to be made conceiving *Kula-kuṇḍalinī* or *Brahmanāḍī* as the thread.[25] It is to be further fancied that

Kuṇḍalinī, raised up to the *Sahasrāra*, is entwining Parama Śiva as a rosary.

One has to hold the breath during *japa*. If one is unable to do so in a hundred *japas*, one may practise *japa* for fifty, twenty-five or even eight times.

Varṇamālā has been praised as the best kind of rosary. Its substitute is *Śaṃkhamālā* (q. v.), *Japa* in *varṇamālā* can be done at any place, pure or impure, and at any time and in the presence of all.

Carā or *Kalpitā mālā* is made with crystal, *Rudrākṣa* beads, etc. It may be of three kinds, viz. *Uttama* (containing 108 or 109 beads), *Madhyama* (55 beads), *Adhama* (28 beads). Such a rosary may contain any of the following number of beads according to necessity: 100, 50, 30, 27, 15, 14, 10, etc.

In such a *mālā*, beads may be of any one of the following, besides those stated above: gold, silver, copper, pearl, coral, *padmākṣa*, *indrākṣa*, red sandal, myrobalan, Tulasī-wood, turmeric, *rāja*-danta (i.e., the four teeth in front), ivory, conchshell, *mahāśaṅkha* (q. v) etc. Different rosaries are commended in different rites. Varying results are said to accrue from different kinds of rosary. In one rosary, there should not be a conglomeration of many jewels. The rosary should always be concealed and never held in hand, head or neck.

For ordinary use are commended rosaries of the wood of Myrobalan, *Tulasī*, Sandal, Bel, etc.

Generally speaking, *Tulasī-mālā* is prescribed for *Viṣṇu-mantra* and *Gajadanta-mālā* for *Gaṇeśa-mantra*. In *Kālī-mantra* and all other *mantras*, metallic rosaries or those made with crystal, *Rudrākṣa*, etc. are commended. *Mahāśankha-mālā* is prescribed for certain *devī-mantras*, e.g. *Chinnamastā-mantra*. It is also prescribed for *Śiva-mantra*.

Karamālā-japa is the name given to *japa* by touching the thumb from the middle *parvan*[26] of the ring finger to the root of the forefinger. *Karamālā* is prescribed for all kinds of *japa—nitya, naimittika* and *kāmya*. *Karamālā-japa* can be done anywhere and at any time. In some Tantras, *Karamālā* has been praised as better than all kinds of *akṣamālā*.

In a rosary, the beads should be beautiful and absolutely free from defect. A rosary should be made to resemble a cow's tail or a serpent. After each bead there should be a knot (*granthi*). A rosary, devoid of knots, is generally forbidden. But, certain authorities recommend such rosaries in connexion with certain deities, e.g. Kālī, Tārā, etc.

The *japamālā* should be preserved in a bag resembling a cow's face (*gomukha*), made of silk cloth, fur or, in some cases, of leather of deer or sheep. The colour of the *gomukha* may be red, yellow or *gairika* (colour of red chalk or red ochre).

One is liable to expiation if one's *japamālā* is stolen, burnt or otherwise spoilt.

Mahāśaṃkha (or, Rahasya) Mālā

Mahāśaṃkha is the name given to a bone of the human skull which has not been burnt. According to the *Triśaktiratna*, it is the name of a bone intervening between the ears and the eyes. In the absence of such a bone, the bone of any part may be used.[27] From certain texts, *mahāśaṃkha* appears to denote also a bone of the forehead or bones of fingers. A *mālā*, made of *māhāśaṃkha*, is recommended for *Vīrācārins* in certain special rites, e.g. māraṇa, uccāṭana, etc. It is also prescribed for *puraścaraṇa* in certain cases. Such a *mālā* is said to produce instantaneous effect. Eight kinds of *siddhi* are stated to be possible by its use.

From a text of the *Yāmala*, it appears that bones of the skulls of elephants, horses and camels, killed in battle, may also be used for the purpose. The bones of the following persons are suitable:

> Killed by thunder-stroke, snake-bite, tigers, drowned in water, slain while fighting in a battle, Caṇḍālas and the like are said to be the most suitable and Śūdras, etc. worst. The corpse of a young and dark-complexioned person and even a Brāhmaṇa will do.

The corpses of people of the following descriptions are to be avoided:

> Those who died as a result of famine, disease, suicide, a two-year old boy, woman, *dvija*,[28] leper, too old, one who died seven days ago.

Siddhi[29]

Ordinarily, *siddhi* means success. In Tantra it also means power. The Tantras of Bengal name several *siddhis* (powers), and lay down the means to their attainment.

The various *siddhis* consist in the power of understanding the significance of the cries of the birds called Khañjana, Mayūra, Sārasa, Kapota, Ṭiṭṭibha, Koka (ruddy goose), Haṃsa, Vidyādhara, aquatic birds, the beasts called Kṛkalāsa (chameleon), Vallī (=*godhikā*), *bhūcaras* (animals like lion, tiger, elephant, buffalo, etc. living on land). *Kaṅkāla-siddhi* appears to mean the power of destroying enemies by propitiating Kālī. *Kṣemaṅkarī-siddhi* seems to mean the power of understanding the significance of the voice of favourable women.

Other powers include the knowledge of the meaning of the cries of cats, mice, jackals, dogs, frogs, *godhā* (*gosāp* in Bengal), cows, deer, sheep, goats, wild cats, bears, crows, cranes, sparrows, parrots, cocks, *cakoras* and insects. *Vāksiddhi* (power of uttering infallible speech) is also stated. One is said to acquire great powers like *mantra-siddhi* or power of making *mantras* fruitful, by resorting to certain practices on the bed, at the root of the *Bel* tree and at the crossing of three or four roads.

It should be noted that the eight well-known *siddhis* viz. *aṇimā*, *laghimā*, etc., have also been stated and means to their acquisition prescribed.

Pūjā

Bengal Tantra ordains both internal (*mānasa*)[30] and external (*bāhya*) *pūjās*, with a preference for the former.

For use in *Pūja* the number of *upacāras* (materials), according to the *Tantrasāra*, may be 64, 18, 16, 10 or 5.[31] Different results are stated to accrue from the offer of jewels, pearls, garments of various kinds, etc.

Flowers appear to be the common factor in all the categories of *upacāras*. Different kinds of flowers are prescribed for different deities and in different seasons.[32] Certain flowers are said to be especially suitable by day or at night. Generally stale flowers are forbidden. But, an exception is made in the case of certain species, e.g. *Padma, Campaka.* It appears that stale buds of flowers are allowed. Flowers, once smelt, are prohibited. Also regarded as very sinful is the worship of deities with flowers grown in a temple. In *gupta-pūjā*, secret worship, certain flowers only can be used.

Generally flowers which are torn or broken (*chinna-bhinna*) are prohibited. This prohibition does not seem to apply to *Jātīpuṣpa*.

Usually, flowers, naturally dropped on the earth, are forbidden. But, such *Bakula* and *Śephāli* flowers are allowed. Tabooed are flowers devoid of fragrance and those whose petals are less than three. Grave sin is said to be incurred by plucking flowers after bath at midday.

In the absence of flowers, fruits can be offered as substitutes. If even fruits are not available, leaves serve the purpose. While stale leaves are generally forbidden, this prohibition does not apply to certain leaves, e.g. *bilvapatra, tulasī.*

In worship, Bengal Tantra seems to lay greater stress on devotion, on mental attitude than on external substances. The *Tantrasāra* cites the authority of the *Navaratneśvara* which clearly asks the *Sādhaka* of steadfast mind (*sthira-mānasa*) to repeat the appropriate *mantra* in the absence of the 64 *upacāras*; such repetition (*japa*) will ensure the intended effect.

In this connexion, it is interesting to note the significance of the terms *puṣpa, dhūpa, dīpa* and *naivedya* as found in the *Prāṇatoṣiṇī.*

Puṣpa is so called as it increases merit (*puṇya*), removes multitudes of sin (*pāpaugha*), puskalārtha (enough of money) and gives.

Dhūpa is so named as it removes great evil arising from putrid smell (*dhūtāśeṣa-mahādoṣa-pūti-gandha-prabhāvataḥ*), and causes immense joy.

Dīpa is so called as it checks the darkness of delusion, prevents decay and (re)birth and grants a divine form.

Naivedya is so designated as, by its *nivedana* (offer), the deity is pleased.

It is interesting to note that betel-leaves constitute one of the *upacāras*. But, those grown on the following trees, are forbidden.

Kalivṛkṣa, Panasa (jack-fruit), *Aśoka, Śālmali.*

The author of the *Prāṇatoṣiṇī* adds that *Kalivṛkṣa* is the abode of *bhūtas* (ghosts), and it is called *Vayaḍā* in Gauḍa.

Regarding cloths to be offered in *pūjā*, it is ordained that a piece of cloth, less than 36 *aṅgulas* in *āyāma* (length ?), should not be given by one who can afford. As regards ornaments, one should not offer such as are smaller in size than those which can be used by an eight-year-old girl. In the matter of offering various articles before deities, one is warned against *vitta-śāṭhya* (deceitful economy). The idea is that one should give things in accordance with one's means, and should avoid niggardliness.

The worship of a pair of the images of certain deities has been forbidden. Such deities are Śakti, Sūrya, Gaṇeśa. Prohibited is the simultaneous worship of two Śālagrāmas, two Śivaliṅgas.

It should be noted that Tāntric *pūjā* must be done by one's ownself or through the medium of the *guru.* If a person is himself unable and his *guru* also is not available, he should appoint, for the purpose, a woman having a son. Grave sin is said to be incurred by getting the *pūjā* performed by *Purohita* or any other person.

Gurupatnī (wife of the *guru*) can be engaged in such worship. But if she does so, then there will be no *homa* nor *balidāna*.

If the worship of a deity is hindered for a period of six months, then one should bathe the deity with eight pitcherfuls of water and then worship it. If the *pūjā* is suspended for over six months, then the image has to be subjected to *saṃskāra* (purificatory rites for revival) before resuming worship.

Images of the following descriptions should not be worshipped:

Broken, cracked, deformed, touched by a leper, fallen on a defiled spot.

The first three are to be thrown into water, while the rest should be worshipped after *saṃskāra*. In a *Mahāpīṭha* and in an *Anādiliṅga* nothing affects the image.

Kumārī-pūjā (worship of virgin girls) figures prominently in Bengal Tantra. The *Tantrasāra* cites authorities to show that the *pūjā* of virgin girls leads to the acquisition of many merits, destruction of many sins and the acquisition of peace and prosperity. The worship of a *kumārī* is to be followed by a feast to her. After that, she should be given a fee (*dakṣiṇā*) consisting of silver, gold or pearls. To arrange for the marriage of such a girl with a suitable person is said to lead to *bhukti* (enjoyment) and *mukti* (salvation). *Homa*, etc., are said to produce complete effect if *Kumārī-pūjā* is done. Virgin girls are stated to have different designations in the successive years following their birth. These are as follows:

One year	Sandhyā
Two years	Sarasvatī
Three years	Tridhāmūrti
Four years	Kālikā
Five years	Subhagā
Six years	Umā
Seven years	Mālinī
Eight years	Kubjikā
Nine years	Kālasandarbhā
Ten years	Aparājitā
Eleven years	Rudrāṇī
Twelve years	Bhairavī
Thirteen years	Mahālakṣmī

Fourteen years	Pīṭhanāyikā
Fifteen years	Kṣetrajñā
Sixteen years	Ambikā

The above list is in accordance with the *Rudrayāmala*.

It is provided that a girl should be worshipped so long as the menstrual flow does not begin in her. *Kumārī-pūjā* is prescribed from the first day to the full moon in the bright half of the month. It is a must on the Mahānavamī day of *Durgā-pūjā*.

The *Prāṇatoṣiṇī* points out that the above designations are given also in the *Bṛhannīla-tantra* with the difference that a fourteen-year old girl is called *Nāyikā* and a sixteen-year old girl is called *Carcikā*. According to the *Kubjikā-tantra*, quoted in the *Prāṇatoṣiṇī*, girls from the age of five up to twelve are *kumārīs* in the real sense of the term. Those, in the age-group of six to nine, are conducive to the fulfilment of the wishes of the *sādhaka*. Girls of the age ranging from eight to thirteen are *Kulajās*. From the tenth year up to the sixteenth they are *Yuvatīs*, and are to be looked upon as goddesses. According to the *Viśvasāra*, cited in the *Prāṇatoṣiṇī*, an eight-year old girl, a nine-year old one and a ten-year old girl are designated respectively as *Gaurī, Rohiṇī, Kanyakā*. After that age-limit girls are *Rajasvalā*, i.e. those in whom menstrual flow appears. Girls of the age-group of twelve to twenty are called *sukumārā*.

It is noteworthy that, in the selection of *Kumārīs*, no caste-distinction is to be observed. On authority, the *Prāṇatoṣiṇī* names the daughters of the following persons, who can be worshipped as *Kumārīs*:

> *naṭi* (dancing woman), *hīna* (low=caste person), *Kāpālika*, *rajaka* (washerman), *nāpita* (barber) *gopāla* (cowherd), Brāhmaṇa, Śūdra, Vaidya,[33] Vaṇik (merchant), Caṇḍala, one's friend.

It may be observed that, in connexion with *Kumārī-pūjā* on the occasion of *puraścaraṇa*, as described in the *Puraścaraṇa-ratnākara*, the *Mahākāla-saṃhitā* prescribes a *kumārī of anīcajāti* (not of a low birth).

Balidāna[34]

Animal sacrifice, according to Bengal Tantra, has been dealt with in connection with *Pañcatattva* and *Durgā-pūjā*.

For *māṃsa*, as a *tattva*, the meat of the following has been prescribed in the *Tantrasāra* as the best: such meat is called *mahāmāṃsa*:

Cow, human being, sheep, horse, buffalo, bear, goat, deer. As an alternative to the above, the same work mentions the following:

Cow, sheep, horse, buffalo, *godhā* (=*gosāp* in Bengal), goat, camel, deer.

It should be observed that cow is the common factor in both. Thus, it is clear that, at some time or other, the cow was slaughtered before the deity and its flesh was offered. It may be presumed that, even at the time of Kṛṣṇānanda, it was not prohibited for Tāntrikas; because there is no prohibition of it in the *Tantrasāra*. It is interesting to note that the *Prāṇatoṣiṇī* does not include cow's meat in the list of animals which should be sacrificed before the deity. Probably, in course of time, due to Brahmanical influence, cow-slaughter was looked down upon by the society.[35]

As regards human flesh, we have noticed, under *Pañcatattva*, that the Prāṇatoṣiṇī forbids it for Brahmaṇas and also in general. This practice might have crept into Tantra from the aborigines among whom Tāntric practices are supposed by some to have originated. In course of time, it was tabooed in the society due to the advancement of culture and Brahmanical influence.[36]

The *Prāṇatoṣiṇī* quotes the *Samayācāra-tantra* which divides *bali* into two kinds—*Sāttvika* and *Rājasa*. The former is devoid of flesh, blood, etc. (*māṃsa-raktādi-varjita*), the latter consists of these things. The *Yoginī-tantra*, quoted in the above work, states the different *balis* most suitable for the different castes. These are as follows:

Brāhmaṇas—milk, *Śāli* rice or *pāyasa* (a preparation of rice with milk and sugar made into a gruel), *caru*[37] saturated with ghee, fruits, flowers, *kṛsara*[38] mixed with honey, *khaṇḍa*,[39] *modaka*.[40]

Kṣatriyas—animals.

Vaiśyas—paddy.

Śūdras—honey.

The text concludes this topic by saying that, as an alternative, all castes may offer animals (*sarveṣāṃ paśavo'thavā*).

The *Yoginī-tantra* appears to allow the offer of even rats, *karāla* (musk-deer?) and small cats.

The above authority prohibits the following birds:

kākola, kalaviṅka, rājahaṃsa, sārika, śuka, gṛdhra, mayūra, citraka, veṇu-pṛṣṭha, kṛṣṇa-pārāvata, bṛhat-kapota, khañjarīṭa, baka, balākā.

An interesting practice is *Śatru-bali*. One is required to make an idol with condensed milk, and perform *prāṇa-patiṣṭhā* (infusion of life by *mantras*) in it in the name of the enemy, and finally cut it with one's own hand with an angry look. This is supposed to ensure the destruction of the enemy.

The offer of eatables, consisting mainly of meat, to jackals at the root of a tree, in a field or a cemetery, in the evening, is stated to be conducive to great merit. Goddess Umā is said to come in the guise of jackals; in fact, a jackal is designated as Śivā and the above articles are called *Śivā-bali*.

Antaryāga

Great importance is attached to *antaryāga* in Bengal Tantra. It means mental worship in which the five *Tattvas* are conceived as abstract and not tangible things. Quoting the *Kulārṇava*, Kṛṣṇānanda says, '*Surā* is *Śakti*, *Śiva māṃsa*, their enjoyer is Bhairava Himself'. Their unity being effected, a peculiar bliss ensues and is called *mokṣa*. This is done in the following process. *Kuṇḍalinī Śakti* repeatedly goes from *mūlādhāra* to *brahma-randhra*. In *antaryāga*, a person drinks the ambrosia flowing from the sky-lotus (*vyoma-paṅkaja*); this is *madhupāna* (drinking of honey). The drink of other kinds of liquor is *madya-pāna* (drinking wine). One, having slain the beast in the shape of merit and sin (*puṇyāpuṇya-paśu*) with the weapon of knowledge, merges his mind in the Supreme Being, and thus becomes *palāśī* (eater of *pala*[41] or meat). One, having restrained the senses, puts them in the soul (*ātmani*), and thus becomes *māṃsāśī* (eater of meat); others, who take meat in the gross sense, are killers of animals. *Yonimudrā* is the *mudrā* to such a person; other *mudrās* are food. Union with the Supreme Soul, *Parāśakti*, is *maithuna*; those who enjoy the bliss of this union are liberated. Others, who enjoy physical copulation, are addicted to women.

In connexion with *antaryāga*, it is said that one who, regardless of the deity residing within oneself, seeks it outside, is like a fool who, ignoring the *Kaustubha* jewel in his hand, roams about for glass.

While describing *antaryāga*, the *Prāṇatoṣiṇī* quotes the following verses from the *Muṇḍamālā-tantra*:

ādhāre kuṇḍalīṃ devīṃ cintayed bhujagākṛtim /
pūrakeṇa maheśāni tayā cakrāṇi saḥ tataḥ /
sahasrānanda-sandoha—mandiraṃ prāpayet sudhīḥ /
yojayitvā pūrakeṇa sādhakaḥ paramātmani /
śivaśakti-samāyogāt sukhī bhuyān-nirantaram /

vikāśitaṃ bhaved dehaṃ sakalaṃ tat prabhāvataḥ /
anāhatād bahiḥ padmaṃ ṣoḍaśāraṃ vicintayet /
tanmadhye cintayen mantrī sudhā-sāgaram uttamam /
śata-yojana-vistīrṇaṃ valayākāram ujjvalam /
tanmadhye parameśāni maṇi-dvīpaṃ manoharam /
pārijātādi—racitair-udyānaiḥ pariśobhitam /
kalpavṛkṣaṃ mahādevi madhyasthāne vicintayet /
suvarṇa-racitaṃ nānā-ratna-sañcaya-rañjitam /
prabāla-mekhalā-yuktaṃ ghaṇṭā-cāmara-rājitam /
tanmadhye parameśāni cintayen-maṇi-vedikām /
tasyopari mahādevi maṇi-pīṭhaṃ manoharam /
śvakalpa-yantramuktaṃ tad yonirūpaṃ vicintayet /
bhrūmadhye parameśāni yaccāndraṃ pātramuttamam /
tatrastham amṛtaṃ devi tatra yonau vinikṣipet /
tenaiva vidyudākāraṃ yonimadhye vicintayet /
ākāśājjāyate vāyur-vayorutpadyate raviḥ /
raverutpadyate nīraṃ nīrād utpadyate mahī /
anenaiva vidhānena pañcabhūtātmakaṃ bhavet /
sarvendriya-samāyuktaṃ sarvāyudha-samanvitam /
sarvālaṃkara-racitaṃ devidehaṃ vicintayet /

Regarding *mānasa-pūjā*, the *Mahānirvāṇa* says (Chap. V) as follows:

hṛt-padmam āsanaṃ dadyāt sahasrāra-cyutāmṛtaiḥ /
pādyaṃ caraṇayor-dadyān-manasārghyaṃ nivedayet /
tenāmṛtenā-camanaṃ snānīyam api kalpayet /
ākāśa-tattvaṃ vasanaṃ gandhaṃ tu gandha-tattvakaṃ /
cittaṃ prakalpayet puṣpaṃ dhūpaṃ prāṇān prakalpayet /
tejastattvaṃ ca dīpārthe naivedyaṃ ca sudhāmbudhim /
anāhata-dhvaniṃ ghaṇṭāṃ vāyutattvaṃ ca cāmaram /
nṛtyam indriya-karmāṇi cāñcalyaṃ manasastathā /
puṣpaṃ nānāvidhaṃ dadyād ātmano bhāva-siddhaye /
amāyām anahaṃkāram arāgam amadaṃ tathā /
amoham adambhaṃ ca adveṣakṣobhake tathā /
amātsaryam alobham ca daśapuṣpaṃ prakirtitam /
ahiṃsāṃ paramaṃ puṣpaṃ puṣpam indriya-nigraham /
dayā-kṣamā-jñāna-puṣpaṃ pañcapuṣpaṃ tataḥ param /
iti pañcadaśaiḥ puṣpair-bhāvapuṣpaiḥ prapūjayet /
sudhāmbudhiṃ māṃsa-śailaṃ bharjitaṃ mīna-parvatam /
mudrā-rāśiṃ subhaktaṃ ca ghṛtāktaṃ pāyasaṃ tathā /

kulāmṛtaṃ ca tat puṣpaṃ pīṭha-kṣālana-vāri ca /
kāmakrodhau tu vikṛtau baliṃ datvā japaṃ caret/
mālā varṇamayī proktā kuṇḍalī sūtrayantritā/
sabinduṃ varṇam uccārya mūlamantraṃ samuccaret/
akārādi kṣakārāntam anuloma-vilomataḥ/
punar-lakāram ārabhya śrīkaṇṭhānta-manuṃ japet/
viloma iti vikhyātaḥ kṣakāro merur-ucyate/
aṣṭa-vargāntimair-varṇaiḥ saha mūlam ahāṣṭakam/
evam aṣṭottaraśatam japtvā tena samarpayet/
sarvāntarātmani laye svāhā jyotiḥ-svarūpiṇī/
gṛhāṇāntarjapaṃ mātar-ādyā kāli namo'stu te/
samarpya japam etena sāṣṭāṅgaṃ praṇamed dhiyā/

The *Prāṇatoṣiṇī* adds that, after performing *antaryajana*, one should commence *bahiḥ-pūjā*.

There is provision for *antar-homa* which is also called *jñāna-homa*. Such *homa* is performed in the vessel in the shape of *ādhāra* (*mūlādhāra* ?) with *cidagni* (fire in the form of consciousness).

Śaiva-vivāha

It has been described in the survey of the contents of the *Mahānirvāṇa-tantra*.

Recognised Subjects of Study

The *Prāṇatoṣiṇī* devotes considerable space to the determination of the subjects of study. On authority, *Vidyās* are said to be eighteen which are as follows: 4 Vedas, 4 Upavedas, 6 Vedāṅgas, Purāṇa, Nyāya, Mīmāṃsa, Dharmaśāstra. Among the Upavedas are included Āyurveda, Gāndharva, Daṇḍanīti, Dhanurveda; these are stated to belong to the following Vedas respectively: *Ṛk, Sāman, Atharvan, Yajus. Darśanas* are Bauddha, Śaiva, Brāhma, Saura, Vaiṣṇava, Śākta. It is also said that, at present (at the time of the author), the following are recognised as *Darśanas*: Vedānta, Sāṃkhya, Mīmāṃsā, Viśeṣa (i.e. Vaiśeṣika), Tarkaśāstra. *Yoga* is conspicuous by its absence. *Cārvāka-darśana* has been characterised as *ati-garhita* (extremely reprehensible). Bauddhaśāstra has been stated to have been propounded by Viṣṇu, in the form of the Buddha, for the destruction of the demons.

Regarding *Ānvīkṣikī*, the author cites authority which condemns it and regards its study as extremely sinful. Authority has been quoted also in support of the study of it. By examining several texts, condemning and commending it, the author comes to the conclusion that *Ānvīkṣikī* has a twofold connotation—*Tarka-vidyā* and *Ātma-vidyā*. *Ātma-vidyā* is, of course, commended. The author seeks to establish that *Tarka-vidyā* as such is not condemned. *Ānvīkṣikī*, which is allowed, does not refer to *Tarka-vidyā*, or *Nyāya-śāstra* propounded by Gautama, but that taught by Dattātreya. By examining certain texts, the author comes to the conclusion that *Tarka-vidyā* as such is not forbidden. If it is studied without any conflict with the import of *āmnāya* (accepted tradition or conventional texts), then it is conducive to welfare. Otherwise, the mere learning of Gautama's *Śāstra*, without any relation to traditional knowledge, will make a person suspicious in all the rites and rituals.

On the authority of the *Meru-tantra*[42] and the *Niruttara-tantra*,[43] *Āgama* (=Tantra) is said to be a Vedāṅga and the fifth Veda respectively.

Sthāpatya (architecture) has been recognised on the authority of Śaṃkarācārya. It means *Viśvakarma-śāstra* which includes *Śāstras* teaching the construction of house, *vāstu, kuṇḍa*, etc.

The author of the *Prāṇatoṣiṇī* concludes that various arts (*śilpa*) like *Kāma-śāstra, Nāṭya-śāstra*, etc., also come within the purview of the approved subjects of study, because these are said to be recognised by Tantra.[44] From the discusson in the *Prāṇatoṣiṇī* it appears that a distinction is made between *Vidyā* and *Śāstra*. While *Vidyās* are the eighteen, enumerated above, all others are included in *Śāstra*.

Deha-tattva

We have said elsewhere that Tantra looks upon the body as the primary requisite of all kinds of *sādhana*. So, attempts have been made to analyse the various elements constituting the body, the bones, flesh, sinews, veins, arteries, various organs, internal and external. Thus, we find anatomy and physiology in Tantra. The entire process of a man's life, since gestation till death, has been analysed. Means have been prescribed to keep the body fit in every way. Torture of the body by penance, as is usually prescribed in the Brahmanical Dharmaśāstra, is not ordinarily countenanced by Tantra.

In the spirit of Tantra in general, the Bengali authors look upon the body as a microcosm. Whatever exists in *brahmāṇḍa* (universe) is found in the *piṇḍa* (body).[45] All the holy places, even gods, are said to reside in the body.

When *sādhana* is properly done, and the mysteries are mastered, one gets an adamantine body (*vajra-deha*) which is not decayed by disease, heat, cold, hunger and thirst. The possessor of such a body can achieve many things at will.

Śava-Sādhana

Śava-sādhana (worship on a corpse) plays an important role in the Tāntric system of worship in Bengal. On the authority of the *Bhāvacūḍāmaṇi*, Kṛṣṇānanda prescribes the following places as suitable for this rite.

> Empty house, river-bank, mountain, lonely spot, root of a bel tree, cemetery, place near a cemetery, battlefield.

The suitable time is the darkness of the night in the eighth and fourteenth lunar mansions of both the bright and dark fortnights. Tuesday is mentioned as propitious for the purpose.

It appears that dead bodies of both human beings and beasts can be used for the purpose. Among human beings, Brāhmaṇas and of the beasts cows are prohibited. Corpses are described as *mahā-śavas*, and are stated to be most suitable in such *sādhana*.[46] Of the human beings, the following are prescribed:

> A Caṇḍāla, dead as a result of being struck with sticks, swords, spears, etc., drowning, struck by thunder, snake-bite, injury; a handsome bright young hero, killed in battle while facing the opposite party, but not escaping.[47]

Forbidden among human beings are woman, thsoe who committed suicide, hen-pecked persons (*strīvaśya*), the apostate (*patita*), the untouchable (*aspṛśya*[48]), beardless men (*tubara*), those whose genital organs are not clearly visible,[49] lepers, the old, those who died in a famine, stale corpses.

Kṛṣṇānanda adds that, according to other Tantras, in the want of the corpses prescribed above, one should perform the rite on an effigy made of *darbha* grass (*darbha-śava*) or barley, rice, etc. (*yava-piṣṭakādinā*). In the absence of suitable carcasses, the body of any animal (*jantumātr*) or a tiny body (*kṣudra-śava*) may be selected.

If, in such *sādhana*, nothing is obtained by the *sādhaka* till midnight, then he should scatter sesamum, walk seven steps and perform *japa*. He should continue *japa* with great concentration so long as the corpse or carcass does not promise to give the desired object or grant a boon. After the purpose of the *sādhaka* is served, he should release the hairs and feet of the dead body, which were tied before commencement of *sādhana*. Then, having washed and bathed it, he should throw it into water or bury it and cast off the articles of worship into water. Last of all, he should bathe and go home. Next day, he should make offerings of these things wanted by those whom he worshipped overnight. The other rites, connected with this *sādhana*, are the drinking of *pañca-gavya*, feeding of twenty-five Brāhmaṇas. God is supposed to reside in the body of such a *sādhaka* for fifteen days since the commencement of *sādhana*. During this period, he is asked not to enjoy his wife, hear songs and witness dance.

Yoginī-sādhana

The worship of Yoginīs occupies a considerable space in Bengal Tantra. According to the *Tantrasāra*, Surasundarī is the foremost of Yoginīs by worshipping whom Kubera is said to have been the lord of wealth. Her appearance is as follows: face like the full moon, complexion white, wearing variegated dress, breasts plump and heaving, she is to be fancied as granting freedom from fear. Meditated upon for a month and duly worshipped on the concluding day of the month, she is stated to appear before the devotee at midnight. She appears only if she knows him to be of firm resolve.

The devotee may worhsip her as a mother, sister or wife. Worshipped as mother, she bestows riches and various other articles, even kingdom, on him, and comes daily and protects him like his mother; looked upon as sister, she gives various things including divine damsels, and takes care of him like a brother. Regarded as wife, she enables him to know the past, present and future, and by her grace he becomes superior even to kings. Moreover, he can traverse everywhere in heaven, on earth and in the nether regions. In union with her, he will enjoy bliss and shall avoid association with other women.

Bhāvas

Tāntric *bhāvas* are attitudes[50] and ways of life. A *bhāva* indicates the habits and practices of a person. Three *bhāvas* are stated in Bengal Tantra. These are *Divya, Vīra* and *Paśu*.

The *Prāṇatoṣiṇī* lays down that, of the *bhāvas, Paśu* is the worst, *Vīra* medium and *Dīvya* best. On the authority of the *Vāmakeśvara-tantra*, it is said that one has *Paśu-bhāva* from birth till the sixteenth year of age. Then a person has *Vīra-bhāva* up to his fifteenth year; for the rest of life he gets *Divya-bhāva*. The *bhāvas* are said to follow one another as boyhood is succeeded by youth and the latter by old age. *Divya-bhāva* is stated to be threefold—caused by Veda, produced by *āgama* and generated by *viveka* (discriminatory knowledge). The first is said to be the worst, the second medium and the third best.

It is further stated that one has to assume *Paśu-bhāva* during the first ten *daṇḍas* of the day. In ten *daṇḍas* at midday, he should have *Vīra-bhāva*. During ten *daṇḍas* from evening one should have *Divya-bhāva*. Again, it is ordained that from birth one should worship deities with *Paśu-bhāva*. Then if *Vidyās* are pleased, then a person should adopt *Vīra-bhāva*. Through the grace of *Vīra-bhāva* he will have *Divya-bhāva*.

Even a person with *Paśu-bhāva* is said to be capable of attaining *Siddhi* provided he always studies and ponders the Veda, abjures speaking ill of others, violence, idleness, greed, delusion and the six internal enemies.

The *Mahānirvāṇa* (iv. 19) states that, in the Kali Age, *Paśu-bhāva* is absent and *Divya-bhāva* scarce. In this age, *Vīra-sādhana* alone is conducive to direct effect.[51] This work, however, advocates *Kulācāra* as superior to all else.

None of the Tantra writers of Bengal appears to have clearly defined the above *bhāvas*. We can, however, gather their characteristics from other sources.

In *Paśu-bhāva* one takes to apparently sensuous and frightful rites. The *Vīra* way is prescribed only for heroic persons who are not deterred in the performance of such rites as sitting on a corpse in a cemetery in a dark night and performing *sādhana* with absolute concentration. A *Vīra* has unflinching zeal in all situations in his search for the eternal soul. In him there is a complete absence of the idea of dualism.[52] *Vīra* and *Divya* have very much in common with the only difference that while the former is haughty, the latter is *śānta* (tranquil), *vinīta* (modest), *madhura* (charming), *kalā-lāvaṇya-saṃyuta* (endowed with *kalā* and grace) and *devavat* (God-like).[53] *Vīras* are threefold, the distinction between the different types being based on the degree of devotional fervour.

It should be noted that some Tantras condemn *Vīra-bhāva* for Brāhmaṇas. According to one Tantra,[54] *Paśu-bhāva* alone should be adopted by them.

Cakra-pūjā

Cakra occupies a very important position in Bengal Tantra. The term literally means 'circle'. In Tantra it came to mean also certain figures and depressions within the human body, conceived for mystical purposes. The term, as used in Bengal Tantra, has threefold connotation.

A. *Cakras* relating to the examination of *mantras* for initiation. These are

(i) *A KA ḌA MA*—Tantrasāra, Śrītattva-cintāmaṇi
(ii) *A KA THA HA* Do
(iii) *Ṛnadhana* Do
(iv) *Kulākula* Do
(v) *Kūrma* Do
(vi) *Nakṣatra* Do
(vii) *Rāśi* Do
(viii) *Varga*—Śrītattva-cintāmaṇi

B. *Cakras* relating to *Yoga*.

These are supposed to be within the human body.[55]

These are as follows, one upon the other —

(i) *Mūlādhara*: Space measuring two fingers between the anus and the genital organ. In it *Kuṇḍalinī* resides.
(ii) *Svādhiṣṭhāna*: A six-petalled lotus in the Suṣumṇā at the root of the genital organ.
(iii) *Maṇipura*: Navel-lotus.
(iv) *Anāhata*: A twelve-petalled lotus in the Suṣumṇā inside the heart.
(v) *Viśuddha*: A sixteen-petalled lotus in the throat.
(vi) *Ājñākhya*: The fontanelle or union of the coronal and sagittal sutures.
(vii) *Sahasrāra*: A sort of cavity said to exist in the top of the head and to resemble a thousand-petalled lotus reversed. Supposed to be the seat of the soul.

Different faculties and deities are supposed to reside in the above *Cakras*. *Ṣaṭcakra-bheda* or *Cakrabheda*[56] denotes the highest stage of *Tāntric sādhana*.

C. Assembly of *Tāntric Sādhakas*.

Bhairavī-cakra and Tattva-cakra

These *Cakras* mean assemblies of Tāntrikas, in which certain rites are performed. The *Bhairavī-cakra*, as described in the *Mahānirvāṇa-tantra* (vii. 154-176), is briefly as follows.

On a beautiful spot (*ramyabhūmi*), the Kulācārya will spread out a seat, purify it with the *mantra Kāmādya astrabīja* (i.e. *klīṃ phaṭ*,- and sit on it. With vermilion, red sandal-paste or with water a triangular *maṇḍala*, and outside it a rectangular *maṇḍala*, should be drawn. The *Sādhaka* will then bring a variegated pitcher which will be filled in succession with curd and *ātapa* rice, fruits and leaves and perfumed water. Then it will be marked with vermilion, and reciting *praṇava* it will be placed on that *maṇḍala* (the outer one?). In front of it should be placed a lamp and burning incense. Having placed sandal-paste and flowers, and meditated upon the desired deity, one should perform a brief *pūjā*. In this rite, nine vessels for *guru*, etc., are not necessary. The worshipper will place the intended *tattva* before him, sprinikle water over it with the *astra* (i.e. *mantra phaṭ*) and look at it with winkless eyes. Then having put flowers and sandal-paste on the drinking vessel, he will meditate upon goddess Ānanda-bhairavī and Ānanda-bhairava. After meditation, he will reflelct upon the unity of the above two deities in the vessel. Then uttering the *nāma mantra*, beginning with *praṇava* and ending in *namas*, and worshipping with sandal-paste and flowers he should purify the wine. The *Kula* worshipper will purify wine by reciting for hundred and eight times the threefold *bīja pāśa*, etc., ending with *svāhā* (i.e. the *mantra āṃ hrīṃ kroṃ svāhā*). This will be followed by the purification, with the above *mantra* recited one hundred times, of meat, etc. Then having thought that all the articles collected are pervaded by Brahmaṇ, one should shut the eyes, offer the articles to Kālī and eat and drink the same.

While in a *Cakra*, one must abjure fickleness, gossip, garrulity, spitting, etc.

Those who are wicked, cruel, sinful, atheistic, speak ill of a *Kula* or follow *paśvācāra* must be expelled from a *Cakra*.

A *Sādhaka*, possessed of true knowledge, will acquire the same merit, by reciting the *mantra* only once in a *Cakra*, as is obtained by a hundred *puraścaraṇas* on *Śavāsana*, *Muṇḍāsana* or *Citāsana*.

By performing the *Cakra* for six months, one can be a king for one year, one can overcome death and by its daily performance one gets liberation. This *Cakra* is stated to be the sole means to the ends of *bhukti* and *mukti*.

Tattva-cakra, also called *Divya-cakra* or *Brahma-cakra*, is regarded as the best among *Cakras* (*cakra-rāja*). (*Mahānirvāṇa-tantra*, vii. 203 ff). Only the *Sādhaka*, possessed of the knowledge of Brahman, is entitled to it. In this rite, there is no provision for the placing of a pitcher and the prolixity of *pūjā*.

The leader of the *Cakra* (*Cakreśvara*) will be a person with his mind fixed on Brahman. He will start the *Cakra* along with *Sādhakas* versed in the knowledge of Brahman. He will sit on a pure and pleasant spot with them, have the *tattvas* brought there and place the same in front. The leader will recite the *mantra*, beginning with *tārā* (i.e. *Om*) and ending in *prāṇabīja* (i.e. *haṃsa*), for a hundred times, over each of the *tattvas*, and then utter the following *mantra* thrice or seven times:

brahmārpaṇaṃ brahmahavir-brahmāgnau brahmaṇā hutam /
brahmaiva tena gantavyaṃ brahma-karma-samādhinā //

Bhagavadgītā (iv. 24)

[(For him) the act of offering is God, the oblation is God, by God is it offered into the fire of God. God is that which is to be attained by him who realises God in his works. Radhakrishnan.] Having thus sanctified the *tattvas*, and consecrated the same to Brahman, he should eat and drink the same with other *Sādhakas*.

It is interesting to note that practices similar, in some respects to *Cakra-pūjā*, prevailed also in some countries of Europe. Some think that this practice was borrowed from the Dravidians of India.[57]

In such a rite in the European countries, *Bacchus* and his consort used to be worshipped by men and women who assembled at a place. A few people worshipped them with austerity and restraint. But, in most cases, at dead of night, men and women used to indulge in unrestrained drinking and promiscuous sexual intercourse. History records such a practice resorted to by the mother of Alexander the Great (4th cent. B.C.).

Yoga

Yoga plays a prominent part in Tantra. Quoting authorities, Kṛṣṇānanda defines and emphasises the importance of *yoga* in the following manner. *Yoga* is stated to be salvation in crossing rebirths (*saṃsārottaraṇe muktir-yoga-śabdena kathyate*). *Yoga* is also described as the identification of the individual with *ātman* (*aikyaṃ vātmanorā-*

hur-yogam). For the realisation of Brahman the practice of both *mantra* and *jñāna* is necessary: success in *Yoga*, is not possible without *mantra* (*na mantreṇa vinā yogaḥ*).

The following are the main types of *yoga* dealt with in Bengal Tantra. We shall name the broad types of *yoga*, state the names of the works dealing with them and set forth briefly the principal characteristics of them.

A. Jñāna-yoga: *Prāṇatoṣiṇī*. It consists in the constant meditation on the Brahman as the one single reality and on the fact that the universe is His manifestation.

B. Mantra-yoga: *Prāṇatoṣiṇī*. Also *Tantrasāra*. It is the designation of the repeated recitation, in the proper manner, of *mantras* followed by *Aṅganyāsa*, etc.

C. Rājayoga: *Prāṇatoṣiṇī*. It consists in the meditation on the six *Cakras, Mūlādhāra*, etc., as connected with *Iḍā, Piṅgalā, Suṣumṇā*.

D. Laya-yoga: *Prāṇatoṣiṇī*. Meditation on the luminous Brahman in the thousand-petalled lotus in the head, after fixing the sight on the tip of the nose or between the eye-brows.

E. Haṭha-yoga: *Prāṇatoṣiṇī*. Performance of the six acts, *Dhauti*, etc., after practising *Pūraka, Kumbhaka, Recaka* in the regular and reverse order in accordance with the rules of *Prāṇāyāma*.

Position of Women and Śūdras

Bengal Tantra accords an exalted place to women. A woman has equality of right with a man in Tāntric *dīkṣa* and other Tāntric rites. Most of the disabilities, to which she is subjected, in the performance of Vedic rites and the recitation of Vedic mantras, have been done away with in Tantra.

To a man his wife is indispensable. A man without wife is like a bird with one wing, a chariot with one wheel. He is debarred from all rites; he cannot be a *gṛhastha*. So, one must get a wife even at the cost of everything (*sarvasvenāpi kartavyo dārasaṃgrahaḥ*).

Ordinarily the father cannot initiate his son to Tāntric *dīkṣā*. But, this restriction does not apply to the mother. In fact, the mother is the best *guru*. A *mantra*, taught by a woman, does not require purification like ordinary *mantras*.

The woman is not only necessary but indispensable for a man in the performance of Tāntric *Sādhana*. Of the five *tattvas*, essential for this purpose, the fifth one, viz. *maithuna*, in the gross sense of the term, is not possible without her. Her position is so high in this matter that she has the honoured designation of *Śakti, Prakṛti, Bhairavī*, etc.

From the *Tantrasāra* we learn that, in the rite *Puraścaraṇa* for *Vīras*, another man's wife can be worshipped. On the authority of the *Gupta-sādhana-tantra*, the *Prāṇatoṣiṇī* holds that, in *Kula-sādhana*, one's own wife or the wife of another person is necessary. A woman of any one of the following classes can be the Śakti for this purpose: Brāhmaṇa, Kṣatriya, Vaiśya, Śūdra, prostitute,[58] barber, washerman and dancing woman.[59] It is further provided that a *Kula* woman of any caste can be the *Śakti* provided she has special accomplishment (*viśeṣa-vaidagdhya*). In the absence of the women of above classes, one is asked to worship any one of the following, each preceding in the list being considered to be better than the succeeding one: daughter, younger sister, elder sister, maternal aunt, mother, step-mother. In the absence of even these women, any woman can be worshipped.

In Smṛti, Vedic *mantras* are not allowed to be recited by women. But, to all Tāntric *mantras* women are equally entitled with men.

Maiden girls, irrespective of caste, are held in high esteem; so much so that their worship (*kumārī-pūjā*) on certain festive occasions is regarded as a bounden duty. Great merit is stated to be acquired by a person who arranges, at his cost, for the marriage of a maiden girl.

Among the disabilities of women, according to Tantra, some are as follows: *Sāvitrī, praṇava*, (i.e. *oṃkāra*), *Lakṣmī-bīja* (i.e. Śrī)—these are tabooed for women. Women are debarred from worshipping, even touching, *śālagrāma* stones.

In certain matters, women are regarded as inferior to men. For example, the dead body of a woman is condemned for *Śava-sādhana*. Again, the corpse of a henpecked (*strī-vaśya*) man is excluded for this purpose.

The *Mahānirvāṇa* (Chap. xi) vehemently denounces the enjoyment of others' wives and sexual intercourse of women with others' husbands. A man shall maintain his wife even if she is raped by another man; in such a case, she will be deprived of conjugal rights over her husband. A man shall be sentenced to death if he forcibly enjoys even a Caṇḍāla woman. If a man finds that his wife has relation with a paramour, then he will desert her, but will be liable to her maintenance provided she abides by his directions.

A girl, married by an eunuch, should be married to a normal person even if a long time expires since the first marriage.

A girl, widowed before associating with her husband, should be married again.

A woman, giving birth to a mature child within six months of marriage or one soon after the death of her husband, will be subjected to social ostracism.

Destruction of the foetus and abetment of the same have been severely condemned.

A widow is required by the *Mahānirvāṇa* to live a life of austerity and self-restraint.

A woman, married according to *Śaiva-vivāha*, is not entitled to the property of her parents (*Mahānirvāṇa*, xii. 60).

The honoured position, accorded to women, is not surprising in a system which regards *Śakti* as the highest divinity. One may think that the predominance of the female sex perhaps points to the matriarchal society in which Tantra may have originated. From this point of view, it may not be quite unjustified to presume that Tantra owes its origin to non-Aryans among whom matriarchy was the commonest pattern. Even today, many aboriginal tribes regard the mother as the supreme personality, indeed the pivot round whom the family moves. A comparison of the society, reflected in the post-Vedic period, particularly the period of Dharma-śāstra, and that envisaged in Tantra reveals that the misogynic tendencies, noticeable in the former, are absent in the latter. Though Manu accords the mother an exalted position, even higher than that of the father,[60] with respect to the son, yet he prohibits religious rites for women independently of their husbands.[61] This attitude is clearly contrary to that of Tantra which allows all Tāntric rites to women subject to limited restrictions, and speaks of initiation by mother as the best. It should, however, be noted that, despite a very honourable position given to women in Tantra, the husband is regarded as a woman's *mahāguru* or the most superior person.

For Tāntric *dīkṣā* Śūdras are equally eligible as members of the highter castes. No disability, attached to the Śūdras, attaches to a Śūdra who is *pūrṇābhiṣikta*. Such a Śūdra can even worship a *Śālagrāma*, recite *praṇava* and perform *homa*. Even a Brāhmaṇa can worship the *Śālagrāma* touched by such a Śūdra. A Śūdra of the above description is entitled to the study of Tantras. The attitude of the Bengali Tāntrikas is that unless a Śūdra becomes free from *aṣṭapāśas* or the eight frailties to which flesh is heir, he cannot enjoy the above privileges even if he is *pūrṇābhiṣikta*.

A Śūdra *kumārī* may be worshipped even by a Brāhmaṇa who can take her *prasāda*.

A Śūdra *Avadhūta* is worthy of salutation by even a Brāhmaṇa.

Tantra has done away with many of the disabilities to which Śūdras are subjected in Smṛti. A Śūdra also is entitled to Tāntric *dīkṣā* and *Śiva-pūjā*. To *Kulācāra* a Śūdra has the same right as that of the upper classes. Among the disabilities of Śūdras, according to Tantra, mention may be made of the fact that they are not allowed to worship or even touch a *Śālagrāma* stone. They can, however, worship it through a Brāhmaṇa. A Śūdra is debarred from reciting the following: *Sāvitrī* (i.e. Vedic *Gāyatrī*), *praṇava* (i.e. *Oṃkāra*). *Lakṣmī-bīja* (i.e. *Śrī*). The *guru* is forbidden to give the following to a Śūdra: *ātma-mantra, guru-mantra, ajapā-mantra, mantra* containing *svāhā*. A Śūdra is allowed to adopt the *mantras* of Gopāla, Maheśvara, Durgā, Sūrya and Gaṇeśa and not of any other deity.

Curbs on Self-indulgence

Tantra advocates the attainment of the goal through enjoyment (*bhoga*) and not by rigorous asceticism. One should not suppose that Tantra encourages levity, lasciviousness or debauchery. We shall point out a few curbs on self-indulgence ordained in Bengal Tantra.

In connexion with *pañcatattva*, we have noticed that wine is condemned in early Tantra for Brāhmaṇas. For them *anukalpa* (substitute) is prescribed. Kṣatriyas and Vaiśyas are allowed to drink only special kinds of wine. Drinking of wine appears to have been compulsory only for *Saṃnyāsins*. The *Mahānirvāṇa* clearly declares that householders (*gṛhastha*) should use *madhutraya* (i.e. milk, sugar and honey) instead of wine. Excessive drinking has been strongly prohibited. According to the *Mahānirvāṇa*, a *Kula* woman should not drink wine, the smell of it is sufficient for her. It appears that wine, which is not consecrated (*asaṃskṛta*) is prohibited. Even when a Brāhmaṇa is allowed to drink wine, he should not do so before undergoing the rite of *abhiṣeka*.

Indiscriminate eating of meat is also forbidden. Of the different beasts, birds and aquatic creatures, only a few are specified. The same remark is applicable to fish.

As regards women, to be associated with or enjoyed by a *Sādhaka*, it should be stated that, while a wide range of choice is allowed, it is ordained that only an initiated woman serves the purpose. Again, one *Sādhaka* is allowed to resort to one woman only. In connexion with

Śaiva-vivāha, the *Mahānirvāṇa* (i. 279) ordains that a man, desiring issue, should meet his wife, but leave her with the expiry of the *Cakra*-period. The *Mahānirvāṇa* strongly condemns the enjoyment of others' wives and sexual union of women with others' husband. A man committing rape on even a *Cāṇḍāla* woman deserves death-penalty.

Thus, we find a spirit of restrained enjoyment of the luxuries of life as a means to the end. Licence has never been granted for the free gratification of the senses.

Bengal Tantra vis-à-vis Dharmaśāstra

The Tantras of Bengal reveal notable departures from the conventional Brahmanical rites and practices laid down in Dharmaśāstra. We shall point out below the marked differences between the two in connexion with certain important matters only.

As regards Varṇāśrama-dharma, we have already noted the salient features of Tantra, which are unconventional. We have noticed also that certain articles are not defiled by the touch of persons regarded as untouchable in Smṛti.

Regarding forms of marriage, the *Mahānirvāṇa* appears to recognise (viii. 150) only *Brāhma-vivāha* among the eight forms stated in Smṛti. It, however, provides also for *Śaiva-vivāha*[62] for the followers of Tantra; the woman, married according to this rite, is commended for all work in *Cakras* called *Bhairavī* and *Tattva*. For other purposes, the woman, married according to the *brāhma* rite, is said to be the most suitable. As stated in connexion with *Śaiva-vivāha* under the *Mahānirvāṇa-tantra*, both *anuloma* and *pratiloma* marriages condemned in Smṛti, are allowed.

Though, in Smṛti, a son born out of *pratiloma* union is regarded with contempt and considered as untouchable, yet according to the *Mahānirvāṇa*, he belongs to the *Sāmānya* caste. According to Smṛti, a man must marry a girl who is not his *sagotrā*, but in *Śaiva-vivāha* a *sagotrā* girl appears to be allowed. Though, in later Smṛti, marriage with a girl of a different caste is not allowed Tantra appears to allow such a marriage. The *Prāṇatoṣiṇī* quotes an authority to say that for a Brāhmaṇa, a wife of the same caste is *dharma-patnī* while one of a different caste is *kāma-patnī*.

Tāntric *dīkṣā* is not ordained by early Smṛti. Again, the provision that women are very suitable as *gurus* and that mother is the best, runs counter to the general attitude of Dharmaśāstra writers.

Purohita is considered to be the best person to serve as one's proxy in the Smārta rites. But, in a Tāntric *pūjā*, *Guru* is to be engaged. Other persons are vehemently condemned.[63]

In connexion with *Kumārī-pūjā*, it is provided that a *kumārī* of any caste, even the daughter of a washerman, barber, a Cāṇḍāla, can be selected for the purpose.[64] A *Kula-strī*[65] of any caste, versed in Tantra and *mantra*, even if she be a prostitute, is to be saluted.

No caste-distinction is to be observed by one who is *pūrṇābhiṣikta*.

The *Śrītattva-cintāmaṇi* prescribes (xxi. 1f) atonement for the sins arising out of *brahma-hatyā* (murder of Brāhmaṇas), etc. It states *brahma-hatyādi*, but does not enumerate all the sins. It, however, seems that the author recognises the sins stated in Smṛti-śāstra. In Smṛti, sins have been divided into several classes, called *Mahāpātaka, Upapātaka*, etc., in accordance with their gravity. The *Mahāpātakas* are five, viz. *brahma-hatyā* (murder of a Brāhmaṇa), *surāpāna* (drinking of wine), *steya* (theft[66]), *gurvaṅganāgama* (adultery with the wife of one's preceptor) and *saṃsarga* (association with the perpetrators of the above four kinds of offence).

The *Mahānirvāṇa* (x. 205) states the five perpetrators of *Mahāpātakas* as—*vīraghātī* (murder of one who is technically called *Vīra*[67]), *vṛthāpāyī* (drinker of unconsecrated wine), *Vīrāṇāṃ strīgama* (one who commits adultery with the wife of a *Vīra*), *steyī* (thief), *tatsaṃsargi* (one who associates with the above four).

The *Prāṇatoṣiṇī* (Kāṇḍa iv, Pariccheda ii) appears to include the following under *Mahāpātaka; vīravadha* (murder of a *Vīra*), *vṛthāpāna* (drinking of unconsecrated wine), *gurusnuṣāgamana* (adultery with preceptor's daughter-in-law), *vīrapatnīgamana* (adultery with the wife of a *Vīra*), *mantra-putrīgamana* (adultery with the daughter of preceptor). The author mentions several other sins of a less grave nature, with their corresponding expiatory rites.

As regards expiation of the sin of the *Mahāpātaka* and other types, Pūrṇānanda ordains the worship of goddess Śivā in a *Cakra*[68] made with all *raśmis* (colour ?), beautified with camphor-dust. The worship is to be done with red flowers, particularly *Javā* flowers, in accordance with *Kulācāra*. Such worship continuously for three months is stated to wash off crores of *Mahāpātakas*. Some other fragrant flowers are also recommended.

Expiation is prescribed for one for the sin incurred by deserting one's *guru*. The atonement, in such a case, is the repetition of a *mantra* for one lac times and the performance of *homa* and *tarpaṇa*. The *Śyāmārahasya* ordains that this expiatory rite applies to the desertion of *gurus* of the *divya* and *vīra* types. For a *Kulaśiṣya*, the desertion of the *guru* of the *paśu* type is but a duty. The *Prāṇatoṣiṇī* holds that it is not correct; because *Kaulikas* are exempted from *prāyaścitta*. On authority, the latter work makes it clear that the deserter of a *paśuguru* is not liable to *prāyaścitta* at all.

Both the *Mahānirvāṇa* and the *Prāṇatoṣiṇī* make a distinction between sin committed with and without knowledge; the punishment for the former is, of course, heavier than that for the latter. Both these works give a rather exhaustive penal code. The offences appear to be twofold, viz. those which harm others and those which cause harm to the perpetrator himself. For the offences of the former kind, the *Mahānirvāṇa* prescribes also punishment by the king besides the expiatory rites. For grave sins, committed without knowledge, the *Prāṇatoṣiṇī* ordains the repetition of the *mūlamantra* for thirteen thousand times. For washing off the sin resulting from offences, wilfully committed, one has to repeat the *mantra* for a lac of times. It is interesting to note that the *Prāṇatoṣiṇī* states bath in the Ganges at holy places like Nandā as capable of redeeming a man even from *mahāpātakas*.

Tantra makes a notable departure in recognising the *Atharvaveda* as a subject of study among the Vedic Saṃhitās. But Dharmaśāstra excludes it, and recognises the Vedic triad,[69] viz. *Ṛgveda, Yajurveda* and *Sāmaveda*.

In Smṛti, *Ucchiṣṭa*, i.e. the remnant of ones' food, is condemned as impure. But, in certain Tāntric rites, e.g. *Bhairava-cakra* and *Tattva-cakra*, ones' *ucchiṣṭa* is allowed to be taken by another.

In Smṛti, the enjoyment by a person of others' wives and of women of other castes is severely condemned. In Tantras, this practice appears to be allowed in certain Tāntric rites. But, the *Mahānirvāṇa* (viii. 173) unequivocally prohibits it in the Kali Age for householders. The reason, underlying the prohibition, is that, in this Age, people are prone to lasciviousness and lack of self-control. For them substitutes are prescribed.[70]

Regarding daily prayer, those who are entitled to *Vaidikī sandhyā* are asked in Tantra to perfom *Tāntrikī sandhyā* too. The latter is ordained for all initiates. The followers of conventional practices have to recite the Vedic Gāyatrī. But, one, initiated to Tāntrism, has to recite also the Tāntric Gāyatri. While Smṛti required the *dvijas* to say Vedic prayer daily, Tantra ordains that it may be given up by a Tāntric initiate who takes recourse to the *Śaiva* way.

No conventional Śāstric injunctions and prohibitions are applicable in the case of one who performs *Brahma-sādhana*.

It has been pointed out, in connexion with *Varṇāśrama-dharma* that, contrary to Smṛti, Tantra recognises a caste, called *Sāmānya*, in addition to the four usual castes. Not only this. The *Mahānirvāṇa* allows (viii. 113) a man of this caste to take to the avocations of any caste other than a Brāhmaṇa, for livelihood.

Contrary to the rules of Smṛti, if a person taking to *brahma-mantra* so desires, his dead body may be thrown into water or buried instead of being burnt (*Mahānirvāṇa*, x. 81).

According to Smṛti, the drinking of certain special kinds of wine, branded as *surā*, causes very grave sin, particularly on the part of Brāhmaṇas. But, the *Prāṇatoṣiṇī* not only allows *surāpāna* to a Tāntric *Sādhaka*, but regards *surā* as the best kind of wine (*surā-madyaṃ sarveśām uttamam*).

NOTES

1. Regarding the significance of the terms and requisite qualities, see accounts of the contents of the *Tantrasāra, Śritattva-cintāmaṇi* and *Prāṇatoṣiṇī*.
2. Vide *Prāṇatoṣiṇī*, Kāṇḍa II, Pariccheda ii.
3. Vide *Prāṇatoṣiṇī*, Kāṇḍa II, Pariccheda ii.
4. It may be pointed out that the *Mahābhārata* allows the desertion of the *guru* in the circumstances stated in the following stanza:
   guror-apy-avaliptasya kāryākāryam ajānataḥ/
   utpatha-pratipannasya parityāgo vidhīyate// Śānti 57/7 cr. edn.
   [The abandonment is ordained of even the preceptor who is proud, ignorant of what should or should not be done (or) who has gone astray.]
5. For details, see under *Śritattva-cintāmaṇi, supra*.
6. See Glossary.
7. cf. *mantrār-canā-sana-nyāsa-dhyāno-pacārakādibhiḥ.*
8. It is thus defined.
   gandhair maṇḍalakaṃ svīyair-vidadhyād dakṣiṇe kare/
   vidhinā tva-rcayed devam itthaṃ syāc-chivahastakam//

[With own perfumed substances (sandal-pasted) one should draw a figure on the right palm (then) worship God according to rule; thus becomes *Śivahasta* (the hand of Śiva).]

9. See in connexion with the contents of the *Śrītattva-cīntāmaṇi*.
10. *Kuṇḍa* is a vessel in which *homa* is performed. *Sthaṇḍila* means sacrificial ground of a vessel used for the purpose.
11. For a lucid description of the devotee in this stage, see *Guru-tantra* — *Saṃśaya-nirāsa*, pp. 20-25.
12. *ādau kālī tatas-tārā sundarī tad anantaram/ kramadīkṣeti vikhyātā.../*
13. cf. *na dadyād brāhmaṇo madyaṃ mahādevyai kathaṃcana / vāmakāmo brāhmaṇo hi madyamāṃsaṃ na bhakṣayet //*
    [A Brāhmaṇa should, by no means, offer wine to Great Goddess. A Brāhmaṇa, desiring (to practise) *Vāmācāra*, should not take wine and meat.]
14. *Makaranda* means juice of flowers. But, the use of *phala* leads one to think that it may be *mākanda* which may mean a mango tree or a myrobalan tree.
15. Some *mantras* are prescribed for removing the curse with which wine is supposed to be tainted.
16. See Glossary.
17. It is interesting to note that Manu (V. 55) derives the word as *māṃ sa bhakṣayitāmutra* (the creature whose meat I eat will eat me in the next world.) This implies his general disapproval of meat-eating. Manu (V. 39), however ordains that the killing of an animal in a sacrifice amounts to non-slaughter.
18. cf. *mahākalyā mahāpīṭhe yatra kutra maheśvari /*
    balidānaṃ narasyāpi haṭhād bādhā bhaviṣyati /
    nivṛttaṃ hi tato devi balidānaṃ narādikam /
19. *na dadyād brāhmaṇo madyaṃ mānuṣam ca etc. Matsya-sūkta* quoted in the *Prāṇatoṣiṇī*.
    [A Brāhmaṇa should not offer wine and a human being.]
20. cf. *ekāṃ śaktiṃ samānīya eka eva tu sādhakaḥ /*
    pūjayed bahuyatnena pañcatattvena kaulikaḥ //
    [One Kaulika should worship, with much care, and five *Tattvas* (i.e. *pañca makāras*), having brought a single *Śakti*.]
21. Also see three kinds in the description of the contents of the *Śrītattva-cintāmaṇi*.
22. Vide Glossary.

23. *Āsana* on human skulls.
24. Also see discussion on this topic in connexion with *Pūjā* in Chapter V.
25. For a clear description, see *Puraścaraṇa-ratnākara*, p. 152.
26. The space in between two lines in a finger.
27. cf. *tadabhāve tu kasyāpi kartavyā-vayavasya vai*. Does *avayava* mean a part of the skull or of the body?
28. But, see 'even a Brāhmaṇa' above.
29. Various *Siddhis* have been stated in the résumé of the contents of *Bengal Tantra*.
30. See in connexion with the contents of the *Śrītattva-cintāmaṇi*.
31. Vide *Tantrasāra*, p. 224 (Vaṅgavāsī Ed.)
32. The topic has been briefly dealt with in connexion with the account of the *Śrītattva-cintāmaṇi*.
33. Name of a sub-caste in Bengal.
34. The word *bali* denotes offering in general, and not necessarily animal-sacrifice.
35. On beef-eating in ancient India, see P.V. Kane, *History of Dharmaśāstra*, Vol. II, pp. 545, 772, 773, 776-7, etc., and the present author's *Dharmasūtras—a study*, etc., pp. 155 ff.
36. It is interesting to note that authoritative texts, quoted in Bengal digests on *durgā-pūjā*, include human beings among the things to be sacrificed before Durgā. This *Pūjā* appears to have been borrowed from or influenced by non-Aryans. Human sacrifice gradually became extinct.
37. Rice, barley or pulse boiled with butter and milk.
38. A dish consisting of sesamum and grain (mixture of rice and peas with a few spices).
39. Treacle or molasses partially dried, candied sugar.
40. A small round sweetmeat; any sweetmeat.
41. In this context, it appears to mean fish, because the next item is *māṃsa*.
42. cf. *vedāṅgaścāgamaḥ smṛtaḥ*/
43. cf. *āgamaḥ pañcamo vedaḥ*/
44. cf. *śilpādi-kriyā tantrābhimatā*/ *Prāṇatoṣiṇī*.
45. cf. *pātālaṃ bhūdharā lokā ādityādi-navagrahāḥ*/ *bhūdharādi-sapta-svargāśca nāgaṃ ca sarvadehinām piṇḍa-madhye sthitāḥ sarve...*/

(The nether world, mountains, the regions, the nine planets, Sun etc; the seven heavens—all this exists in the bodies of all corporeal beings.)

Śāktānanda-taraṅgiṇī quoted in the *Prāṇatoṣiṇī*.

jantor-ākāraṃ brahmāṇḍaṃ nānā-varṣma ca pārvatī/
brahmāṇḍaṃ vigrahaṃ proktaṃ sthūla-sūkṣmā-dikaṃ hi tat/
[O Pārvatī, the form of a being, the universe containing various bodies is called body, gross, subtle etc.]

Nirvāṇa-tantra quoted in Ibid.

Prakṛtiḥ puruṣo dehe brahmā viṣṇuḥ śivastathā

* * *

brahmāṇḍe ye gaṇāḥ santi te tiṣṭhanti kalevare/
[*Prakṛti* and *Puruṣa* are in the body. Brahmā, Viṣṇu, Śiva and the *Gaṇas*, who are in the universe, exist in the body. (*Gaṇas* are a class of demigods who are regarded as Śiva's attendants and under the special superintendence of Gaṇeśa).]

Tattvasāra quoted in Ibid.

46. cf. *mahāśavā-manuṣyāh syuḥ praśastā vīrasadhane* — (In *Vīra-sādhana* the *Mahāśavas* of human beings are commended.)

Kālītantra quoted in the *Tantrasāra.*

47. cf. *palāyana-viśūnyaṃ ca sammukhe raṇavartinam* —

Bhāvacūḍāmaṇi quoted in the *Tantrasāra.*

48. It is difficult to be reconcile with the above rule prescribing the body of a Caṇḍāla who is regarded as untouchable in Dharmaśāstra.
49. Eunuchs?
50. cf. *bhāvo hi manaso dharmo manasaiva sadābhyaset/*
51. It may be noted that the *Rudrayāmala* (Uttara Khaṇḍa, Paṭala I) ordains *Divya* and *Vira-bhāvas* as leading to the goal.
52. *Puraścaryārṇava*, pp. 862-63.
53. *Kalā* may mean skill or the three constituents of sacrifice, viz. *mantra, dravya, śraddhā.*
54. *Puraścaryārṇava*, p. 855.
55. Also see p. 6 *supra.*
56. See Glossary.
57. Svāmī Sāradānanda, *Gītātattva O Bhārate Śaktipūjā*, p. 151.

58. Of *Veśyās*, on the authority of the *Gupta-sādhana-tantra*, the *Prāṇatoṣiṇī* distinguishes seven kinds, viz. *gupta-veśyā, mahā-veśyā, kula-veśyā, mahodayā, rāja-veśyā, deva-veśyā, brahma-veśyā*. See in connexion with *Kula-nirṇaya* in the *Prāṇatoṣiṇī*.
59. Regarding *Kula-śaktis*, the *Prāṇatoṣiṇī*, on the authority of the *Revatī-tantra* (Paṭala iii), names 64 types of women including Caṇḍālī, Dhīvarī, Kocāṅganā, Bauddhā, Yavanī.
60. cf. *sahasraṃ tu pitṛn mātā gauraveṇā-tiricyate/* (ii. 145).
    [The mother surpasses a thousand fathers in honour.]
61. cf. *nāsti strīṇāṃ pṛthag yajño na vrataṃ nāpyu poṣaṇam/* (v. 155).
    [For women there is no separate sacrifice nor vow nor fasting.]
62. For description, see account of the contents of the *Mahānirvāṇa-tantra*.
63. cf. *ṛtvik-putrādayo devi smṛtyuktā bahavaḥ priye/*
    tantroktā parameśāni pūjādau naiva kārayet//
    purohitaṃ samānīya yadi pūjādikārayet/
    tasya sarvā-rtha=hāniḥ syāt kruddhā bhavati kālikā//
    [O dear Goddess, O Supreme consort of Lord, many persons, viz. *Ṛtvik-putra* (son of a Ṛtvik priest) etc. are stated in Smṛti and Tantra; one should not engage them in (Tāntric) worship, etc. If after having brought the priest one performs (Tāntric) worship, etc., then all his objects will be lost, (and) Kālī becomes angry.]
    Gupta-sādhana-tantra quoted in the *Prāṇatoṣiṇī*.
64. *Kumārī tu sarvajātiyā eva pūjyā praśastā* (Prāṇatoṣiṇī).
    [Virgin girls of all castes are to be worshipped and are commendable.]
65. A woman practising *Kulācāra*.
66. Theft of gold belonging to Brāhmaṇa.
67. See Glossary.
68. It is called *Cakrarāja*.
69. cf. *traividyebhyas-trayīṃ vidyām*, etc., *Manu-smṛti*, vii. 43.
    catvāro veda-dharmajñāḥ parṣat traividyameva vā /Yājñavalkya-smṛti, 1.1.9.
    (*tisro vidyā adhīyanta iti traividyāḥ teṣāṃ samūhaḥ traividya* — Mitākṣarā).
70. See our observations on *Pañcatattva*.

VI. Kālī: The Favourite Mother-Goddess

The Śākta cult is very popular in Bengal. The worship of Śakti as Kālī is widespread.[1] There are countless temples containing images of Kālī who is regularly worshipped. We hear of *mānats*,[2] made to Kālī, among all classes of people. Stories are current about devotees having got the *darśan* of Kālī in dream. Rāmakṛṣṇa Paramahaṃsa dedicated his life to the meditation on, and the worship of, this goddess. He is reported to have shown the goddess, in her orginal form, to his famous disciple, Vivekānanda. We find the mass worship of her by people in marketplaces, particularly on the Diwāli day. Some unforgettable devotional songs, particularly those of Rāmprasād, were inspired by devotion to Kālī. Her worship has been the bounden duty, nay an indispensable part of life of the descendants of such Kālī-sādhakas. as Pūrṇānanda, Sarvavidyā, etc. In Calcutta, the locality called Kalighat, has been named after Kālī established there. It is one of the Śākta Pīṭhas. Thousands of people throng there, particularly on *Amāvasyā*[3] and other days regarded as especially favourite to Kālī. In some temples, images of the deity, made of clay, stone or metal, are established permanently. On festive occasions, and when epidemic diseases like Cholera take heavy toll of lives, Rakṣā-Kālī or Śmaśāna Kālī is publicly worshipped.

It is worthwhile to see how and when Kālī was conceived as a deity. It is also interesting to trace the origin of her great popularity in Bengal. In doing so, we shall also consider her different forms and briefly deal with the rites and customs connected with her worship.

The tendency of tracing the origin of all deities in the Veda has prompted some to identify Kālī with Rātri-devī who owes her existence to the Rātri-sūkta (x. 127) of the *Ṛgveda*. Apart from the dubious propriety of this identification, the great question that confronts us is whether the above *Sūkta* at all forms an integral part of the *Ṛgveda*. It is a *khila* (supplement) supposed to be a later interpolation. Some scholars are inclined to find, in the fierce goddess Nirṛti of the Veda, the precursor of the later Kālī.[4] Nirṛti is mentioned as dark and dreadful in the *Śatapatha Brāhmaṇa* (vii. 2.7). She is represented as *pāśahastā* (with a noose in hand) in the *Aitareya Brāhmaṇa* (iv. 17).

The word Kālī occurs, for the first time, in the *Muṇḍakopaniṣad* where it is the designation of one of the seven tongues of the sacrificial fire.

Kālī is mentioned at some places of the *Mahābhārata*.[5] Her description in the epic reminds one of the description in the Purāṇas. She has red eyes and face, red garland and unguents, has a noose in hand and is terrible.

Kālidāsa has mentioned Kālī and Kālikā[6] in the *Kumārasambhava* (vii. 39) and the *Raghuvaṃśa* (xi. 15) where the descriptions *Kapīlābharaṇā* and *Calakapālakuṇḍalā* occur respectively.

References to this goddess directly or indirectly are scattered in Sanskrit literature. Caṇḍī, whose worship with blood has been described in the *Kādambarī* of Bāṇabhaṭṭa (first half of the seventh century), appears to be identical with Kālī. The awesome, dark goddess Karālā, described in *Mālatīmādhava* (act V) of Bhavabhūti (*c.* seventh century) as being worshipped with human flesh, in a shrine close to a cremation ground, is none but Kālī. According to the *Adbhuta-rāmāyaṇa* (xxv. 29-31), Sītā, having assumed her own form as *Kālī*, slew Rāvaṇa.

Kālī, in her fierce aspect, is mentioned in the Kinsariya stone inscription of 999 A.D.[7]

Kālī appears to be a curious blend of Umā, Nārāyaṇī, Cāmuṇḍā, Satī, Durgā, etc.[8] All these have been fused into this Mahādevī.

It is in the Purāṇas, that Kālī appears in her various forms and full glory. Among such Purāṇas, the most noteworthy are the *Mārkaṇḍeya, Viṣṇudharmottara, Bhaviṣya, Devī* and *Kālikā*. Her origin is described in the Devīmāhātmya or Caṇḍī of the *Mārkaṇḍeya Purāṇa* (vii.5 pp.). To repel the attacking demons, led by Caṇḍa and Muṇḍa, she came out of the forehead of the Divine Mother who became dark with indignation. Kālī had a huge and horrible face and a fearful look. With red and sunken eyes and lolling tongue, she had a sword, a noose and a club. She put on tiger-skin, and had a garland of human heads. Her raucous voice filled the directions. In the *Viṣṇudharmottara*, Bhadrakālī appears as charming and noble. In works like the *Karaṇāgama, Caṇḍīkalpa*, etc., there are descriptions of Mahākālī and Bhadrakālī.

The importance of Kālī[9] in the Purāṇas is indicated by the fact that she heads[10] the list of ten Mahāvidyās.

Regarding the forms of the deity, current in Bengal, and the mode of worship, the following works are authoritative: *Mahānirvāṇa-tantra, Kālī-tantra, Tantrasāra* of Kṛṣṇānanda and the *Śyāmārahasya* of Pūrṇānanda. Other works also on this subject exclusively, or along with other topics, were written in Bengal. Some of these are the *Prāṇatoṣiṇī* of Rāmatoṣaṇa. *Śyāmākalpalatikā* of Mathurānātha, *Śāktānanda-taraṅginī* and *Tārā-rahasya* of Brahmānanda, *Kālīkādi-sahasra-nāma-stuti-ṭīkā*[11] of Pūrṇānanda, *Tārā-rahasya-vṛttī* of Gauḍiya Śaṃkara, *Abhijñāna-ratnāvalī* of Rāmānanda, *Kālī-tattva-sudhābindu* of Kālīprasāda, *Kālī-sarvasva-sampuṭa* of Śrīkṛṣṇa, *Tārārcana-candrikā* of Jagannātha. *Tārāvilāsodaya* of Vāsudeva, *Tārā-bhakti-taraṅgiṇī* of Kāśīnātha, *Śyāmākalpalatā* of Rāmacandra, *Śyāmā-pūjā-paddhati* of Cakravartī. *Śyāmā-ratna* of Yādavendra, *Śyāmārcana-candrikā* of Ratnagarbha, *Śyāmā-santoṣaṇa-stotra* of Kāśīnātha Tarkapañcānana, *Śyāmā-saparyāvidhi* of Kāśīnatha Tarkālaṃkāra, *Śyāmā-stava-ṭīkā* of Durgārāma and the *Pañcamaveda-sāra-nirṇaya* of Haragovinda Rāya. The number of the above works and their manuscripts, preserved at various places, are an index to the wide popularity of the Śākta cult in Bengal.

The forms of Kālī, mentioned in the Tāntric works of Bengal, are as follows: Dakṣiṇakālikā, Siddhakālī, Guhyakālī, Bhadrakālī, Śmaśānakālī, Rakṣākālī or Mahākālī. Other forms are described in the *Śyāmārahasya* (vi. 5, xv. 22).

The most popular form in Bengal is Dakṣiṇakālikā.[12] She is described as follows: four hands, hideous face, dark like cloud, lolling tongue, a garland of human heads, body smeared with blood dripping from these heads, two corpses used as ear-ornaments, girdle of hands of dead bodies, blood trickling through corners of the mouth, three eyes bright as the orb of the rising sun, hair hanging loose on the right side, protruding teeth, large heaving breasts, naked, placed on the chest of Mahādeva lying like one dead, surrounded on all sides by howling and terrible jackals. According to the *Tantrasāra*, her upper left hand holds a sword, the lower left one holds a severed human head, hte right upper hands are represented as granting freedom from fear and boon. She is stated to live on the cremation ground. According to the *Gupta-sādhana-tantra* (vi), quoted in the *Tantrasāra*, she is stated to have her left foot as *ālīḍha*[13] and the right as *pratyālīḍha*.[14] There is a tradition that Kṛṣṇānanda, author of the *Tantrasāra*, conceived the form of *Dakṣiṇakālī* for the first time, and since then it has been widely current in Bengal. This view is, perhaps, not correct; because this form occurs in pre-Kṛṣṇānanda works also. May be that, owing to the tremendous influence of Kṛṣṇānanda, the worship of this form gained in popularity.

To even a casual observer it may appear ludicrous and incongruous with the Indian tradition that Śiva, husband of Kālī, should lie under the feet of his consort, Kālī. Ancient India looked upon the husband as highly venerable to the wife; *patireko guruḥ strīṇām*. Manu says (v. 155)- *patiṃ śuśrūṣate yena tena svarge mahīyate*; by serving the husband a woman is honoured in heaven.

A *dhyāna* of Kālī represents her as engaged in *viparīta-rati* or *puruṣāyita* position in sexual union with Mahākāla (Śiva). An image of Kālī representing her as sitting naked on Śiva lying on his back, with his penis thrust into her sex-organ.

Mythological accounts state that Kālī, having defeated the demons and killed them, trampled over their corpses. In course of time, perhaps, the idea of *viparītarati* and demons' corpses under her feet were confused and Śiva was represented as a corpse.

About the peculiar appearance of Dakṣiṇā Kālī, the most popular image, there is a legend. One night, Kṛṣṇānanda Āgamavāgiśa (or, some other devotee) was thinking about the form of the image of Kālī when the goddess appeared and asked him to make it, on the model of the first person to be met by him the next morning. Next morning he saw a woman, with one foot on the ground and the other on the dung heap and with her right hand raised and holding cowdung, engaged in sticking cowdung cakes on the walls of her house. At the sight of him, she became ashamed and pressed her tongue between her teeth. This position of the woman supplied the model of the Kālī-image.[15]

A conjecture may, perhaps, be hazarded that the woman-superior position of the image indicates a society in which matriarchy prevailed.

Besides the daily worship of Kālī,[16] in the images established in shrines or residential houses, she is particularly worshipped on the following occasions: Diwāli[17] night, *Raṭantī caturdaśī* and the fourteenth night of the dark half of the month of Jyaiṣṭha. The deity, worshipped on *Raṭantī caturdaśī* (i.e. 14th day of the dark fortnight of the month of Māgha) is designated as Raṭantī. In the fourteenth night of the dark half of the month of Jyaiṣṭha, she is called Phalahāriṇī. The worship on the Diwāli night is by far the most popular. It is performed with great gusto and grandeur; but, this practice does not seem to be based on any old authority. Chintaharan Chakravarti has found[18] the oldest reference in the *Śyāmā-saparyā-vidhi* of Kāśīnātha, composed as late as Śaka 1699 (=1777 A.D.). C. Chakravarti has found, in the above work,[19] passages quoted from Purāṇas and Tantras in support of the worship on the Diwāli day. Rājā Kṛṣṇacandra of Nadiya (eighteenth century), to whom tradition attributes many good ritualistic practices prevalent in Bengal, is said to have ordered all his subjects to perform this worship, and threatened them with penalty on their failure.[20] Since then, thousands of images began to be worshipped on this occasion in the district of Nadiya alone. The Rājā's grandson, Īśānacandra, is reported to have lavishly spent money on offerings to the deity on this occasion.

Animal-sacrifice is an indispensable part of Kālī worhsip. Goat, sheep and buffaloes are the animals commonly sacrificed.[21] There are stories about human sacrifice too.[22] Some well-known shrines of Kālī are said to stand on five human heads (*pañca-muṇḍī*). These heads were probably of the persons sacrificed in honour of Kālī. There is a *pañca-muṇḍī āsana* at Halisahar, a suburb of Calcutta, where the famous devotee-singer Rāmprasād is said to have attained *Siddhi*.

The *Mahānirvāṇa-tantra* explains[23] the significance of the current form of Kālī in an interesting manner. The form of the goddess is determined, for the benefit of devotees, in accordance with qualities and activities. The colours white, yellow, etc., are merged in black. Similarly, all beings enter into Kālī. That is why, for the benefit of the Yoginī, the goddess, who is in reality devoid of attributes and form, has been represented as black. The moon-mark on the forehead of this symbol of eternity, the benign and changeless Devī, signifies the repository of nectar. She views this world, made with a limitation of time, clearly with the eternal sun, moon and fire; hence she has three eyes. She chews and devours all creatures; therefore, she is represented as wearing a cloth in the shape of their blood. Her activity in saving the creatures from danger and impelling them to action are represented by the hand-poses of *vara-dāna* (gift of boon) and *abhaya-dāna* (granting freedom from fear). She pervades the worlds produced by the quality of *rajas*; so, she is placed on a seat of red lotus. The goddess, witnessing everything, drinks wine that causes *moha*, and looks upon the creation arising from Kāla (Time) and engaged in various sports. The Tantra says that, for the benefit of the devotees of small intellect, various forms of the goddess have been conceived.

Some are of the opinion that Kālī was originally a non-Aryan goddess. She was subsequently admitted to the Aryan pantheon. After her recognition within the Aryan fold, spiritual significance was imparted to her traits and appearance. The following non-Aryan elements in her conception and worship are pointed out. In the first place, her very appearance — dark with a hideous face, decked with human heads, having blood-stains—fits ill with the general Aryan conception of gods.

Indeed, the very word *deva*, denoting god, is derived from the root *div* to shine. The Vedic conception of gods and goddesses is quite opposed to the description of Kālī. It has been held that the human heads, associated with her, point to the period when the aborigines resorted to head-hunting. The howling jackals, surrounding the goddess, also remind one of forest-life. Contrary to the usual practice, Kālī is worshipped at night. This, according to the advocates of the non-Aryan origin of Kālī, appears to hint at the fact that the uncivilised people, who lived by plunder and pillage, used to reside in hideouts where, under the cover of darkness, they used to worship the deity. The use of wine, as an essential offering to her, seems to indicate a non-Aryan practice. Wine, according to Dharmaśāstras, is not only a taboo for the upper classes of people, particularly for Brāhmaṇas; the drinking of *surā* constitutes a *Mahāpātaka* (grave sin) for which the maximum penalty is death. The practice of sacrificing human beings before the goddess appears to have been borrowed from the non-Aryans.

The very designation Śmaśāna-Kālī[24] appears to hint at her non-Aryan origin. The description of the appearance of this deity and the rites and practices relating to her worship seem to be offensive to Aryan taste. She is jet black, and naked with a skull filled with wine and a human head severed a short while ago. She chews raw flesh, and is always intoxicated. She resides in the cremation ground which is the fittest place for her worship.

In this connexion, it may be noted that there is evidence of the worship of Devī by the aborigines. The *Harivaṃśa* (Viṣṇuparvan, III. 7-8 Vaṅgavāsī Ed.) mentions the worship of Kātyāyanī[25] and Kauśikī[26] on the Vindhya mountain by aboriginal tribes like Śabaras, Barbaras and Pulindas. Kātyāyanī and Kauśikī are designations of Durgā. As stated before, Durgā and several other goddesses have been fused into a single Kālī. In his Prākrit poem, *Gaüḍavaho*, Vākpatirāja (eighth century) has mentioned the worship of goddess Parṇaśabarī, covered with leaves, by Śabaras. This might be a form of Kālī. The worship of Kālī by dacoits and robbers is too well known to be dealt with in detail. This practice may be a survival of her worship by the plundering aborigines.

We shall conclude this chapter with the following hymn[27] in honour of Kālī. It is interesting in that every word begins with *Ka*, the initial letter of the name Kālī and the first consonant in the alphabet.

hrīṃ kālī śrīṃ karālī ca krīṃ kalyāṇī kalāvatī/
kamalā kali-darpaghnī, kapardīśa-kṛpānvitā//
Kālikā kālamātā ca kālānala-samadyutiḥ/
Kapardinī karālāsyā karuṇāmṛta-sāgarā//
Kṛpāmayī kṛpādhārā kṛpāpārā kṛpāgamā/
Kṛśānuḥ kapilā kṛṣṇā kṛṣṇānanda-vivardhinī//
Kālarātriḥ kāmarūpā kāma-pāśā-vimocinī/
Kādambinī kalādhārā kali-kalmaṣa-nāśinī//
Kumārī-pūjana-prītā kumārī-pūjakālayā/
Kumārī-bhojanānandā kumārī-rūpa-dhāriṇī//
Kadamba-vana-saṃcārā kadamba-vana-vāsinī/
Kadamba-puṣpa-santoṣā kadamba-puṣpa-mālinī//
Kiśorī kālakaṇṭhā ca kalanāda-ninādinī/
Kādambinī-pāna-ratā tathā Kādambarī-priyā//
Kapāla-pātra-niratā kaṅkāla-mālā-dhāriṇī/
Kamalāsana-santuṣṭā kamalāsana-vāsinī//
Kamalālaya-madhyasthā kamalāmoda-modinī/
Kala-haṃsa-gatiḥ kalivya-nāśinī kāmarūpiṇī//
Kāmarūpa-kṛta-vāsā kāma-patha-vilāsinī/
Kāmanīya kalpalatā kāmanīya-vibhāṣaṇā//
Kāmanīya-guṇārādhyā komlāṅgi kṛśodarī/
Karuṇāmṛta-santoṣā kāraṇānanda-siddhidā//
Kāraṇānanda-japeṣṭā kāraṇārcana-harṣitā/
Kāraṇārṇava-sammagnā kāraṇā-varta-pālinī//
Kastūrī-saurabhamodā kastūrī-tilakojjvalā/
Kastūrī-pūjana-ratā kastūrī-pūjaka-priyā//
Kastūrī-dāha-jananī kastūrī-mṛga-toṣiṇī/
Kastūrī-bhojana-prītā karpūrā-moda-moditā/
Karpūra-mālā-bharaṇā karpūra-candano-kṣitā//
Karpūra kāraṇā-hlādā karpūrā-mṛta-pāyinī/
Karpūra-sāgara-snātā karpūra-sāgarālayā//
Kūrca-bīja-japa-prītā kūrca-japa-parāyaṇā/
Kulīnā kaulikā-rādhyā kaulika-priya-kāriṇī//
Kulācārā kautukinī kulāmārga-pradarśinī/
Kāśīśvarī kaṣṭa-hartrī kāśīśa-vara-dāyinī/
Kāśīśvara-kṛtāmodā kāśīśvara-manoramā//
Kala-mañjīra-caraṇā kvaṇat-kāñcī-vibhūṣaṇā/
Kāñcanā-dri-kṛtāgārā kāñcana-cala-kaumudī//
Kāmabīja-japānandā kāmabīja-svarūpiṇī/
Kumatighnī Kulīnāri-nāśinī kulakāminī//

There is a vivid description of the image of Kālī in the following lines of her *dhyāna:*

> *Śavārūḍhāṃ mahābhīmāṃ ghoradaṃṣṭrāṃ varapradām/*
> *hāsyayuktāṃ trinetrāṃ ca kapālakartṛkākarām/*
> *muktakeśīṃ lolajihavāṃ pivantīṃ rudhiraṃ muhuḥ/*
> *caturbāhuyutāṃ devīṃ varābhayakarāṃ Smaret//*
> [*Kartṛkā*—small sword, knife.]
> *Karālavadanāṃ ghorāṃ muktakeśīṃ caturbhujām/*
> *kālikāṃ dakṣiṇāṃ divyāṃ muṇḍamālāvivhūṣitām//*
> * * *
> *evaṃ saṃcintayet kālīṃ śmaśānālayavāsinīm/*

NOTES

1. The *Brahmayāmala* states *Kālikā vaṅgadeśe ca* : it means that Devī is worshipped under the designation of Kālikā in Bengal.
2. Resolve to worship a deity or to offer certain articles on the fulfilment of a desire.
3. New-moon day.
4. Vide Appendix II (by B.L. Mukherji) to Woodroffe's *Shakti and Shākta.*
5. e.g. in the Sauptika-parvan. Here the sleeping heroes were being killed by Aśvathāman. Then the heroes visualised the fierce Kālī. Kālī, Mahākālī, Bhadrakālī are mentioned among the epithets of Durgā in the Durgāstotra of Arjuna in the Bhīṣmaparvan (23).
6. Explained by Mallinātha as *ghanāvālī* (mass of clouds).
7. *Epigraphia Indica,* XII, p. 59.
8. The *mantra,* with which salutation is made to Kālī, is
   sarvamaṅgala-maṅgalye śive sarvārtha-sādhike/
   śaraṇye tryambake gaurī nārāyaṇi namo'stu te//
9. The derivative meaning of the term is given as follows in the *Mahānirvāṇa-tantra* (iv. 32) — *Kāla-saṃgrasanāt kālī* (Vaṅgavāsī ed.). The *Prāṇatoṣiṇī* reads *saṃkalanāt* for *saṃgrasanāt.* Kālī is so called as she devours or seizes time.
10. The *Mahānirvāṇa* (iv. 32) describes her as *sarveṣām ādirūpiṇī.*
11. This and the following works are yet unpublished. For MSS of these works, see Appendix I.
12. See *Kālī-tantra,* i. 27 ff., quoted in the *Tantrasāra.* According to the *Śyāmārahasya* (iv. 5), Kālī is called *dakṣiṇā* as she is generous in granting boons.

13. 'A particular attitude in shooting (the right knee advanced, the left leg drawn back.' M. Williams.
14. Opposite of *ālīḍha* above.
15. For the conception of Kālī image, see N.N. Bhattacharya, *History of Tāntirc Religion*, pp. 349, 383.
16. For elaborate procedural matters, see N.K. Lahiḍi, *Kālyarcana-candrikā*.
17. *Amāvasyā* of the month of Kārtika. The word is from *dīpāvalī* (rows of lights). On this day, also called *dīpānvitā* (with lights), series of lights are placed in the house. The idea is that these lights show the paths, leading to heaven, to the spirits of the ancestors who are supposed to have come on the occasion of Mahālayā i.e., on the previous *Amāvasyā* day.
18. See his *Tantras—Studies*, etc., p. 92.
19. MS in Asiatic Soc., Calcutta, fol. 94a.
20. W. Ward, *A View of History . . . Religion of the Hindoos*, II, p. 124.
21. The *Viśvasāra-tantra* (Paṭala V) states that Guhyakālī is pleased with the meat of *godhā*.
22. On human sacrifice, see *Pañca-tattva* under Principal Topics of Bengal Tantra.
23. Vaṅgavāsī ed., xiii. 2-13.
24. Described in *Śyāmārahasya*, vi. 21, 22; *Tantrasāra*, Vaṅgavāsī Ed., p. 157.
25. Supposed by some to be so called after the tribe known as Kātya.
26. Believed by some to be so called after the tribe known as Kauśika.
27. *Mahānirvāṇa-tantra* (Vaṅgavāsī Ed.), vii. 12-31.

VII. Bengal Tantra and Durgā[1]

The name 'Durgā' occurs in many of the Tantras of Bengal. The *Tantrasāra* mentions *Durgā-mantra*, *Mahiṣa-mardinī-mantra*, *Jaya-durgā-mantra* and *Śūlinī-mantra*. The following forms of Durgā emerge from the *dhyānas* stated respectively in connexion with the above.

1. Resting on a lion, moon-crested, having complexion like *marakata* (emerald), holding *śaṅkha, cakra, dhanus*, and *śara* in her four hands, three-eyed, wearing ornaments like necklace, bracelet, girdle and anklet, jewelled earrings, etc.

2. Possessed of complexion like cloud (?)[2] causing fear to enemies with crooked look, having a digit of the moon on the crest, holding a conch-shell, a disc, a sword and arrow with her four hands, three-eyed, riding on a lion's neck, filling the three worlds with lustre, surrounded by gods, served by those desirous of success.

3. Riding on a lion, having complexion like clouds surcharged with water, moon-crested, three-eyed, causing fear to fighters of the opposite side.

In connexion with other *Durgā-mantras*, laid down in the *Tantrasāra*, the following *dhyāna* occurs:

> Riding on a lion's neck, decked with many ornaments, four-armed, having a serpent-like sacred thread, putting on a red cloth, possessed of body shining like the morning sun, holding in her hands deer's hair, bow, noose and goad (*aṅkuśa*), served by sages like Nārada.

A *Durgā-homa* is also mentioned in the *Tantrasāra*. Different results are obtained by performing this *homa* with different substances and flowers. For example, by using lotuses one can vanquish enemies. By using *marīca* one can secure the death of the enemy. By using *palāśa* flowers one can acquire prosperity.

The *Tantrasāra* contains also a *Śatanāma-stotra* of Durgā, a *Mahiṣa-mardinī-stotra*, a *Durgā-kavaca* and a *Mahiṣa-mardinī-kavaca*. It also states a *Durgā-yantra* or a diagram in which Durgā is to be meditated upon and worshipped.

Though *Durgā-pūjā* as such has not been dealt with in the work, the following facts about it can be gathered from incidental remarks. The articles, to be offered in the worship, are: fish, meat, soup, cakes, etc. The animals, to be sacrificed, are *mṛga* (deer), *śaśaka* (hare) *sal-*

yaka (porcupine), buffalo, goat, horse, elephant, camel and ass. Among the birds to be offered are the crow, the parrot and the vulture. What is remarkable is that Tantra mentions human beings among the offerings to the goddess.

Durgā has been conceived as destroying enemies, saving a person from distress, helping one in the acquisition of whatever is desired, bringing even kings under the control of the worshipper, granting all material welfare, etc.

The *Prāṇatoṣiṇī* is the only published work among the Tantras of Bengal, which deals systematically with *Durgā-pūjā*. The question may arise—why *Durgā-pūjā* was not dealt with as a separate topic by the authors of Tāntric works preceding the *Prāṇatoṣiṇī*. The reason seems to be that *Kālī* having dominated in the Tāntric pantheon, the earlier authors naturally were more concerned with her. But, *Durgā-pūjā*, the procedure of which was marked by Tāntric elements, being current in Bengal, they could not dispense with this goddess.

The *Prāṇatoṣiṇī* came into being in 1821 A.D. i.e. about a century later than the probable introduction of *Durgā-pūjā* in a pompous form by Kṛṣṇācandra (1710-1783 A.D.). So, by the time of origin of the *Prāṇatoṣiṇī*, this *Pūjā* became the major annual festival of the Bengals. This was, perhaps, the reason of its elaborate treatment in this work.

Even if we are to believe that Kaṃsanārāyaṇa, a local chief, who was a contemporary of Akbar (reign 1556-1605) according to some or of Shahjahan (reign 1628-1657) according to others, introduced this *Pūjā* our above argument does not lose force; because while the latter is supposed only to have introduced this *pūjā* in this province, the former is believed to have added a new dimension to it. In this connexion, it cites the *Matsya-sūkta-mahātantra, Devipurāṇa* and the *Durgā-bhakti-taraṅgiṇī* as the principal authorities. The rules and regulations about the *pūjā* are substantially the same as those given in the works on *Durgā-pūjā*, composed by the writers of Bengal.[3] A few interesting facts, found in the *Prāṇatoṣiṇī*, are stated below.

The symbols, on which Durgā can be worshipped, are as follows: picture, image, bel (tree ?), *mahāyoni, candrabimba* (manuscript?), stone-slab, *yoni-maṇḍala, pādukā* (mark like foot-print ?), sword, *mahābimba* (?), holy place, bank of the Ganges. A householder is prohibited to use an earthen image. The author adds that an earthen image, with straw within, is not forbidden. Also prohibited for a householder is an image measuring three cubits and a half; a smaller image is allowed for him.

As regards the number of arms of the goddess, the following rules are given on authority; the number varies in accordance with the region in which the goddess is worshipped.

Eight arms: Orissa, Bihar, Madhyadeśa, Ayodhyā, Saurāṣṭra, Cohāra (?), Sylhet, Kośala, Savavallaka?

Eighteen arms: Mahendra, Himālaya, Kuru land, Mathurā, Kedāra, Rāmaṭha.

Twelve arms: Makaranda, Virāṭa.

Ten arms: Kaumāra, Gauḍa, Pāripātra, Dakṣiṇa (?), Mahārāṣṭra, Gajāhvaya (?).

Four arms: Pūrṇa (?), Nepāla, Kacchameśa, Kaṅkana.

Two arms: Near the ocean.

The author adds that, in *Durgā-pūjā*, a kind of sound, made by the voice of women[4], is auspicious.

The image, described in the *Prāṇatoṣiṇī*, corresponds to the image usually worshipped at present in Bengal. The image of the goddess is accompanied by those of Kārtika, Gaṇeśa, Lakṣmī, Sarasvatī, Brahmā, Sāvitrī, demon, lion, buffalo, peacock, rat, etc.

A noteworthy fact about the *Prāṇatoṣiṇī* is that, though the earlier authorities mention human beings and wine among the offerings to the goddess, the author clearly forbids these two things for Brāhmaṇa worshippers.[5]

It should be noted that *Śabarotsava* is ordained in the Bengal works on *Durgā-pūjā* as a festival on the *Daśamī* or last day of the *Pūjā*. In it the participants are required to besmear their bodies with mud and dust, cover the same with leaves of trees, and abuse one another in filthy language. This does not occur in Tantra.

NOTES

1. For the curious we set forth the following information.
   The term *Durgā* (fem.) and *Durga* (neuter) appear to have the same basic meaning. Also used in the masculine gender, the word *Durga* appears to have been used in the earliest times in the *Atharvaveda, Manu-smṛti, Mahābhārata* etc. Its general meaning is difficult of access, impassable, unattaintable. In the well-known Upaniṣadic line *durgaṃ pathastat kavayo vadanti* also, the word conveys the same meaning. Subsequently it came to mean a difficult narrow passage, citadel, stronghold, fort etc. In the

masculine gender, it means a demon of this name supposed to have been slain by Goddess Durgā, as stated in the *Skandapurāṇa*. *Durgā*, when denoting a deity, means One who can be approached or whose favour can be obtained through great pain. We do not know how and when Durgādevī was included in the Brahmanical pantheon. The words 'Durgā' and 'Durgi', as the name of a deity, appears to have been used, for the first time, in the *Taittirīya Āraṇyaka* X. 2, 3 and X. 1,7 respectively. *Durgā* is identified with *Umā* who appears to have been mentioned in the *Harivaṃśa*, *Kumārasambhava*, *Raghuvaṃśa*, etc.

Eulogies of Goddess *Durgā* occur in the Bhiṣmaparvan and Virāṭaparvan of the *Mahābhārata* which contains earlier and later portions, its present form dating back, according to Winternitz, to about the fourth century A.D.

A numismatic evidence points to the prevalence of *Durgā-pūjā* at least about 300 A.D. A *Siṃhavāhinī* Goddess is found on the reverse of the coins of Candragupta I of the Gupta dynasty (C. 305-325 A.D.) Vide Altekar's *Gupta Gold Coins* etc. (pp. xliv-v) and Allan's *Catalogue of Gupta Coins*, lxxxiii.

Still earlier prevalence of the worship of this deity seems to be proved by a coin of the Kuṣāṇa king Kaniska (1st or 2nd cent. A.D.). Its reverse depicts the figure of a goddess with a lunar crescent seated full face on a lion crouching left and the goddess appearing with a noose and a sceptre. Thus, the figure seems to be that of *Durgā*.

According to the *Kālikā Purāṇa* (X. 26.3), dating back to about the tenth century A.D., whose earlier version is, perhaps, hinted at by Raghunandana (16th cent.) as *duṣprāpya*, Durgā was awakened in autumn, which is not the proper season, and worshipped for favouring Rāma against Rāvaṇa. Similar stories occur also in the *Devī-bhāgavata* (iii. 30) and *Mahābhāgavata Purāṇas* (36, 42). Curiously enough, all these Purāṇas were probably composed or compiled in Bengal. It may be noted that the unseasonal worship of the goddess, most popular in Bengal, does not occur in the original *Rāmāyaṇa* but in its Bengali version by Kṛttivās, a pre-Caitanya writer.

Durgā-pūjā, in the present form, was introduced in Bengal by Kṛṣṇacandra, a big landlord of Nadiyā in W. Bengal, in the 18th century.

The Smṛti digests of Bengal, dealing with the *Pūjā*, are the following:
Kālaviveka of Jijūtavāhana (c. bet. 11th and 13th cent.) *Durgotsava-viveka* of Śūlapāṇi (C. bet. the 11th and 15th cent.), a work of the same title by Śrīnātha Ācāryacūḍāmaṇi (c. bet. 15th and 16th cent.), the *Durgotsava-tattva* by Raghuvandana (16th cent.)

2. *Kāmābhrabhā* — meaning is not clear.
3. On this subject, the present author has written a work which is proposed to be published shortly.
4. It is popularly called *ulu* in West Bengal and *jokāra* in East Bengal. In dictionaries, it is variously referred to as *hulahuli, hulihuli, huluhulu,* etc. the word *Ulūli,* in this sense, occurs in the *Atharvaveda* (xxxi. 9.6). This peculiar sound is mentioned in the *Naiṣadha-carita* (xiv. 49), *Chāndogya Upaniṣad* (iii. 19.3.) For a discussion on it, see K.K. Handiqui's introduction to *Naiṣadhacarita*, Eng. Trs.
5. *na-dadyād brāhmaṇo madyaṃ mānuṣaṃ ca/* 1

VIII. Varṇāśrama-Dharma and Ācāras

The Tantras of Bengal do not recognise the four conventional stages of life. The *Mahānirvāṇa*, followed by the *Prāṇatoṣiṇī*, recognises two stages, viz. *Gārhasthya* (householdership) and *Bhaikṣya* (living on alms, mendicancy).[1] All people are said to be entitled to the duties of these two *āśramas*.[2] Those who have resorted to the last stage of life are designated as *Avadhūta*. In Kali Age, *Avadhūtāśrama* has been stated as *Saṃnyāsa*. It is interesting to note that even a householder, observing certain practices, can be an *Avadhūta* if *Brahmajñāna* dawns upon him. Escapism has been strongly condemned. One is doomed to hell if one leaves behind the old parents, minor children, devoted wife and retires to the forest. A person is allowed to receive the initiation of *saṃnyāsa*, and take to the forest only when he has completed his duties towards his family and is permitted by relatives to do so.

Avadhūtas

Avadhūtas are divided into two broad classes, viz. *Gṛhastha* and *Sadāśiva*. A *Gṛhastha* will be devoted to *guru*, acquire knowledge, be pious both internally and externally, devoid of desire, engaged in the worship of Śiva. He will also practise obeisance with eight parts, viz. knees, feet, hands, chest, mind or intellect, head, speech and sight. An *Avadhūta* of the second class is naked, takes to *pañcatattva*, is always joyful, calm. He will give away everything, enjoy everything; he will have no distinction of caste, and should be engaged in religious practices. In the Kali Age, an *Avadhūta* of the former type is debarred from taking wine. *Saṃvit* (knowledge) has been said to be superior to wine.[3]

Those, living in the house (*gṛhastha*), worship *Brahma-mantra* and are called *brahmāvadhūta*.

Those who have undergone *pūrṇā-bhiṣeka* are called *Śaivāvadhūtas*. Again they can be *pūrṇa* (complete) and *apūrṇa* (incomplete) the former being called *Paramahaṃsa* and the latter *Parivrāṭ*.

The fourth kind of *Avadhūta* is designated as *Haṃsa*. The other three practise *yoga* and take to *bhoga*. A *Haṃsa* is debarred from association with a woman; he cannot possess anything. He should give up all the duties and signs of a householder. To him no Śāstric injunction nor prohibition applies. He should roam the world at will without any desire and effort to do anything. Devoid of grief and delusion, he will always be self-contented. He will be without a house, have fortitude, be devoid of attachments, tranquil, unaffected by pleasure and pain, cold and heat, etc. He has nothing to meditate upon, and is absolutely free.

A *Śaivāvadhūta* has got to do no rite connected with gods, manes and sages.[4]

Men, who are foolish or learned, whether belonging to a high or low caste, even if they are Caṇḍālas, are equal if they resort to *Kulācāra.*

All the rites, performed by *Avadhūtas*, are completed with the *mantra Oṃ tat sat* which is stated to be the great *mantra*, the cause of all causes (*sarva-kāraṇa-kāraṇam*); by practising it one can be Śiva (*bhaven mṛtyuñjayaḥ svayam*). *Japa, homa, pratiṣṭhā, saṃskāra*—in fact, all the rites are supposed to be performed only if this *mantra* is recited. It is easy to use (*sukhasādhya*), free from prolixity (*abāhulyam*) and conducive to complete effect (*saṃpūrṇa-phala-dāyaka*). This *mantra* is the quintessence (*sārāt sāratara*) of Nigamas, Āgamas and Tantras. It is the sanctifier of all objects including the *tattvas*. One repeating it, with its meaning comprehended, becomes identified with Brahman.

The *Kulayogins* are regarded as such holy persons that by merely seeing, touching and talking with them or by causing their satisfaction one secures the result of visiting all the holy places.

As regards the caste-system, Bengal Tantra makes a considerable departure from the conventional *varṇa-dharma*. The following facts about the attitude of Tantra towards *varṇa-dharma* can be gleaned from the *Mahānirvāṇa-tantra.*

Besides the four conventional castes, the *Mahānirvāṇa* provides for a caste called *Sāmānya* (viii. 5). Though the people coming under *Sāmānya* are not specified, yet it seems to include all beyond the pale of the four castes.

In respect of the *prasāda* of Kālī no caste distinction is observed. Same is the case with *Śaiva-vivāha*,[5] the two *Cakras* called *Bhairavī*[6] and *Tattva.*[7] For use in Cakras, articles for worship, raw or cooked, can be brought by a member of any caste, even by those beyond the fold of caste-system, viz. Mleccha, Śvapaca (Caṇḍāla), Kirāta or Hūṇa. Such articles are purified as soon as put into the hands of one who is technically designated as *Vīra*. Observance of distinction, based on caste or pedigree, is prohibited also in *Brahmacakra*.[8] Wine, as one of the *Pañcatattvas*, is not defiled by the touch of anybody. The same remark is applicable to *māṃsa*; it may be collected from any place, anybody can slaughter the animals whose meat is offered to deities. No caste-distinction is observed in the case of *mahāprasāda* of the Supreme Brahman. Even the best of Brāhmaṇas can partake of it even if it is offered by a man of inferior caste.

All castes, including *Sāmānya*, are entitled to *Kulāvadhūta-saṃskāra*. It should be added that Brāhmaṇas are held in high esteem.[9] Excepting certain Tāntric rites, people are directed to do the duties of their respective castes. For a Brāhmaṇa only a wife of the Brāhmaṇa caste is *dharma-patnī*; she can participate in religious rites with the husband. His wife of a different caste is *Kāma-patnī*, i.e. for enjoyment only.

Ācāras

Various *ācāras* (forms of worship and ways of life) have been recognised in Bengal Tantra. *Kulācāra*, the *ācāra* par excellence, has been dealt with or referred to in almost all the works. Various ācāras have been enumerated[10] and described in the *Prāṇatoṣiṇī*. *Kulācāra* has been described in detail in the *Tantrasāra* and, to some extent, in the *Mahānirvāṇa* also. These are briefly described below:

Vedācāra—rising in *brāhma muhūrta*, salutation of *guru*, worship of deity meditating upon it in the *sahasrāra* lotus, with five articles. *Vāgbhava-bīja* is to be recited and *paramā kalā* to be meditated upon. On another authority, it is stated that, after finishing morning duties, he should again be on the bed, meditate on *guru* and the desired deity in the thousand-petalled lotus in the head. According to various authorities, the following practices are recognised: meditation on Ugratāriṇī, in the form of a lotus fibre, from the *mūlādhāra* to *brahma-randhra*; she has the brilliance of a crore of suns and the coolness of a crore of moons, etc. Mental worship of the *guru* has been commended. Different *dhyānas* and *stotras* of the *guru* are laid down by different authorities.

Vaiṣṇavācāra—sexual intercourse and talk of it, violence, speaking ill of others, crookedness and meat-eating should be avoided. The rosary and *yantra* should never be touched at night. One should worship Viṣṇu, offer all actions to Him and always look upon the world as pervaded by Him.

Śaivācāra—it is the same as *Vedācāra* with the only difference that, in the *Śākta ācāra*, animal sacrifice is prescribed while it is prohibited in the *Śaiva ācāra*.

Dakṣiṇācāra—it is so called as it was practised by sage Dakṣiṇāmūrti.

Vāmācāra—the Supreme Goddess is to be worshipped according to *Vedācāra*. By day one should be austere like a Brahmacārin, and practise concentration. At night the Goddess should be worshipped with the substitutes of *pañca-tattva*.

Siddhāntācāra—it appears that, for people practising it, animal-sacrifice is allowed in a religious performance.[11] It is further said that what is pure and what is impure are purified by *Śodhana* (purificatory rite). One should be engaged in *devapūjā* and meditate upon Viṣṇu.

Kulācāra[12]—for a person practising it there is no restriction relating to directions, time, *tithi*, etc. Nor is there any fixed rule about the *sādhana* of *mahāmantra*. Such a man is sometimes virtuous, sometimes fallen from the right path, at times like a ghost or goblin. Such persons move about in various garbs.[13] They make no distinction between mud and sandalpaste, son and enemy, cremation ground and home, gold and grass. One, observing *kulācāra*, practises whatever *ācāra* is ordained in respect of deities. A *Kaula* is sometimes regarded as belonging to the fifth *Āśrama*.[14]

The practice of *Kulācāra* is prohibited by day[15] and in the presence of others.[16]

A *Kaula* should look upon women with great respect. They are to be regarded as goddesses. He should avoid beating them and speaking ill of them. All sorts of rude dealings with women and crookedness towards them should be avoided.

Such a person should not while away his time by indulging in dice-play, etc. He should spend time by worship of deities, *japa*, *stava*, etc. *Japa* is allowed at all times and at all places. In the worship of the goddess, there is no restriction as to day and night. *Pūjā* is allowed even without bath and with a loaded stomach. *Mahāpūjā* is, however, to be performed at night only. *Mahāniśā* (i.e. two middle *praharas* of the night) is the time when Mahākālī is supposed to arrive with her retinue, and grant boons to devotees.

A *Kaula* should fearlessly move about alone in a cremation ground, solitary forest, empty house, river-bank, etc.

He should be generous, tolerant of censure by others and follow *Vaiṣṇavācāra*.

Worship of Yogini is hightly beneficial on *Kulavāra* and in *Kulāṣṭamī*, particularly *caturdaśī*. Tuesday and Friday are *Kulavāras*,

Tithis of even number, excepting *dvitīyā, daśamī* and *ṣaṣṭhī*, are *Kual-tithis* propitious for religious performances by a *Kaula*.

A *Kaula* should shun hate, shame, fear, sleep, disgust, family, caste, (conventional) conduct; these eight are the fetters getting rid of which *jīva* can become Śiva. Also to be avoided by a *Kaula* are expiation, fall from a precipice, renunciation (*saṃnyāsa*) use of an umbrella, visit to a holy place.

The salutation of a *kula* tree is one of the morning duties of such a man. The *kula* trees are: *śleṣmātaka, karañjaka, nimba, aśvattha, kadamba, plakṣa, vaṭa, udumbara, ciñcā.*

Kulācāra has been extolled lavishly. It has been stated to be the highest religion.[17] Even a Caṇḍāla, versed in it, is superior to a Brāhmaṇa devoid of it. As all rivers merge into an ocean, as the footprints of all animals are lost in those of an elephant, so all other *ācāras* are lost in *kulācāra*. The difference between *kulācāra* and other *ācāras* is like that between mount Meru and oilseeds, between the sun and firefly. According to all systems of philosophy, one attains it immediately (*sadya eva*). A *yogin* is not a *bhogin*, nor a *bhogin* is a *yogin*. But, one practising *kulācāra* is a combination of both. A *Kaula* has been stated to be *Śiva* Himself.[18] The honouring of a *Kaula* is said to produce the result of worshipping all the gods and goddesses.

In connexion with *kulācāra*, the *Prāṇatoṣiṇi* quotes the *Samayācāra-tantra* which divides *ācāra* as *ārdra* (moist) and *śuṣka* (dry). In the former, one resorts to *pañcatattva*, while in the latter, *pañcatattva* is absent. In the Kali Age, however, *ārdrācāra* has been declared as especially effective.[19]

Some raise the question as to whether or not the above *ācāras* are to be adopted in succession. The spirit of Tantras in this respect seems to be this. One, possessed of *paśubhāva*, has to adopt any one of the following—*vedācāra, vaiṣṇavācāra, śaivācāra*. After *śāktābhiṣeka*, everyone becomes inclined to *dakṣiṇācāra*. After *pūrṇābhiṣeka*, a follower of *dakṣiṇācāra* takes to anyone of the following—*vamācāra, siddhāntācāra, kaulācāra.*

NOTES

1. cf. *jātamātro gṛhasthaḥ syāt saṃskārād āśramī bhavet/ gārhasthyaṃ prathamaṃ kuryāt... tattva-jñāne samutpanne vairāgyaṃ jāyate yadā/*

tadā sarvaṃ parityajya saṃnyāsā-śramam āśrayet/
[AS soon as born, one becomes a *gṛhastha*, due to sacrament one belongs to a stage. One should at first resort to *gārhasthya*. When true knowledge arises, *Vairāgya* (spirit of renunciation arises. Then, having renounced every thing, one should resort to the stage of renunciation.)

— Mahānirvāṇa, viii. 14, 15.

2. cf. *viprāṇām itareśāṃ ca varṇānām prabale kalau/*
ubhayatrā-śrame devi sarveṣām adhikāritā/

Ibid., viii. 12.

[Kalī being powerful, O Goddess, the Brāhmaṇa and all other castes are entitled to both the stages.]
3. cf. *saṃvidā-savayor madhye saṃvideva garīyasī/*
4. *Mahānirvāṇa*, xiv. 166.
5. For description, see in connexion with the contents of the *Mahānirvāṇa* in the chapter on Tāntric Texts of Bengal.
6. See Glossary.
7. *Ibid.*
8. *Ibid.*
9. For example, see *Prāṇatoṣiṇī* (Brāhmaṇa-praśaṃsā).
10. See description of the contents of the work.
11. cf. *aśvamedhakratau naiva vājihatyā yathā bhavet/*
tathaiva parameśāni yajñe doṣo na vidyate//
[As in *Aśvamedha* sacrifice, there is no slaughter of a horse, so also, O Consort of Supreme Lord, there is no fault (in animal sacrifice) in a sacrifice.]

— (*Prāṇatoṣiṇī*, 1266 B.S., p. 561)

12. Also see description of *Avadhūtas*, *Supra*.
13. cf. *antaḥ śāktāḥ bahiḥ śaivāḥ sabhāyāṃ vaiṣṇavā matāḥ/*
nānārūpadharāḥ kaulā vicaranti mahītale/
[*Kaulas*, assuming various guises, roam the world—they are *Śāktas* inwardly, *Śaivas* outwardly and regarded as *Vaiṣṇavas* in an assembly.]
14. cf. *kaulastu pañcamāśramaḥ* — *Niruttaratantra* quoted in the *Prāṇatoṣiṇī*.
15. cf. *rātrau kulakriyāṃ kuryāt divā kuryācca vaidikīm/*
[At night, one should practise *Kula* rite, by day Vedic rite.]
Niruttara-tantra, quoted in the *Prāṇatoṣiṇī*, p. 599.
na divāyām kulācāraḥ — *Vāmakeśvara-tantra* quoted in *Ibid.*

16. It should be noted that the *Mahānirvāṇa* condemns the secret performance of such rites. Vide
tasmāt prakāśataḥ kuryāt kaulīkaḥ kulasādhanam//
kuladharmasya guptyarthaṃ nānṛtaṃ syāj jugupsitam/
yaduktaṃ kulatantreṣu na śastaṃ prabale kalau//
iv. 79.80.
[So, *Kaulikas* should openly perform *Kula* rite. For the secrecy of *Kuladharma*, there should be no falsehood which is hated. What is stated in *Kulatantras* is not commendable while *Kalī* is powerful.]
17. *Kauladharmāt paro nāsti.*
18. *kulācaraṇa-pūtātmā sākṣāt śivamayo bhavet/* On the persons fit to be *Kaulas*, see *Guru-tantra, Saṃśaya-nirāsa*, pp. 18-19.
19. cf. *Kalau viśeṣato devī ārdrācāraḥ phalapradaḥ/*

IX. Bengal Tantra: Philosophy and Theology

Of the published Tantras of Bengal, containing philosophical ideas, the following are noteworthy:

Śrītattva-cintāmaṇi of Pūrṇānanda,

Mahānirvāṇa-tantra.

Prāṇatoṣiṇi of Rāmatoṣaṇa.

The *Tantrasāra* and other works dwell on the common places of Tantra, and deal in detail with the ritualistic aspect. It should, however, be noted that the very ideas of *Kulakuṇḍalinī*, the dormant power in human beings, and the mystic *Cakras* within the body are philosophical. These occur in many of the works.

Of the four main branches of philosophy, viz. metaphysics, epistemology, ethics and eschatology, Bengal Tantra deals, to some extent, with metaphysics and ethics. Eschatological ideas are incidentally found in them. So far as epistemology is concerned, we find no discussion as such. But, as we have seen above, *jñāna* (knowledge) has been divided into two kinds—that derived from scriptures and that arising from discrimination. The means of attaining the highest form of knowledge is Tāntric *sādhanā*. The means of valid knowledge, which has been discussed at length in the orthodox schools of philosophy, does not appear to have engaged the attention of the writers on Tantra.

Pūrṇānanda begins with a discussion about the nature of *ātman*, or Parama Brahman, who is immanent, but is neither gross nor subtle; he is eternally pure, enlightened and free, beyond the three qualities which lead to the states of wakefulness, sleep and deep slumber. He is formless, devoid of origin, middle and end, and is changeless. His parts are called *jīva* which, under the influence of *avidyā* (nescience), assumes different bodies and enjoys happiness and suffers pain. *Avidyā* covers the *jīvātman* by the force of *āvaraṇa*, and keeps it off by the force of *vikṣepa*. *Avidyā* is non-material, but by reflection in *Ātman*, it appears to be like something material. It is like the reflection of a thing in a clear mirror.

That, which is consciousness reflected in the constituent *Sattva-guṇa* of *Avidyā*, which is the cause, is called Īśvara as there is firm *adhyāsa* as 'That am I'. Having the attribute of *Sattva-guṇa* he is ominiscient, omnipotent and the doer of all deeds.

When that, which appears as consciousness, is reflected in the qualities of *Rajas* and *Tamas*, the effects of *Māyā*, the cause, owing to the influence of action, is shorn of its fullness, and becomes subject to the limitations of space, time and substance, gets the distinctions of *sajātīya* (of equal type) *vijātīya* (of a different type) and *svagata* (own form). Then it has the false notions 'I', 'mine', and is called *jīva*. Having the attribute of effect it has dullness by which it thinks — I am the doer, I am the enjoyer, I am happy, I am sorry, I do not know myself.

Īśvara, due to the differences of attributes of three qualities, assumes the forms of Brahman, Viṣṇu, Rudra, etc; under the force of *āvaraṇa* and *vikṣepa* belonging to *avidyā*, creates, preserves and destroys the ninefold *saṃsāra* from Brahman to grass.

The author poses the question—how is it that Paramātman, who is indifferent, eternal, pure, free, enlightened, beyond *guṇas*, devoid of ego, desire, jealousy, efforts, etc., comes under the influence of *āvaraṇa* and *vikṣepa*? The author solves the problem thus. The above twofold effect of *avidyā* has no real existence. But, it is wrongly perceived to exist due to lack of discrimination on the part of one who does not know the Ātman. When a man dreams a dream, it appears to be true to him. A man, witnessing magic, for the time being thinks it to be true. The dream having gone and the influence of the magician having ceased, the falsity of the things seen is realised. Similarly, a man, before the rise of knowledge, thinks *avidyā* and its effects to be true. But when the falsity is realised, *avidyā* and its effects disappear.

Pūrṇānanda states that salvation (*mukti*), according to some, consists in the absence of infinite misery. Accoring to others, it means the destruction of hankering (*tṛṣṇā-nāśa*). His own opinion is that it means the merger of the individual soul in Paramātman, the mass of deep bliss.

Salvation is attained not by self-mortification, sacrifice, observance of various practices, study of scriptures, but by knowledge alone (*jñānameva hi kāraṇam*). *Jñāna* is twofold—arising out of discrimination and arising from scriptures. Knowledge of Śabda-brahman arises from scriptures and that of Parama-brahman from discrimination. According to learned persons, Śabda-brahman is sound which is inaudible (*avyakta*) and rises from Para Bindu when it is split (*bhidyamāna*). According to others, Śabda-brahman is *Sabdārtha*[1] (meaning of words). The author rejects both the views, because both identify Śabda-brahman with something unconscious or insentient (*jaḍa*). He avers that it is the consciousness of all beings. According to him, it, assuming the form of *Kuṇḍalī* within the human body, manifests itself as *varṇas* or letters which appear in the forms of prose, poem, etc. In other words, it is the sole producer of energy in every creature.

As regards Parama-brahman, the author says that some[2] look upon it as non-dual while others[3] have a dualistic outlook. From the manner of his references to these views it appears that the author looks upon it as beyond dualism and non-dualism.[4]

The author holds that *nirmama* (nothing is mine) and *mama* (mine) are the two ideas which lead respectively to emancipation and bondage. That action, which causes bondage, is called *avidyā* while that which does not do so it *vidyā*. Bondage lasts so long as desire (*saṃkalpa*) exists, and freedom arises as soon as that desire ceases. The actions of *japa, homa, pūjā, tīrtha-darśana, veda-śāstrādhyayana*, etc., are resorted to so long as the knowledge of reality is not acquired. So, one, desiring emancipation, should make all-out effort to acquire true knowledge.

True knowledge is this. Parama-brahman, which is eternal and of the form of *Rasa*, becomes manifest and non-manifest by Prakṛti. So, through Prakṛti, one should directly perceive the Supreme Being. Without the quality of a *ghaṭa*, it cannot be perceived as a *ghaṭa* although it is different from other objects. So, without Śakti, Puruṣa cannot be perceived. In other words, Śakti is inseparable from Puruṣa; the latter is the substratum of the former. Every object of the phenomenal world has Prakṛti or Śakti underlying it. Prakṛti absorbs in her all that is manifest. There are diverse means of knowing Brahman, but these help in the indirect knowledge of it. Thus the outward means, the evolutions of Prakṛti, help the realisation of Brahman mediately. The perceptible phenomena thus help in the realisation of the Brahman which is ordinarily imperceptible. That Prakṛti or Śakti can be known through *dīkṣā* (initiation).

The *Prāṇatoṣiṇī* cites several authorities in connexion with the order of creation. The following order emerges. From Parameśvara, who is full (*sakala*) and consists in existence (*sat*), consciousness (*cit*) and bliss (*ānanda*), arose Śakti. Then appeared *nāda* which gave rise to *bindu. Saccidānanda* implies that *avidyā* does not impair the real nature of Īśvara. *Sakala* indicates *Īśvara* with Prakṛti. Śiva is twofold—*nirguṇa* (attributeless) and *saguṇa* (possessed of attributes). In the latter form, he is connected with Prakṛti. The question arises—how is it that

Śakti arose from one who was possessed of Śakti? The reply is that eternal Śakti remained in a subtle form in the Great Dissolution. Then, due to the disparity of *guṇas*, she became manifest. Though eternal, she is said to be produced (*utpanna*) when she appears for accomplishing the work of gods. It is said that Parā Śakti is identfied with Śiva through this desire. At the time of creation, she emerges like oil from sesamum. According to another opinion, the first principle was *bindu* whence arose *nāda* which gave rise to Śakti. From three *bindus* and a half arose the serpent-power *Kulakuṇḍalī*. *Bindu* is threefold—*Śivamaya, Śaktimaya, Ubhayamaya*. *Śakti* is threefold—*jñānaśakti, icchāśakti* and *kriyāśakti*.

From the union of Śiva and Śakti was born the first son called Brahman. Mother gave Brahman Śakti called Mohinī. The second son was Viṣṇu who protects the entire world having resorted to Śakti given to him by Śiva's consort. The third son was Sadāśiva who was given Śakti called Bhuvanamohinī. The consorts of Brahman, Viṣṇu and Śiva respectively create, preserve and destroy. The males are absolutely incapable of any work without Prakṛti. Lord (Viśveśa or Viśvātman) has been stated to be one and one alone (*eka eva*). He is the one real principle free from dichotomy (*advaita*), higher than the highest (*parāt paraḥ*), self-luminous, (*sva-prakāśa*), always full (*sadā pūrṇa*) and *saccidānanda* (existent, conscious and blissful). He, the formless and changeless one, devoid of attributes and *guṇas*, is eternal and immanent, being the soul of all. He is not perceived by speech and mind. He is omniscient, but none knows Him. The three worlds are upheld by him. All gods, headed by Indra, are under his control. They rule at his command. Śiva says that from Him emanated the above three who respectively create, preserve and destroy. To Pārvati Śiva says that She is the Supreme Prakṛti of the Supreme Lord. The principles beginning with *Mahat* and ending with five *bhūtas* are creations of Prakṛti, Brahman having been only the *nimitta*. Prakṛti is said to assume different forms through illusion (*māyā*).

As regards Śabda-brahman, the views of the author are similar to those of Pūrṇānanda. The same remark applies to the twofold Brahman — Śabda-brahman and Parama-brahman. The author devotes considerable space to a discussion of the threefold *Śabda*, viz. *nitya, anitya* and *prasiddha*.

Śiva is twofold—*nirguṇa* and *saguṇa*, the former being unconnected with Prakṛti. Śiva and Jīva are thus distinguished. Śiva is free from any cover (*kañcuka*) while Jīva has a cover which is fivefold,[5] viz. *avidyā, rāga, kāla, māyā, niyati*. According to the *Kulārṇava*, quoted in the work, *jīva* is restrained by eight fetters (*pāśa*) which are *ghṛṇā, lajjā, bhaya, śoka, jugupsā, kula, śila, jāti*. Sadāśiva is free from these fetters. Thus, *jīva* is Śiva only with the difference that the former is fettered while the latter is unfettered. On authority the author mentions 50 forms each of Viṣṇu, Śiva and Śakti.

As regards the order of creation, the author states the views of different authorities, especially the Sāṃkhya theory.

Mukti is attained by those who concentrate on those which are beyond *guṇas*. *Jīva* can attain Śivahood by knowledge which is imparted by Tantra alone and not by any other scripture, not even by Veda. *Tantra* yields knowledge of the Supreme Being. According to the author, *jīvanmukti* (salvation in life) is possible.[6] The body is indispensable for salvation. As fragrance is in flowers, as fire is in wood so *ātman* is in the body.

In the matter of salvation, Tantra considers the body as indispensable. This sharply distinguishes it from the six schools of Indian philosophy none of which shares the view. Like Vedānta and Sāṃkhya, Tantra believes in *jīvanamukti* or salvation in life. The idea of *jīvanmukti* implies that the preservation of the body is necessary; the Tantra argues—if the body does not exist, how can the fruits of *jīvanmukti* be enjoyed?

Of ethical principles, we have a lot in Bengal Tantra. These are evident in the qualities and merits required in a guru and a *śiṣya*, which have been described in connexion with the contents of the different works. Rigorous self-discipline and various qualities of head and heart are indispensable for a person to be a *guru* in the truest sense of the term. To his disciple he is Śiva incarnate. He has the capacity for leading his disciple along the right path to salvation. A true *Śiṣya* will also have to acquire certain qualities to make himself fit for *dīkṣā*. Disrespect and speaking ill of the *guru* is not only a great hindrance to the achievement of the goal, it also reduces the longevity of the disciple. Among other factors, causing loss of longevity, are acceptance of gifts from a person averse to the duties of his caste and stage of life, lust for other men's wives, covetuousness for wealth, negligence of the study of scriptures, lack of self-restraint.

Time is fleeting; it is the destroyer of all. So, one should not while away time in lethargy, inaction and self-indulgence. One should be fearless where fear exists, and should always be alive to duties.

A man, desiring salvation, should avoid associations, and devote himself to true knowledge; he should be peaceful. Association leads to many sins. If association has to be made, one should keep the company of the virtuous and cultivate the power of correct judgement. Such an association will chasten his mind, and he will be able to discern a thing in its true perspective. Thus, he will come to realise the evanescence of the relation of the soul with his own body, the hollowness of the association of friends and relatives. In this way, with worldly attachments gone, he will not be subjected to worldly bondage and will enjoy the calm and tranquility through renunciation.

Worldly objects are a source of infinite misery. A person who realises this truth renounces the world, and becomes a recluse. Then he does his duties with an indifference towards the fruits of action. In such a state, he can overcome all passions which are a source of suffering and bondage.

Everyone in the world has to satisfy some passions. One, who does so without losing control over the senses, deserves honour. But, he, who indulges in the gratification of his senses, without the power of discrimination, is a beast who is sure to be subjected to infernal tortures in the end.

Some people look upon the enjoyment of worldly pleasures as the only pursuit in life. They are subjected to repeated births and deaths. Other people think that the mere performance of the duties of their caste and order is enough for realising the Supreme Brahman. Yet, others believe that self-mortification by rigorous austerities will lead them to the goal. But, none of the above can lead to the highest end of human life. True knowledge alone is necessary, and all efforts should be directed towards that end.

Ethical principles are elaborately laid down in connexion with the various Tāntric *ācāras* which have been dealt with elsewhere in this book. It should be noted that the Tantra writers were fully alive to the difference in the mental make-ups of different persons. So, they prescribed different modes of discipline for people of different mental powers and attitudes, as will be evident from an account of the different *ācāras*.

To say that Tantra encourages lasciviousness by allowing people to indulge in their natural instincts is to miss the true spirit of Tantra. In fact, self-restraint characterises the Tāntric prescriptions which allow a man to satisfy his instinctive urges no doubt, but always seeks to curb excesses or overindulgence.

A noteworthy feature of Bengal Tantra, as of Tantra in general, is that it lays greater stress on mental purification than on the external means of a purificatory nature. Mental *pūjā* has been extolled as superior to physical worship. The salient features of mental worship are contained in the following quotations from the *Mahānirvāṇa* (v):

hṛtpadmam āsanam dadyāt sahasrāra-cyutāmṛtaiḥ/
pādyam caraṇayor dadyān-manasārghyaṃ nivedayet/
tenāmṛtenācamanam snānīyam apo kalpayet/
ākāśa-tattvaṃ vasanaṃ gandhaṃ tu gandha-tattvakam/
cittaṃ prakalpayet puṣpaṃ dhūpaṃ prānān prakalpayet/
tejastattvaṃ ca dīpārthe naivedyaṃ ca sudhāmbudhim/
anāhata-dhvaniṃ ghaṇṭāṃ vāyutattvaṃ ca cāmaram/
nṛtyam indriya-karmāṇi cāñcalyaṃ manasas tathā/
puṣpaṃ nānāvidhaṃ dadyād ātmano bhāvasiddhaye/
amāyam anahaṃkāram arāgam amadaṃ tathā
amohakam adambhaṃ ca adveśā-kṣobhake tathā/
amātsaryam alobhaṃ ca daśapuṣpaṃ prakīrtitam/
ahiṃsām paramaṃ puṣpaṃ puṣpam indriya nigraham/
dayā-kṣamā-jñānapuṣpaṃ pañcapuṣpaṃ tataḥ param/
sudhāmbudhiṃ māṃsaśailaṃ bharjitaṃ mīnaparvatam/
mudrārāśiṃ subhaktaṃ ca ghṛtāktaṃ pāyasaṃ tathā/
kulāmṛtaṃ ca tat puṣpam pīthakṣālana-vāri ca/
kāmakrodhau tu vikṛtau baliṃ dattvā japaṃ caret/

Processes of mental *japa* and mental *homa* (*jñānahoma*) have also been described in other works on Tantra quoted in Bengal Tantra. Silent *japa* has been stated to be far more effective than loud *japa*. Tantra appears to prohibit all sorts of ostentation and pomp in religious performances; austerity is ordained, but not at the expense of physical health. A *kaula* has been asked to practise *kulācāra* in the solitude of night. The *mūlamantra* should be concealed from others like the paramour of one's mother (*mātṛjāravat*).

Respect for women characterises the conduct of a *Tāntrika*, particularly of one who practises *kulācāra*. They are to be looked upon as embodiments of goddesses.[7] *Kumārīs* or virgin girls of certain age limits are to be honoured on special occasions for the acquisition of merit.[8]

The *Mahānirvāṇa* (iv. 100 ff) condemns the enjoyment of public women, and holds that one, indulging in this vice, incurs sin and loses the fitness of performing religious duties. The son, born of such a union, is called *Kānīna*, and is excluded from all religious rites.

The Tantra further holds (iv. 73 ff) that, in the Kali Age, there is laxity of all religious principles; only truth will remain so that all efforts should be made to uphold truth. Truth, indeed, is Supreme Brahman; it is the greatest austerity; nothing is higher than truth (*satyāt parataraṃ nahi*). *Pūjā, japa* and *tapas*, bereft of truth, are futile like seeds sown in a barren field. This work does not favour the idea of performing Tāntric rites in secret; in its opinion, truth suffers from concealment, no concealment is possible without untruth.[9]

So far as theology is concerned, Bengal Tantra, like Tantras in general, recognises two primeval principles, Śiva and Śakti, corresponding, to a great extent, to Puruṣa and Prakṛti of Sāṃkhya.[10] Śiva and Śakti are regarded as the forms assumed by the Supreme God. This Śakti has been called Ādyā Śakti, Ādi Vidyā, Tripurasundarī, etc. The Supremacy of Śakti is conveyed by the conception that she stays upon Śiva who willingly lays Himself down under her feet. She is an object of meditation to gods Indra and others and is adored by Brahmā himself.

They are but different forms of the Supreme Being. The Supreme Being has been said to have assumed the form of Viṣṇu out of compassion for those who like to adore Him in that form.

The goddesses Durgā, etc., of the Brahmanical pantheon have been conceived as manifestations of this Śakti.[11] As stated in the Chapter on Kālī, she has been represented in this form. Of Kālī again, various forms have been recognised. Bengal Tantra recognises Brahmā, Viṣṇu, Maheśvara as the gods respectively of Creation, Preservation and Destruction. The general attitude is that no deity of the pantheon is denied. Thus, we find Gaṇeśa, Sarasvatī, etc., in the Tantras of Bengal. Kālī, however, is the most prominent figure among the various divine beings.

It should be noted that, though regarding Śakti as the all-powerful Energy of Śiva, Bengal Tantra accords an honoured place to Viṣṇu and Kṛṣṇa also. We have already seen that Viṣṇu has been spoken of as an emanation of the Supreme Being, meant for the preservation of what was created. The *Tantrasāra* gives *mantras* in honour of the various aspects of Viṣṇu, e.g. Dadhivāmana, Varāha, Nṛsiṃha, Harihara, Hayagrīva and Rāma. We find *mantras* also in honour of Kṛṣṇa, Bālagopāla and Vāsudeva. In connexion with Kṛṣṇa, we find the mention of Nanda, Yaśodā, Devakī, Vanamālin, *go-cāraṇa*. A Kṛṣṇa-*mantra*, recited for a lac of times, is stated to be conducive to all success.[12] Such well-known exploits of Kṛṣṇa as *Rāsa-līlā, Viśvarūpa-dhāraṇa, Pūtanā-vadha, Kāliya damana*, destruction of the city of demon Bāṇa, *Govardhana-dhāraṇa*, various activities in Vṛndāvana and Dvārakā, stealing of *Kalpadruma*, etc., are mentioned. Different results are said to accrue from the meditation on Kṛṣṇa in his various forms and engaged in various exploits.

On the authority of the *Prapañca-sāra*, the *Prāṇatoṣiṇī* lays down the fifty aspects of Viṣṇu and his fifty *Śaktis* (powers). It also states the glory (*māhātmya*) of the different names of Viṣṇu. We find in it also a Śatanāma-stotra of Kṛṣṇa. The recitation of the hundred names of Kṛṣṇa is regarded as highly conducive to merit among the pious Vaiṣṇavas.

The *Mahānirvāṇa*, however, does not mention Kṛṣṇa.

The importance, given by Kṛṣṇānanda to Kṛṣṇa, is not difficult to explain. Having flourished either contemporaneously with Caitanya or a little later than him, Kṛṣṇānanda could not naturally escape the tremendous influence of the Vaiṣṇavism as preached by the great religious reformer. Caitanya's preachings centred round Kṛṣṇa.

It is rather curious that Pūrṇānanda, in his voluminous *Śrītattva-cintāmaṇi*, does not deal with Kṛṣṇa. He appears to have flourished a little later than Caitanya. Nevertheless, Caitanyaism flooded the religious soil of Bengal for a long time to come. May be that having been a *Kālī-sādhaka*, who attained *Siddhi*, he thought it fit to dwell on the glorification of Śakti alone to the exclusion of other deities revered in his times.

As we have said elsewhere, the profound influence of Vaiṣṇavism on Bengal Tantra is evidenced by the compilation of the *Rādhā-tantra* and the inclusion of *Vaiṣṇavācāra* among the seven Tāntric Ācāras. In connexion with the *Prāṇatoṣiṇī*, we have noticed the substitutes for the conventional *pañcatattvas* of Tantra, for the Vaiṣṇavas.

It deserves notice that the formlessness of God is recognised. But such a god is beyond the ken of the people in general, because he is *avāṅ-manasa-gocara* (not comprenhesible by speech and mind). Such a divinity is either incomprehensible (*agamya*) or *yogi-nirgamya* (comprehensible to Yogins). The meditation on such a divinity has been termed *arūpa* in the *Mahānirvāṇa* (ch. V). So, for the benefit of the lay people, different forms of the divine being have been conceived. The meditation on such a divinity has been termed in the above work as *svarūpa*. Forms have been fancied in accordance with the quality and action of Devī.

The mother-goddesses (*mātṛkās*) are prominent in Tantra. They are Gaurī, Padmā, Śacī, Medhā, Sāvitrī, Vijayā, Jayā, Devasenā, Svadhā, Svāhā, Śānti, Puṣṭi, Dhṛti, Kṣamā, Ātmadevatā, Kuladevatā.

Of considerable importance among the lesser divinities are the Yoginīs. In the *Śrītattva-cintāmaṇi*, we find that these divinities are classed as follows:

A. *Prakaṭa*—ten. These are Aṇimā, Laghimā, Mahimā, Iśitva, Vaśitva, Prākamya, Siddhi, Icchāsiddhi, Prāpti-siddhi, Sarvakāma-Siddhi. It is noteworthy that these include the eight conventional *Siddhis*.

B. *Gupta*—sixteen, viz. Kāmākarṣaṇa-rūpā, Buddhyākarṣaṇa-rūpiṇī, Ahaṃkārākarṣaṇī, Śabdākarṣaṇa-rūpiṇī, Sparśākarṣaṇa-rūpā, Rūpākarṣaṇa-rūpiṇī, Smṛtyākarṣaṇa-rūpā, Nāmākarṣaṇa-rūpiṇī, Ātmākarṣaṇa-rūpiṇī, Amṛtākarṣiṇī, Śarīrākarṣiṇī.

The text of the *Śrītattva-cintāmaṇi* appears to be defective, as it enumerates only eleven Gupta-yoginīs. The other five are stated in the *Jñānārṇava* (Paṭala xvi) as follows: Rasākarṣakārī, Gandhākarṣaṇa-kāriṇī, Cittākarṣiṇikā, Dhairyākarṣiṇikā, Bījākarṣiṇikā.

C. *Kulakaulika*—ten. Six of them grant respectively *sarvasiddhi, sarva-sampat, sarva-priya* (objects), *sarva-maṅgala*, *sarva-kāma*, *sarva-saubhāgya*. One relieves all kinds of sorrow, another destroys all obstacles. One averts death. One is Sarvāṅga-sundarī.

D. *Nigarbha*—ten, viz. Sarvajñā, Sarva-śakti, Sarvaiśvarya-pradāyinī, Sarvajñānamayī, Sarva-vyādhi-vināśinī, Sarvādhāra-svarūpā, Sarva-pāpa-harā, Sarvānanda-mayī, Sarvarakṣā-svarūpiṇī, Sarvepsita-phala-pradā.

E. *Rahasya*—eight, viz. Vaśinī, Kāmeśvarī, Modinī, Vimalā, Aruṇā, Jayinī, Sarveśvarī, Kaulinī.

Bengal Tantra recognises some lesser Śaktis supposed to reside in the body. These are Ḍākinī, Rākiṇi, Lākinī, Kākinī, Śākinī, Hākinī. On their positions within the human body, we have the following stanzas in the *Śrītattva-cintāmaṇi* and the *Śāktānanda-taraṅgiṇī*:

dvipatradala-madhyasthā *lalāṭa-tala-vāsinī/*
ḍākinī rākiṇī caiva *lākinī kākinī tathā//*
śākinī hākinī caiva *ṣāṭcakra-vinivāsinī/*
sṛṣṭi-sthiti-vināśā ca *sṛṣti-sthity-antakāriṇī//*

Śrītattvacintāmaṇi, xxv. 66.

viśuddhau ḍākinī devī anāhate tu rākiṇī/
lākinī maṇipurasthā kākinī liṅgagocare//
ādhāre śākinī devi ājñāyaṃ hākinī tathā//
śākinī brahmarandhrasthā sarva-kāma-phala-pradā//

Śāktānanda-taraṅgiṇī.

Each of the above is supposed to have a distinct form.

A noteworthy deity is Mañjughoṣa (lit. one whose voice is pleasant). Under this the lexicon, *Śabdakalpadruma*, quoting the *Trikāṇḍa-śeṣa*, notes *pūrvajinabhedaḥ*. *Jina* refers to the Buddha. It seems that the Buddha was, though indirectly, recognised as a deity in Bengal Tantra. A *mantra*, in honour of Mañjughoṣa, as found in the *Tantrasāra*, is as follows:

jāḍyaugha-timira-dhvaṃsī saṃsārāraṇava-tārakaḥ/
śrī-mañjughoṣo jayatāṃ sādhakānāṃ sukhāvahaḥ//

His dhyāna is given as follows:

śaśadharmiva śubhraṃ khaḍga-pustāṅga-pāṇim/
suruciram ati-śāntaṃ pañcacūḍaṃ kumāram/
pṛthutara-vara-mukhyaṃ padmapatrā-yatākṣam/
kumati-dahana-dakṣaṃ mañjughoṣaṃ namāmi//

Khaḍga may be symbolic of the enlightenment of the Buddha, with which he destroyed the darkness of ignorance. *Pusta* may refer to his immense learning. *Atiśānta*, *Kumāra* and *Kumati-dahana-dakṣa* suit the Buddha admirably. It appears to be significant that *puraścaraṇa* relating to *Mañjughoṣa-mantra* consists of only four *aṅgas* instead of the usual five; *brāhmaṇa-bhojana* is prohibited[13] presumably because of the animosity between the Brahmanical religion and Buddhism. The *Gandharva-tantra* (Paṭala I), quoted in the *Prāṇatoṣinī*, describes the Buddha as an incarnation of Viṣṇu.[14]

The *Śrītattva-cintāmaṇi* (xviii. 356-58) enjoins the worship of not only the Buddha, but also of Buddhist philosophy. The word *jineśa*[15] occurs as an epithet of Viṣṇu in the *Śrītattva-cintāmaṇi* (xviii. 401). Does it mean the Buddha? If so, he has perhaps been regarded as an incarnation of Viṣṇu.

It is nothing surprising to find provision of the worship of the Buddha in Hindu Tantra. This is because the Buddha has long been admitted as one of the ten *avatāras*.

NOTES

1. This is the view of *Sphoṭavādins*.
2. viz. *Māyāvādins*.
3. viz. *Naiyāyikas*, etc.
4. cf. *Kulārṇava-tantra* — *mama tattvaṃ na jānanti dvaitā-dvaita-vivarjitam/*
5. cf. *pañca-kleśa* of Sāṃkhya philosophy—*avidyā-asmitā-rāga-dveṣa-abhiniveśaḥ/*
6. The *Mahānirvāṇa* also says—*brahma-jñāna-yuto martyo jīvanmukto na saṃśayaḥ* (iv. 2.1.).
7. cf. *śriya etāh striyo nāma satkāryā bhūtimicchatā/*
   [These women are indeed goddesses of fortune; they should be honoured by one who wishes prosperity.]
   Mahābhārata, Cr. ed., Anu., 46/14.
   yatra nāryastu pūjayante ramante tatra devatāḥ— Manusmṛti.
   [Gods are pleased where women are honoured.]
8. On *kumārī-pūjā*, see under *puraścaraṇa* in Chap. V.
9. *gopanād hīyate satyaṃ na guptir anṛtam vinā.*
10. On the relation of Tantra and Sāṃkhya, see this topic discussed earlier.
11. cf. *tvaṃ kālī tāriṇī durgā ṣoḍaśī bhuvaneśvarī/*
    dhūmāvatī tvaṃ vagalā bhairavī chinnamastakā/
    tvaṃ annapūrṇā vāgdevī tvaṃ devī kamalālayā/
    sarva-śakti-svarūpā tvaṃ sarva-devamayī tanuḥ//
    Mahānirvāṇa, iv. 13-14.
12. cf. *lakṣaika-japanād asya kiṃ na siddhyati bhūtale/*
13. See p. 4 of the *Puraścaraṇa-ratnākara*.
14. cf. *daityānāṃ nāśanārthāya viṣṇunā buddha-rūpiṇā/*
    bauddha-śāstraṃ tathā proktam, etc.
15. The alternative reading is *dineśa* (sun) which does not seem to yield a happy sense.

X. Popular Beliefs and Mystic Practices

Magic has been a part of folk-life perhaps ever since the dawn of civilisation. Some of the magical ideas may have been obtained from earlier aborigines. Sorcery, witchcraft, etc., have a long history in all countries. India is no exception in this respect. The earliest recorded magical rites are found in the *Atharva Veda*. The more primitive a people the more widespread is the belief in such rites and practices. Even today, in the rural life of India, we find a section of people practising these rites as a family vocation. Various tribes preserve such mystic rites with zeal.

The Tantras are a rich store-house of such magical and mystical beliefs and practices. So far as Bengal is concerned, we shall confine ourselves only to the *Tantrasāra* of Kṛṣṇānanda and the *Prāṇatoṣiṇī* of Rāmatoṣana. We shall briefly describe such rites and practices, dealt with in these two works, so that the reader may have an idea of the real popular belief reflected therein. In doing so, we shall not repeat those which have already been referred to while describing the contents of the above two compilations.

Magic is twofold, white and black. The former is designed to secure good health, prosperity and other kinds of material well-being. The latter is calculated to cause harm to hostile people, bring others under control, etc.

Bengal Tantra deals with the magic of both the above kinds.

White magic, according to the authors of Bengal, consists in the rites to ensure the following:

(i) Victory in disputes. The plants *go-jihvā* or *śikhimūlā*, collected in Puṣyā *nakṣatra* and held in the mouth or on head, ensure victory. In the month of Agrahāyaṇa, *śikhimūlā* should be gathered on the Full Moon day and held in the arm, head, the tuft of hair on head—this leads to victory. In the fourteenth night of the dark half, the root (?) of *Mahānīlī* should be gathered from a burning ground and tied round the hand—this ensures victory in disputes. The *mantra* is *Om sudarśanāya hūṃ phaṭ svāhā.*

(ii) Counteracting the menace of theft. Under Puṣyā *nakṣatra*, in the bright half, one should collect the root of the *guñjā* plant which should be tied on the head.

(iii) Cure of diseases. One should drink ghee measuring one *pala* with an incantation.

(iv) Removal of thirst. One should rub red sandal with water, mix it with a *tolā* of water, recite a *mantra* over it for 108 times and drink it saying *tṛṣṇāṃ nāśaya.* In a week the thirst of such a person will disappear.

(v) Prevention of hunger. The following alternative processes are prescribed:

(a) *Kṛṣṇacitrā* measuring half a *tolā* or half or one-fourth of it should be mixed with ghee and made into pills. Then, uttering *Kāmabīja mantra* and saying *kṣunnāśini nivāraya svāhā*, these should be taken.

(b) First, one should have a meal of *haviṣya,* then perform *mātṛkājapa* and take ghee with a *mantra.*

(c) With the tongue one should stir ghee so that the lips are smeared with it, then rub the tongue so as to make it lick the lips.

(d) Every day one should drink *Vijayādhūma*, purified by a *mantra* through *brahma-randhra.*

(vi) Prevention of urination. One should collect *Aśvagandhā*, consecrate it with a *mantra*, mix a *tolā* of it with ghee and drink it. At the root of the penis, he should recite *kāmabīja* and mentally effect stagnation. Mix 32 *tolās* of milk with two *tolās* of *marica* and heat the mixture till it is dried up. Then after reciting a *mantra*, it should be eaten.

(vii) Prevention of motion. Make a mixture of the following: 2 *tolās* of *Viḍaṅga*, 1 *tolā* of *Pippalī*, 3 *tolās* of *Śuṇṭhī* and the juice exuded from *Tejapatra.* The mixture should be made with a *mantra* recited for 108 times. Then, after reciting a *mantra*, it should be taken.

(viii) Prevention of semen-flow. The root of *Eraṇḍaka* is to be crushed and applied to the root of the navel. The bile of *Rohita* fish should also be rubbed over the place. A *mantra* is, of course, to be recited.

(ix) Removal of laziness. After making *Hum* sound and producing a sound with palms, one should take the crushed root of *Vetāla.* With the *Phaṭ mantra* the root of *Tāla* is to be taken. Then one should take honey.

(x) Prevention of sleep. Mix *Śvetadhūpa* with half a *tolā* of *Kaṭutaila.* After uttering a *mantra* for 108 times, one should apply the mixture on both eyes daily. A *mantra* is to be recited in between the eyes and the family preceptor and the family deity are to be meditated upon.

(xi) Freedom from all diseases. Described in connexion with the contents of the *Prāṇatoṣiṇī*.

(xii) Reviving the life of a dead person. This consists in recitation of Mṛtyuñjaya-mantra, invocation and worship of Tryambaka (Śiva).

In white magic are included the various *Siddhis* or powers. Certain *sādhanas* are prescribed for acquiring these *Siddhis*. Some such *Siddhis* are the powers by which one can understand the significance of the cries of various beasts, birds, aquatic creatures, etc.[1] As a specimen, we state below *Kṛkalāsa-siddhi* or the power of understanding the meaning of the cries of a *kṛkalāsa* (chameleon).

One should go alone, with a mind free from fear, to a cremation ground at dead of night on the third lunar mansion of Kārtika and Phālguna. There he should sit and meditate upon goddess Carcikā who is described as having a white throat, a fierce voice, terrible eyes. She is young, two-armed, has shanks long as a palm tree, her hairs are dishevelled. Then he should recite a *mantra* for a thousand times with great concentration. Thus he attains this *siddhi* by which he can quickly bring under control a king and a woman.

One of the *siddhis* is *Khecara-siddhi* by which one can fly like a bird (*Śrītattva-cintāmaṇi*, xxii. 140-42).

Black magic is of the following kinds:

(i) *Māraṇa*—killing. First of all, cinders of *Khadira* wood have to be collected, particularly on *Kujāṣṭamī* day (i.e. in *Aṣṭamī tithi* falling on Tuesday). Then, on an iron plate, the likeness of the enemy has to be drawn. At dead of night, the letters of the *mantra* concerned are to be written in order in the following spots of the picture: head, eyes, forehead, heart, hands, navel, anus, hip, back, two feet. After this, one should form *saṃhāra-mudrā* (hand-posture for destruction) and meditate upon the goddess who gives victory. The goddess, to be meditated upon, is tall, dark, with head turned upward, holding a pair of human heads in hand, naked. Next brick-powder is to be given to the goddess saying *Śatrunāśakaryai namaḥ*. Then, this powder should be mixed with pulverised turmeric and the mixture given before the goddess *amukasya śoṇitaṃ piba piba māṃsaṃ khādaya khādaya hrīṃ namaḥ* — after worshipping the goddess this *mantra* is to be recited at noon and midnight for 108 times. On the eleventh day, the enemy will surely be attacked with a disease. He will die after one *daṇḍa* following the 21st day.

Other methods for *māraṇa* are also prescribed. First of all, the head of a cat, killed for the purpose, is to be obtained. Colouring its tongue with vermilion, one should write on it the name of the intended person. Then one should recite the name of Kālī 10,000 times.

Śmaśānakālī is to be invoked and worshipped with cloth accompanied by iron ornaments. Then one should recite the *mantra* facing south in order to achieve the object.

Having cooked rice, one should offer it to creatures in a lonely spot, and put it into a pit at midnight in the enemy's house. If this is done, the enemy will die within a week.

Having worshipped the great goddess with *pañca-tattva*, one should purify own wine with the seeds of *kūrca*. Then, having pleased the fierce Bhairavī with it, one should drink it uttering the name of the enemy. One should also sprinkle it in all directions in a *Mahāpīṭha*. Then one should walk there in a naked state.

One should write the name of the person concerned on an earthen vessel. Putting own urine into small containers one should throw them there. Then one should recite *Māyābīja* for 108 times. By pleasing Bhairavī thus one can cause insanity and even the death of the person intended.

According to the *Śrītattva-cintāmaṇi*, one should face southward, write the name of the enemy with *mahānīra-rasa* (?) in a *cakra* which is to be burnt in fire. Thus, an enemy can be killed.

(ii) *Utsādana* (destruction). The dung of a bull is to be collected with the *mantra mahādevyai namaḥ*. It is to be worshipped with warm water. On an iron vessel, the picture of the enemy is to be drawn with *Khadira* cinders. Then Śiva is to be mentally placed on it, and with a concentrated mind one should meditate upon Mahārudra, who is to be conceived as staying like fire ablaze on the chest of the enemy seizing his hair with the left hand and drawing his vital breath with the right, surrounded by big fierce animals, holding the *Pināka* bow. After invoking the deity one should bathe him with the *mantra Śūlapāṇaye namaḥ*, and worship him with water for washing feet, etc., uttering the *mantra Maheśvarāya namaḥ*. The *mantra Namaḥ śivāya* is to be recited 21 times. *Huṃ kṣamasva* — with this *mantra visarjana* is to be done with the left hand. The following *mantra* is to be recited once—*ajita keśava viṣṇo hare satya janārdana haṃsa nārāyaṇa svāhā*. Also to be recited is *Huṃ namo bhagavate vāsudevāya svāhā*. On the eleventh day the enemy will be destroyed.

(iii) *Stambhana* (rendering motionless or causing paralysis). A pot is to be obtained from a potter. In it one should put dry lotus-stalks and leaves. Then the pot, resting on ashes, should be placed, along with a shallow dish (*sarāva*) on it, on an iron rod planted into a hole dug to the north-east of the house on a Saturday just at noon when no one else is there.

(iv) *Vaśīkaraṇa* (bringing under control). The process, according to the *Tantrasāra*, has been described under that work. We briefly describe the processes stated in the *Prāṇatoṣiṇī*.

The image of the object is to made with a *pala* or half a *pala* of silver. *Haritāla* and half a *pala* of powdered turmeric should be thrown into a pit 1.5 cubits deep. Placing a red seat therein, one should enter into it and have flags planted all around. Facing eastward and placing a pitcher, filled with sesamum, one should commence *Japa*. Then, after worshipping deities, including Cāmuṇḍā, with certain *mantras*, one should name the object and pray for bringing him under control. *Japa* should be done from morning till midday. Then *homa* is to be performed with *Jāti* flowers. Feeding of Brāhmaṇas is a part of the rite. A paste, made of the crushed roots of white *Aparājitā* plant and *rocanā* (a yellow pigment), should be consecrated with a *mantra* recited hundredfold and used as *tilaka* (a mark on the forehead). Gold of such a quantity as is permitted by the financial condition of the person concerned should be offered as sacrificial fee. The rite should be preceded and followed by elaborate *pūjās*. After five days, a king can be brought under control.

Pūrṇānanda gives certain novel methods. Some of these are stated below briefly. With *mahānīlī* and *rocanā*, mixed with milk, alkaline substance, one should write the name of the person concerned, hold it in his person uttering a *mantra*. Or, the name so written should be kept in water with which he should bathe and which he should drink.

One, facing northward, should write the name of the intended person with vermilion powder and worship it properly.

One should draw a *Cakra* with *rocanās*, and throw it into milk.

One part of *rocanā* and one part of *kuṃkuma* are to be mixed with sandal-paste. The mixture should be used as *tilaka*. Then a *mantra* is to be recited 108 times.

Any one of the following substances, duly consecrated with *mantra* recited 108 times, should be given to the intended person: betel-leaf, incense, flowers, fruit, curd, milk, ghee, cloth, camphor, musk, clove, etc.

One should write on a birch-leaf with *rocanā, aguru,* and *kuṃkuma,* the name of the city, country or any other intended region. It should be worshipped properly and put underground. Thus, the entire region can be brought under control.

In order to bring a woman under control, one should take betel-leaves, with her name in mind, sitting on the bed in a lonely house where none else is present. Or, having recited a *mantra* for 108 times, one should drink water with the name of the woman intended.

One can win the hearts of all women, by the following method: one should face westward, write with sandal-paste the name of the intended woman and worship the goddess duly.

(v) *Vidveṣaṇa* (causing enmity). Some methods for this have been laid down among the contents of the *Tantrasāra.* We state below the method as found in the *Prāṇatoṣiṇī.*

On a *bhūrjapatra* (birch-leaf) the figures of a crow and an owl are to be written with the juice of *Karavīra* or *Dhustūra.* Then, writing the names of the persons concerned, along with a *mantra,* one should wish as follows—let there be enmity between those two persons like that existing between these two birds. The *mantra* in question should be recited 5,000 times. The worship of *Mahākālī* is propitious in this connexion.

With a *mantra* one should write the name of the person concerned with cow's urine mixed with the fluid extracted from the excretion of buffaloes and horses. Then it is to be thrown into *Palāśa* flowers.

(vi) *Uccāṭana* (expulsion). According to Pūrṇānanda, painting the wing of a *droṇakāka* (a kind of crow) in the middle with *rocanā* (a pigment), it should be hung in the air. According to the *Tantrasāra,* the name of the person concerned should be written on a *neem* leaf with the excretion of buffaloes and horses. The pen will be made of a crow's wing. The *mantra* is—*kākatuṇḍi dhavalāmukhī amukam uccāṭaya uccāṭaya hrīṃ phaṭ.* Fire should be brought from the cremation ground and fed with the wood of *Dhustūra.* Human oil or other oil should be poured into it. In this rite, goddess Dhavalāmukhī is to be worshipped. After this the ashes are to be thrown on the enemy's house.

Another method is this. On a particular day a human bone measuring four *aṅgulas* is to be collected. On it the name of the enemy is to be written at the end of night. Then the bone should be thrown into the principal residential house of the enemy.

(vii) *Mahāhāni-karaṇa* (causing great mischief). Facing westward one should worship a black *Cakra* uttering the name of the intended person.

It should be noted that rites are prescribed also for counteracting the effects of hostile magic. These consist in *japa*, and propitiation of goddess Annapūrṇā with various dainty dishes, etc.

Śānti, Vaśīkaraṇa, Stambhana, Vidveṣaṇa, Uccāṭana and *Māraṇa* — these six together are called *Ṣaṭkarma* in the *Tantrasāra*.

NOTE

1. Enumerated in connexion with the contents of the *Prāṇatoṣiṇī*.

XI. Tantra Vis-a-Vis Bengali Cultural Life

Bengal may not have been the birth-place of Tantra, as is supposed by a section of scholars. Nevertheless, the fact remains that the soil of this region was very favourable for the growth and spread of Tāntrism. Tāntric practices permeated the society of Bengal. The religious rites of this province were deeply hued with Tantra. The worship of Kālī, in accordance with the prescriptions of Tantra, became popular not only among the upper classes, but also among the common folk. Tāntric rites to ward off evil, ensure welfare and cause harm to enemies were widely practised. As we have seen above, Sanskrit scholars of Bengal wrote treatises on Tantra.

In short, people thought of Tantra, dreamt of Tantra, talked Tantra, wrote Tantra, sang Tantra, and adopted Tantra for religious purposes.

The Sanskrit works of Bengal, particularly the works of the followers of Bengal Vaiṣṇavism, show widespread influence of Tantras. Besides the ritualistic works on Bengal Vaiṣṇavism,[1] their great devotional, philosophical, theological and literary works are replete with references to, and quotations from, various Tantras, especially the Vaiṣṇava Tantras. Of the works revealing Tāntric influence, mention may be made of the *Bhakti-rasāmṛtasindhu, Ujjvalanīlamaṇi* and *Saṃkṣepabhāgavatāmṛta* of Rūpa Gosvāmin, the *Ṣaṭ-sandarbha* and *Gopāla-campū* of Jīva Gosvāmin.[2]

Some of the Purāṇas and parts of others are supposed to have been composed or compiled in Bengal. Among these works, some reveal profound Tāntric influence.[3] Such Purāṇic works are: the *Devī purāṇa, Bṛhaddharma, Mahābhāgavata, Devībhāgavata*, and the *Kālikā-purāṇa*. The *Devī-purāṇa* mentions several Tantras like *Kālatantra, Mūlatantra, Bhūta-tantra*, etc. It prescribes Tāntric *mantra, nyāsa, mudrā*, etc. Meat and wine also are prescribed in certain cases. Like Tantra, it speaks highly of *Kumārī-pūjā*. It also mentions magic spells like *Kāmikā, Aparājitā* and *Mṛtyuñjaya*. In the worship of the goddess, it accords a higher place to even a qualified Śūdra than one of a higher caste devoid of merit. According to it, the woman has an exalted position; it even provides for the worship of women. It allows even the people of such low classes as Caṇḍāla, Pukkasa, etc., to worship the goddess.

Like Tantra, the *Bṛhaddharma-purāṇa* seeks to determine the proper *guru*. It describes, *inter alia*, the image of Kālī, and provides for her worship to the accompaniment of Mālsī (i. 23) songs; these songs are devotional and suffused with Tāntric ideas. It also contains (iii. 16. 37-45) an eulogy of Kālī. One of the appellations of this Purāṇa is Śāktaśāstra. The *Mahābhāgavata* deals, *inter alia*, with the ten *Mahāvidyās*, the creation of Chāyā Kālī, the origin of 51 Mahāpīṭhas. It is clearly a Śākta work. In it, Kālī is Supreme Brahman and Parā Prakṛti. Puruṣa of threefold quality is created by her. The urge of Puruṣa for creation is due to the impetus provided by the goddess. This work appears to syncretise Vedic religion with the Tāntric. The *Devībhāgavata* is a Śākta work. According to it, the goddess is the highest Divinity, and is the Śakti of all other gods.

The Kālikā-purāṇa describes *Kālī-pūjā* in detail, and provides for the sacrifice of not only animals but also of men in her honour.

The *Vidvan-moda-taraṅgiṇī*, a Campū by Cirañjīva, a Bengali author of the seventeenth-eighteenth century, deals with the *Śākta* as a prominent cult. The *Sadukti-karṇāmṛta* of Srīdharadāsa, an anthology of verses dating back to the thirteenth century A.D., contains several verses describing Kālī in her various forms and activities. Of the authors of such verses, Umāpatidhara is definitely a Bengali. Bhāsoka, author of another verse, is supposed by some scholars to have been a Bengali. The authors of the remaining two stanzas, quoted anonymously, may also have been Bengali. As the anthology originated in Bengal, it is but natural that Kālī should figure prominently among the gods with whom verses are associated.

In Bengali literature, the influence of Tantra is varied and widespread. As we shall see, even scholars, educated in western methods, were deeply influenced by Tāntric ideas. The *Caryāpada*, also called *Caryāgīti*, *Caryācarya-viniścaya*, *Bauddha Gān o Dohā*, which is believed to have been composed about 1000 A.D., contains much that betrays its indebtedness to the Buddhist *Sahajiyā* cult. In certain portions of the work, the firm faith of the author concerned in nihilism is reflected. Even its language resembles the *sandhā* (or *sandhyā*) *bhāṣā* of Tantra. In many cases, religious principles, influenced by Tantra, particularly the Nātha cult, have been mainly drawn upon by Bengali authors. In the Nātha literature, some noted Bengali works are *Māṇikcandra rājār Gān*, *Mayanāmatīr Gān*, *Gopīcandrer Gīt*, *Gorakṣavijaya*, etc. In the well-known *Śrīkṛṣṇa-kīrtana*, which is pre-Caitanya according to some and post-Caitanya according to others, and is attributed to Vaḍu Caṇḍīdāsa, there is indication of the Tāntric mode of *Sādhana*.[4]

In the Bengli *Rāmāyaṇa* of Kṛttivāsa, we find that, goddess Ambikā, whose help is sought by Rāvaṇa in distress, is Kālī or Śyāmā who figures prominently in Tantra. In the same work, the goddess, awakened and worshipped by Rāma out of season, is no other than Kālī. Kṛttivāsa writes about the effect of the hymn, recited by Rāvaṇa, in honour of Ambikā —

asitavaraṇā kālī kole daśānan.

After the goddess concealed one of the blue lotuses, with which Rāma wished to worship Devī in autumn,

Hanumān says —

hena lay cite tomāre herite
paṅkaj harilā kālī//

[To my mind it seems that, to test you Kālī took away the lotus.]

The *Meghanādavadha* (canto V) of Madhusūdana, *Daśamahāvidyā* of Hemacandra, the *Kapālakuṇḍalā* of Baṅkima, *Mā Nā Mahāśakti* of Kālīprasanna Ghosh, the poems *Śavasādhana, Nācuk tāhāte śyāmā* by Navīnacandra and Vivekānanda bear eloquent testimony to Tāntric thought. The *Dasa-mahāvidyā* of Vijayakṛṣṇa, the great devotee of Mother Goddess, is another instance in point. Poet Surendranāth Majumdar appears to have been influenced by the two Tāntric principles of Śiva-Śakti as well as by Puruṣa and Prakṛti of Sāṃkhya philosophy. He says in his poem entitled *Mahilā*:

saṃsāre ye dike cāi, kari vilokan
viparīt duī bhāv melā;
* * * *
hara-gaurī-rūp viśve puruṣ-prakṛti!

[Wherever I cast my eyes, I find that two opposite attitudes are manifest. In the world, there are Hara and Gaurī, Puruṣa and Prakṛti.]

In his conception of Sāradā, as the Universal Energy, in his *Sāradā-maṅgal* and *Sādher Āsan*, poet Vihārīlāl shows his indebtedness to Tāntric ideas. He writes —

kabhu varābhay kare,
cānde yena sudhā kṣare —
karen madhur svare abhay pradān,
* * *
dīpta sūrya hutāśan
dhvak dhvak du-nayan
* * *

kabhu āluthālu keśe
śmaśāner prāntadeśe
jyotsnāy āchen vasi...

[Sometimes she grants boon and freedom from fear with her hand as though the moon exudes ambrosia. She gives freedom from fear with a sweet voice. Her two eyes shine like the blazing sun and fire. At times, she sits with dishevelled hair in moonlight on the outskirts of the cremation ground].

The poet was imbued with the idea of the complete form of the goddess as described in Purāṇa and Tantra. At several places, he characterises her as *yogeśvarī*.

Vihārīlāl appears to be affiliated to the *Śrīvidyā-kula*. The *Latāsādhana* or *Yoginī-sādhana* of Tantra have culminated in *prema-yoga* in his writings. The idea of *prema* may have come from the Vaiṣṇava Sahajiyā cult. The blissful state, acquired by a devotee from the realisation of Śiva-Śakti, is referred to in the following lines of his *Sādher Āsan*:

tomāre hṛdaye rākhi,
sadāi ānande thāki,
āmār prāṇe pūrṇa candroday, sārā divā rajanī.'

Satyadev Ghosh,[5] a scholar-devotee, writes —

āy mā sādhan-samare
dekhvo, mā hāre ki putra hāre!
ārohaṇ kariye kālī-sādhana rathe,
tap jap duṭā aśva yute tāte,
diye jñān-dhanuke ṭān, bhakti-brahma-bāṇ
vasechi dhare[6]*//*

[Come, Mother, to the battle of *Sādhana*. I shall see whether the mother or son is vanquished. Having climbed the chariot of *Kālī-sādhana*, yoked to it the two horses in the form of *tapasyā* (penance) and *japa* (repetition of *mantras*), and drawn the bow of knowledge, I have sat down holding the arrow of devotion and Brahma.]

The main idea of Satyadeva is to transform the individual consciousness to Śakti-consciousness which again is to be realised as Mother consciousness. She is at once the giver of energy and the dispenser of well-being.

In recent times, Yatīndranāth Sen Gupta has composed a poem, called *Bhikhāriṇī* in his poetical work, entitled *Triyāmā*; the theme of the poem is the hunger-stricken goddess Kālī.

Ravīndranāth sometimes betrays a penchant for an outlook on life, which resembles the Tāntric view; the resemblance might, of course, be accidental. For example, we may quote the following lines:

vairāgyasādhane mukti se āmār nay — mine is not salvation through renunciation.

indriyer dvār ruddha kari yogāsan, se nahe āmār — mine is not the yogic posture shutting the doors of the senses.

It is a clear denial of the ascetic ideal of the orthodox Brahmanical religion. The same lust for sensuous enjoyment finds expression in such lines as *śūnya vyom apariamāṇ, madya-sama kariva pān* — I shall drink like wine the limitless sky that is void.

The *Caṇḍīmaṅgala* works clearly reveal the influence of Tantra, e.g. the work of Mukundarāma (late 16th cent.), Dvija Mādhava (late 16th century). Works on *Manasāmaṅgala*, e.g. one by Ketakādās Kṣemānanda (17th cent.), *Ṣaṣṭhī* and *Śītalā maṅgalas*, etc. also contain Tantric ideas.

Bhāratcandra's *Annandā-maṅgala*[7] has been deeply influenced by Tantra. His *Vidyāsundara*[8] also amply shows its indebtedness to Tantra.

The *Kālikā-maṅgalas*, composed by various authors, are clearly influenced by the Śākta cult. Dvija Rādhākānta has characterised his *Kālikā-maṅgala* as *Śyāmār saṁgīt* (song in honour of Śyāmā, i.e. Kālī). The class of literature, known as *Corer Pāñcālī*, in old Bengali, deals with goddess Kālī as the divinity of bandits and thieves. The *Tantrasāra* states that such a goddess, who originated in a Tāntric mileu, used to be worshipped with Tāntric rites.

Quite a number of works chiefly in prose, relating to *Sahajiyā* cult, arose about the seventeenth and eighteenth centuries. Their very titles, *Deha-kaḍcā, Ātma-jijñāsā*, etc., hint at their contents. The Vaiṣṇava Sahajiyā cult obviously bears the deep impress of Tantra. Its philosophy of love is basically Tāntric. The dualism of Śiva-Śakti of Tantra finds a parallel in the dichotomy of *Rasa* and *Rati* in the *Sahaja* in the form of *Mahābhāva. Rasa* and *Rati* correspond to Kṛṣṇa and Rādhā respectively. Tāntric *Sādhanā* assumes energy in the woman and realises it. Again, it assumes and realises Śivahood in man. Likewise, the fundamental thing in the *Mahābhāva-sādhana* of *Sahajiyā* is the realisation of *sva-rūpa* (own real form) in the *rūpa*. The *svarūpa* of woman is Rādhā, and that of the male is Kṛṣṇa. *Mahābhāva* arises out of the union of the pair established in *Svarūpa*. The Nātha literature of Bengal shows that the Nātha cult, which appears to have originated in Bengal, is deeply indebted to Tantra.

A large number of devotional songs, relating to *Śākta* cult, bespeak Tāntric influence and have enriched Bengali literature. Among the writers of such songs, the most famous is Rāmprasād[8] who was at once a poet and a devotee. He was a follower of the *Kaula* way of Tantra. Kālī, a form of Śakti, was his object of meditation. That he was a *Sādhaka* is proved even today by the *pañcamuṇḍī-sādhanā-sana* at the place called *Śiver gali* at Hālisahar, a suburb of Calcutta. His religious outlook appears to have been influenced by the monistic doctrine of Vedānta philosophy. He appears to have looked upon Kālī as one Brahmamayī Śakti behind all the diversities of the universe. The poetical work, called *Kavirañjana*, attributed to *Rāmprasād*, is said to have been a part of his *Kālikā-maṅgal* which is lost. Rājā Kṛṣṇacandra of Nadīyā was a composer of such devotional songs. His two sons, Śivchandra and Śambhuchandra and some other members of the family, notably Narachandra, Śrīśchandra and Nareśchandra, have also left some songs for us. A few songs of such devotional strain are marked with the *bhaṇitā* of Mahārāj Nandakumār. The writers of such devotional songs can be broadly divided into two groups—one of Nadīyā and the other belonging to Burdwan. Some songs were written by Dewān Raghunāth Roy of Burdwan. Mahārāj Mahātabchānd of Burdwan was himself a composer of considerable merit. Of the Burdwan group, and indeed among all such song-makers, a very prominent figure was Kamalākānta Bhaṭṭāchārya.

These devotional songs, particularly those of Rāmprasād, have a charm peculiar to themselves. Their devotional fervour gives rise to rapturous delight in the mind of the devotee and contain immense emotional possibilities. Rāmprasād exquisitely portrays the *Mātṛ-bhāva* (motherhood) of the goddess, and gives a delicate expression to the *Vātsalya-bhāva* of the devotee whose childlike appeal to the mother stirs the soul. It should be noted that the sentiment of tender devotion, called up by Rāmprasād, is in contrast to the terrible aspect of Mother as found in king Suratha's worship of Ādyā Śakti in the *Devīmāhātmya*.

It should be noted that the Tāntrikas and Vaiṣṇavas of Bengal exercised mutual influence, that of the latter on the former being more marked. A few writers even attempted a fusion of the two with a view to removing conventional intersectarian animosities. The Vaiṣṇava poet, Caṇḍīdāsa, used Tāntric imagery and referred to the Tāntric idea of *Ṣaṭcakra-sādhana.*[9] In his *Kālī-kīrtan* and *Kṛṣṇa-kīrtan*, Rāmprasād reveals his deep indebtedness to Vaiṣṇava ideas. He imitates not only the style and imagery of Vaiṣṇava poems, but also attributes to the goddess the characteristics of Kṛṣṇa as revealed in his *Vṛndāvana-līlā.* Thus, he depicts the *goṣṭha, rās*, and *milan* of Bhagavatī. The placing of the flute and cows' goad (*pācanbāḍi*) and the imagery of a female, grazing cows, have exposed him to sarcastic comments,[10] no doubt. Yet, here, as in *Āgamanī* songs, the adaptation of the popular Vaiṣṇavite ideas was not without a purpose; it was not merely an effusive outburst. Apart from the fact that, in the highest form of devotion, the devotee loses all distinctions of names and objects, there were Rāmprasād's solicitations for bringing about rapprochement between the two warring sects. A typical example of this attempt of doing away with all distinctions between Viṣṇu and Śakti, Kṛṣṇa and Kālī is furnished by the following quotations:

prasād bhaṇe abhedjñāne kālarūpe meśāmeśi/
ore eke pāñc pāñcei ek man karo nā dveṣā-dveṣi//
kālī hali mā rāsvihārī
naṭavar-veśe vṛndāvane/

[Prasād says—thinking of non-difference, there is intimate mixing with black form. O man, in one there are five, in five indeed is the one. O mind, do not indulge in hatred. Mother Kālī, thou hast become Rāsvihārī (i.e. Kṛṣṇa) in the guise of the master-dancer at Vṛndāvana.]

Rāmprasād identifies Kālī with not only Kṛṣṇa; according to him, she is the one principle which is manifested in the forms of different deities. He sings —

ai ye kālī kṛṣṇa sivrām-sakal āmār elokesī/

[That Kālī of mine, with dishevelled hair, is all, viz. Kṛṣṇa, Śiva Rāma.]

A few specimens of devotional songs, betraying Tāntric ideas, are given below:

kālībrahma jene marma
dharma karma sav cheḍechi/
ṣaṭcakra-rathmadhye śyāmā mā mor virāj kare/
tinṭi kāchi kāchākachi bāndhā āche mūlādhāre//
hṛtkamalmañce dole karālvadanī śyāmā

* * *

iḍā piṅgalā nāmā suṣmṇā manoramā
tār madhye gānthā śyāmā brahma sanātanī O mā.

[Having known the quintessence that Kālī is Brahman, I have given up all *dharma* (religious practices) and *karma* (action). My mother Śyāmā, resides in the six-wheeled chariot. Three strong ropes, near one another, are tied in *Mūlādhāra* (see Glossary). The fierce-faced Śyāmā swings in the heart-platform. (The *Nāḍis*), named *Iḍā*, *Piṅgalā* and the pleasing *Suṣumna*; into these is stuck the eternal Śyāmā who is Brahman, O Mother.]

— Rāmprasād

tumi cit-abhimukhī kāryahetu cit-vimukhī
cidānande piche rākhi cittānande unmādinī/
tyajya kara nirvikāre mahat hate ahaṃkāre
sṛṣṭi kara savikāre vikār rūpiṇī//

[You are turned towards consciousness, for the sake of work, turned against consciousness. Keeping the joy of consciousness behind you are mad in the joy of mind. Give up *Nirvikāra* (the changeless) from *Mahat* to *Ahaṃkāra*; O (Mother) with the form of change, create, what has change.]

— Rasik Ray

śyāmā mā ki āmār kāla re
ore śyāmā mā ki āmār kālo/
loke vale kālī kālo —
āmār man to māne nā kālo—
kālorūpe digambarī hṛdipadma kare ālo/

[Is my mother Śyāmā black; O, is my mother Śyāmā black? People say that Kālī is black, but my mind does not admit blackness. The naked one, with her black form, illumines the heart-lotus.]

— Kamalākānta

tīrthe gaman duḥkha-bhramaṇ, man ucāṭan hayo nāre
tumi ānanda-triveṇīr snāne, śītal hao nā mūlādhāre//[11]

[Visiting a holy place is painful travel; O mind, don't be restive. Why do you not be cool by bath in the *Triveṇī* of bliss in *Mūlādhāra* (see Glossary) ? Note: *Triveṇi* is the name of the confluence of rivers Gaṅgā, Yamunā and Sarasvatī at the holy place called Prayāga (in Allahabad). The author appears to hint punningly at the terminal point of the three *Nāḍis*, *Iḍā*, *Piṅgalā* and *Suṣumnā* at *Mūlādhāra.*]

— Kamalākānta

Attempts at syncretism are found also in the following:

jāna nā re man param kāraṇ śyāmā kabhu meye nay/
se...kakhan kakhan puruṣ hay//
kabhu bāndhe dhaḍā kabhu bāṇdhe cūḍā...
haye elokeśī kare laye asi...
vrajapure āsi vājāiyā vānśī...

[O mind, you know not that Śyāmā, the Supreme Cause, is never a woman. She sometimes becomes a man, (and) sometimes ties a *dhaḍā* (strip of coth fastened round the lions) and sometimes *cūḍa* (diadem). Having dishevelled hair and holding a sword in hand, coming to *Vrajapura* (Vṛndāvana) and playing on the flute....]

— Kamalākānta

In some works of the *Pāñcālī* class also, we find the same tendency. In Dāśarathi Rāya's *Pāñcālī*, we have the following:

kuñjakānane kālī, tyaje vānśī vanamālī,
śyām śyāmā bhed kena karare jīv bhrānta//
bhuvan bhūlāli go bhuvanmohinī/
mūlādhāre mahotpale vīṇāvādya-vinodinī//
śarīre śārīrī yantre suṣumṇādi traya-tantre
guṇabhede mahāmantre tinagrāma-sañcāriṇī//
ādhāre bhairavākār ṣaḍdale śrīrāg ār
māṇipurete mallār vasante hṛt-prakāśinī//
viśuddha hillolasvare karṇāṭik ājñāpure/
tāl mān lay sure trisapta surabhedinī//

[Vanamālī (Kṛṣṇa), giving up the flute, is Kālī in the bower forest. O confused creature, why do you discriminate between Śyāma and Śyāmā? O Goddess, taking delight in playing the lute in the great lotus of *Mūlādhāra* (see Glossary), O enchanter of the world, you have charmed the world. You are moving in the three villages, with the great *mantra* which is different in accordance with the difference of qualities, in the three strings of *Suṣumṇā* in the body-machine. You are of the form of *Bhairāva* (*rāga*) in *Mūlādhāra*, in the *ṣaṭdala* (six *Cakras*) *Śrīrāga, Mallāra* (*rāga*), in *Maṇipura* (see Glossary) and the revealer of heart in *Vasanta (rāga)*. In *Hillola* note in the *Viśuddha* (*Cakra*) and in the *Karṇāta* (*rāga*) in the *Ājñācakra* you distinguish between thrice seven (i.e. 21) melodies in *tāla* (beating time), *māna* (measure), *laya* (time) and *sura* (melody).]

— Nandakumar

Kālī Mirjā (Kalidas Chatterji), well known for his *ṭappās* and *śyāmā-saṃgīta*, follows the tradition of Rāmprasād with a considerable degree of success. The following lines are quoted from one of his songs:

āre man tui maje yāre kālīpada-sudhārase
caturvarga phal pāvi mukta havi bhava-pāśe/

[O mind, plunge into the ambrosia of Kālī's feet. (Thus) you will get the result of the four ends of life (and) be liberated from the snare of existences (or, rebirths.)]

A class of versifiers and singers in Bengal was known as Kaviwālās. The *Kavi*-songs began to be composed as early as the eighteenth century or even a little earlier. But, the period of its luxuriant growth extended between 1760 and 1830 A.D. One of the several topics of *Kavi*-songs was *Mālsī* which means songs on Rādhā-Kṛṣṇa and other deities. Vaiṣṇava influence on the Kaviwālās was predominant. But, they also wrote on Śākta and Tāntric themes. Lālu Nandalāl, a well-known Kaviwālā, composed songs on the common theme of the identity of Kṛṣṇa and Kālī.[12] About the glory of Devī, Raghunāth Dās sings —

tomār apār lile,
āvār śuni sītā uddhārite, abhay diye akālete,
laṅkāpure raghunāthe, āpani saday hole//

[Your sport is endless. Again, I hear, to rescue Sītā, granting freedom from fear out of season to Raghunātha (i.e. Rāma) in Laṅkā, you yourself became kind.]

Anthony Phiriṅgī, another famous Kaviwālā, sings —

mā rāvaṇ rājā antimkāle raghunāther raṇasthale
durgā vale ḍekechila vadane,
tavu tār pāne phire cāili ne,
tār duḥkha bhāvli ne.

[O Mother, King Rāvaṇa, at the final hour, in the battlefield of Raghunātha, called (Thee) as Durgā with his mouth. Yet, Thou didst not look back at him, didst not think of his misery.]

Nīlmaṇi sings —

mā harārādhyā tārā,
tomār nām, mokṣadhām, tantre śunte pāi/

* * *

tumi tārā, tvaṃ triguṇadhārā

* * *

tārā go mā keval gaṅgājal añjali kare
mānase naivedya kare,
diva mā tor caraṇ dhare, nirmal gaṅgājal//

[O Mother Tārā, adorable to Śiva, I hear in Tantra that your name is the abode of salvation. You are Tārā in whom flows the stream of three qualities. O Mother Tārā, with only a handful of Gaṅgā-water and making *Naivedya* (eatables offered to a deity) of the mind, I shall holding your feet, offer the clear water of the Gaṅgā.]

There are many Bengali patriotic songs composed by different persons. These began to be composed about the middle of the nineteenth century when the spirit of nationalism inspired many a Bengali patriot. In these songs, the native country is looked upon as mother (*deśa-mātṛkā*) and Śakti (Energy). These are clearly influenced by the Śākta cult. In some of them, the influence of Tantra, particularly of Kālī as conceived in Tantra, is discernible. Baṅkim Chatterji (1838-1894 A.D.) was, perhaps, the first noted Bengali litterateur who sang such a patriotic song. His famous *Vande Mātaram* song enthralled countless people, and provides inspiration even today. D.L. Roy was the next great figure who eulogised *Deśa-mātṛkā*. We quote below a few songs which bear clear evidence of Tāntric inspiration.

cala samare diva jīvan ḍhāli —
jay mā bhārat, jay mā kālī!

Rāṇā Pratāp — D. L. Roy

[Let's go, we shall lay down our lives in battle.
Victory to Mother India, victory to mother Kālī.]

śmaśāṇ to bhālavāsis mā go,
tave kena cheḍe geli?
eta vaḍa śmaśān
e jagate kothāy peli?

Asvini Kumar Datta

[Here the author is extremely pained at the miserable condition of the country groaning in thraldom of the foreign rulers. He looks upon Kālī as the Presiding Deity of the country. It means — Mother, you love the cremation ground. Then, why have you deserted it? Where have you got such a huge cremation ground in the world?]

jāgo go, jāgo janani!
tui nā jagile śyāmā
keha jāgive nā mā,
tui nā nācāle kāro
nācive nā dhamanī!

Mukunda Das

[Mother, wake up, wake up. O Śyāmā, unless you awake, none will awake. Unless you make people dance, the vein of none will pulsate.]

The popular folk songs, called *Bāül*[3] *gān*, bear the indelible imprint of Tāntric ideas of the *Sahajiyā* type. A few Bāül songs, containing Tāntric ideas, are quoted below:

1. *gurur hāter pradīp laiyā*
   dekhare aṭhāi guhāy vaiyā
   ātmayoge sacet haiyā
   tave param maram pāvi/
   (dekhvi) saras daraś hṛdmājhāre
   (āvār) apār caudda bhuvan-pāre/
   yogalīlā tor sahasrāre
   ātmā-nātma bhed ghucāvi.

[Taking the lamp of the preceptor's hand (and) sitting in the fathomless cave, look. Being conscious of self-yoga, you will get the greatest secret. (You will have) the sight of the delightful (one) in the midst of the heart (again) at the end of the boundless fourteen worlds. your *Yoga*-sport in *Sahasrāra* (see Glossary); you will put an end to the discrimination between the soul and non-soul.]

(Attributed to Ādyanātha)

2. *ye āche ṣaḍdale, tāre lao ulṭā kale,*
   yadi se yāy dvidale
   uṭhve jvale vāti/

[Take him, who is in the six-petalled (*Cakra*, i.e. *Svādhiṣṭhāna*-*Glossary*), in the reverse machine. If he goes to the two-petalled one, then the lamp will start burning.]

3. *mṛṇāl hāoyār gati, triguṇ-dhāriṇī śakti yathāy vasatī*
   tāre jāgāle yoganidrā, sādhyadhan vādhya hay/

[If the movement of the breeze of the lotus-stalk, where resides *Śakti*, possessed of three qualities, be awakened, then *Yoga-nidra* (see Glossary) (takes place and) the accomplishment of the desired object comes under control.]

(Attributed to Hāüḍe Gosāin)

4. *śata kiṃvā sahasra dal*
   rasa-rati kare calācal
   dvidalete sthiti vidyut-ākṛti
   ṣaḍdale se to ṣaṭtattva hay,
   daśam dale mṛṇāl — gati gaṅgā vay
   tira-dhārā tār śriguṇ vicār
   lālan vale guru anusār/

[Hundred or thousand petals—the delight of charm makes movement. (Its) stay is in the two-petalled one in the form of lightning; in the six-petalled (*Svādhiṣṭhāna Cakra*) it becomes the sixfold principle. In the ten-petalled (*Maṇipura cakra*—see Glossary), the Gaṅgā of the movement of lotus-stalk flows. Its flow, along the bank, is the consideration of *Śrīguṇa* (the three qualities of *Śakti*?). So says Lālan according to his preceptor.]

5. *tũi tāre dharivi keman kare*

* * *

jāne cakrabhedī śikṣā yārā
dharle dharte pāre tārā/
āge caturdale dhar ge goḍā
ṣaḍdale lāgva joḍā
rasik havi torā/

[How shalt thou catch him?

* * *

Those, also possess the knowledge of the penetration of *Cakras*, may catch if they like. At first, go and catch hold of the root in the four-petalled (*Cakra*, i.e. *Mūlādhāra*—see Glossary); (then) there will be union (or joining) in the six-petalled (*Cakra*, i.e. *Svādhiṣṭhāna*) (and) you will be possessed of delight.]

6. *dvidale triveṇi-mahātīrthadhāme*
śaśāṅkaśekhar gaurī laye vāme
nirakhi nayane sei rādhāśyāme
ānandasalile bhāse anukṣaṇ//

[In the two-petalled great holy place of *Triveṇī* (i.e. *Iḍā, Piṅgalā, Suṣumṇā*), the moon-crested (Śiva), with Gaurī on his left, seeing that (couple of) Rādhā and Śyāma, floats in the water of joy at every moment.]

7. *mūlādhāre caturdal padma-pare*
sāpinī nidrita chila nataśire
doleri golete jāgiyā śihari
uccamukhe preme kare nirīkṣaṇ//

[On the four-petalled lotus in the *Mūlādhara*, the female serpent was asleep with its head bent low. In the tumult of swing, having awakened being horripilated looks on in love with its upturned face.]

8. *nā jene gharer khavar tākāo kene āsmāne*
cānd rayeche cānder kole īśān koṇe
prathame cānd uday dakṣiṇe

śuklapakṣe āse neme vāme
āvār dekha kṛṣṇapakṣe
kirūpe yāy dakṣiṇe/
* * *
khuñjile āpan gharkhānā,
tumi pāve sakal ṭhikānā.

[Without knowing the news of the house why do you look at the sky? The moon is in the lap of the moon in the north-east corner. At first, the moon rises in the south; it descends to the left in the bright fortnight. Again, see how it goes to the right in the dark fortnight.]

* * *

If you search your own house, you will get all whereabouts.]

(Lālan Phakir)

9. *suṣumṇā dhariye mṛṇāl vāhiye, uṭha sei padma' pare*
* * *
rūpāśray kari, cal adhaḥ chāḍi —
rūp dhare cal maṇipure/

[Holding the *Suṣumṇā* and proceeding along the lotus-stalk, get upon that lotus.

* * *

Resorting to form, proceed leaving the bottom. Assuming form go to *Maṇipūra* (see Glossary).]

10. *guru, tumi tantrer tantrī,*
guru, tumi mantrer mantrī,
guru, tumi yantrer yantrī
* * *
āmār janma-andha man-nayan,
guru, tumi nitya sacetan,
caraṇ dekhva āśāy kay lālan,
jñān-añjan dāo nayane/

[O preceptor , you are the possessor of *Tantra*; you are the possessor of *Mantra*; you are the possessor of *Yantra* (diagram used in Tantric rites; see illustration v).

* * *

My mind's eye is blind since birth. O preceptor, you are ever-conscious. In the hope of seeing the feet, Lālan says — give the collyrium of knowledge in my eye.]

(Lālan)

11. *amāvasyāy candra uday,*
dekhte yār vāsanā hṛday,
lālan vale theko sadāy —
triveṇite theko vase/

[To one, whose heart's desire is to see moon-rise in the new moon, Lālan says — always keep on sitting over *Triveṇī* (i.e. *Īḍā, Piṅgalā, Suṣumṇā*).

(Lālan)

12. *ṣaḍa cakra pare āche ādi vidhān,*
tāte pūrṇa rekhe ṣola kalā
bhed kare sapta tālā,
tār upare kare khelā kālācānd/

[Over the six *Cakras* is the primeval precept. Keeping it full with sixteen digits (and) penetrating seven storeys, upon that plays Kālācānd.]

(Lālan)

The following are some of the exquisite lines of Nazrul Islam, which echo Tāntric sentiments:

1. *āmār hṛday adhik rāṅā māgo, rāṅājavār ceye/*
[O Mother, my heart is redder than the red *Javā* (flower).]
2. *ore sarvanāśi mekhe eli e kon culor chāi,*
śmaśān chāḍā khelār tor jāygā ki ār nāi?
[O all-destroying lady, you have come besmearing (your body) with the ash of which hearth? Have you got no other playground than the funeral place.]
3. *kālo meyer pāyer taāy, dekhe yāre ālor nācan/*
[See the dance of light under the feet of the dark girl.]
4. *bal re javā bal, kon sādhanāy peli śyāmā māyer caraṇ tal/*
[O *Javā* flower, say, by what penance have you got the soles of the feet of Mother Syāmā?]
5. *Śmaśāne jāgiche śyāmā, antime santāne nīte kole/*
[Śyāmā is keeping awake in the funeral place in order to take (her) children into her lap at the end.]

The idea of *Cāri Candra* (lit. four moons, i.e. four states of mind), found in some Bāül songs, and the concept of *Candrabheda* according to some, echo the Tāntric conception of mental discipline and *Cakrabheda.*[14]

Tantra as religion influenced the conventional religious practices, rites and customs of the Bengalis. The wide use of *maṇḍalas, mudrās, yantras* and the cryptic and mystic syllables in the religious rites of Bengal is a clear proof of the penetration of Tantra into the social and religious life of this province. *Durgotsava*, the greatest festival of Bengal, is marked by Tāntric practices. The *Śabarotsava* on the *Daśamī* day of the *Pūjā*, in which people are required to besmear their bodies with mud and leaves and abuse one another in filthy language, appears to indicate the degeneration of Tāntric practices. Similar indication is found in a provision in the *Bṛhaddharma-purāṇa* which is, in all probability, a work of Bengal. Regarding some vulgar words, it provides that these should not be normally uttered before others. But, on the occasion of the autumnal Durgā worship, these should be uttered except in the presence of one's mother, sister and a female disciple not initiated to *Śakti-mantra*.

Raghunandana, the celebrated social leader of this land, recognised Tāntric initiation (*dīkṣā*) which has since been regarded as indispensable for full spiritual training.

The Vaiṣṇavas freely adopted Tāntric elements in their rites and practices. The *Haribhakti-vilāsa*, the most authoritative work on their rites and customs, openly acknowledges debt to Tantra, among other works, in his prescriptions. In matters of *dīkṣā*, *pūjā* and certain duties, the author draws upon Tantra as on Smṛti, Purāṇa, etc. At several places, he refers to this Śāstra by such general terms as Tantra, Āgama, Nigama, Pañcarātra, etc., while at others, he specifically mentions such Tāntric works as *Kramadīpikā*, *Gautamīya Tantra*, *Trailokyasammohana Tantra*, *Nārada-pañcarātra*, *Rudra-yāmala*, *Viṣṇu-yāmala*, *Śāradātilaka*, *Śaivāgama*, *Hayaśīrṣa-pañcarātra*, etc. Tāntric diagrams, circles, spells, *mudrās*, *nyāsa*, etc., find prominent places in the work. Twenty types of Tāntric *mantras* have been recognised by the author. He dwells on the Tāntric mode of *dīkṣā* (initiation) besides the Purāṇic. The Vedic mode was the most ancient one. He also accepts the Tāntric mode of bath besides the Vedic. In Vilāsa V of the work, he deals mainly with the Tāntric method of the daily worship of Gopāladeva. He follows the *Gautamīya Tantra* for the modes of meditation and worship at the three junctures of the day (*trisandhyā*). The main subject of Vilāsa XVII is the Tāntric rite *Puraścaraṇa*[15] which is an essential prerequisite of *mantrasiddhi* (successful attainment of *mantras*). In this, he takes the *Kramadīpikā* as the principal authority. After the manner of Tantra, it prescribes the worship of the sixteen Mātṛkās before the consecration of images.

The *Satkriyā-sāra-dīpikā*, another work on Vaiṣṇava rites and customs, also utilises Āgama, Yāmala, etc. The *Rudra-yāmala* is a prominent Tantra drawn upon by its author. In almost all of the sacraments, dealt with in it, Tāntric *mantras* have been copiously used.

In Bengal (including the present Bangladesh), there are many centres of Śakti-worship, including some *pīṭhasthānas*. Some of these are: Mehar, Kirīṭeśvarī, Kaṅkālitata, Tārāpīṭha, Kālīghāṭ, Bhavānīpur, Serpur, etc.

Of the above places, Kālīghāṭ is very well-known, and has a long history. Thousands of devotees throng the temple of Kālī every day, particularly on days regarded as very auspicious for Kālī-worship or for *Kālī-darśana*. Situated at the south-western fringe of old Calcutta, it is one of the fifty-one *pīṭhas*. It is said that a toe of the right foot of the dead body of goddess Satī, cut into pieces by Viṣṇu, fell here. Here, the deity is Kālī and Śiva or Bhairava is Nakulīśa, Nakuleśa or Nakuleśvara. It should be noted that this place is not mentioned in any work of ancient times, dealing with holy places. The earliest reference to it, as a renowned holy place, occurs in some Bengali works dating back to 17th-18th centuries, e.g. *Kālikāmaṅgala* of Kaviśekhara, *Anādimaṅgala* of Rāmdās. The art of *Paṭa* or pictures, which has been inspired by the temple and the deity, forms a class by itself. Makers of such *paṭas*, known as *Paṭuyās*, are widely known among the lovers of art.

The Tāntric way of life and the Tāntric mode of *sādhana* were resorted to by certain Bengali families. Generations of members of such families used to cling to this mode as a precious heritage. For a good span of time, the scions of these families enjoyed great reputation and prestige among the people. They were held in high esteem by those who set store by religious practices. One such family is known as *Sarvavidyā-vaṃsa*. The most prominent *Sādhaka* in this family was *Sarvānanda*.[16]

Another such family was resident of village Kāṭihālī in Netrakonā subdivision of the Mymensing district of Bangladesh. It is known by the name of Pūrṇānanda Paramahaṃsa Parivrājaka (c. middle of sixteenth century) who is reported to have been a Tāntric *sādhaka* of a very high order. He composed quite a number of works on Tantra.

Some other families, well-known for Tāntric *Sādhanā*, are the descendants of Ardhakālī, Bhaṭṭācārya family of Meḍtalā, the group of *premikas* of Āndul, etc.

There were some Bengali adherents of Tantra who initiated a number of disciples. They devoted their energy to the study of Tantras and the Tāntric mode of *sādhanā*. The greatest of these figures is Rāmkrishna Paramahaṃsa whose disciples included the famous scholar-preacher, Svāmī Vivekānanda. The most noteworthy feature of Rāmkrishna's religious thought is that he used to look upon Kālī as the Supreme Being. According to him, She is the symbol of unity among the diversities of the phenomenal world. Among those who came into close contact with Rāmkrishna, Giriś' Ghosh was very deeply influenced by Tantra.

It is believed by some that Kesab Sen, founder of Navavidhān Brāhma Samāj, having come into contact with Rāmkrishna, took to the worship of Kālī. Other well-known Tāntric *Sādhakas* were Ratnagarbha, popularly known as Gosāin Bhattacharya, Vāmā Khyāpa.[17] Ratnagarbha is said to have been the spiritual preceptor of Cānd Rāy and Kedār Rāy, famous among the Vāra Bhuiñyās (Chiefs) of Bengal who flourished towards the end of the sixteenth century. A follower of the *Vīrācāra* form, he is stated to have attained *Siddhi* in the temple of goddess Digambarī at Mayaisar in Dacca district. Vāmācaraṇa, known as Vāmā Khyāpā, was born about the middle of the nineteenth century in a Brahmin family of a village in the district of Birbhum in West Bengal. He attained *Siddhi* at Tārāpīṭha, a well-known centre of Tāntric worship, near his native village. It should be noted that a lady, generally known as Ardhakālī,[18] attained considerable fame as a follower of the Tāntric mode of *sādhana*. This in brief is the anecdote associated with her. She was daughter of Dvijadeva, a traditional Sanskrit scholar of village Panditbāḍī (Parganā Ālāpṣing) in Mymensing district of Bangladesh. She was married to Rāghava, a pupil of Dvijadeva. After the marriage, the usual *pākasparśa* (=*boubhāt*) was held at Rāghava's house. While the newly married girl was serving food to the guests, a gusty wind blew off her veil. The girl naturally felt uncomfortable. But, both her hands were engaged, and could not be used to set the veil in the proper position. Then, two more hands emerged from her body, and the needful was done. Thenceforward this miraculous girl had been known as Ardhakālī and much venerated by the people. Her family came to be known as *Ardhakālī-vaṃśa*.

In village Kṣīragrām in Burdwan (West Bengal), there is a very ancient Kālī temple. The story goes that goddess Kālī, whose image is installed there, assumed the form of a girl, introduced herself as daughter of her worshipper and got conch-bangles from a dealer. The place is a holy spot to devotees.

Kudi Mā is known to have been the human incarnation of Kālī in village Tilak on Khulna-Bagerhat railway in Bangladesh.

The sceptic may not place any credence on these anecdotes. Nevertheless, these testify to the Tāntric influence among the mass of people; Kālī is a Tāntric deity.

Among the individual Tāntric Sādhakas, we should mention also Satyadev Ghosh and his disciple, the famous Vijaykṛṣṇa.

Our treatment of this topic will remain incomplete without a reference to the world-famous Aurobindo Ghosh. He appears to have been considerably influenced by Tantra. Tāntric rites and rituals were not his concern. The philosophy of Tantra, particularly Tāntric *Sādhana*, played a great role in moulding his spiritual life. The quintessence of the Yogic *sādhana*, taught by him, is founded on Tantra. The main teaching of Tantra is *kāya-sādhana*, to make the body fit for the abode of God. With it is inextricably bound up the ideal of the fusion of *bhava* (being) and *nirvāṇa* (liberation), of *bhukti* (enjoyment) and *mukti* (salvation). Ghosh also teaches this ideal; he advocates the complete transformation of one's being for the purpose of divine life. Tantra prescribes the drinking of divine *Somarasa*. Ghosh holds that the flow of this divine juice pervades the universe as the divine lustre, divine bliss. One has to prepare oneself for receiving it. After getting it, one tastes divine life. Like Tantra, Aurobindo teaches us *ādhāra-śuddhi* which means the purification of the body and the mind. He looks upon Divine Mother as the Supreme Being to whose will one desiring to reach the goal shall surrender oneself completely and unconditionally.

The Smārta rites and customs of Bengal, dating back from medieval times bear the deep imprint of Tantra. We have already referred to Tāntric *dīkṣā*, prescribed by Raghunandana. Here we shall examine the extent to which the Smṛti digests of Bengal were influenced by Tantra.[19] Bhavadeva Bhaṭṭa, the upper limit of whose date is tentatively fixed in the third decade of the eleventh century, and who flourished probably before 1100 A.D., is the earliest Bengali digest-maker whose works have survived. The prominent Smṛti writers of Bengal, preceding the great Raghunandana and following Bhavadeva, are Jīmūtavāhana, Aniruddha, the royal scholar Vallālasena, Halāyudha, Śūlapāṇi, Bṛhaspati Rāyamukuṭa and Śrīnātha Ācāryacūḍāmaṇi. Govindānanda appears to have been a senior contemporary of Raghunandana or preceded him by a short period. It should be noted that the influence of Tantra is more marked on later writers than on the earlier ones. As a matter of fact, no writer before Śūlapāṇi mentions a single Tantra, although traces of Tāntric influence are noticeable in the pre-Śūlapāṇi digests. Only a few works, among the many attributed to Śūlapāṇi, mention Tantra. Tantras have been mentioned by Śrīnātha, Govindānanda and Raghunandana, the last one most profusely.

The cause of Tāntric influence on these works is not far to seek. As we have stated elsewhere, Tantra invaded every nook and corner of Bengal society. So, the social leaders could ignore it only at a great peril to orthodox Brahmanical rites and customs. Some scholars are of opinion that Tantra found its way into Smṛti works through the medium of Purāṇas,[20] which constituted one of the authorities in socioreligious matters so that Purāṇic authority could not be accepted without recognising Tantra. This view does not seem to be tenable. It is believed that Tantra had been exercising influence on Purāṇa ever since the end of the eighth century A.D.[21] In that case, pre-Śūlapāṇi Bengal writers, who flourished in the period between the eleventh century and the fourteenth century, might have easily absorbed Tāntric rites and customs. So, it seems that Tantra influenced Bengal Smṛti not because of Purāṇas, but in spite of them. Social compulsion seems to have been at the root of the recognition of Tantra by the Bengal writers.

The *Haratattva-dīdhiti*, by Harakumar Tagore of the famous Tagore family of Bengal, is a work on the various rites, rituals and practices of the Hindus. The author lays down the rules and regulations, and freely quotes the authority of various Tantras, Purāṇas, Smṛti and other ancient works. The work deals, *inter alia*, with such well-known Tāntric topics as *Guru, Dīkṣā Sādhana, Sādhaka, Śāktas, Ṣaṭcakra, Nyāsa, Praṇāyāma, Yantra, Pīṭhas, Japa, Kālī-pūjā, Puraścaraṇa, Pañca-tattva, Avadhūta*, various *Ācāras*, etc. The work is an index to the profound influence of Tantra on the religious rites. Had it been otherwise, the author would not have taken pains to consult and cite so many Tantras.

It should also be noted that many festivals of Bengal are Tāntric in character. Some such festivals date back to the fifteenth or sixteenth century.[22]

In an Appendix, we shall state the Tantras mentioned in the various Smṛti digests of Bengal.

In the domain of Bengal sculpture, the influence of Tantra is widespread. Images of the various forms of Devī are scattered all over Bengal.[23] The image, found at Deulbāḍī in Tippera district, appears to be like the goddess described in the *Śāradātilaka-tantra* as Bhadradurgā, Bhadrakālī, etc. Ugratārā, worshipped at village Sikarpur in Bakharganj, is a Tāntric deity. Many pieces of stone, with the figures of seven Mātṛkās engraved side by side, have been discovered in various parts of the province. The Mātṛkās are conceived as the energies of gods.

There are countless images of the various forms of Kālī in every nook and corner of Bengal.

Besides Hindu deities, images of Buddhist Devīs also exist in a good number. Mention may be made of Tārā, Vajratārā, Bhṛkuṭitārā, Parṇaśabarī, etc. There are also statues of Heruka, Hevajra, etc.

NOTES

1. We shall deal with Tāntric influence on such works later on.
2. For details, see S.B. Das Gupta, *Obscure Religious Cults*, etc.
3. For the Purāṇas, supposed to have originated in Bangal, see the present writer's work entitled *Saṃskṛta Sāhitye Vāṅgālīr Dān*, Calcutta.
4. For example, *iḍāpiṅgalāsusamaṇā sandhi*
   manpavan tāte kaila vandī/
   [Iḍā, Piṅgalā and Suṣumanā are united, therein mind-wind was made captive.]
5. Author of *Sādhan-samar*, published in three volumes in Calcutta.
6. Vide *Śākta-padāvali* (Calcutta University).
7. See S.K. De, *Bengali Literature in the Nineteenth Century*, Calcutta, 1962, p. 420.
   The following lines of the *Annadā-maṅgala* are interesting:
   Mṛṇāler tantumadhye sadā āse yāy//
   prakṛtipuruṣrūpā tumi sūkṣma sthūl/
   ke jāne tomār tatva tumi viśvamūl//
   [Always it comes and goes through the lotus-fibre. In the form of Prakṛti and Puruṣa you are subtle and gross: who knows the truth about you. You are the root of the world.]
   More eloquent testimony to Tāntric influence is borne by the following lines:

Kauśiki kālike caṇḍike ambike prasīda naganandīnil
Caṇḍa-vināśini muṇḍa-nipātini Śumbha-Niśumbha-ghātini.
[O Kauśiki, Kālikā, Caṇḍikā Ambikā, O daughter of the mountain, O destroyer of Caṇḍa and Muṇḍa, O slayer of Śumbha and Niśumbha, be pleased.]
In the above lines, Kālī has been identified with Durgā.
The following lines from the *Kālī-stuti* in Vidyāsundara are typically Tāntric:
Kāli Kāli Kālike
Caṇḍa-muṇḍa-muṇḍa-khaṇḍi khaṇḍamuṇḍa-mālike,
laṭṭa paṭṭa dīrgha jaṭṭa mukta-keśa-jālike
[O Kālī, the beheader of Caṇḍa and Muṇḍa, wearing a garland of severed heads, with dishevelled long matted locks from which the mass of hair has been let loose.]
In connexion with the boon given by goddess to Sundara, the poet writes :
lolajihvi lak lak bhāle agni dhak dhak
kaḍ kaḍ vikaṭa daśan//
mukh ati suvistār sṛkkete rakter dhār
Śava-śiśu śravaṇa kuṇḍal/
[The tongue is lolling, fire blazing in the forehead, fierce teeth are making a rattling sound, blood is flowing in the lips. The dead body of a child is very widely used as ear-ring.]

8. For an exposition of *Prasādī Saṃgīt*, see *Vīrabhūmi*, (new Series), Vol. II.
9. *kivā kārikarer ājav kārikuri/*
tār madhye chay padma rākhiyāche pūri//
sahasrāre hay padma sahasrak dal
tār pare maṇipur param śiver sthal//
[What workmanship of the craftsman! Into it, he has put six lotuses. In *Sahasrāra* (see Glossary) there is a thousand-petalled lotus. On it is the *Maṇipura* (see Glossary), the place of Supreme Śiva.]
Lines quoted from Caṇḍīdāsa in *Vīrabhūmī* (New Series), ii, p. 15. Which Caṇḍīdāsa is meant is not clear.
10. For example, *nā jāne tattva kānṭāler āmsattva*
meye haye dhenu ki carāy, etc.

[He does not know the truth (as one who says) *āmsattva* prepared with jackfruit. Note: *Āmsattva* is a preparation of the juice of mangoes dried in the sun.]

— Āju Gosvāmī

11. cf. *agādhe vimale śuddhe satyatoye dhṛti-hrade/*
snātavyaṃ mānase tīrthe sattvam ālambya śāśvatam//
[One should, having resorted to eternal spirit, bathe in the mental holy place which is fathomless, limpid, pure and a lake of fortitude in which truth is the water.]

Mahābhārata, Anuśāsana, III 3.

tīrthaṃ paraṃ kim — svamano viśuddham/
[What is the best holy place; one's own pure mind.]
12. Vide *Prācīn kaviwālār Gān*, compiled by P.C. Pal, pp. 42-46. Kṛttivās calls her Ambikā who is none but Kālī, as stated elsewhere.
13. The word is, perhaps, derived from *Vātula* (mad); some would take it to have been derived from *Vyākula* (Very eager). The corresponding Hindi word appears to be *Vaurā.* He is a Bāül who is mad for realising the proximity or favour of God who is full of love and is his *maner mānuṣ* (the man most desired by mind). Bāüls form a class by themselves. Though mostly illiterate or uneducated, they are adepts in composing songs. With a single-stringed instrument, they go about singing songs in their own way. They do not observe caste-distinctions. Yet some of them belong to different Hindu sects, e.g. *Kartābhajā, Sahajī, Balarāmī,* etc. Some of them are Muslims of whom the most famous is Lālan Phakir (1774-1890). He is said to have been a Hindu by faith; but being orphaned in childhood he was brought up by a Muslim family. Their songs are a curious medley of Tāntricism of the Sahajiyā type, Sufism and Vaiṣṇavism. On Bāüls and their songs, see Tagore, *The Religion of Man;* Ksitimohan Sen, *Bāṃlār Bāül* and his *Līlā Lectures.*
14. See H.C. Paul in *Journal of Asiatic Society of Bangladesh,* XVIII, No. 1.
15. It consists of the following five rites: *traikālika pūjā* (worship of the deity at three junctures of the day), *japa, tarpaṇa* (offer of libations), *homa* (offering oblations) and *brāhmaṇa-bhojana.*
16. For details, see under 'Tantras of Bengal'.

17. For his life, see the Bengali books *Vāmā Khyāpā* and *Śrī Vāmā-līlā* by J.N. Chatterji and H.C. Ganguli respectively.
18. For her biography, see A.C. Mukherji, *Ardhakālī* (in Bengali) and *Rāghava-dīpikā* (in Sanskrit) attributed to Viśvadeva Ācārya.
19. On this question, see R.C. Hazra, *ABORI*, xv, Pts. iii-iv, and *IHQ*, ix, pp. 678-704.
    Also see the present writer's work, entitled *Smṛtiśāstre Vāṅgālī*, Calcutta, 1368 B.S., Chap. V.
20. See R.C. Hazra, *Studies in the Purāṇic Records*, etc. p. 262.
21. *Ibid.*, p. 250.
22. For such festivals and their antiquity, see C. Chakravarti, *IHQ*, xxvii.
23. Vide R.C. Majumdar, *Vāṅglā Deśer Itihās*, in three volumes.

XI. Tantra Vis-a-Vis Bengali Cultural Life

Supplement

Tantra and Sister Niveditā

In connection with Tāntric influence on the life of the people of Bengal, a word must be added about Sister Niveditā[1] (1867-1911). Although a foreigner, yet her relation with the Bengalis was so close that, for all intents and purposes, she was regarded as inseparable from the society of Bengal. While introducing herself, she would write - Sister Niveditā of Rāmakrishna and Vivekananda. She was an ardent devotee of Kālī. She has deftly analysed the conception of Kālī in her celebrated work, entitled *Kālī, The Mother*. Her speech about Kālī, delivered in Calcutta, stirred the soul of the Bengalis, and generated in them a new enthusiasm and devotion to this deity. Many men and women became her disciples.

Tantra and Tagore

Rabindranāth did not support outrageous and barbarous activities perpetrated on the pretext of Tāntric rituals. His attitude of protest is clear from his dramatic compostion, entitled *Vālmīki-pratibhā* and *Rājarṣi*. That he did not fully endorse the Tāntric conduct is obvious from the following lines written by him:

ye jāti calenā kabhu, tāri patha-pare
tantra-mantra-saṃhitār caraṇ nā sare/

'Dui Upamā', 1302 BS.

(The feet of *Tantra, Mantra* and *Saṃhitā* do not move on the path of that nation which never moves forward.)

More about Kālī[2]

At various places in Bengal (West Bengal and Bangladesh taken together), Kālī is worshipped in images[3], symbols[4] or trees.[5] Besides the Kālī image at Kalighat, Calcutta, there are several other renowned Kālī images in West Bengal. These are

the image at Birsimhapur in Birbhum district, the image of Ambikā or the wooden Siddheśvarī at Ambikā-Kālnā, the image of Mayda Kālī at South 24 Parganās, the image of Bargabhīmā[6] at Tamluk, the image at Hālisahar in North 24 Parganas district.

The popularity of Kālī is not confined merely to the Hindu community. Even today, many Muslims, desiring to get over serious difficulties, offer *pūjā* to Kālī. Some of them offer even goats which, instead of being sacrifice in the Hindu way, are set free.

It is said that the renowned Kabiwallāh, Anthony Firiṅgi, was a devotee of Kālī. The song about Bhavānī, which he used to sing before starting *Kavigāna*, is as follows:

bhajan pūjan jānine mā, jātete firiṅgi/
yadi dayā kare taro more e bhave mātaṅgī//

(Mother, I do not know how to serve or to worship; by caste I am an Anglo-Indian. O Mātaṅgī, it depends on your mercy to save me in this existence or earth).

In central Calcutta, an established Kālī image is called *Phiriṅgi Kālī*; it is said that the aforesaid Anthony used to worship it.

Kālīghāt

It is the most well-known place of Kālī-worship in Bengal, and is regarded as one of the fifty-one *Pīṭhasthānas*. It is said that the goddess's right toe fell on this spot. Curiously enough, there is no mention of this holy place in any old work. Comparatively late works on places of pilgrimage also are silent about it. The *Tīrtha-tattva* of the famous scholar, Raghunandana (16th cent.), of medieval Bengal does not refer to it. An oft-quoted line is *Kālikā vaṅadeśe ca*. It refers to Kālī as the dominating deity of Bengal, but gives no hint about Kālīghāṭ. The Bengali poet, Mukundarām (16th cent.) is, perhaps, the earliest author to mention Kālīghāṭ in the following line:

Kālīghāṭer vandiva pratyakṣa mahābalā

(Caṇḍimaṅgala)

It appears to be the earliest literary reference to Kālīghāṭ. In works like the *Kālkāmaṅgala* of Balarāma Kaviśekhara, *Anādimaṅgala* of Rāmadāsa Adaka, Kālīghāṭ[7] iṣ mentioned among the prominent places where Kālī is worshipped, and salutation to the goddess is written. These works date back to seventeenth or eighteenth century.

Rathin Mitra informs[8] us that the present Kālī temple at Kālīghāṭ was built by a Sāvarṇa landlord of Barishā, a suburb of Calcutta, in or about 1809 A.D. In fact, however, this temple is the result of the renovation of the temple originally built in the 16th century.

Pīṭhasthānas

Many of the *Pīṭhasthānas*, mentioned in Purāṇa and Tantra, are *Mātr-pīṭhas*, In Bengal (including Bangladesh), there are the following *Kālī-pīṭhas* : Candraśekhara-Sītākuṇḍa in Caṭṭala (Chittagong), Mehar in Tripurā district, Yaśoreśvarī of Jessore, Bhavāni or Aparṇā of Bhavānīpur in Baguḍā district, Kirīṭeśvarī of Kīrtikona in Mursidābād district, Mahābalā Bhadrakālī of Kālighāṭ (Calcutta), Nalāteśvarī of Nalhāṭ Yodādyā of Kṣīragrāma.

Kālī and Dacoits

In connexion with Kālī, it should be noted that some dacoits of Bengal were worshippers of this deity. They used to invoke Kālī before undertaking operation, and worshipped her with a portion of their booty. It is said that some of them resorted to human sacrifice for pleasing Kālī. The stories of the dacoits, named Raghu, Viśe, Buddho, etc. have become a part of the folk-tales of Bengal. Some of the notorious hide-outs of dacoits were at the following places in West Bengal:

Kānchḍāpāḍa (24 Paraganas, North)
Moynāpur (Bānkurā-Visnupur), Bagati (Hughli),
Singur (Hughli), Cakrapur (Ārāmbāg, Hughli),
Bhātendā (24 Paraganas), etc.[9]

Śyāmā-Saṅgīta

It should be noted, in connexion with songs about Kālī, that She was not looked upon merely as Mother. In the poem, captioned 'Kālī the Mother; penned by Svāmī Vivekānanda, in extreme anguish and agony, invokes[10] Kālī symbolising Death. A portion of this poem, as translated by Satyendranāth Datta, is as follows:

nāce tārā unmād tāṇḍave-mṛtyurūpa mā āmār āy!
karālī ! karāl nāmtor, mṛtyutor niśvāse praśvāse,
tor bhīm caraṇ nikṣepe pratipale brahmāṇḍa vināśe!
Kālī tui pralayarūpiṇī, āy māgo, āy mor pāśe!

Tāntric influence on Caryāpada

The *Cakra* (nerve-plexuses) and *Padmas* (lotuses), conceived in Tantra to be within the body, are mentioned in the following line of the *Caryāpada*, the earliest extant work in Bengali literature:

eko so padumā, cauṣāṭi pākhuḍi (No. 10)

The Tāntric devotee aims at rousing *Kuṇḍalinī*, slumbering in the base,

Mūlādhāra, and raising it to the apex, *Sahasrāra*. The *Caryāpada* also hints at directing the awakened *Bodhicitta* to the *Mahāsukhacakra*:

> *duhila dudhu ki beṇṭe sāmāe* (No. 33)

Tantra recognises three principal *Nāḍīs* : *Iḍā* on the left, *Piṅgalā* on the right and *Suṣumnā* in the middle. The vital breath and Śakti move through *Suṣumnā*. In the following lines, quoted from the *Caryāpada*, there is the direction, according to the Buddhist *Sahajiyā* doctrine, for resorting to the middle path of *Sahaja* after leaving the right and the left

> *Sāṅkamata caḍhile dāhin vām māhohi* /
> *niyaḍḍi sohi dūr mā jāhi*/ (No. 5)
> *vām dāhin cāpi mili māṅgā*/
> *vāṭata milila mahāsuha sāṅgā*/ (No. 8)

Sculpture and Tantra

In the realm of Bengal sculpture, impact of Tantra is noticeable in various images[11] of the goddesses mentioned in Tantra. The image at Deubāḍī, in the district of Tripurā, reminds one of Bhadradurgā and Bhadrakālī mentioned in the *Śāradātilaka*. The image of Ugratīrā at Sikārpur, in the district of Bākharganj (now in Bangladesh), is a Tāntric deity. The figures of the seven *Mātṛkās*, in many pieces of stone and terracotta found at several places, testify to the influence of Tantra; the *Mātṛkās* have been conceived as *Śaktis* of gods. In the different nooks and corners of Bengal, there are countless images of Kālī, the typical Tāntric deity. Not only Hindu deities, there are many images of Buddhist deities, which bear the impress of Tantra. As instances, we may mention Tārā, Vajratārā, Bhṛkuṭitārā, Parṇaśabarī, etc. Mention may also be made of the images of Heruka, Hevajra, etc.

Architecture and Tantra

Tantra made its impact on Bengal architecture too. There is a temple, dedicated to goddess Haṃseśvari, at Bānsebriyā (Vaṃśavāṭī) in the district of Hughli, to the west of the Ganges, about fifty kilometers from Calcutta. A landlord, named Nṛsiṃha Devrāy, who was a Tāntric devotee, planned this temple, and began its construction in 1799 A.D. It was completed by his widow in 1814 A.D.

The interior of the temple is built like six Tāntric *Cakras*. The deity has been represented as *Kuṇḍalinī* which is rising upward. Besides the three principal *Nāḍis*, called *Iḍā*, *Piṅgalā* and *Suṣumnā*, two other *Nāḍis*, called *Vajrākhya* and *Citriṇī*, have been shown by means of a ladder within the temple. The aforesaid deity is represented as seated on a lotus on the navel of Śiva lying in a triangular *Yantra* (Tāntric diagram). In the lower left hand of the goddess, there is a human skull, the upper right hand is shown in the pose of *Abhayamudrā*. One of the two other hands holds a sword, and the remaining one clutches a conch-shell. The very name Hamseśvarī is Tāntric. *Haṃ* is a Tāntric *Bīja*, and *Sa* indicates *Śakti*. The union of *Haṃ* and *Sa* is considered to be the means of attaining the untlimate goal.

Painting and Tantra

The art of painting, prevailing in Eastern India in the Pāla period (c. 750 – c. 1155 A.D.), reveals the impact of Tantra. Some paintings, contained in manuscripts, reflect the model of Prajñāpāramitā on the one hand, and faith in Tantra on the other. An example is furnished by the picture of Lokanātha, dating back to the 12th-13th cent. It is preserved in the posture of *Ardhaparyaṅka*. The right hand is in the boon-giving pose, and the left holds a lotus with stalk.[12] Figures of deities in accordance with Vajrayāna-Tantrayāna, are painted in some Buddhist manuscripts of the 11th-12th cent. Two manuscripts of *Aṣṭasāhasrikā-prajñāpāramitā* have been found; one of them dates back to the 39th regnal year or Rāmapāla c. 1077-1120 A.D.), and the other to 19th regnal year of Harivarman. A manuscript of the *Pañcaviṃśati-sāhasrikā prajñāpāramitā* harks back to the 8th regnal year of Harivarman.[13] These testify to Tāntric inspiration in the domain of the art of painting. That the votaries of Tantra used to cultivate the art of painting is indicated by the paintings contained in some Tāntric mansucripts or on their wooden covers, dating from the medieval period. Such a painting appears in a manuscript (1443 A.D.) of the *Kālacakra-tantra*.

The well-known *Paṭ* paintings of Kālīghāṭ, Calcutta, originally centred around Kālī and her temple. In course of time, however, many other motifs, besides Kālī, were adopted by the artists.

Minor religious sects influenced by Tantra[14]

Tantra has a philosophy. Rites and rituals are not all that Tantra teaches us. Justice Woodroffe (1865-1936), his preceptor, Sibchandra

Vidyārṇava (b. 1860 A.D.) and Manmathanath Datta, among others, tried to bring out the philosophy of Tantras. But, most of the common people took the enjoyment of the five *Tattvas* (*Pancamakāras* as these are generally known) as the be-all and end-all of Tāntric *Sādhana*. This attitude to Tantra reminds one of the fact that a girl, after listening to the story of the *Mahābhārata*, remarked that the lesson, derived from it, is that a girl can marry five men. The inevitable result of the above attitude was levity, licence and lasciviousness that corrupted the society.

About the horrible nature of the Tāntric rites in the nineteenth-century Bengal, Ward has given a vivid picture in his work, *A View of the History, Literature and Mythology of the Hindoos.* Here is a brief account, according to Ward's Report, of the then society reeking and reeling with Tāntric practices of incredible indecency.

For the purpose of such a rite, a woman would be brought to the chosen place. The devotees of the righthanded sect (*dakṣiṇācārī*) would bring their own wives. Those of the left-handed one (*vāmācārī*) would select a woman from anyone of the following communities:

barber, washerman, Caṇḍāla, Muslim, etc.

The woman, meant for the ritual, would be seated and worshipped with various articles including eatables of various sorts. After the worship, the woman would eat fish, meat etc.; and drink wine. The remnants of her food and drink would be put by the devotees into the mouth of one another irrespective of caste. Then the woman was stripped of her clothes, and orgy ensued in which the first participant was the priest followed by others.

Ward concludes his account by writing that very few people followed the precepts of the Śāstras. They considered the ritual as a licence for enjoying wine and sex, etc.

En passant, it may be added that some degenerated Tantras held out the hedonistic ideal embodied in such statements as *vāme rāmā ramaṇakuśalā dakṣiṇe pānapātram* (to the left is a woman skilled in sexual intercourse and to the right a goblet).

Ward has also cited examples of human sacrifice in Tāntric worship.

A reprehensible fall-out of the degenerated Tāntric practices was what was known as *Guruprasāda*. It is reported that a newly married girl would be, at first, enjoyed by the *Guru*, and then she would be allowed to lie down with her husband.

Inspired by new values in the wake of the Renaissance in Bengal in the nineteenth century, some young men tried to eradicate the loathsome practices to which the gullible people resorted under the guidance of the so-called *Gurus* who were unscrupulous, and exploited the devotees' naive beliefs to fill their pockets.

A funny incident in connexion with dealing a blow to the vicious system of *Guruprasāda*, referred to above, may be related here. It is reported that a newly married girl was lying with the *Guru* on a bed under which a young man was hiding with a stick to teach a lesson to the *Guru*. While courting the girl, the *Guru* asked her to say *āmi rādhā tumi śyām* (I am Rādhā, you are Kṛṣṇa). As soon as he uttered it, the young man pounced upon him saying - *ei kāndhe lāṭhi balarām* (here is Balarām with a stick on his shoulder).

Here we shall briefly describe some little known or unknown religious sects which were influenced by Tantra. It should be stated that corruption did not infiltrate into each and every one of these sects. Some of them adopted the liberal Tāntric principles of giving women right to religious practices, denied in the orthodox Śāstras, and doing away with the caste distinctions and untouchability which, according to Mahātmā Gandhi, is a blot on Indian society. Besides Tantra, the *Sahajiyā* doctrine also appears to have produced considerable impact on them.

Kartābhajā Sect

A fairly large number of adherents were claimed by the sect in the eighteenth and early nineteenth century.

One, Āulacānd (d. 1769 A.D.), founded this sect, and preached this religion in the district of Nadīyā. After his demise, one, Rāmśaraṇ Pāl, of Ghoshpāḍā near Naihāṭi, became the leader of this sect. He did not recognise caste distinction, and used to initiate both Hindus and Muslims. The adherents of this sect looked upon their *Kartā* or *Guru* as God incarnate or the embodiment of Kṛṣṇa. Low-class women would serve him even as *Gopīs* are stated to have done towards Kṛṣṇa. The influence of the *Guru* was so great that the devotees did not call their begetters father. To them, the *Guru* was the father of all. The conduct of the *Gurus*, as laid down in contemporary newspaper (*Somaprakāśa*, 1863 A.D.) is briefly as follows.

Kartā is lying on bed, surrounded by a host of women. Some of them are shampooing his feet, some rubbing sandal-paste on his body, while others are garlanding him. Some *Kartas* carry away the clothes of their female devotees, and climb trees. Devotees of all castes sit together for worship. The precepts of this sect are, of course, noble and point to a righteous way of life. Akshay Datta has remarked that immoral practices have eclipsed whatever good is there in the doctrine of this sect.

Rāmavallabhī Sect

One, Rādhāvallabha, of village Bānsberiya in Hughli district of West Bengal, was the founder. In it, Kṛṣṇa, Christ and Muhammad were regarded as equal, and the *Gītā, Bible* and *Qurān* used to be studied with equal reverence. In course of time, the sect came to be called Rāmavallabhī. Guru Nānak also was an object of adoration. Among other things, beef was also offered in religious rites, and used to be eaten as *prasāda*. The song, current in this sect, was - *Kālīkṛṣṇa God Khodā, kona nāme nāhi vādha* (Kālī, Kṛṣṇa, God Khodā - there is no bar to any name). This attempt at religious symbiosis reminds one of Ramkrishna's (1835-1886) oft-repeated remark *'yata mat, tata path'* (there are as many ways as there are doctrines), as also of Kesab Sen's (1838-1884) *Navavidhān*, as a religious system.

Sāhebdhani sect

The story is that one, named Sāhebdhani, who was indifferent to worldly life, founded this sect in the forests of the villages, Sāligrām, Dogāchiyā etc., in Nadīyā district. Both Hindus and Muslims were inducted into its fold. The adherents of this sect did not worship images; they looked down upon images and *Mantragurus*.

Vaiṣṇava sect

Some small sub-sects, belonging to the Vaiṣṇava community, made considerable impact on the populace. These were called

Spaṣṭadāyaka, Sakhībhāvaka, Āul, Bāul,
Sahaji, Sāin, Nyada, Darveś, etc.

These sects had the following common features :

Prakṛti-sādhana (worship in the company of women), absence of caste-distincion, taking food from one another, etc.

Spaṣtadāyaka

In this order, *Guru* was not looked upon as an incarnation of God; his authority was limited. Its founder was Rūparam Kavirāja, disciple of Kṛṣṇa Cakravartin of Saidābad in the district of Murshidābād. A band of ascetics, male and female, used to control the adherents. The adherents used to live in *Maṭhas* as brothers and sisters.

Sakhībhāvaka

The male adherents of this order used to dress themselves as females.

Having experienced delight in reciting the names of Kṛṣṇa and Caitanya, they used to sing and dance. Low-class people were initiated into this order. Their main centre was at Jangaliṭolā in the district of Māldā. The sphere of their influence extended to Jaipur and Vārāṇasī.

The English version of the remarks of Aksay Datta[15] about the Order of *Āul*, may be quoted:

> "Their other name is Sahaja Kartābhajā . . . Many prostitutes overtly or covertly are engaged in their *Sādhana*. They do not drudge their wives even attached to other men."

There were some other minor Vaiṣṇava sub-sects, too. These were as follows :

(1) Khusiviśvāsī : Founded by a Muslim named Khusi Viśvās, of village Bhaga near Devagrāma, in the district of Nadīyā. In this Order, Khusi is regarded as an incarnation of Caitanya, and caste distinction is not recognised.

(2) Gauravādī : In this Order, Gaurāṇga is looked upon with greater reverence than even Kṛṣṇa. The image of Gaurāṅga is worshipped, and his name is constantly recited.

(3) Balarāma sect : Founded by Balarāma Hāḍi of village Meherpur in the district of Nadīyā. In it, he is worshipped as if he is Rāma. The adherents do not recognise caste distinction. Most of the disciples are householders, some are indifferent to the world. The people of the latter class are unmarried, but free from sexual indulgence. There is no image-worship. After the demise (1851) of Balarāma, a woman, named Brahmaka Maloni was given the status of *Guru*.

(4) Pāgalpanthī : This sect prevailed among the Muslims of Serpur in the district of Mymensing in Bangladesh. Its founder was Ṭipu Pāgal of the village. Letiyakanda in Pargana Susang. The central teaching of the sect is this; all men are created by God, nobody is under the control of anybody, the discrimination as high and low is meaningless.

(5) Miscellaneous : Three Muslims, Hajrat, Gobrā, Pāgalnāth, founded three independent sects in imitation of the aforesaid *Kartābhājā* sect.

Tilak Dās, belonging to the Kartābhajā sect, having renounced it, founded a sub-sect called Tilakdāsī, and proclaimed himself as incarnation of Śaiva, Viṣṇu, etc. Darpanārāyan Muchi of Sāntipur was a strong exponent of this sect.

NOTES

1. Vide Samkariprasād Basu, *Niveditā Lokamāṭā.*
2. For details, see the following Bengali books:
   Diptimay Rāy - *Paścim Vaṅger Kālī O Kāliksetra*;
   Bratindra Mukherji - *Śaktir Rūp bhārate O Madhya Esiyāy.*
   Also see the Bengali journal, *Desh,* Calcutta, dated 17.10.87 (B.N. Mukherji's article - Kālī devir mūrtitattva).
3. Usually made of stone, metal or earth.
4. E.g. stone-phallus or other forms. There is a phallus-symbol at Kirtikon.
5. As in Mehar. At Sītākuṇḍa, the goddess is supposed to be in the form of fire. In rare cases, the goddess is worshipped also in water.
6. According to some, it is Buddhist Ugratārā. It is worshipped with *Tārā-mantra* contained in the *Nīlatantra.* But, from the following *Dhyāna-mantra* in the *Devi-māhātmya,* the image appears to be that of Kālī :
   vicitra-khaṭvāṅgadharā asipāśinī, dvīpi-carma-paridhānā, jihvā-lalana-bhīṣaṇā/
7. A tradition would have us believe that the image at this place was installed by Gorakṣanātha (c. 11th or 12th cent.), a renowned *Guru* of the *Nātha* Order.
8. Vide *Telegraph,* a Calcutta daily, dated 23.12.90 (Magazine).
9. For details, see Diptimoy Roy, *Paścim Vaṅger Kālī O Kālīkṣetra* (1391 B.S.), p.185 ff.
10. For the attitude of Svāmījī vis-a-vis Śakti, see *Svamijike yerup dekhiyāchi,* Svami Mādhavānanda's Bengali trs. of *The Master as I Saw Him* by Sister Niveditā, chap. XI.
11. Vide R.C. Majumdar, *Baṃla Deśer Itihas, Madhyayug, Adhunik yug.*
12. Vide S.K. Sarasvati, *Pāl Yuger Citrakalā* (in Bengali), p. 125.
13. Vide R.C. Majumdar, *Baṃla Deśer Itihās,* Prācīn Yug, p. 236.
14. For details, see R.C. Majumdar, *Bāṃlā Deśer Itihās,* vol. 3, pp.243-64; Aksay Datta's *Bhārtavarṣīya Upāsak Sampradāy* (in Bengali); newspaper entitled *Somaprakāśa,* 1863 A.D.
15. Vide *Bhārtavarṣīya Upāsak Sampradāy,* (Bengali), p. 175.

APPENDICES

I. Unpublished Tantras of Bengal

We have given accounts of the published Tantras of Bengal along with the personal history of their authors. Besides these works, some are available in manuscripts, while others are known only from references to them contained in other works. In addition to these little known or unknown works of Bengal, which are mostly digests or compendia for ritualistic purposes, there are commentaries by Bengal writers on some well-known Tāntric works. We set forth below the titles of the unpublished Tāntric works of Bengal with such details about their places of deposit, authors and contents as could be gleaned from various sources. The following abbreviations have been used here:

AS: *Asiatic Society Catalogue*, Calcutta.

CC: *Catalogus Catalogrum* by T. Aufrecht.

IO : *India Office Catalogue*, London.

N: *Navadvīpa Sādhāraṇa Granthāgāra*, Navadwip, Nadiya, West Bengal.

NCC: *New Catalogus Catalogrum* by V. Raghavan.

NM: *Notices of Skt. MSS.* by R. L. Mitra.

NP: *Catalogue of Skt. MSS. in Private Libraries of NW. Provinces.*

NS: *Notices of Skt. MSS.* by H. P. Sastri.

SC: (Government) Sanskrit College, Calcutta.

SKR: A Handlist of MSS. with Sarat Kumar Roy, 1-4. European Asylum Lane, Calcutta.

SKRDC: An Unfinished Descriptive Catalogue of the above collection.

SSP: Handlist of Skt. MSS. in Sanskrit Sāhitya Pariṣat, Calcutta.

Varendra: A Handlist of MSS in Varendra Research Society, Rajshahi, Bangladesh.

VSP: Catalogue of MSS. belonging to Vaṅgīya Sāhitya Pariṣat, Calcutta.

VSP Sup: *A Supplementary Handlist of MSS.* in Vaṅgīya Sāhitya Pariṣat, Calcutta.

Titles are in Devanāgari Alphabetical Order

Title	*Author*	*Reference to MS.*	*Remarks*
Abhijñāna-ratnāvalī	Rāmānanda Tarkālaṅkāra	AS 3603 G viii.A 6211 NM xi. Pref. 15 Varendra 1217	An extensive work on the worship of Śakti. The AS MS. contains only fragments of Chapters i- iv.
Amarasaṃ-graha	Amara Maitra		Author, son of Viṣṇvānanda.For MS. and bio-graphy of author, see under Tāntric Texts of Bengal.
Āgama-candrikā	Kṛṣṇa-mohana	AS 6209 viii. i. 6209 VSP p.187 and Intro. pp. xxv-xxvi	Author, a Kāyastha of Pūrvasthalī in West Bengal. He appears to have been well off and to have appointed Pandits for com-piling works for himself. In this work, it is stated to have been compiled by Pandits. To Kṛṣṇamohana are attributed as many as eighteen works including the *Kamalodaya* and the

			Nītiśataka; these two mention some of the eighteen works. Vide AS vii. 5250, 5251, 5508-9; VIII. 6209; NS II. 41; VSP, pp. 125, 187. The *Āgama-candrikā* deals with rules of initiation and the worship of deities of the group of Mahāvidyā.
Āgamacandrikā	Rāmakṛṣṇa Tarkālaṃ-kāra	NM I 269. CCI. p. 273 AS 6214 VSP Sup No. 1879 Intro. p. xvii.	From it we learn that the author was son of Raghunātha and a resident of Napāḍā, popularly known as Dakṣiṇa Navadvīpa, in Andul near Calcutta. It is a summary of Raghunātha's *Āgama-tattva-vilāsa*. The date of composition of the *Āgama-candrikā* is *munivedanṛpe śāke*, i.e. Śaka 1647 (=1725 A.D.).

Āgama-tattva-vilāsa	Raghunātha Tarkavāgīśa	SC 1053 AS G viii. i. 6214 1611 NM IX. 3186 (1st, etc.) NS I 22 (5 chaps) SKR 172	Author, son of Śivarāma. Written in 1687 in 5 chaps; it deals with Tāntric modes of worship and *mantras* for various deities. In the beginning, the author is stated to have consulted 160 works including the *Tārārahasya* and *Śyāmā-rahasya*. Part of it printed. See *Cat. of Printed Books in British Museum.*
Ādyākā-raṇa-tantra-Ānanda-laharī-ṭīkā	Vidyāvāgīśa Mahādeva Vidyāvāgīśa	SSP A 1389 AS G 6582 IO IV. 2624	From the work it is learnt that the author was son of Yādavānanda Chakravarti, grandson of Vidyāsāgara and great-grandson of Subuddhimiśra. Author said to have obtained the title Vidyāvāgīśa from his preceptor at Viṣṇupura,

			situated within Māndāraṇa. Date of composition — 1527 Śaka (=1605 A.D.). Said to have been written in Jahangir's reign. Vide *Indian Culture*, IV, p. 322.
(Hari-bhakti-Śuddho-dayā)	Harinārāyaṇa	SS G 3973 NS II 17	
Do	Govinda Tarkavāgīśa	AS G 3694, 5204 NM X 3373 VSP 334	
Do	Śrikṛṣṇa Tarkālaṅkāra Bhaṭṭācārya	AS G 3905	
Amari-saṃhitā	Amara Maitra		For MS. and biography of author, see under Tāntric Texts of Bengal.
Kakārādi-Kālī-sahasra-nāma	Pūrṇānanda		
Kaṅkāla-mālinī-tantra	Rāmasvarūpa	SSP 375	

Karpūrādi-stava-ṭīkā (Prabodhinī)	Rāmakiśora	NS III 48 Dacca University Handlist, No. 3967	Author appears to have been a descendant of Sarvavidyā.
Do	Yādavendra Bhaṭṭācārya	Sanskrit College, Benares, 1916-17, p. 3 (No. 2624) with text	
Kāmya-yantro-ddhāra	Mahāmahopādhyāya Parivrājakācārya	NS III. 53	Dated 1375 A.D.
Kālikā-rahasya	Pūrṇānanda		
Kālikādi-sahasra-nāma	Pūrṇānanda	NP V 138 AS VIII B 6643-46 Dacca University No. 552 B NS I 61 Travancore University No. 7799 Viśvabhāratī 509, 510.	
Kālī-tattva-sudhā-bindu	Kāliprasāda Kāvyacuñcu	NM IX. 2956	
Kālī-sarvasva-sampuṭa	Śrīkṛṣṇa Vidyālaṅkāra	NS I. 60 Varendra 979 Dacca DR 33	Author, son of Nyāyavāgīśa.

Kulapūjanacandrikā or Kulapūjācandrikā	Candraśekhara	NS II. 37 SSP I. J. 53	
Kulamūlāvatāra	Śaṃkara		
Kaulikārcanadīpikā	Rāmaratna	SSP 411	
Kramacandrikā	Ratnagarbha Sārvabhauma	NM I. 331 SC 761	Contains *mantras* applicable in Tāntric rites. Author appears to have been the preceptor of the famous Cānd Rāy and Kedār Rāy of Vikramapura, now in Bangladesh. He is also known as Gosvāmī Bhaṭṭācārya.
Kramastava	Śaṃkara		
Gururājatantra	Rāmalocana	SSP A 1183	
Gurupādukāstotraṭīkā	Durgādāsa Vidyāvācaspati	Viśvabhāratī Annals 190 (b) VSP p. 267 SSP III. U. 52 Dacca University	

		MS. 1350 AS 3401, 6118, 5289, 3917A VIII. B. 6798 5799 -6801, 6802	
Do (-pañcaka)	Raghunandana Nyāyapañcānana	Dacca University MS. No. 1974, 2964 NS I. 97.	
Gautamīya-tantra-tattva-dīpikā	Rādhāmohana	VSP 39 (117), 40 (335)	Author seems to be identical with the Vaiṣṇava author of this name, who wrote the *Kṛṣṇabhakti-sudhārṇava* and commentaries on the *Śuddhitattva* of Raghunandana and the *Gautamanyāyasūtra*. Rādhāmohana was a writer of the nineteenth cent. and a friend of Colebrooke. Vide VSP, p. 16.
Cakra-dīpikā	Rāmabhadra Sārvabhauma	ASG 141 VIII R 6622 Dacca University 187 A. 1884	Quoted in *Tantrasāra* Aufrecht's Bodleian Cat.95a.
Cakra-dīpikā	Ratneśvara	SC 633	
Jñānā-dīpikā	Amara Maitra		For MS. and biography of

			author, see under Tāntric Texts of Bengal.
Jñānā-nanda-taraṅgiṇī	Śiromani	NM I 286	
Tattva-prakāśa	Jñānānanda Brahmacārī	NS I 137	Composed in 1730 Śaka (=1808 A.D.) in 12 Chapters.
Tattvā-nanda-taraṅgiṇī	Pūrṇānanda	AS Cat. VIII. 6200	
Tantra-kaumudī	Govindacandra	SSP A. 1184	
Tantra-candrikā	Rāmagati Sena	AS 6274	Author, perhaps identical with that of the *yoga-kalpalatikā* (NS. I. 299). He is said to have been a resident of East Bengal (Bangla-desh). Vide NS.I, Preface p. 21.
Tantra-dīpanī	Rāmagopāla Śarmā	NS II 79	Composed in 1626 Śaka (=1794 A.D.) in 11 Chapters. Author, a disciple of Kāśi-nāthānandanātha

			otherwise known as Paramaniranjana
Tantra-dīpikā	Gopāla pañcānana	ASG 5097 NS I 138 NM VI 2262 SC 874	Author, grandson of Kṛṣṇānanda Āgamavāgīśa and son of Harinātha Bhaṭṭācārya.
Tantra-pradīpa	Jagannātha Cakravartī	NS I 139	
Tantra-pradīpa-prabhā	Sanātana Tarkācārya	NS II 80	
Tantra-prakāśa	Govinda Sārvabhauma	ASG 5641	Deals with *dīkṣā*, *puraścaraṇa*, etc., and the worship of Tārā and Tripurā.
Tantra-ratna	Kṛṣṇa Vidyāvāgīśa	ASG 10494 IO IV 2573 NMI 240 SC 913	Deals with worship of Kālī and Tārā.
Tantra-saṃkṣepa-candrikā	Bhavānīśaṃkara Vandyopādhyāva	NS II 81	
Tantra-sāra	Rāmānanda Tīrtha	AS II A 48	Complete in 10 Chaps. On page 93, there is a quotation from the *Śrī-tattva-*

			cintamāṇi of Pūrṇānanda. Author was a protégé of Kṛṣṇacandra (eighteenth century), king of Nadīyā.
Tārārcana-candrikā	Jagannātha Bhaṭṭācārya	ASG 6537	
Tārārahasya-vṛtti	Gauḍīya Śaṃkara	VSP 33-35 (108, 732, 1267) IO IV 26038. See Cat. of Skt. MSS., Asiatic Society, Calcutta, Vol.VIII, p. xli	
Tārābhakti-taraṅgiṇī	Kāśīnātha	NM IV 1607	Date 1737 Śaka (=1815 A.D.) Kṛṣṇacandra, king of Nadīyā, mentioned as the author's patron.
Tārāvilāsodaya	Vāsudeva Kavikaṅkaṇa Cakravartī	ASG 790, 3455	
Tīkṣṇākalpa	Rādhāmohana	NS II 90	Written in Śaka 1732 (=1810 A.D.). Author, a landlord of Candrapratāpa in Dacca district (Bangladesh).

Tripurār-cana-rahasya	Brahmānanda	NM VII 2487	
Dakṣiṇā-kalpa	Haragovinda Tantravāgīśa	NM I 291	
Dīkṣā-tattva-prakāśa	Rāmakiśora		Author, a member of the Sarvavidyā family of Mehār (Bangladesh). Vide K. Sen, *Cinmay Vaṅga*, p.173.
Pañca-kalpataru	Rāghava Devaśarmā	NS X 3311	Author, son of Rāmānanda Tarkapañcānana. It is a digest on Tāntric rites, and contains a fairly elaborate account of mystic *maṇḍalas* and *Durgāpūjā* with those *maṇḍalas*.
Pañca-maveda-sāra-nirṇaya	Haragovinda Rāya		For MSS. and biography of the author, see under Tantras of Bengal.
Puraś-caraṇa-prayoga-darśa	Vāsudeva Sārvabhauma	VSP 39 (1309)	Author identified as *Sarvā-nandika sādhusāgnika-*

			jñānānanda bhaṭṭācāryā tmaja.
Puraś-caraṇa-dīpikā	Candraśekhara	CC I p.340 SC 1058	
Puraś-carṇo-llāsa-tantra	Kāśīcandra	SSP 1383	
Prāṇa-kṛṣṇa-vaiṣṇa-vāmṛta	Bholānātha Brahmacārī		Composed for Prāṇakṛṣṇa Biswas in 1748 Śaka (=1826 A.D.). Deals with Tāntric rites of Vaiṣṇavas.
Bhāva-nirūpaṇa		ASG 4660	Appears to be a part of Rāmagati Sena's *Tantra-candrikā (Supra).*
Mantra-kośa	Jagannātha Cakravartī	VSP 43 (1548 Kha) NM VII 2378	In the second MS., the author's name ends in Bhaṭṭācarya. In the contents are mentioned, *inter alia, Tāntric bīja-mantras* and their explanation. It also contains a brief account of the origin and nature of alphabet.

Mantra-ratnākara	Yadunātha Cakravarti	ASG 6028	
Mahimnaḥ-stotra-ṭīkā	Raghunandana Nyāyavāgīśa	VSP 55 (1482)	
Muṇḍa-mālā-tantra	Nyāyavāgīśa	SSP 417	
Mudrā-prakāśa	Rāmakiśora		See *Dīkṣātattva-prakāśa* (*Supra*).
Yakṣiṇī-tantra	Āditya	SSP 774	
Yogakal-palatikā	Rāmagati Sena	NSI 299	
Rahasyā-rṇava	Vanamālī Ācārya	VSP 60 (1408)	
Lalitā-rahasya	Rājendra Tarkavāgīśa	VSP 64 (753) NM IV 1674	A digest, in nine chapters, based on various Purāṇas and Tantras. In it attempts have been made to establish the predominance of Kṛṣṇa.
Varṇa-bhairava	Rāmagopāla Pañcānana	NM I 280	Deals with origin of sound and the significance of letters starting with 'a'.

Varṇā-bhidhāna	Yadunandana Bhaṭṭācārya	ASG 8144 NM II 560 IO II 1046 SC 1492	In the last two MSS., the author's name is Śrīnandana Bhaṭṭācārya.
Vaśa-kārya-mañjarī	Rājārāma Bhaṭṭācārya	ASG 3463	
Śākta-krama	Pūrṇānanda	NM VI 2067	
Śivār-cana-mahāratna	Śaṃkara		
Śaiva-ratna	Do		
Śyāmā-kalpalatā	Rāmacandra Kavicakra-vartī	ASG 3459 NS I 372	
Śyāmā-kalpa-latikā	Mathurānātha	Pub. Guptapallī Śaka 1825 (with Bengali translation)	
Śyāmā-pūjā-paddhati	Cakravartī	ASG 5958 Indian Museum Collection No. 4590	
Śyāmā-ratna	Yādavendra Vidyālaṃkāra	NM I 377	
Śyāmār-cana-candrikā	Ratnagarbha Sārvabhauma	NM I 220	For particulars about the author, see *Krama-candrikā (Supra).*

Śyāmā-santoṣaṇa stotra	Kāśīnātha Tarkapañcānana	ASG 3540	
Śyāmā-saparyā-vidhi	Kāśīnātha Tarkālaṃkāra	ASV vii 3603	Composed in Śaka 1699 (=1777 A.D.) in seven chapters.
Śyāmā-stava-ṭikā	Durgārāma Siddhānta-Vāgīśa Bhaṭṭācārya	AS 6628-29	Text of *Karpūra-stotra* and its comm.
Srī-tattva-bodhinī	Kṛṣṇānanda	NM 281	
Ṣaṭkarma-dīpikā	Srī Kṛṣṇa Vidyāvāgīśa	NM IV 309 VSP 85 (363) ASG 3881 Calcutta Sanskrit College MS. 410	
Ṣaṭ-karmollāsa	Pūrṇānanda	NS IV 308	
Ṣaṭcakra-dīpikā	Brahmānanda		
Ṣaṭcakra-dīpikā-ṭikā	Pūrṇānanda		
Ṣaṭcakra-nirūpaṇa	Nandarāma Tarkavāgīśa	AS 6367 SC 446	With the author's name are associated the works *Ātma-*

			prakāśikā (IO IV. 2400), *Sāṃkhya-prakāśikā* (*Ibid.* IV 2457), etc. Author perhaps identical with the author of *Svarūpākhya-stava-ṭīkā*. In the *Ṣaṭcakra-nirūpaṇa*, he has mentioned Hari-vallabha Rāya as his patron. He appears to have flourished before Śaka 1638 (=1716 A.D.).
Ṣaṭcakra-krama-dīpikā	Rāmabhadra Sārvabhauma	NS I 386 SC 619	
Ṣaṭcakra-bheda (Ṣaṭcakra)	Pūrṇānanda		
Ṣaṭpadya-mālā	Rāmarāma Bhaṭṭācārya	NS I 387	
Sanātana-dharmānu-ṣṭhāna	Jaganmohana Tarkālaṃkāra		First part deals with the procedure of ten-fold *Saṃskāra* in accordance with Tantra. Second part deals with procedural

			matters relating to *Śrāddha* in conformity with Tāntric practices.
Sarvā-nanda-taraṅgiṇī	Śivanātha	NS iii 336	A biography of Sarvānanda by his son.
Sādhana-mālā	Vinodacandra	SSP 634	
Sundarī-rahasya-vṛtti	Ratnaṇābha Āgamācārya	AS 6350	Account given by himself — Vārendra Brāhmaṇa, Maitreya. Son of Nārāyaṇa, grand-son of Mukunda, disciple of Gopīnātha.
Sundarī-śakti-varadānam	Ādinātha	SSP A 1237	
Svarūpā-khya-stava-ṭīkā	Nandarāma	VSP 154 (1356 Ka) 155 (1356 Kha) NS I 39	

II. Tantras Mentioned in the Smṛti Digests of Bengal

Abbreviations

DK : *Dānakaumudī* of Govindānanda, Bib. Indica, Calcutta.
DV : *Durgotsavaviveka* of Śūlapāṇi, Skt. Sāhitya Pariṣat, Calcutta.
ET: *Ekādaśītattva* in *Smṛtitattva* of Raghunandana.
SK: *Śrāddhakaumudī* of Govindānanda, Bib. Indica, Calcutta.
TT: *Tithitattva* in *Smṛti-tattva* of Raghunandana.
VK: *Varṣakriyākaumudī* of Govindānanda, Bib. Indica, Calcutta.
VV: *Vratakālaviveka* of Śūlapāṇi.

(In Devanāgari alphabetical order)

Kapilapañcarātra
DK–5,13,126,129,130, 180,192,204,205
DV–23
Gavākṣatantra
DV–12
Gāruḍatantra
VK–283
Gautamītantra
VK–146
Nāradapañcarātra
VK–150
Nāradīya-saṃhitā
TT–51
Nigamapariśiṣṭa
SK–53, 317
VK–17
Puraścaraṇa-candrikā
VK–118, 152, 158, 176, 179
ET–74, 85
Bhuvaneśvarītantra
VK–160
Matsyasūkta
DK–206
DV–7, 11, 13, 23
Mahākapilapañcarātra
DV–23
Yoginītantra
VK–120, 132, 149, 157, 175, 372, 440, 441, 442
Rudrayāmala
SK–266
VK–157, 284
Śāradā (Tilaka?)
DV–11

Śāradātilaka
VK–118-21, 126-28, 134
136, 139, 145, 149, 150,
152, 153, 157, 159, 162,
170, 171, 173,174,176,
190, 384, 385, 391, 565
DK–9,10, 68, 74, 75, 89,112,
124, 125, 126, 128, 130,
131, 141, 144, 146, 149,
150, 151, 153, 154, 155,
156, 158, 159, 164, 176,
178, 179, 180, 182, 185
188, 190, 191,

Śivāgama
VK–76

Hayaśīrṣapañcarātra or
Hayaśīrṣa
VV–24

Tantras cited in the Haratattva-dīdhiti

(In Devanāgarī alphabetical order)

Little known works have been left out

Āgamakalpadruma
Āgamatattva-vilāsa
Āgamadvaita-nirṇaya
Āgama-sandarbha
Āgamasāra
Uttarakāmākhyā-tantra
Uttara-tantra
Utapatti-tantra
Umājāmala
Kaṅkālamālini-tantra
Kamalā-tantra
Kamalāvilāsa-tantra
Kātyāyanī-tantra
Kāmadhenu-tantra
Kāmākhyā-tantra
Kālīkalpa-tantra
Kākulāmṛta-tantra
Kālīkulārṇava-tantra
Kālīkrama-tantra
Kālītantra
Kālīvilāsa-tantra
Kubjikā-tantra
Kumārī-tantra
Kulaprakāśā-tantra
Kulācāra-tantra
Kulārṇava-tantra
Kulāvalī-tantra
Gandhāra-tantra
Gāyatrī-tantra
Guptadīkṣā-tantra
Gupta-sādhana-tantra
Guptārṇava-tantra
Guru-tantra
Gotamīya-tantra
Gaurījāmala
Gheraṇḍa-saṃhitā
Cīnatantra
Jāmala
Jñānatantra
Jñanārṇava-tantra
Ḍāmara-tantra
Tantra-kaumudī
Tantracūḍāmaṇi
Tantradīpikā
Tantrapramoda
Tantraratna

Tantrarāja
Tantrasāgara-saṃhitā
Tantrasāra
Tantrādarśa
Tāntrikadarpaṇa
Tārāgama
Tārātantra
Tārārahasya
Tārārahasya-vṛtti
Tārārṇava
Toḍala-tantra
Trailokya-sammohana-tantra
Dakṣiṇāmūrtikalpa
Dakṣiṇāmūrti-saṃhitā
Dattātreya-jāmala
Durgā-kalpa-tantra
Devījāmala
Devyāgama
Navaratneśvaratantra
Nārāyaṇī-tantra
Nigamakalpalatā
Nigamakalpasāra
Nigamatattvasāra
Nityātantra
Nibandha-tantra
Niruttara-tantra
Nirvāṇa-tantra
Nīlatantra
Picchilā-tantra
Puraścaraṇa-candrikā
Puraścaraṇa-bodhinī
Puraścaraṇa-rasollāsa-tantra
Phetkāriṇī-tantra
Bṛhat-tantrasāra
Bṛhat-toḍala-tantra
Bṛhad-gautamīya-tantra
Bṛhad-rudrajāmala
Bṛhannirvāṇa
Bṛhannīla-t
Bṛhanmāyā-t
Brahmajāmala
Brahmāṇḍa-tantra
Bhagavad-bhakti-vilāsa tantra
Bhuvaneśvarī-tantra
Bhūtasuddhi-tantra
Bhairavajāmala
Bhairava-tantra
Bhairavī-tantra
Matsyasūkta
Mantratantra-prakāśa
Mahākālamohinī-tantra
Mahānirvāṇa-tantra
Matānīla-tantra
Mahāliṅgeśvara-tantra
Mahiṣamardinī-tantra
Mātṛkābheda-tantra
Māyātantra
Mālinī-tantra
Muṇḍamālā-tantra
Mṛḍānī-tantra
Meru-tantra
Yoginī-tantra
Rudrayāmala-tantra
Revā-tantra
Liṅgārcana-tantra
Varadā-tantra
Vāmakeśvara-t
Vāmadeva-t
Vārāhī-t
Vidyotpatti-t
Vimalā-t
Viśvasāra-t
Viṣṇujāmala-t
Vīra-t

Vyomaratna-t
Saktijāmala
Śakti-t
Śakti-saṃgama-t
Śāktānanda-t
Śāmbhavī-t
Śāradā-t
Śāradā-tilaka
Śāśvata-t
Śikhariṇī-t
Śyāmā-kalpalatā
Śyāmārahasya
Śyāmarcana-candrikā
Śyāmā-saparyā-krama
Śyāmā-saparyā-vidhi
Śrītattva-cintāmaṇi
Sanatkumāra-t
Samayā-t
Samayācāra-t
Sammohana-t
Sārasvata-t
Sarasvatī-t
Siṃhavāhinī-t
Siddhalaharī-t
Siddheśvarī-t
Svacchanda-maheśvara-t
Svatantra-t
Haṃsamaheśvara
(Haṃsaparameśvara)
Hayaśirṣa-pañcarātra

Tāntric authors mentioned in the *Haratattva-dīdhiti*
Tantradīpikākāra
Pūrṇānanda
Brahmānandagiri

III. Works and Authors Cited in the Tantras of Bengal[1]

(Arranged in English Alphabetical Order)

N.B—The figures refer to the pages of the work against which these are mentioned.

A. WORKS

Title	*Tantra in which mentioned with reference*
Ācāracintāmaṇi	PV Kanda v
Ācārasāra	P 344
Ādityapurāṇa	S 41
Ādiyāmala	T 611
Adhyātma-viveka	P 12, 28
Āgamakalpadruma	T 16, 35, 240, S 5 PV Kanda ii
Āgamasaṃhitā	T 1, S 4
Āgamasandarbha	P 195
Āgamasāra	P 239, T 4
Āgama-tattva-vilāsa	T 75
Āgamottara	T 583
Agastya-saṃhitā	T 37, 38
Agnipurāṇa (Āgneyapurāṇa)	P 349, S 8, 18, 41
Akṣayā	SU 124
Ānandapaṭala	SU 120
Annadākalpa	P 104. PV Kanda ii
Arṇava	S44
Bhagavadbhukti-vilāsa	P 181
Bhāgavata	P 9. S 39, 42
Bhairavīya	T 467, 511
Bhairavatantra	P 63. T 461, 463, 472. S 19, 21, 31. SU 33, 66. SR 7
Bhairavītantra	T 9
Bhārata	S 18
Bhāṣya	S 10
Bhāvacūḍamaṇi	P 511. T 153, 545. SU 24, 43, etc., SR 5

Title	*Tantra in which mentioned with reference*
Bhāvasārāvalī	TR 56
Bhaviṣyapurāṇa	P 88. S 14, 18
Bhūtabhairava	T 40. PV Kanda ii
Bhūtaḍāmara	T 640. S 24
Bhūtaśuddhitantra	P 189. SS 8, 11, 17
Brahmajñānatantra	P 22, 23, 24, 25
Brahmajāmala	P 104. T 57, 384
Brahmapurāṇa	T 686. S 183
Brahmasaṃhitā	T 693, 776
Brahmavaivartapurāṇa	P 346
Bṛhacchaṃkara-vijaya	P 495
Bṛhadyoni	SU 57, 107, etc.
Bṛhannīlatantra	P 5
Bṛhat-stavarāja	T 414
Bṛhat-toḍalatantra	S 15
Bṛhacchrīkrama	T 20. S 21, 34. PV Kanda ii. SR 20, 50/(*Saṃhita*)
Bṛhadgautamīya	T 255
Cāmuṇḍātantra	T 48, 492, 708
Caraṇavyūha	P 62
Chandaḥsāra	T 51
Chinnamastātantra	SR 41
Cidambara-naṭa-tantra	PV Kanda ii
Cintāmaṇi	PV Kanda i
Dakṣiṇāmūrti	T 375, 377, 404. SU 134 (*Saṃhita*)
Dakṣiṇāmūrtisaṃhitā	T 160, 204
Dakṣiṇāmūrtitantra	P 160, 204
Dakṣiṇāmūrtitantra	P 206
Ḍāmara	SR 22
Daśapaṭalī	P 174
Dattātreyasaṃhitā	P 406, A
Devīpurāṇa	P 110
Dharmapurāṇa	S 14
Dharmasaṃhitā	T 351
Divyācāratantra	·PV Kanda i, iv
Divyatantra	T 575
Ekavīrakalpa	T 50, 504, SR 33

Title	*Tantra in which mentioned with reference*
Gaṇeśa	SU 1
Gandharvamālikā	T 11. S (Gandharva) 5, 15, 18, 37, 42
Gaurījāmala	P 196. S 15. PV Kanda iii
Gāndharva	T 937. S 5, 13, 18, 37, 42, 8, 17, 18, 20, 31A
Garuḍatantra	T 622
Gāruḍa	S 59
Gāyatrītantra	P 83
Gandharvatantra	P 6
Gaṇeśavimarśinī	P 162. T 7, 114. S 44. PV Kanda ii
Garuḍapurāṇa	P 182
Gautamīya	P 178. T 34 39. S 14, 19, 30, 43, 45. A. SU 77, 94, 99, 205, 212. SR 6
Gheraṇḍasaṃhitā	A
Gītā	P 9
Gopālatāpanīya	S 8
Gorakṣasaṃhitā	P 8, 198. A
Govindavṛndāvana	T 83. S 42
Grahajāmala	P 126. A
Gupta-dīkṣātantra	P 144. S 31
Guptarahasya	SR 48
Guptārṇava	T 446. SR 16
Gupta-sādhana-tantra	P 11. SU 36, 76, etc.
Gurudīkṣātantra	P 5
Gurugītā	P 99
Gurutantra	P 94. SU 31, 32, 150
Haṃsamaheśvara	SU 67, 89, etc.
Haṃsatantra	PV Kanda iii
Haṃsamaheśvara	SU 67, 89, etc. T 48. S 28
Haṃsaparameśvara	P 73. SR 20
Hanūmatkalpa	T 757
Hastihṛdaya-prabandha	P 292
Haṭhadīpikā	PV Kanda vi
Hayaśīrṣa-pañcarātra (Hayaśīrṣa)	P 150. T 6
Īśānasaṃhitā	P 22
Jāmala	P 17, 97
Jñanadīpa	SU 7, 14 etc.

Title	*Tantra in which mentioned with reference*
Jñanabhāṣya	P 27. S 1. A
Jñānapradīpa	S 31
Jñānārṇava	P 174. T 2, 127. S 14, 19. SU 46, 68, etc. SR 2
Jñānamālā	T 702
Jñānasaṃkulī	P 177. PV Kanda v
Jñānatantra	PV Kanda iv
Jñāneśvarī-saṃhitā	PV Kanda iii
Jñānottara	P 321, 326
Jyotiṣtattva	p 49
Kaivalyatantra	P 509
Kālāgnirudropaniṣat	P 184
Kālikā-kula-sarvasva-saṃpuṭa	PV Kanda iii. P 62. S 5. SU 49, 82, 94, 126
Kālikā (Kālī)—(kulasarvasva)	S 41. SR 32
Kālīkalpa	T 486. SU 83, 89, 107, 169
Kālikāpurāṇa	T 46, 51
Kālikopaniṣat	SR 16
Kālīhṛdaya	T 147. PV Kanda ii
Kālikāpurāṇa	S 3, 41. SR 5
Kālikulāmṛta	PV Kanda iii
Kālītantra	P 230. T 473, 475, 499, 522, 934. SU (simply Kali) 109, 111. S 31. SR 4
Kālīvilāsatantra	P 272. SU 136
Kālikrama	SR 7
Kālikulāmṛta	PV Kanda iii
Kālīrahasya	T 488
Kālottara	P 321, 326
Kalpa	171, 302, 365
Kalpasūtra	P 17. T 445. T 699
Kalpasūtraṭīkā	P 12
Kalpataru	P 369
Kāmadatantra	P 188
Kāmadhenutantra (or Kāmadhenu)	P 15. S 24. PV Kanda ii
Kāmākhyā-mūla	TR 23
Kāmākhyātantra	P 91, 92, 149

Title	*Tantra in which mentioned with reference*
Kaṅkālamālinītantra	P 94
Karmavipāka	P 26
Kāśīkhaṇḍa	P 182
Kaṭhopaniṣat	P 449
Kaulatantra	SR 34, 39
Kāvyaprakāśa	P 11
Kedārakhaṇḍa	P 322
Kramadīpikā	T 152, 167, 255. S 5
Kriyāsāra	T 3, 75. S 4. P 7
Kriyāsāra-samuccaya	T3
Kṛkalāsadīpikā	P 243
Kṛṣṇārcana-candrikā	P 179
Kubjikātantra	P 6. T 55, 381. S 10. SU 128, 136, 138, 196, 206
Kukkuṭa	SU 72
Kukkuṭeśvaratantra	P 339. T 586
Kulacūḍāmaṇi	P 157. T 6, 59, 20, 37, 38. SU 58, 73, 92, 174, 207. SR 2
Keralāgama	P 95
Kulāmṛta	T 112, 130. PV Kanda i
Kulamūlāvatāra-kalpasūtraṭīkā (or Kulamūlāvatāra)	P 17. S 6
Kulānandasaṃhitā	T 799
Kulaprakāśa	T 71. SR 33
Kularahasya	SU 103, 213
Kulārṇava	P 9. T 40. S 4, 5, 8, 21, 23, 33, 37, 44. A. SU 26, 400, etc. SR 5
Kulasadbhāva	SR 50
Kulasāra-saṃgraha	SR 46
Kulasambhava	SR 11, 32
Kulasarvasva	PV Kanda v. SR 45
Kulasāra	P 542. PV Kanda v. SR 22
Kulatattvasāra	SU 83, 105, 148, 178
Kulāvalī	T 115, 659
Kuloḍḍīśa	T 389, 396. SR 22, 41
Kulottama	P 542. PV Kanda v
Kumārī-kalpa	T 478, 482. SR 3

Title	*Tantra in which mentioned with reference*
Kumāritantra	P 511. T 508, 934, 949. S 41. SU 27, 69, 135. SR 1
Kūrmapurāṇa (Kaurma)	P 186. S 9
Laghukalpasūtra	P
Laiṅgapurāṇa	S 8
Lakṣmīkulārṇava	T 125
	S 15
	P 187
Lalitā	SU 167
	T 958
Liṅgāgama	P 240
Liṅgapurāṇa	P 326. T 96, 656
Liṅgārcanacandrikā	TR 29
Liṅgārcanatantra	P 327. S 41
Liṅgatantra	TR 1
Mādhavīyasaṃhitā	S 45
Mahābhārata	P 45. A
Mahācīna	TR 8
Mahākapila-pañca-rātra	P 97
Mahāliṅgeśvaratantra	TR 30
Mahānīla	TR 4
Mahānirvāṇa	P 6. PV Kanda iv. A. SU 21, 222, 225
Mahāphetkārīya	T 506
Mahātārārṇava	TR 8
Mahogra	T 930. 931
Mahogratarākālpa	T 930
Mahiṣamardinītantra	P 96. S 7, 31, 39
Mālinītantra	T 125
Malini-vijaya	P 186. T 14
Mānasollāsa	S 18. T 318
Maṅgalatantra	S 26
Mantramuktāvalī	S 4
Mantraprakāśa	PV Kanda iii
Mantraratnāvalī	SR 16
Mantra-tantra-prakāśa	P 165. T 656. S 13
Mantrataraṅgiṇī	PV Kanda i
Mantracūḍāmaṇi	T 191

Title	*Tantra in which mentioned with reference*
Mantradeva-prakāśikā	T 203, 327
Mantradeva-prakāśinī	T 614
Mantramahodadhi	P 251
Mantrakośa	S 24. PV Kanda ii
Manusaṃhitā	P 63
Mārkaṇḍeyapurāṇa	P 7. S 3, 4, 8, 9, 39, 42. A
Mātṛkābheda	SU 61, 87, 117, 194
Mātṛkābhedodaya	P 27
Mātṛkodaya	P 17
Matsyasūkta	P. 5 T 8, 12, 153, 508. S 6, 41. SR 4
Māyātantra	T 379, 498, 532
Merutantra	P 21
Mṛḍānītantra	A
Mṛtyuñjayāgama	PV Kanda iv
Mṛtyuñjayasaṃhitā	P 12
Muktitantra	PV Kanda iv, vi
Muṇḍakopaniṣat	P 451
Muṇḍamālātantra	P 5. T 14, 42. S 22, 30, 33. A. SU 48, 66, 191. SR 4
Nandikeśvarasaṃhitā	T 127. SR 3
Nandikeśvara-tantra	P 239
Nandyāvarta	T 832
Nārada-pañcarātra	P 18
Nāradīyatantra	T 246, 650
Narapati-jayācārya-svarodaya	P 33, 104
Nārāyaṇa-kalpa	T 71
Navaratneśvara	P 187. T 11, 96, 418. S 4, 19, 20, 40
Nibandha	T 15, 20
Nārāyaṇīya	P 65, 117. T 18
Nārāyaṇītantra	T 188. SU 4, 29, etc.
Navacakreśvara	P 92, 93, 189
Nigama-kalpadruma	P 447, 555. T 3. PV Kanda v. SU 33, 85
Nigama-kalpa	SU 71, 108
Nigama-kalpalatā	SU 76, 129
Nigama-kalpānanda	SU 23
Nigamānanda	SU 63, 93

Title	*Tantra in which mentioned with reference*
Nigama-tattva	SU 41, 42
Nigama-tattvasāra	PV Kanda iv. SU 214, 217, 239
Nīlasarasvatītantra	TR 11
Nīlasārasvata	T 488. TR 1
Nīlatantra	SR 2, 51. TR 15. P 149. S 13, 15. SU 228. T. 84, 130
Niruttaratantra	P 32. SU 32, 35, etc.
Nirvāṇatantra	P 5. SU 17, 59, etc.
Nityātantra	P 149
Nṛsiṃhapurāṇa	P 354
Nṛsiṃha-tāpanīya	S 4
Padārthādarśa	P 43
Padmapurāṇa	P 180. T 65 (Padma), 762, 765. S 9 (Padma). A
Padmavāhinī	P 151
Pañcadaśī	P 23
Parākrama	P 17
Parāpañcāśikā	P 63
Parāparimalollāsa	P 12
Parāśarabhāṣya	T 72
Parimalollāsa	P 61
Phetkāriṇī	P 13. T 556, 559. S 19, 33, SR 3
Phetkārīya	T 488, 511
Picchilā	P 93. SU 41, 55, 56, 161
Piṅgalā	P 67. T 21, 30, 31
Prapañcasāra	P 9. T 90, 197
Prayogapārijāta	P 360
Prayogasāra	P 7
Purāṇa-saṃgraha	P 352
Puraścaraṇacandrikā	T 140, 158. PV Kanda ii
Paraścaraṇalaharī-tantra	P 185
Puraścaraṇarāsollāsa	P 6. PV Kanda i
Rādhā	SU 9, 59
Rāghavīya	S 44
Rāmārcanacandrikā	P 92. T 35
Ratirahasya	P 558
Ratnāvalī	T 38, 40

Title	*Tantra in which mentioned with reference*
Revatītantra	P 548
Rudrādhyāya	TR 6
Rudray (j)āmala	P 17. T 5, 7, 16, 26, 30, S 4, 5, 6, etc. A. SU 145. SR 27. TR 7
Ṣaḍanvaya-mahāratna	P 118
Śaivāgama	T 36. P 172
Śāktakramacandrikā (tantraka)	SU 208, 211, 220
Śāktānanda-taraṅgiṇī	P 27. PV Kanda ii
Śaktikalpa	TR 1
Śaktikāgamasarvasva	P 554
Śaktisāra	TR 5
Śaktitantra	PV Kanda iii
Śaktiyāmala	T 8. SI. PV Kanda v. TR 38
Samayācāratantra	P 64. T 954, 961. SU 27, 31, etc.
Samayāṅka	T 404, 441
Samayāṅkamātṛkā	S 19
Samayatantra	T 4. S 10, 12, 15, 16, 37, 45
Śāmbhava	T 153
Śaṃkaratantra	A
Saṃketacandrodaya	T 506
Sammohanatantra	P 93. T 94, 127. S 15, 43, 32
Sanatkumāratantra	T 44, 773
Sanatkumārīya	P 230. T (Sanatkumarasaṃhita) 31, 36, 42. S 29
Saṅketapaddhati	S 12
Śāradātilaka	P 7. S 20. PV Kanda ii
Śāradā	S 6, 10, 19, 42, 43, 44, 45
Śāradā-ṭīkā	SR 2
Sārasaṃgraha	P 92. T 4, 54
Sārasamuccaya	T 656. PV Kanda iii
Sārasvata	P 115. S 27, 25
Sarasvatītantra	P 223
Sārāvalī	T 673. S 20
Ṣaṭkarmadīpikā	P 117
Sautrāmaṇitantra	P 287
Setumaṅgala-tantra	S 27
Siddhalaharī	SU 232

Title	*Tantra in which mentioned with reference*
Siddhāntaśekhara	P 113, 179. T 686. S 42
Siddhasārasvata	T 13, 530, 680. SR 37
Siddhayāmala	T 8, 385, 797
Siddheśvartantra	T 490. SR 35
Śikṣāsūtra	P 46
Śivadharma	P 186. T 64. S 14
Śivadīkṣā-ṭīkā	S 6
Śivāgama	T 937, 961. SR 40
Śivarahasya	P 198
Śivatantra	PV Kanda iii
Skandapurāṇa	P 180. T 842. S 41. A
Smṛtisāra	P 288. 543
Ṣoḍhā-tantra	TR 1
Somabhujagāvalī	T 415, 687
Śrībījārṇava	S 31
Śrīkrama	T 2, 9, 42. T 378 (-*saṃhita*). S 39. SR 2, 34
Śrīrāmatāpanīya	S 8
Śrītattvacintāmaṇi	T 155. P 32. SR 20
Sūkṣmasvarodaya	P 420
Sūtasaṃhitā	P 322
Svacchandabhairava	P 63. T 402
Svacchandasaṃgraha	T 536. PV Kanda i
Svarodaya	P 105
Svarodayaṭīkā	P 106
Svatantratantra	P 179. T 93, 408. SR i
Svāyambhuva-mātṛkā-tantra	T 603
Śyāmākalpalatā	PV Kanda ii
Śyāmāpradīpa	P 180
Śyāmārcanacandrikā	PV Kanda v
Śyāmārahasya	P 179. S 10. SU 159
Taittirīyaka	P 448
Tantradevaprakāśika	S 22
Tantragandharva	S 6, 13, 17, 18, 20
Tantracūḍāmaṇi	P 234. T 515. SR 40
Tantrakaumuḍī	T 374
Tantrarāja	T 18

Title	*Tantra in which mentioned with reference*
Tantrārṇava	T 5. SR 19
Tantrasāra	P 67
Tārānigama	TR 4
Tāpanī	P 61
Tārākalpa	T 826. TR I
Tārākrama	PV Kanda iii
Tārākula-sarvasva	TR I
Tārāsāra	TR 6
Tārāyoga	TR 81
Tāriṇītantra	T 593
Tārāpradīpa	T 5
Tārārṇava	T 504. TR 8
Tāriṇī-nirṇaya	T 527
Tārātantra	T 529
Tattvabodha	T 397
Tattvānanda-taraṅgiṇī	SR 15
Tattvasāra	P 39. T 116. S 5. PV Kanda i, iv, vi
Tīkṣṇakalpa	PV Kanda ii
Tithitattva	P 21
Toḍalatantra	P 173
Traipurīśruti	T 379
Tripurākalpa	TR 30
Tripurārṇava	T 358
Tripurāsārasamuccaya	P 419. T 139
Tripurāsāra	T 362, 364
Triśaktitantra	T 361
Udayākarapaddhati	P 188. SR 9, 21
Uḍḍāmareśvaratantra	P 256
Ūrdhvāmnāyatantra	S 32. TR 1
Utpattitantra	PP 231
Uttarakalpa	S 7, 24
Uttarakhaṇḍoḍḍīśa	PV Kanda iii
Uttaratantra	P 511. T 948. SR 5
Vābhaṭa	P 28
Vaikhānasagrantha	P 199
Vaiśampāyanasaṃhitā	T 3, 9, 34, 45, S 28

Title	*Tantra in which mentioned with reference*
Vaiśvānarasaṃhitā	P 201
Vājasaneyasaṃhitā	P 448
Vāmakeśvaratantra	P 22. T 61, 410, 4, 555, 651. SU 36, 80
Varadātantra	P 47. SU 60, 63, 165
Vāräha	S 10
Vārāhītantra	T 12, 13, 28, 32, 41, S 4, 6, 22, 27. SU 124. SR 32
Varṇabhairava	PV Kanda ii
Varṇavilāsatantra	P 131
Varṇoddhāratantra	P 49
Vaṣiṣṭha	T 72, 116
Vaśiṣṭhasaṃhitā	P 172, T 674
Vaśiṣṭharāmāyaṇa	S 18
Vāstuyāgapradīpikā	P 105
Vijayamālinī	PV Kanda i
Vijayakalpa	T 946
Vīrabhadratantra	PV Kanda ii
Vimalānandabhāṣya	S i
Vedāntavṛtti	P 16
Vidyāgama	T 5
Vidyānandanibandha	T 159
Vīramitrodaya	P 179
Vīrasarvasva	PV Kanda iv
Vīratantra	T 72, 475, 506, 516, SU 82, 100. SR 8, 40
Viṣṇudharmottara	P 346. S 42
Viṣṇuyāmala	T 40. S 9. SU 129
Viśuddheśvara	T 45, 54, 66. S 15, 19, 23, 27, 29. SR 20 (*-mahatantra*)
Viśvasāra	P 13. T 22, 43. S 5, 6, 13, 18, 21, 28, 38. SU 58, 149, etc.
Viśvasāroddhāra	T 685
Viśvadarśa	PV Kanda ii
Viśvaśvarakalpadruma	PV Kanda iii

Title	*Tantra in which mentioned with reference*
Yajurvedīya hiraṇya-keśīyaśākhā	P 152
Yāmala	T 3, 28, 32, SU 2, 77, etc. SR 13. TR 30
Yogacūḍāmaṇi	PV Kanda vi
Yogārṇava	P 28
Yogasāra	P 323
Yogeśvarodaya	P 431. A
Yoginīhṛdaya	P 144. T 49, 56. S 5, 8, 29, 30, 36, 37, 39, SR 46
Yoginījalandhara	T 388
Yoginītantra	P 8. T 7, 8, 34, 38, 41
Yoginī	SU 126
Yonitantra	P 495. TR 1

B. AUTHORS

Abhinavaguptācārya	P 41
Amarasiṃha	P 11
Baudhāyana	P 111
Bhadrācārya	P 318
Bhartṛhari	P 46
Dattātreya	P 117
Durgasiṃha	P11
Gopīnātha Tarkācārya	P11
Himādri	P 321
Jābāla	T 10
Kṛṣṇānanda Āgamavāgīśa	P 75
Mādhavācārya	T 83
Maitreya	P 18
Nārada	T 17, 45
Narahari	P 107
Nityānanda	T 6
Pūrṇānanda	SR 15
Puṣpadanta	P 17
Rāghavabhaṭṭa	P 7. T 661. SR 2
Rāmakṛṣṇa Paṇḍita	P 36
Rāmalocana Vidyābhūṣaṇa	P 105

Title	*Tantra in which mentioned with reference*
Rāyamukuṭa	P 11, 35
Śaṃkarācārya	P 12. T 515
Smārta Bhaṭṭācārya	P 277
Śrīdharasvāmī	P 18
Suśruta	P 29
Udayabhānu	P 179
Vidyānandasvāmī	P 36
Vidyāraṇyasvāmī	P 495
Yajñapārśva	P 180
Yogiyājñavalkya	P 28

NOTES

1. The following abbreviations have been used —
   A=*Āmarī-saṃhitā*, as described in *Vaṅgīya Sāhitya Pariṣat Patrikā*, vol. 58/3-4, p. 41.
   P=*Prāṇatoṣiṇī*, Vasumatī ed., Calcutta, 1335 BS.
   PV=*Pañcama-veda-sāranirṇaya* as described in *Vaṅgīya Sāhitya Pariṣat Patrikā*, Vol. 59/3-4, p. 71.
   R=*Rādhātantra*, ed. R. Chattopadhyaya, Calcutta.
   S=*Śāktānanda-taraṅgiṇī*, ed. R. Chattopadhyaya, Calcutta.
   SR=*Śyāmārahasya* of Pūrṇānanda, ed. R.M. Chattopadhyaya.
   SU=*Sarvollāsa-tantra*, ed. R.M. Chakravarti, Comilla, 1941.
   T=*Tantrasāra*, Vaṅgavāsī ed., 1334 BS.
   TR=*Tārārahasya*, ed. J. Vidyasagara, Calcutta, 1896.

IV. Tantras Mentioned in the Sanskrit Works on Bengal Vaiṣṇavism

Some of the important Sanskrit works, relating to Bengal Vaiṣṇavism, contain copious references to Tāntric works. This is particularly true in the case of the works dealing with the rites and rituals. For the present purpose, We shall collect the references to Tantras contained in the following works against which the respective abbreviations are noted.

1. *Bhaktirasāmṛta-sindhu* of Rūpa Gosvāmin (Murshidabad ed., Radharaman Press)	BS (The references are to the pages of the edition used.)
2. *Haribhakti-vilāsa* of Gopāla Bhaṭṭa[1] (Ed. R. Vidyāratna, Behrampore, West Bengal)	HV (The references are to the pages of the edition used here).
3. *Saṃkṣepa-bhāgavatāmṛta* of Rūpa Gosvāmin (Murshidabad ed., 1303 B.S.)	SB (References are to pages).
4. *Sat-kriyā-sāra-dīpika*, ascribed to Gopāla Bhaṭṭa[2] (Ed. Gauḍīya Maṭh, Calcutta, 449 Gaurābda).	SD (References are to pages).
5. *Ṣaṭ-sandarbha* of Jīva Gosvāmin (Tattva, Bhagavat, Paramātma, Rādharaman press ed.) Śrīkṛṣṇa-ed. P. G. Gosvamin, Navadvīpa, 1332 B-S. Bhakti—ed. S. Gosvāmin, Calcutta, Śaka 1822. Prīti—ed. P. Gosvāmi, Noakhali).	SS (The Arabic numerals refer to pages and the Roman figures to the Sandarbhas in the order shown here).
6. *Ujjvalanīlamaṇi* of Rūpa Gosvāmin (Kāvyāmālā ed., Bombay, 1913).	UN

The *Gopāla-campū* of Jīva Gosvāmin contains references to several Tantras all of which have been referred to also in his *Sandarbhas*. So, for the present purpose, we need not take the *Gopāla-campū* into consideration.

(In Devanāgarī alphabetical order)

Aśvaśiraḥ-pañcarātra: Same as *Hayaśīrṣa* (q.v.)

Āgama:	HV. I. 41-42, 79, 82-83, 154-55, 267, 516-19, 548, 552, 582-83, 750, 789-90, 807-09, 811-13, 1170-71, 1178-79
	III. 110-14
	IV. 2-3, 8-9, 21-22
	SB 393
	SS IV. 76, 255, 271, 335, 565. V. 626, 634. VI. 477, 958
Kramadīpikā:	HV. I. 15-16, 28, 71, 78, 353, 397-98, 405-06, 519-20, 723
	IV. 5
	UN 349
Gautamīya:	HV. I. 83-84, 330-31, 475, 703
	III. 44, 60, 164, 285
	IV. 21, 30, 32-33, 67, 184-85
Gautamīya-tantra:	HV. I. 58, 192, 236, 237, 432-35, 462, 913, 1146-50, 1208, 1344
	II. 9-10
	III. 4, 220-23
	IV. 100-02
	SS IV. 220, 423. V. 547, 640, 651. VI. 959, 1074
Tantra:	HV I. 70, 1176-77
	III. 183-84
	IV. 12
	SB 374
	UN 61
	BS 21, 24, 111, 170, 187
Tantra-bhāgavata:	SS. I. 53, 72. IV. 224, 421
Tantrāntara:	SS. V. 627
Tāntrikāḥ:	HV. I. 92-93

Trailokyamohana-pañcarātra: HV. II. 179

Trailokya-sammohana-pañcarātra: HV. I. 60-62, 71-73, 377-78 IV. 39-40, 46-49, 58, 60
SS. IV. 220. V. 523, 630. VI. 725
Navapraśna-pañcarātra: HV III. 151
Nārada-tantra: HV I. 85
Nārada-pañcarātra: HV. I. 20-22, 32, 34, 44-45, 123-125, 151-152, 199-201, 233, 286-87, 359-63, 436, 449, 552, 790, 822, 1087-88, 1352
IV. 13, 20, 24-25, 28-29, 35-36, 41, 52-53, 54, 68-69, 175-76
BS 11, 23, 59, 107
SS II. 182, 257, 386. III. 25, 127. IV. 299, 466
V. 576, 595, 596, 628, 629, 630, 633, 640, 650
VI. 225, 246, 247
Nāradīya-tantra: SS III. 33
Nāradiya-pañcarātra: HV. I. 187
III. 136
Nārāyaṇa-pañcarātra: BS 218
Nigama: HV III. 359
Pañcarātra: HV. I. 39, 125-26, 267, 349, 745-46, 777-78
II. 5-6
BS 36, 129, 213, 216, 217
SS III. 75, 80. V. 472, 625, VI. 417, 426
Prahlāda-pañcarātra: HV. I. 907
Bṛhat-tantra: SS VI. 239
Bṛhad-gautamīya-tantra: SS IV. 305, 309, 567, 568. VI. 239, 564
Brahmayāmala: BS 79
SS V. 628
Bhagavat-tantra: Same as Tantra-bhagavata (q.v.)
Bhāgavatādi-tantra: HV II. 106
Bhārgava-tantra: SB 244
Mṛtyuñjaya-tantra: SS IV. 296
Yāmala: SS IV. 463, 567, V. 650
Rudrayāmala: SD 39, 50, 108. HV I. 86
Viṣṇuyāmala: HV. I. 80-81, 126-34, 354, 1245
IV. 491
BS 334
SS V. 613, 640
SD 20, 107

NOTES

1. The identity of the author is controversial. Some think that he is one of the six Gosvāmins of Vṛndāvana, while others think that he was a different person. Yet others think that it was really a work of Sanātana Gosvāmin who associated it with the name of Gopāla Bhaṭṭa. There is an opinion that it was their joint work.
2. The authorship is doubtful. Even if it was written by Gopāla Bhaṭṭa, his identity with Gopāla Bhaṭṭa, one of the famous Gosvāmins of Vṛndāvana, has not yet been established conclusively.

V. List of Holy Places Mentioned in Bengal Tantra

Only the major published works have been taken into account

The following abbreviations are used:

P: *Prāṇatoṣiṇī*
S: *Śrītattva-cintāmaṇi*
SR: *Śyāmārahasya*
ST: *Śāktānanda-taraṅgiṇī*
T: *Tantrasāra*
TR: *Tārārahasya*

(In Devanāgarī alphabetical order)

Akṣayavaṭa	P	Kālamādhava	P
Agastyāśrama	P	Kālīghāṭa	P
Aṭṭahāsa	P	Kāverī	P, SR, TR
Ayodhyā	P	Kāśī	T, P
Avanti	P	Kāśmīra	P
Amarakaṇṭaka	P	Kubjaka	P
Aśvatīrtha	P	Kurukṣetra	T, P
Āryāvarta	P	Kuśāvarta	P
Ujjayinī	P	Kedāra	P
Uḍḍīyāna	P	Kauṣikī	P
Elāpura	P	Gaṅgā	T, P, SR, TR
Oghavatī	p	Gaṇeśvara	P
Kanakhala	P	Gaṇḍakī	P
Kanyāśrama	T, P	Gayā	T, P
Kamalā	P	Godāvarī	P, SR
Karavīra	P	Govardhana	P
Karatoyā	P	Gautameśvara	P
Karṇatīrtha	P	Candrabhāgā	P
Karṇasūtra	P	Candraśekhara	T, P
Karṇāṭa	P	Jayantī	P
Kalamba	P	Jālandhara	P
Kāñcī	P	Jvālāmukhī	P
Kāmākhyā	P	Trikoṇa	P
Kālañjara	P	Tripurā	P

Triveṇī	P	Mathurā	P
Trisrotā	P	Madhupurī	P
Durgā	P	Mānasa	P
Dvāravatī	P	Māyā	P
Nandipura	P	Māhiṣmatī	P
Narmadā	P, SR, TR	Mithilā	P
Nalāhāṭī	P	Yamunā	P, SR
Nāgatīrtha	P	Yaśor	P
Nāgarasambhava	P	Ratnāvalī	P
Nepāla	P	Ramaṇaka	P
Naimiṣāraṇya	P	Rāmagiri	P
Pañcavaṭī	P	Rāmatīrtha	P
Pañcāpsara	P	Rāmeśvara	P
Pāṭala	P	Lagnikāśrama	P
Piṅgā	P	Laṅkā	P
Piṇḍārakavana	P	Viraja (Virajā)	T, P
Puṣkara	P	Śukratīrtha	P
Prabhāsa	P	Śoṇa	P
Prayāga	T, P	Śrīśaila (Śrīgiri)	T,P
Brahmaśira	P	Sarayū	P
Brahmāvarta	P	Sāradātīrtha	P
Bhadreśvara	P	Sindhu	SR, TR
Bharatāśrama	P	Haratirtha	P
Bhāskarakṣetra	T	Haridvāra	P
Bhairavaparvata	P	Haṃsatirtha	P
Maṇipura	P	Harita	P
Maṇibandha	T	Hiṅgula	P
Mataṅga	T	Hṛṣīkeśa	P

VI. Pantheon in Bengal Tantra

The major published works have been utilised here

The following abbreviations have been used:
P: *Prāṇatoṣiṇī*
PU: *Puraścaraṇa-ratnākara*
S: *Śrītattva-cintāmaṇi*
SR: *Śyāmārahasya*
ST: *Śāktānanda-taraṅgiṇī*
T: *Tantrasāra*
TR: *Tārārahasya*

Besides the deities mentioned here, there are many demigods, minor deities, etc. The different *Avatāras* have been mentioned in some texts. We have not stated them separately. Of Vāmana, there are the aspects of Dadhivāmana, Ṣaḍvāmana. The various weapons and other things, supposed to be held by different deities, e.g. Ṣaṃkha, Cakra, Khaḍga, Dhanus, etc., have been deified and mentioned in some texts. We do not set forth these deities here.

Some texts mention the different planets as deities, which we do not state here.

A separate list is given of those deities whose *mantras* are mentioned.

(In Devanāgarī alphabetical order)

Name	*Work in which mentioned*	*Name*	*Work in which mentioned*
Agni	PU	Indra	T, PU
Agnidurga	PU	Indrāṇī	PU
Ananta	PU	Ucchiṣṭa Gaṇeśa	T
Aniruddha	PU	Ucchiṣṭa Caṇḍālinī	PU
Antarikṣa Sarasvatī	PU	Ucchiṣṭa Mātaṅgī	PU
Annapūrṇā	T, PU	Ekajaṭā	PU
Annapūrṇā Bhairavī	T	Kamalātmikā (Kamalā)	T, P, PU
Aparājitā Vaiṣṇavī	PU		
Aśvārūḍhā	PU		

Name	*Work in which mentioned*	*Name*	*Work in which mentioned*
Karṇapiśācī	T	Gāyatrī	P, S, PU
Karṇamātaṅgī	PU	Gorakṣanātha	PU
Kātyāyanī	T, PU	Gopāla	PU
Kāma	PU	Govinda	PU
Kāmeśvarī Bhairavī	T, PU	Gaurī	T, S, PU
Kārtavīrya	PU	Graha	P
Kārtikeya	PU	(Sūrya, Candra,	
Kālī	TR, T, P,	Maṅgala, Budha,	
	PU, ST.	Bṛhaspati, Śukra,	
	S, SR	Śani, Rāhu, Ketu)	
(Bhadrakālī,		Caṇḍikā	S
Dakṣiṇakālī,		Caṇḍeśvara	T, PU
Mahākālī, Siddhikālī,		Candramauli	T
Śmaśānakālī,		Cāmuṇḍā	S, PU
Guhyakālī		Cintāmaṇi	PU
Kāmakalā Kālī)		Cintāmaṇi	
		Sarasvatī	PU
Ketu	PU	Caitanyabhairavī	PU
Kauleśa Bhairavī	T, PU	Chinnamastā	PU
Kaumārī	PU	(See Pracaṇḍa	
Kuvera	PU	Caṇḍikā)	
Kṛṣṇa	T, S	Jayadurgā	T, PU
Keśava	PU	Jñānasarasvatī	PU
Kṣetrapāla	T, S, PU	Tārā	T, P
Gaṅgā	T, P, S, PU		PU, TR
Gaṇapati	PU	Tumburu	PU
(Śakti-gaṇapati,		Tulasī	P
Mahāgaṇapatī,		Trikaṇṭakī	PU
Vighnagaṇapati)		Trikūṭā Sarasvatī	PU
Gaṇeśa	T, P	Tripuṭā	T, S, PU
(Śaktigaṇeśa,		Tripurabhairavī	T, PU
Lakṣmīgaṇeśa,		Tripurasundarī	T, P, S,
Vighnagaṇeśa,			PU
Ucchiṣṭa-gaṇeśa,		Tryambaka	T
Kṣipra-prasāda		Tvaritā	PU
Gaṇeśa Vakratuṇḍa)		Dadhivāmana	T, PU
Garuḍa	T		

Name	*Work in which mentioned*	*Name*	*Work in which mentioned*
Durgā	T, P, PU	Dāmodara	PU
Dhanadā	T, PU	Bhairavī	T, S, PU
Dharaṇī	PU	(also see	
Dhūmāvatī	T, P, PU	Sakalasiddhidā and	
Nārāyaṇa	PU	Sampatpradā	
Nityaklinnā	PU	Bhairavīs)	
Nityā	T	Mañjughoṣa	T
Nityābhairavī	T, PU	Maṇikarṇikā	PU
Nīlakaṇṭha	T, S	Madhusūdana	PU
Nīlasarasvatī	PU	Mahākāla	
		Bhairava	T, P, S
Nṛsiṃha	T		PU, SR
Nairṛta	PU	(Kālī-bhartṛdeva)	
Padmāvati	PU	Mahālakṣmī	T, S, PU
Pārijāta Sarasvatī	PU	Mahāsarasvatī	PU
Pārvati	PU	Mahiṣa-mardinī	T, PU
Puruṣottama	PU	Mātaṅgī	T, P, S, PU
Pracaṇḍacaṇḍikā	T, P		
(Chinnamastā)		Mādhava	PU
Pratyaṅgirā	PU	Maheśvarī	PU
Pradyumna	PU	Mukhya	
		Vāgīsvarī	PU
Bāṇaliṅga Śiva	P, S	Mṛtyuñjaya	T
Bālagopāla	T, PU	Yama	PU
Bālā	PU	Yoginī	T, S
Brāhmā	T, P, S, SR	(As companion	
Brahma	PU	goddesses, Yoginīs	
Brāhmā	PU	are of many kinds,	
Bhaya-vidhavaṃsinī		e.g. Prakaṭa-yoginī,	
Bhairavi	T, PU	Dakṣiṇī, etc.)	
Bhāratī	PU	Rājamātaṅgī	PU
Bhuvanéśvarī		Rāhu	PU
Bhairavī	T, PU	Rudra	T, S, PU
Bhairava	T, S	Rudrabhairavī	T, PU
(Many kinds, e.g.		Rudravāgīśvarī	PU
Asitānga, Rudra,		Lakṣmī	T, S, PU

Name	*Work in which mentioned*	*Name*	*Work in which mentioned*
Caṇḍa, Krodha,		Śītalā	PU
Unmatta-bhairava,		Śūlapāṇi	T, PU
etc.)		Śeṣa	PU
Lakṣmī		Śeṣikā	PU
Vāsudeva	T, PU	Śrīkara	PU
Laghuśyāmā	PU	Śrīdhara	PU
Vagalāmukhī	T, P, PU	Śrīrāma	T
Vajraprastāriṇī	T, PU	Śrīhari	PU
Vaṭuka	T, S, PU	Ṣaṭkūṭā Bhairavī	T, PU
Vanadurgā	PU	Sakalasiddhidā	
Varāha	T	Bhairavī	T, PU
Varuṇa	PU	Sadāśiva	PU
Vaśyamātaṅgī	PU	Sampatpradā	
Vahnivāsinī	PU	Bhairavī	T, PU
Vāgīśvarī	T, S, PU	Sarasvatī	PU
Vāgmatī	PU	Sāmrājya-lakṣmī	PU
Vāgvādinī	PU	Sītā	PU
Vāsudeva	T	Sūrya	T, S
Vāyu	PU	Svapnavārāhī	PU
Vārāhī	PU	Hanūmat	T, PU
Viśālākṣmī	T	Hayagrīva	T, PU
Viṣṇu	T, P, S	Haridrāgaṇeśa	T, PU
	PU, SR, T	Harihara	T, PU
Viṣṇu Vāgīśvarī	PU	Haṃsa Vāgīśvarī	PU
Vaiṣṇavī	PU	Heramba	T
Vyāsa	PU	Hṛṣīkeśa	PU
Śarabha	PU		
Śiva	SR, T, P, S, PU		
(Tryambaka, Pārvatīśvara, Mṛtyuñjaya Mahāmṛtyuñjaya, Paśupati, Ardha-nārīśvara, Aghora, Nīlakaṇṭha, Īśāna)			

List of Deities whose *Mantras* are Mentioned in Bengal Tantra

(The names of deities are in Devanāgarī alphabetical order)

Name	*Work in which mentioned*	*Name*	*Work in which mentioned*
Annapūrṇā	T	Pārijāta Sarasvatī	T
Annapūrṇābhairavī	T	Pracaṇḍacaṇḍikā	T
Indra	T	Bālagopāla	T
Ucchiṣṭagaṇeśa	T	Bhadrakālī	T
Ucchiṣṭacaṇḍālinī	T	Bhayavidhvaṃsini	
Karṇapiśācī	T	Bhairavī	T
Kātyāyanī	T	Bhuvaneśvarī	T
Kāmeśvarī	T, S	Bhuvaneśvarī	
Kṛṣṇa	T	Bhairavī	T
Kauleśa Bhairavī	T	Bhairavī	T
Gaṇeśa	T	Mañjughoṣa	T
Garuḍa	T	Mahākāla	
		Bhairava	T, SR
Guhyakālī	T	Mahālakṣmī	T
Gaurī	T	Mahiṣamardinī	T
Caṇḍeśvara	T	Mātaṅgī	T
Candramauli	T	Mṛtyuñjaya	T
Jayadurgā	T	Yogin	S
Tārā	T, TR	Rudrabhairavī	T
Tripuṭā	T	Lakṣmī	T
Tripurabhairavī	T	Lakṣmī Vāsudeva	T
Tripurasundarī	T, S	Vagalāmukhī	T
Tryambaka	T	Vajraprastāriṇī	T
Dakṣiṇāmūrti	T	Vaṭuka	T
Dadhivāmana	T	Varāha	T
Durgā	T	Vāgīśvarī	T
Dhanadā	T	Vāsudeva	T
Dhūmāvatī	T	Viśālākṣī	T
Nityā	T	Viṣṇu	T
Nityābhairavī	T	Śiva	P
Nīlakaṇṭha	T	Śūlinī	T
Nṛsiṃha	T	Śmaśānakālī	T

Śyāmā	T, SR	Sūrya	T
Śrīrāma	T	Hanūmat	T
Śrīvidyā	T, S	Hayagrīva	T
Ṣaṭkūṭā Bhairavī	T	Haridrāgaṇeśa	T
Sakala-siddhidā Bhairavi	T	Harihara	T
Sampatpradā Bhairavī	T	Heramba	T

VII. List of Mudrās, Yantras and Maṇḍalas Mentioned in Bengal Tantra

The major published works have been taken into account

The following abbreviations are used:
P : *Prāṇatoṣiṇī*
S : *Śrītattva-cintāmaṇi*
T : *Tantrasāra*
TR : *Tārārahasya*
SR : *Śyāmārahasya*
ST : *Śāktānanda-taraṅgiṇī*

(In Devanāgarī alphabetical order)
The principal *mudrās* only are listed here

Aṅkuśa	T	Nāda	S
Añjali	T	Padma	T
Apāna	S	Prāṇa	S
Abhaya	T, SR	Prārthanā	T, S
Avaguṇṭhana	T, S, SR	Bali	S
Āvāhanī	T, S, ST, SR	Bindu	S
Udāna	S	Bīja	S
Kumbha	T, SR	Bhūtiṇī	T
Kauliki	T	Mahāṅkuśā	S
Khaḍga	T, SR, TR	Mahāmudrā	T
Khecarī	T, S	Muṇḍā	T, SR
Gajatuṇḍā	S	Muṣala	T
Gadā	T	Mṛga	TR
Gālinī	T, S	Yoga	S
Cakra	T, S	Yoni	T, S, ST, SR, TR
Carma	T	Lakṣmī	T
Jñāna	T	Lelihā	T, S, SR
Tattvamudrā	T, S, SR, TR	Vara	T, SR
Trikhaṇḍā	T,S	Vismaya	S
Durgā	T	Vīṇā	T
Dhenu	T, SR, TR	Vyāna	S
		Śaṃkha	T, S, SR, TR
		Śrīvatsa	T

Sarva vidrāvaṇī	S	Sarva saṃkṣobhaṇī	S
		Sarvonmādinī	S
Saṃbodhinī	T, P, SR	Saṃhāra	T, TR
Sakalīkaraṇī	T, S, S, T	Sundarī	S
Sannidhāpanī	T ,S, ST, SR	Sthāpanī	T, S, ST, SR
Samāna	S		
Sammukhī-karaṇī	T, S, ST, SR		
Sarvavaśyakaraṇī	S		

MAṆḌALAS

The prominent *maṇḍalas*, mentioned in the *Tantrasāra*, are *Navanābha*, *Sarvatobhadra* and *Svalpa-sarvatobhadra*. The *Śrītattva-cintāmaṇi* mentions *Guru-maṇḍala*.

YANTRAS

The Yantras can be broadly divided into two classes—*Pūjā-yantra* and *Dhāraṇa-yantra*. As will be seen, some names are common in both the classes.

Pūjā-yantras

Annapūrṇā Bhairavi	T	Rudrabhairavi	T
Gaṇeśa	T	Lakṣmī	T
Guhyakālī	T	Vagalāmukhī	T
Tārā	T	Vajraprastāriṇī	T
Tāriṇī	T	Vaṭuka	T
Tripuṭā	T	Vāgīśvarī	T
Tvaritā	T	Viśālākṣī	T
Durgā	T	Śmaśānakālī	T
Dhanadā	T	Śyāmā	T
Pracaṇḍacaṇḍikā	T	Śrīvidyā	T, S
Bhuvaneśvarī	T	Ṣaṭkūṭā Bhairavī	T
Mātaṅgī	T	Hanūmat	T

Dhāraṇa-yantras

Kālī	T	Mṛtyuñjaya	T
Tārā	T	Lakṣmī	T
Tvaritā	T	Śiva	T
Nṛsiṃha	T	Śrīrāma	T
Bhuvaneśvarī	T	Śrīvidyā	T
Bhairavī	T		

VIII. List of Kavacas Mentioned in Bengal Tantra

Abbreviations:
P : *Prāṇatoṣiṇī*
S : *Śrītattva-cintāmaṇi*
SR : *Śyāmārahasya*
T : *Tantrasāra*

(In Devanāgarī alphabetical order)

Name	*Work in which mentioned*	*Name*	*Work in which mentioned*
Akṣaya	P	Pracaṇḍacaṇḍikā	T
Annapūrṇā	T	Brahma	P
Kārtikeya	T	Bhuvaneśvarī	T
Kuṇḍalinī	P	Bhairavī	T
Gaṅgā	T	Mahāvidyā	P
Gāyatrī	T	Mahiṣamardinī	T, SR
Guru	P	Mātaṅgī	T
Tārā	T	Yoni	P
Tripuṭā	T	Lakṣmī	T
Tripurasundarī	T, S	Vaṃśalābhākhyā	T
Trailokya-maṅgalā	T	Śiva	P
		Śmaśānakālī	T, P
Dakṣiṇakālikā	SR	Śyāmā	T, SR
Durgā	T	Śrīvidyā	T
Dhanadā	T	Sarasvatī	T
Nāyikā	T	Sūrya	T
Nṛsiṃha	T	Haridrāgaṇeśa	T

IX. List of Hymns and Protective Mantras Mentioned in Bengal Tantra

Abbreviations:
P : *Prāṇatoṣiṇī*
S : *Śrītattva-cintāmaṇi*
SR : *Śyāmārahasya*
ST : *Śāktānanda-taraṅgiṇī*
T : *Tantrasāra*

(In Devanāgarī alphabetical order)

Name	*Work in which mentioned*	*Name*	*Work in which mentioned*
Ānanda	P	Bhairavī	T
Kiṅkiṇī	T	Manasā	T
Kuṇḍalinī	P	Mahākālī	T
Kumārī	P	Mahāvidyā	P
Gaṇeśa	T	Mahiṣamardinī	T, SR
Guru	P, ST	Mātaṅgī	T
Gopāla	T	Yoni	P
Tārā	T	Lakṣmī	T
Tulasī	P	Vagalāmukhī	T
Tripuṭā	T	Vaṭuka	T
Tripurasundarī	T, S	Viṣṇu	T
Dakṣiṇā	T	Śānti	P
Durgā	T	Śiva	T, P
Dhanadā	T	Śyāmā	T, SR
Dhūmāvatī	T	Śrīkṛṣṇa	T
Nāyikā	T	Śrīrāma	T
Nṛsiṃha	T	Śrīvidyā	T
Pracaṇḍacaṇḍikā	T	Ṣaṣṭhī	T
Balarāma	T	Sarasvatī	T
Bāṇaliṅga	P	Svāhā	T
Brahma	P	Hanūmat	T

X. Profiles of Tāntric Devotees

Bengal produced not only an abundance of Tantras, both Buddhist and Hindu, but also gave birth to a galaxy of Tāntric devotees. Some of them were of a very high order, and have carved out a permanent niché in the shrine of human memory. Of them again, some were scholar-devotees like Pūrṇānanda, Sarvānanda, etc. They reached a spiritual height not comprehensible to ordinary people, inspired a band of illustrious disciples, and wrote treatises. Others were immersed in the nectar of thought of the Mother Goddess in whose honour they composed and sang songs. Even under adverse circumstances, they went on singing with sang-froid and unparalleled abandon. Yet others devoted a lifetime to silent meditation.

Unfortunately, we have very little information about them beyond stories about their mystic and superhuman powers which commanded the naive and complacent attention of the devoted souls. The Bengalis loved *Caritāmṛtas*, containing more of fiction and fancy than of sober facts, rather than serious or faithful *Caritas*. Here we shall try to give short life-sketches of a very few eminent *Sādhakas* leaving aside all fanciful accounts of them. No account of Bengal Tantra can be complete without information about these devotees of immortal fame, whose names have become household words in Bengal, and whose teachings and songs have become a current coin the Bengali society.

Rāmprasād[1]

Rāmprasād (C. 1720-81. Date of birth according to others 1723 or 1718. Death 1775 according to some, 1782 according to others). A poet, Śākta devotee and a singer, all rolled into one, Rāmprasād was born to Rāmrām Sen at village Kamarhati in Hālisahar in the district of 24 Parganās, West Bengal. At first a clerk under a wealthy person (Gokul Ghosal, Dewan of Bhukailash, according to some or Durgacharan Mitra, accorting to others), he subsequently enjoyed the patronage of a few other landlords including Krishnacandra Rāy. Kṛishnachandra offered him a job. Rāmprasād having declined, he gave him 100 bighas of rent-free land and conferred on him the title Kavirañjana. In recognition of this honour, Rāmprasād composed, 1293 B.S./ a poetical work on Vidyāsundar, and named it Kavirañjana. Nawab Siraj-u-ddaula is said to have been very much delighted by his *Śyāmā-saṃgīta*.

The time of Rāmprasād was full of trouble. He lived through the battle of Plassey (1757 A.D.) and the Great Bengal Famine of 1770. The resulting distress is echoed in some of his poems.

Quite early in age he is said to have acquired proficiency in Sanskrit, Persian and Bengali. In his teens, he could compose poems of a high class. Gradually he was attracted to Tantra and the Tāntric mode of worship. He is said to have practised *Sādhana* on a *pañcamuṇḍī Āsana*. His spiritual preceptor was Śrīnātha, according to some, Kṛpānātha according to others. His two sons were Ramdualal and Rammohan.

He was reputed as a Śakti-devotee of high order, and composed many songs on the deity of his devotion. His songs, imbued with Tāntric ideas, became a genre. He used to say *na vidyā saṃgītāt parā*; no other ore is higher than music. In Bengal, *prasādī sur* (tune or melody of Ramprasad's songs) has become proverbial. He is, indeed, the pioneer in the introduction of a new mode of Śākta songs. 'Kālīkīrtan' is a small work by him. Of more than 300 songs, passing by his name, probably some are not genuine. Most of his songs are marked by passion or effusion relating to Kālībhakti. A few of his songs relate to the *Āgamanī* (arrival of Umā) and *Vijāyā* (departure after *Durgāpūjā*. He is known to have composed also a *Kṛṣṇakīrtana*.

Kamalākānta Bhaṭṭācārya[2] (C. 1772-1821)

Born at village Cānnā in Burdwan district of West Bengal, he was a native of the village Ambikā-Kālnā. His father and mother are said to have been named Maheśvara and Mahāmāyā.

He studied Sanskrit in the traditional way, and became a teacher. At first, an initiated Vaiṣṇava, he later became a dedicated devotee of Kālī having received *dīkṣā* at Tārāpīṭha in Birbhum district of West Bengal. He is said to have achieved *siddhi* on a *Pañcamuṇḍī Āsana*. With a background of training in vocal music, he wrote many songs which are known as *Śyāmāsaṃgīta*. Besides these, he worte also *Samara-saṃgīta*, *Śivasaṃgīta*, *Kṛṣṇapadāvalī*, *Daśamahāvidyā-saṃgīta*.

Hearing of his spiritual attainment, Tejchand (1764-1832), the then Rājā of Burdwan was attracted to him, appointed him his court-Pandit, built for him a residential house at village Koṭālhāṭ near the town of Burdwan, and granted him an allowance. Here he spent the rest of his life, and was highly respected by the Rāj family.

He composed songs not as a pastime, but as part of his *Sādhanā*. Written in *Tappā* style, his *Śyāmāsaṅgīta* was not looked upon as pedestrian, but also found respectful access into the soirées.

A work by him is entitled *Sādhanarañjana.*

Rāmakrishna[3]

Nothing can be more sacrilegious than the idea expressed in some quarters that Rāmakishna (1836-86) was an unlettered village priest masquerading as a Sadhu.

Born at village Kāmārpukur in the district of Hughly (West Bengal), in 1836 (18th February), he was named Gadādhara. Though of indigent circumstances, his parents, Kṣudirām Caṭṭopādhyāya and Candramaṇi, were very pious.

In his very boyhood, Gadādhara had a spiritual bent of mind, and liked the company of learned men and divines. For quite sometime he studied Sanskrit Śāstras in the traditional way.

The reputation of the piety and devotion of the young Gadādhara attracted the attention of Rāṇī Rashmani who was a pious and prosperous lady. She engaged him as priest at the newly built Kālī temple of Dakṣineswar, a northen suburb of Calcutta, on the Ganges. It was here that the spiritual eye of the priest opened. In the lifeless image, he perceived the pulsation of a living goddess.

A remarkable fact of his life is that, though born and bred in a conservative Brahmin family in the early 19th century, he was absolutely free from bigotry. He tasted the sweet fruits of all the major religions, viz. Islam, Christianity, Sikhism, Buddhism, etc., and openly declared that there were as many ways as there are religious doctrines.

His simple life, precepts of epigrammatic brevity yet pregnant with noble thoughts and sincerity, and, above all, catholicity of heart soon attracted many disciples.

Vivekānanda,[4] an intellectual of high order and having liberal education, was at first sceptic about the existence of God, and had scant regard for the Daksineswar priest. But, the magic wand of Rāmakrishna's spiritual genius soon converted him, and enlisted him as his foremost disciple. Himself great, this saint came to be glorified thousandfold through Vivekānanda.

It was, indeed, a misfortune for the people of Bengal that this great man (Ramkrishna) fell a victim to the fatal malady of cancer, and breathed his last at the comparatively early age of 50.

Vivekānanda[5] (1863-1902)

He was one of those men who never die, though their physical frame perishes.

Born as Narendranath Dalla, in 1863 (Jan. 12), to Visvanath Datta of Simulia in Calcutta and Bhuvaneśvarī, he imbibed a liberal outlook on life from his father and religious bent of mind from his mother.

As a young man, he reluctantly paid a visit to Ramkrishna through the insistence of his friends. This was a turning point of his life.

The early death of his father plunged the family into penury. One day, unable to bear the pinch of poverty, he asked Ṭhākur Ramkrishna to intercede, on his behalf, to Mother goddess for removing his dire poverty. Ṭhākur asked him to go to the nearby temple, and plead his own case. He did go to the Goddess, but he could ask for nothing material. The only things which came out of his mouth were *Jñāna* (knowledge) and *bhakti* (devotion).

After the demise of the master, he, through the munificence of people and the cooperation of his co-disciples, established (1886) a Ramkrishna Maṭh at Baranagar.

Towards the middle of 1890 he, as a wandering mendicant, traversed many regions of India, and acquired first-hand knowledge about the country and its people. At this time, he studied many Śāstras.

In 1893 (May), he went to America to represent Hinduism in the Parliament of Religions at Chicago (September). His soul-stirring speech there dispelled many wrong notions of the western people about the outlook of the Indians.

After that he spent some more time in America and Europe lecturing, interpreting Śāstras and writing books.

A great event of this odyssey was his acquaintance with Margaret Noble, later known as Sister Nivedita who became his disciple, came to India and dedicated herself to social service. Her book, '*The Master as I saw him*' throws light on the many-faceted life of Vivekānanda.

Having returned to India in 1897, Svāmījī, as he was popularly called, devoted himself, heart and soul to the moral regeneration of the people and social reform. A powerful speaker and writer, he urged the people to adhere to truth, sacrifice, acquire mental and physical strength and to shake off superstitions and redeem the country from political bondage and internal dissensions and discords caused by sectarian and communal feelings. He tried, by his speeches and writings, to remove the social blots of untouchability, child marriage, and insisted on liberal and scientific education. Above all, he insisted on the uplift of the downtrodden, and on the service of *Jīva* as Śiva.

The foundation of the Ramkrishna Maṭh and Mission (1897) is a monument to his organising ability and breadth of vision.

He was one of the pioneers in the use of spoken Bengali for literary purposes. He wrote in English also.

In 1899 (June) he again visited western countries, and founded some centres for teaching Vedānta.

Towards the end of 1900, he came back to India. The onslaught of diabetes and the stress and strain of a stormy career were too much for him to bear. His mortal frame gave way, and his soul left it in 1902 (July 4) at Belur Maṭh.

Of his several works, the *Parivrājaka* (1903), *Prācya O Pāścātya, Karmayoga, Jñānayoga, Rājayoga* and *Bhakti-yoga* deserve special mention. His English works have been published in eight volumes.

Vāmā Kṣyāpā[6] (1838-1911)

His full name was Vāmācaraṇa Caṭṭopādhyāyā. Son of Sarvānanda Caṭṭopādhyāyā, grandson of Rāmānanda, and a native of village Āṭlā near Tārāpīṭha in Birbhum district (West Bengal), he, even as a boy showed a sort of divine frenzy. So he was described as Kṣyāpā (mad).

In his very boyhood, he renounced the householder's life, and resorted to the cemetery at Tārāpīṭha.

His father having died, the family faced dire distress. Driven by desperate penury, he got a job at the Kālī temple of village Muluṭi. But, he was so engrossed with the thought of Mother Goddess that he could not fulfil his obligations. As a result, he lost the job.

Now his only shelter was his maternal uncle's house where it was his duty to tend cattle. But, while on duty he used to be immersed in the thought of Kṛṣṇa grazing cows at Vṛndāvana. His indifference led the cows astray, which caused damage to others' crops. So, his maternal uncle drove him away.

Then he accepted the job of plucking flowers for the worship of Tārā for which he was to get food. Here also he could not stick.

He was then appointed cook in the Kāchāri at Mursidabad. But, though physically working there, his mind was drawn to Mother Tārā. He was then sent back to the above temple.

He received Tāntric initiation from the anchorite, Vrajavāsī Kailāsapati, who came to Tārāpīṭha for *Sādhana*. Since then he devoted himself to *Sādhana* in the local cemetery. Then he formally renounced the world, and became a full-fledged *Sannyāsīn*.

He visited Varanasi and Hardwar, but returned to the place of his Mother Goddess.

Rājā Yatīndramohan of Calcutta once had him brought to the city. But, the din and bustle of the city-life was not liked by him. So, he went back.

Rāmakrishna Ray (d. 1795 A.D.; according to some, 1800)

Adopted son of the celebrated Rāṇī Bhavānī of Nāṭor (Bangladesh), he was a big landlord and earned the title of Mahārājādhirāja Pṛthvīpati Bāhādur from the then Mogul King. His fame, however, rests on his Tāntric *Sādhanā*.

He performed *Sādhana* in the Kirīṭeśvarī temple on the west bank of the Bhāgīrathī, some three miles away from village Ḍāhāpāḍā. This temple was regarded as an Upapīṭha, because a part of the crown of Satī is said to have dropped there.

Ramakrishna is known to have practised *Śavasādhana* on a *Pañcamuṇḍī āsana* (seat over five heads or skulls).

NOTES

1. See *Bhāratkoṣ*, *Mātṛgāthā* by Omkārnāth
2. See S.K. De, *Bengali Literature in the Nineteenth Century*; *Mātṛgāthā* (in Bengali) by Omkārnāth.
3. See R. Rolland's Life of Ramakrishna, Calcutta, 1929, and Achintya Sen Gupta's *Paramapuruṣa Rāmakrishna* (in Bengali), Calcutta. There are several other biographies both in English and Bengali.
4. See R. Rolland, *Life of Vivekānanda*, Calcutta, 1931; M.L. Burke, *Svāmī Vivekānanda*, pt. I; Calcutta, 1983 (3rd. ed.), *Svāmī Vivekānanda in the West*, 1982 (2nd. ed.).
5. R. Rolland, *The Life of Vivekānanda*, etc.; There are many other biographies.
6. See H.C. Gangopadhyay, *Śrīvāmālīlā*, I, II, Calcutta, 1340, 1370 B.S.

XI. Buddhist Tāntric Works of Bengal[1]

This topic has been discussed in a chapter of this book. Some more facts are laid down here.

The Tibetan *Tanjur* testifies to the fact that the following Bengali scholars were Buddhist, and composed Tantras.

Candragomin	Author of the following
It is not definitely known whether or not he was identical with the grammarian or the logician of this name.	works on *Abhicāra*: *Abicāra-karma, Camūdhavmsopāya, Bhaya-trānopāya, Vighna-nirāsaka-pramathanopāya.* Some mystic hymns in honour of Tārā, Mañjusrī, etc. are also attributed to him. A few magical works relating chiefly to medicine are also believed to have been penned by him; e.g. *Jvara-rakṣā-vidhi, Kuṣṭhacikitsopāya.*
Dānaśila	
Described as a native of 'Bhagala' in Eastern India, and as belonging to Jagaddala Vihāra in the East.	Sixty works are attributed to him. He appears to have written also a Pustakapāṭhopāya.
Jnanaśri	
Kambala or Kambalapāda	Ten Vajrayāna works. From his works, he appears to be a Bengali. Eight works are attributed to him. These are related mainly to *Heruka* (or Cakrasamvara) *sādhana.* In Proto -Bengali there is a collection of *Dohās, Collet Kambala-gitika.* Of these Dohas, one

	(No.8) occurs in the *caryācarya*, the earliest known Bengali work of c. 1000 A.D.
Kumāracandra Described as an *Avadhūta* of Vikramapuri Vihāra of Bengal.	Stated to have written three Tāntric *Pañjikās* or commentaries.
Śantideva Perhaps different from Śantideva, author of the *Bodhicaryāvatāra* and *Śikṣasamuccaya*. Stated to be a resident of Zahor which, according to H. P. Sastri, was identical with Sābhār in the district of Dacca, Bangladesh.	Author of three Vajrayana works.
Ṭankadāsa or Ḍaṅgadāsa Described as *Vṛddha Kāyastha* and a contemporary of Dharmapāla, ruler of Bengal. There is no certain evidence of his birth in Bengal.	Commentary, called Suviśadasamputa, on *Helvajra-tantra*
Vibhuticandra Stated to belong to a Vihara of Eastern India. It is not clear whether or not he was a Bengali.	Stated to have authored twenty-three works.

NOTE

1. See S.K.De, Buddhist Tāntric Literature of Bengal, *New Indian Anthropology*, April 1938.

Glossary of Select Technical Terms

(English alphabetical order)

ABHICĀRA

Magic spell or rite designed to cause harm to others, e.g. killing an enemy.

ABHIṢEKA

A kind of Tāntric *Dīkṣā* (initiation). The *Guru* performs different kinds of it in the different stages of the spiritual life of his disciple. It is of eight kinds.

ĀCĀRA

Way of life or mode of Tāntric *Sādhana*. Generally of seven kinds: *Veda, Vaiṣṇava, Śaiva, Dakṣiṇa, Vāma, Siddhānta, Kaula*. These are broadly divided into two groups, *Dakṣiṇa* and *Vāma*. Usually those, who use five *Makāras*, are regarded as followers of *Vāmācāra*. A twofold division into *Aghorācāra* and *Yogācāra* is found in some works.

Vide *Mahānirvāṇa* (4/36-37), *Kaulamārga-rahasya* (p.11), Prāṇatoṣiṇī (7/4, p. 532), *Mātṛkābheda* (p. 6).

ADHVA ŚODHANA

Method of purifying the body consisting of six *adhvas*, viz. *varṇa, pada, mantra, kalā, tattva* and *bhuvana.*

AGHORA

A form of Śiva, which is dark and of a fierce nature.

AṄGANYĀSA

Feeling the existence of God in different limbs.

AJAPĀ

The *mantra* called *Haṃsa*. Spontaneous meditation taking place within the body.

ĀJNĀ

Name of a *Cakra* supposed to exist at the joint of the eyebrows. It is like a lotus with two petals.

AKULA

Śiva aspect of Śakti.

ALI

Spirituous liquor used in Tāntric worship.

ĀLĪḌHA

A posture of legs. The right leg is stretched out and the left one is slightly bent.

ĀMNĀYA
Five or six regions where Tāntric culture exists.

ANĀHATA
A *Cakra* supposed to be in the region of the heart. It is like a deep red lotus of twelve petals.

ANTARYĀGA
Mental worship in which the five *Tattvas* are conceived as abstract and not tangible things.

ANUKALPA
Substitute of something; e.g. garlic in place of meat, coconut-water instead of wine.

ĀSANA
Posture necessary for the facility of the circulation of energies. It ensures physical comfort and psychic protection.

AṢṬASIDDHI
See *Siddhi*.

AṢṬAPĀŚA
See *Pāśa*.

AŚVAKRĀNTĀ
According to *Śaktimaṅgala-tantra*, name of the part of India from the Vindhya Hill to the great ocean. It is one of the three regions into which India is divided in certain Tantras.

ĀVARAṆA-CAKRA
Same as *Navacakra* (q.v.).

AVADHŪTA
A Tāntric devotee of a very high order. He is an object of respect of all, free from *Saṃskāras* and possessed of self-knowledge. *Avadhūtas* are of two kinds—*gṛhī* (householder), and *Saṃnyāsī* (ascetic). An *Avadhūta* of the highest order is called *Kulāvadhūta* who is possessed of *divyabhāva*. Vide *Kulārṇava* (17), *Prāṇatoṣiṇī* (7/4, p. 325), *Mahānirvāṇa Tantra* (7/27-83).

ĀVARAṆA-DEVATĀ
Goddesses also known as Yoginīs presiding over the nine *cakras*.

BĀṆALIṄGA
A kind of Śiva-phallus. According to Tantra, it is located in a triangle within *Anāhata Cakra* (q.v.).

BHAIRAVĪ-CAKRA
A *Cakra* ritual in which *Pañcamakāras* are resorted to, and male and female devotees participate.
See *Mahānirvāṇa* (8/54-206), *Kaulāvalī-nirṇaya* (7), *Kulārṇava* (8).

BHŪPURA

A quadrangle with four doors and a triangle within.

BHŪTĀPASARAṆA

Warding off ghosts with the help of *mantras*. Scattering white mustard at the time of sacrifice is a part of the rite. Vide *Tantrasāra* (Kṛṣṇānanda), p. 616; *Śāradātilaka*, 4/10—Rāghava's comm., *Puraścaryārṇava*, III, p. 154.

BHŪTA-ŚUDDHI

A rite for purifying the five elements of the body.

See *Tantrasāra* (Kṛṣṇānanda), pp. 85, 87; *Prāṇatoṣiṇī*, 3/5, p. 202.

BĪJA

A mystical letter forming an essential part of the *mantra* of a deity, e.g. *Hrīṃ*. Different *bījas* have different designations, e.g. *Kāma, Māyā, Lakṣmī, Kālī*, etc. In it the deity is revealed in a subtle form.

BRAHMADVĀRA

The passage through which *Kuṇḍalinī* (q.v.) is supposed to move.

BRAHMANĀḌĪ

Same as *Suṣumnā* (q.v.).

BINDU

(i) Condensed form of *Nāda* (q.v.). In Śaiva philosophy, an evolute of *Nāda* (q.v.), produced by the *Kriyāśakti* of Śiva. According to the *Śāradātilaka* i, 7ff, *Bindu*, characterising Parāśakti, is divided into three parts, *Bindu* (Śiva-oriented), *Bīja* (Śakti-oriented) and *Nāda* (a combination of both). *Bindu* has three forms, *Prakāśa* (static), *Vimarśa* (dynamic) and *Prakāśa-Vimarśa* (combination of both). It is the cause of the origin of letters and elements.

(ii) Dot. One dot represents Śiva. A double dot (*Visarga*) represents Śakti. According to *Śāradātilaka* (ii.6), the former is a symbol of solar power and the latter of lunar.

(iii) Male organ.

(iv) One among *Daśa Mahavidyās* (q.v.) in Kashmir Śaivism—vide *Śāradātilaka*, 1/7 onward, 2/6, 7/9; *Tantrāloka*, 1/216.

BRAHMAPURA

Human body.

BRAHMARANDHRA

Supposed to be at the centre of the head. Through it the vital breath or life is believed to exit at death.

CAKRA

(a) Mystical nerve-cycle or nerve-plexus; the human body is stated to contain the following *Cakras*:

(i) *Mūlādhāra*
(ii) *Svādhiṣṭhāna*
(iii) *Maṇipūra*
(iv) *Anāhata*
(v) *Viśuddha*
(vi) *Ājñā*

(b) Designation of an assembly of Tāntric *Sādhakas* for certain rites, e.g. *Bhairavī-cakra*
(c) Endless rotation of Śakti.
(d) Mystic diagram or *Yantra*, as *Trikoṇacakra, Aṣṭakoṇa cakra.*

CAKRA-BHEDA
Literally, penetration of *Cakras*. Manifestation or activation which is necessary for keeping the body fit and for the attainment of *Siddhis.* Name of a stage of Tāntric *Sādhana.*

CANDRANĀḌĪ
Name of *Iḍā* (q.v.).

CARAMĀLĀ
A rosary made of *rudrākṣa*. (fruits of *Elaeocorpus ganitrus Roxb.*), conch-shells or some other thing meant for the recitation (*japa*) of *mantras.*

CATUṢKUṬĀ
A particular arrangement of letters in connexion with the worship of *Śrīvidyā.*

CĪNĀCĀRA, CĪNAKRAMA
A form of *Kaulācāra*. A follower of it follows *Tārākrama* and *Chinnamastākrama.* That aspirant is eligible for it, who is free from the sense of duality and sin, has given up caste-distinction, is calm and detached. Vide *Tārātantra*, p. 20; *Śaktisaṃgama* (Sundarī, 1/188 onward), *Puraścaryārṇava*, I, p. 20.

CITRIṆĪ
A *Nāḍī* (q.v.) supposed to be within the body, also called *Brahmanāḍī*. It is like a lotus fibre. Generally identified with *Suṣumṇā* (q.v.). It is also stated that *Suṣumṇā* is constituted of the three *Nāḍīs*; viz. *Citriṇī Vajrā* and *Brahma* possessed respectively of the qualities of *Sattva, Rajas* and *Tamas*. Vide *Prāṇatoṣiṇī*,1/4, p. 32.

ḌĀKINĪ
Designation of various goddesses. Ḍākinī occupies a special position in Buddhist Tantra. At some places, She is a companion of Pārvatī and is connected with the manifestation of the goddess as

Chinnamastā. Regarded as a particular form of *Parā* or Supreme *Śakti*. Resorts to *Mūlādhāra* (q.v.) She is supposed to impart spiritual knowledge to the devotee. Vide *Prāṇatoṣiṇī* (5/6, pp. 378-79), *Tantrasāra* (Kṛṣṇānanda), p. 338; *Ṣaṭcakra-nirūpaṇa* (8).

DAKṢIṆĀCĀRA

Worship of Śakti according to the right-hand ritual. Some explain it as the way prescribed in Veda, Smṛti and Purāṇa. It is a way of spiritual attainment without the use of *Pañcamakāra* and extreme forms of rituals.

DAŚA MAHĀVIDYĀ

The following ten female deities are called *Mahāvidyā*: Kālī, Tārā, Ṣoḍaśī, Bhuvaneśvarī, Bhairavī, Chinnamastā, Dhūmavatī, Vagalā, Mātaṅgī, Kamalā. See *Prāṇatoṣiṇī*, 5/ p. 374. The names of *Mahāvidyās* differ in different Tantras.

DHĀRAṆA-YANTRA

The *Yantra* (q.v.) that is generally worn as a talisman or amulet for ensuring well-being. Such a *Yantra*, written on the leaf of a tree, is dedicated to a deity.

DHĀRAṆĪ

Mystic protective spells.

DHYĀNA

Meditation on a deity. Different deities are to be meditated upon in different forms. It is the basic element in *Sādhana*.

DĪKṢĀ

Initiation to Tāntric *Sādhana*. According to *Viśvasāratantra*, it is of four types—*Kriyāvatī, Kalāvatī, Varṇamayī* and *Vedhamayī*. According to *Rudrayāmala*, it is of three types—*Āṇavī, Śāktī, Śāmbhavī*. According to the *Kulārṇava* (XIV) it is of seven kinds—*Kriyā, Varṇa, Kalā, Sparśa, Vāk, Dṛk, Mānasa*.

DIVYACAKRA

A *Cakra* ritual meant for those who have achieved considerable spiritual progress. In it, *Pañcamakāras* are used.

DIVYAUGHA

A kind of succession of *Gurus*. Vide *Śyāmārahasya* (3).

GAJAKRĀNTĀ

Same as *Aśvakrānta* (q.v.).

GĀYATRĪ

Mantra in honour of a deity recognised in Tantra; e.g. *Kālikāyai vidmahe, Śmaśānavāsinyai dhīmahi*.

GAUḌA SAMPRADĀYA

A sect of the *Vāmācārī* Tāntrikas of eastern India. The devotees of this sect believe only in rituals involving *Pañcamakāras*. According to them, the deity, preceptor and *mantra* are identical, and are the manifestations of Mahādevī. Vide *Puraścaryārṇava*, 9, p. 866; *Śaktisaṃgama*, Sundarī, 3/15-18.

GURU

Preceptor who initiates a person to Tāntric *sādhana*, is regarded as Śiva. *Gurus* are of four kinds, viz. *Sākṣātguru* (direct preceptor), *Paramaguru* (*Guru* of *Guru*), *Parāpara Guru* (third *Guru* in ascending order), *Parameṣṭhi-guru* (fourth *Guru* in ascending order). See *Tantrasāra* (Kṛṣṇānanda), pp. 2, 3; *Prāṇatoṣiṇī* (2/2, 6/4), *Mahānirvāṇa* (6/98), *Rudrayāmala* (Uttara 2), *Kulārṇava* (11-14, 17), *Tantrarāja* (1), *Gandharvatantra* (26), *Śāradātilaka* (2 and *Rāghava's* comm. on 2/143-44); *Prapañcasāra* (36/50), *Kāmākhyātantra* (4), *Kaulāvalī-nirṇaya* (10), *Paraśurāma-kalpasūtra* (10/74,75), etc.

HĀDIVIDYĀ, HĀDIMATA

A Tāntric school so called after its symbol HA representing Śiva. It was influential in Kerala and Kashmir.

Vidyā (*jñāna*, *mantra* or *devatā* arising from *Kāmarāja Bīja*, vide *Śaktisaṃgama* (Tārā, 58/81).

HĀKINĪ

Presiding deity of *Ājñā-cakra* (q.v.). She is conceived as having six-faces and white colour.

HAṂSA

Same as *Ajapā* (q.v.). Regarded as *parama mantra*. It is of two kinds—*Vyakta* (manifest) and *gupta* (hidden). So called from *Ham* (inhalation) and *Saḥ* (exhalation). *Ham* is the symbol of *Bindu* (male principle) and *Saḥ* of *Visarga* (female principle).

HAṬHAYOGA

A kind of forced *yoga* or abstract meditation performed with great self-torture such as standing on one leg, holding up the arms, inhaling smoke with the inverted head, etc. In it, the mind is forced to withdraw from external objects.

According to the *Yogaśikhopaniṣat* (i.133), *Haṭha* means the unity of the Sun (*Ha*) and the moon (*Ṭha*).

IḌĀ

One of the three principal arteries, supposed to be on the left side of the spinal cord. One of the main channels of the vital spirit, also called *Candranāḍī*. Conceived to be of white colour and representing the *amṛta* aspect of Śakti.

JAPA

Repeated mental recital of the specified *Bīja* (q.v.) with the sense that *Guru, Devatā* and *Mantra* are identical. For details about *Japa*, see *Puraścaryārṇava* (6, p. 541), *Kulārṇava* (15, 17) *Śaktisaṃgama* (Tārā 46/2-3), *Gandharvatantra* (18/3-4, 28/9), *Rudrayāmala* (Uttara 26), *Śāradātilaka* (4/55; 56 – Rāghava's comm).

JĪVANMUKTI

Liberation in life, attaining which one acquires the knowledge of self, dispels the darkness of false knowledge. Also used to denote immortality that can be achieved by transmuting the mortal body by chemical processes into a divine one.

KĀDIMATA

A principal Tāntric school mentioned in *Śaktisaṃgama*, Tārā, LVIII. 81-82. This school has *KA* as the symbol (3).

KĀDIVIDYĀ

Knowledge of a special kind. Named after the initial letter (KA) of *Vāgbhava-bīja*. Vide *Śāradātilaka* (1/1 – comm.).

KAHĀDIMATA

A Tāntric school, mentioned in *Śaktisaṃgama*, Tārākhaṇḍa, LVIII. 81-82. Also called *Tāriṇīmata, Ibid.* Kālī, VI. 125.

KĀKINĪ

Presiding deity of *Anāhata Cakra* (see *Cakra*). She is conceived as three-eyed, yellow-coloured and dwelling in a 12-petalled red lotus, Vide *Ṣaṭcakra-nirūpaṇa*, 24.

KALĀ

Evolute of *varuṇa*. 38 *Kalās* are supposed to emanate from letters.

KĀLACAKRA

A nerve-cycle situated above the *Viśuddhacakra* (q.v.).

KĀLĪMATA

Same as *Kādimata*.

KĀPĀLIKA

Śaiva sect holding extreme views, following the Tāntric cult of Śakti, defying Vedic authority, drinking wine from human skulls.

Some take them to belong to the Nātha sect. Vide *Gorakṣa-siddhānta-saṃgraha*, p.16 onward; *Śaktisaṃgama*, Kālī, 8/9-10.

KĀLIKĀ

A kind of Tāntric *Nyāsa* (q.v.).

KĀLĪKULA

A Tāntric sect in which Kālī is the Supreme Deity. The noted works of this school are *Jayadratha-yāmala, Uttaratantra, Śaktisaṃgama* (Kālīkhaṇḍa).

KARAMĀLĀ

Designation of the parts of the fingers used in counting the number of times of recitation of *mantras* at the time of *Japa*. See *Puraś-caryārṇava* (6, pp. 447-49), *Tantrasāra* (Kṛṣṇānanda), p. 27 onward.

KĀRAṆA

Wine. So called as it is the cause of all knowledge of *dharma, artha, kāma* and *mokṣa*. (*Prāṇatoṣiṇī*, vii.2).

KAULA, KAULIKA

One who follows Tāntric *Kulācāra*. The adherents of the *Kula* path are divided into many sects, e.g. *Kāpālika, Kṣapaṇaka, Digambara*, etc.

KAULAMĀRGA

Sevenfold *Tāntric Ācāra* or spiritual effort. Otherwise called *Kulācāra*. Vide *Kaulamārga-rahasya* (p. 5) *Kulārṇava* (17), *Rudrayāmala* (Uttara 17), *Praṇatoṣiṇī* (7/4, p. 531), *Kaula-jñāna-nirṇaya* (ed. Bagchi) 14,16,21; *Mahānirvāṇa* (14/184) etc.

KAVACA

Prayer with certain mystic syllables, supposed to protect the devotee as an armour protects the body. Protective spell.

KHAPUṢPA

Menstrual blood.

KHECARĪ MUDRĀ

A yogic posture helping in spiritual attainment and in overcoming disease and death.

It is necessary in the meditation on Tripurasundarī. See *Mudrā-nighaṇṭu* (14-16), *Haṭhayoga-pradīpikā* (3/67), *Gheraṇḍasaṃhitā* (3/1-3).

KLEŚA

Five causes of suffering: *Avidyā* (false knowledge), *Asmitā* (egotism), *Rāga* (attachment), *Dveṣa* (hatred), and *Abhiniveśa* (adherence).

KOṢA

Sheath. The human body is supposed to consist of five sheaths which are:

(i) *Annamaya*
(ii) *Prāṇamaya*
(iii) *Manomaya*
(iv) *Vijñānamaya*
(v) *Ānandamaya.*

KULA

(i) Family and the mode of worship handed down by the tradition of the family. Spiritual lineage.
(ii) Tāntric rites obtaining in a particular region with reference to a particular deity.
(iii) It denotes the Śāstra which expounds the group of objects including the knower, the known and the knowledge or the worshipper and the object of worship.
(iv) It denotes body.
(v) It means the *ādhāra-cakra.*

The term is constituted by *Ku* (earth) and *līyate* (merged).

KULĀCĀRA

See *Kaulamārga.*

KULADRAVYA

Kulatattva, Pañcatattva or *Pañcamakāra.* Vide *Kaulāvalīnirṇaya* (8).

KULA-VṚKṢA

The following trees, regarded as sacred for *Kaulas,* are so called: *śleṣmātaka, karañjaka, plakṣa, vaṭa, nimba, aśvattha, kadamba, udumbara, ciñca.*

KULLUKĀ

Designation of certain mystic syllables preceding *mantras* to be used in *Śakti-pūjā.*

KUMBHAKA

See *Prāṇāyāma.*

KUṆḌALINĪ

Dormant spiritual energy supposed to encircle the *Mūlādhāra* (q.v.) like a serpent. The Mahākuṇḍalinī is believed to be at the root of the universe.

LĀKINĪ

Presiding deity of *Maṇipura Cakra.* See *Cakra.*

LATĀ

Same as Śakti or Dūtī, the female partner in Tāntric *sādhana.*

LIṄGA PUṢPA

The flower *Raktakaravī* (Red *Nerium indicum*) used as a substitute for sexual union.

LIṄGATRAYA

Threefold Śiva-phallus, viz. *Itara, Svayambhū* and *Bāṇa.*

MADHYAMA

A special type of sound between *Paśyantī* and *Vaikharī.* See *Śabdabrahma.*

MAHĀCAKRA

One of the five *Cakra* rituals; the others are *Rāja, Devī, Vīra* and *Paśu.* In it, one's mother, sister, daughter, daughter-in-law and wife are to be worshipped as *Pañcaśakti.*

MAHĀMĀṂSA

The flesh of eight creatures, viz. man, cow, horse, buffalo, boar, goat, ram and deer. See *Tantrasāra* (Kṛṣṇānanda), p. 630, *Śyāmārahasya* (3).

MAHĀMUDRĀ

See *Mudrā.*

MAHĀSETU

Name of a *mantra.* See *Setu.*

MAHĀVIDYĀ

A manifestation of Śakti.

MĀLĀ

Impurities or fetters which cause suffering and lead to re-births. It is of three types—*Āṇava, Kārma, Māyīya.*

MĀNAVAUGHA

Literally, human stream. Name of a succession of *Gurus.* See *Śyāmārahasya* (3).

MAṆIPURA

A *Cakra* supposed to exist in the navel. It is like a golden lotus of ten petals.

MAṆḌALA

(i) A mystic diagram like *Sarvatobhadra* or an otherwise enclosed space used in certain rites and modes of worship.

(ii) A gathering of devotees who collectively perform rites, and resort to the five *Makāras* and sit, along with their female partners around the leader (*nāyaka* or *adhīśvara* and his consort).

MANTRA-CAITANYA

Consciousness lying in *Mantra*. It has to be awakened by a Tāntric process. Vide *Prāṇatoṣiṇī* (4/1, p. 222), *Puraścaryārṇava* (6, p. 528), *Gandharvatantra* (29/24-25).

MANTRAYĀNA

Name of Tāntric Buddhism.

MAṆIPURA

See *Cakra*.

MĀNTRĪ

A kind of *Dīkṣā*.

MĀRAṆA

See *Ṣaṭkarma*.

MĀTṚKĀ

Divine Mothers or mystic letters. Each of the letters from *A* to *Kṣ* represents an aspect of Śakti. Divine Mothers are eight in number; viz. Brahmāṇī, Maheśvarī, Kaumārī, Vaiṣṇavī, Vārāhī, Aindrī, Cāmuṇḍā, Mahālakṣmī.

MERU

The central bead in a rosary is so called.

MOKṢAMĀRGA

Same as *Suṣumṇā* (q.v.).

MUDRĀ

(i) Formed from the root *mud*, it literally means that which causes delight. It generally stands for particular positions of the fingers used in worship. Some *mudrās* are *Matsya*, *Śaṃkha*, etc.

(ii) It denotes some postures of the body at the time of *yoga*, e.g. *Aśvinī-mudrā*.

(iii) Designation of parched grains or fried cereals as one of the five *tattvas*.

(iv) Diagram used in Tāntric rites.

(v) Woman, particularly in Buddhist Tantra.

(vi) *Mahāmudrā*, in Buddhist Tantra, means female organ.

MUKTA-TRIVEṆĪ

Same as *Ājñā* (q.v.).

MŪLĀDHĀRA

A mystic circle believed to be above the genital organ.

NĀBHI CAKRA

Same as Manipura (q.v.).

NĀDA
(i) Sound.
(ii) First vibration of Parā Śakti when it goes to express itself in creation.
(iii) Manifestation of the consciousness of the Supreme Being, revealed as sound. This manifestation is conceived as sexual union of Śiva-Śakti (Static and dynamic aspects, also known as *Prakāśa* and *Vimarśa* of the same ultimate reality); the thrill of the pleasure of this union is known as *Nāda*. The abbreviated form of *Nāda* is called *Bindu*. Vide *Śāradātilaka*, 1/6 onward; *Ṣaṭcakra-nirūpaṇa*, 39 (remark of Kālīcaraṇa); *Prapañcasāra*, 1/41. See *Bindu* and *Bīja*.

NĀḌĪ
Vein.The human body is supposed to contain 72,000 veins. Of these, 72 are prominent. Of them again, fourteen are important in consideration of the others. These are *Iḍā, Piṅgalā, Suṣumṇā, Gandhārī, Hastijihvā, Yaśasvinī, Alambusā, Kuhu, Śaṃkhinī, Sarasvatī, Vāruṇi, Pusā, Viśvodarā, Payasvinī,* Among them, the most important are *Iḍā, Piṅgalā*, and *Suṣumṇā*. Vide *Prāṇatoṣiṇī* 1/4, pp. 32-33.

NAṬĪ
Actress or female dancer. Applied to Śakti who is supposed to dance out of delight at the performance of rituals related to Her.

NAVACAKRA
Nine *cakras* (actually triangles) as constituents of *Śrīyantra* (q.v.). Of these, five pointing upward belong to Śakti and four, pointing downward, to Śiva. According to Lakṣmīdhara on *Saundaryalaharī*, ix, this *cakra* has three parts, each symbolically connected with creation, preservation and destruction. Also called *Āvaraṇacakra*.

NYĀSA
Designation of the process by which the *Sādhaka* fancies the different parts of body as identical with those of the body of the deity meditated upon or worshipped. There are many kinds of *Nyāsa*, e.g. *Aṅga-nyāsa, Kara-nyāsa, Mātṛkā-nyāsa*. It may also mean subtle identification with the *Cakras*.

PADMĀSANA
A posture suitable for the practice of *Yoga*. In it, the right foot is placed on the left thigh, and left foot on the right thigh.

PAÑCAMUṆḌĪ
A kind of seat suitable for Tāntric *sādhana*. It is prepared with the severed heads of the following creatures: two Caṇḍālas, one jackal, one monkey and one snake.

PAÑCATATTVA (or MAKĀRA)
Also called *Kula-dravya* or *Kulatattva*. It is commonly called *Pañca-makāra*. The five *tattvas* are: *madya* (wine), *māṃsa* (meat), *matsya* (fish), *mudrā* (position of fingers or particular kinds of parched grain), *maithuna* (sexual union).

PARĀ
See *Śabdabrahma*.

PARAMAHAṂSA
One who has attained perfection in *Haṃsa* mantra (q.v.).

PARAMAKULA
Same as *Ājñā* (q.v.).

PARAMEṢṬHĪ GURU
See *Guru*.

PARĀPARA GURU
See *Guru*.

PARĀŚAKTI
(i) Supreme Śakti.
(ii) Female partner of the male devotee.

PĀŚA
Eight fetters causing bondage: *ghṛṇā* (hatred), *lajjā* (shame), *bhaya* (fear), *śaṅkā* (apprehension), *jugupsā* (aversion), *kula* (pedigree), *śīla* (conduct), *jāti* (birth or caste). Vide *Paraśurāma-kalpasūtra*, 10/70.

PAŚU
Designation of a man in whom the animal propensities are predominant. Regarded as the meanest type of human beings.

PAŚYANTĪ
A kind of sound in the region of the navel. Having little vibration, it is connected with *Nādatattva*.
See *Śabdabrahma*.

PIṄGALĀ
One of the main arteries supposed to be on the right side of the spinal cord and rising from the *Mūlādhāra* and terminating in the right nostril. Also called *Sūryanāḍī*, it symbolises the waking state, and leads one to violent action.

PĪṬHA-NYĀSA
It means feeling the *Pīṭha-sthānas* in different parts of the body, as Kāmarūpa in the heart, Jālandhara on the forehead.

PĪṬHASTHĀNA
Holy places of Śakti, generally regarded as 51 in number. Each such place is supposed to contain a limb of Satī. (See the Purāṇic legend of *Dakṣayajña*). *Pīṭhas* are divided into two classes, *Mahā* (major) and *Upa* (minor). *Pīṭha* means a seat. The place at which or the seat on which a great devotee attained *Siddhi*, is regarded as a holy *pīṭhasthāna*. Of the 51 *Pīṭhasthānas*, quite a few are in Bengal (including Bangladesh).

PRAKṚTI
Designation of the woman with whom a Tāntric *Sādhaka* performs sexual intercourse as a *tattva*. Female Principle of creation often identified with Śakti.

PRĀṆĀYĀMA
Breath exercise. It is threefold: *Pūraka* (inhalation), *Recaka* (exhalation) and *Kumbhaka* (holding the breath). An accessory of *Yoga*. Vide *Prāṇatoṣiṇī* (6/1, p. 408). *Gheraṇḍa-saṃhitā* (5/46) mentions eight kinds of *Kumbhaka* and the *Haṭhayoga-pradīpikā* two more.

PRATYĀHĀRA
Yogic process of withdrawing the senses from their contact with external objects.

PRATYĀLĪḌHA
Reverse of *Ālīḍha* (q.v.). In it, the left leg is outstretched, and the right one is slightly bent.

PŪRAKA
See *Prāṇāyāma*.

PŪRAŚCARAṆA
A rite in which the *Sādhaka* goes through five steps, viz. *japa, homa, tarpaṇa, abhiṣeka, brāhmaṇa-bhojana*. In some works, five extra steps are added. Different degrees of *japa*, etc. are prescribed for the different types of aspirants according as they are *Divya, Vīra* and *Paśu*. There are elaborate rules for a devotee undergoing *Puraścaraṇa* regarding food, habits, conduct etc. Its purpose is *Mantrasiddhi*.

PŪRṆĀBHIṢIKTA
See *Abhiṣeka*.

RĀJAYOGA
Highest form of *yoga*, as laid down in *Pātañjala Yogasūtra*. By it the mind is merged in Brahman.

RATHAKRĀNTĀ

Name of the tract of land from the Vindhya hill to Mahācīna, including Nepal.

RECAKA

See *Prāṇāyāma*.

ŚABDABRAHMA

Brahman or Force regarded as the source of sound. This sound-producing Force, identified with *Kuṇḍalinī* (q.v.) is fourfold, viz. *Parā* (in *Mūlādhāra*, q.v.), *Paśyantī* (in navel), *Vaikharī* (carried by wind within the body and sounded in throat), and *Madhyamā* (in between *Paśyantī* and *Vaikharī*). According to Rāghavabhaṭṭa, *Para* is unmanifested sound, *Paśyantī* reveals letters, *Madhyamā* words and *Vaikharī* sentences.

SĀDIVIDYĀ

A system of knowledge, so named after the symbolic first letters of Śakti-bīja.

SAHAJA

Easy and natural way of spiritual exercise. The followers of this path are called *Sahajiyās*. According to them, the Superme Reality is known as *Sahaja*. There were adherents of this doctrine among both Hindus (*Vaiṣṇavas*) and Buddhists.

SAHASRĀRA

A supposed multicoloured lotus of a thousand petals. It is believed to be contained in *Brahma-randhra* (q.v.).

ŚĀKTEYĪ

A kind of *Dīkṣā*.

ŚAKTI

(i) Female Energy of Śiva, the Supreme Being.

The universe is manifested through Śakti. The main characteristics of Śakti are *Cit* (consciousness), *Ānanda* (joy), *Icchā* (desire), *Jñāna* (knowledge) and *Kriyā* (action).

(ii) Female associate of a Tāntric devotee. She may be *Svakīyā* (own wife), *Parakīyā* (other's wife), *Sādhāraṇī* (public woman, prostitute) or a low-class woman. Generally, a woman of a despised profession is regarded as Śakti par excellence. Vide *Tantrasāra* of Kṛṣṇānanda (p. 627), *Prāṇatoṣiṇī* (7/4, p. 548), *Kulārṇava* (7), *Niruttara* (14), *Gandharvatantra* (23/19).

(iii) One of the six limbs of *mantra*.

ŚAKTICAKRA

The five *Śakti* triangles in *Śrīyantra* (q.v.).

SAMĀDHI

Thus defined in *Pātañjala-Yogasūtra* (3/3): *Tadevārthamātra-nirbhāsaṃ svarūpa-śunyanaiva samadhih.*

The very same thing (i.e. *Dhyāna*), when conscious only of the object, as if unconscious of itself, is *Samādhi*. It is mainly twofold—*Saṃprajñāta* (when there is perception of meditator as different from the object of meditation) and *Asaṃprajñāta* (when the above perception is absent). These two types are also called *Savikalpa* and *Nirvikalpa* respectively.

SĀMARASYA

State of equilibrium of Śiva-Śakti (Male and Female Principles) corresponding to the Buddhistic conception of *Upāya* and *Prajñā*, generally conceived in sexual union the complete comprehension of which leads to the feeling of non-duality.

SAMAYĀCĀRA

A way of the followers of the *Śrīvidyā* cult.

ŚĀMBHAVĪ

A kind of *Dīkṣa*.

ṢAṬCAKRA

See *Cakra*.

ṢAṬ CAKRABHEDA

See *Cakra-bheda*.

ŚAVASĀDHANA

Performance of a Tāntric rite with a corpse. It has been described in the book. Vide *Kaulāvalīnirṇaya* (14), *Śyāmārahasya* (14), *Tārābhakti-sudhārṇava* (9), *Puraścaryārṇava* (9).

SETU

According to the *Tantrasāra* of Kṛṣṇānanda, *oṃkāra*, preceding a *mantra*, is called *setu*. Again, fourteen vowels, followed by *anusvāra* and *nāda*, are called *setu* in the case of Śūdras. According to the *Prāṇatoṣiṇī*, *praṇava* (i.e. *oṃkāra*) is called *setu* for Brāhmaṇas and Kṣatriyas. For Vaiśyas, *phaṭ* is *setu*. So called as it is regarded as a bridge of knowledge to cross the ocean of misery. Its higher form is called *Mahāsetu*.

SIDDHAUGHA

Name of a succession of *Gurus*. Vide Śyāmārahasya (3).

SIDDHĀNTĀCĀRA

One of the sevenfold *Ācāra* (q.v.). Regarded as a variety of *Vāmācāra*, suitable for a devotee of the *Vīra* (q.v.). In it there is greater stress on *Antaryāga* (q.v.) than on external rites. The adherents worship Viṣṇu by day, and resort to *Pañcamakāra* (q.v.). See *Puraścaryārṇava*, I, p.22; *Kaulamārgarahasya*, p.10.

SIDDHI

(i) Extraordinary or supernatural power acquired by a *Sādhaka*. The following eight are the principal *Siddhis*: *Aṇimā* (assuming an atomic figure), *Laghimā* (assuming excessive lightness of body), *Garimā* (excessive heaviness), *Mahimā* (increasing one's size at will), *Prāpti* (obtaining everything at will), *Prākāmya* (having irresistible will), *Īśitva* (superiority over others), *Vaśitva* (keeping others under control), some substitute *Kāmāvasāyitā* (suppression of passion or desire) for *Garimā*.

ŚIVACAKRA

The four Śiva-triangles in *Navacakra* (q.v.).

ṢOḌHĀNYĀSA

In this kind of *Nyāsa* (q.v.), the presence of deities is separately felt in the body. It has six varieties. Vide *Tantrasāra* (Kṛṣṇānanda), pp. 272, 309 onward; *Tārābhakti-sudhārṇava* (5, p.163), *Śāradātilaka* (7), *Puraścaryārṇava* (12, p.1165).

ŚRĪCAKRA

The most important diagram relating to Śrīvidyā. It symbolises the body of the goddess. Of the nine triangles or *yonis*, contained in it, five are in the name of Śakti and four in that of Śiva. The Śakti triangles point upwards and the Śiva triangles downwards.

ŚRĪKULA

A principal Tāntric school.

ŚRĪYANTRA

Same as *Śrīcakra* (q.v.).

STAMBHANA

Causing paralysis, obstruction. One of the six Tāntric acts.

ŚUDDHI

Designation of meat, fish, *mudrā*, fruits, roots, etc., which are offered while offering wine to the goddess. *Pañcamakāras* are also designated as Śuddhi.

ŚŪNYATĀ

According to Buddhists, it is the Female principle and is known as *Prajñā*. It is symbolised by the forms of different female deities. According to Buddhists, the Male principle is conceived as *Karuṇā* or *Upāya*.

SŪRYANĀḌĪ

Same as *Piṅgalā* (q.v.).

SUṢUMṆĀ

The most important artery supposed to be in the middle of the human body. It is called *Brahma-vartma* (the path of Brahman) or *Brahamanāḍī* or *Mokṣamārga*, and is supposed to extend from *mūlādhāra* to *sahasrara*.

SVĀDHIṢṬHĀNA

A *Cakra* supposed to exist between the *mūlādhāra* (q.v.) and the navel. It is like a lotus of six petals.

SVAPUṢPA

The first menstrual blood of a newly married woman.

TĀḌANA

A process connected with *Mantra*. By it a letter of the *mantra* concerned is recited ten or hundred times. In it, the letters may be written, and sandal-water sprinkled over them.

TĀRIṆĪMATA

Same as *Kahādimata* (q.v.). *Śaktisaṃgama, Kālī*, vi. 125.

TARPAṆA

Offering libation of water to departed ancestors.

TATTVA

See *Pañcatattva*.

TATTVACAKRA

Most important *Cakra*, also called *Divyacakra*. It is confined only to those who have advanced far in *Tāntric Sādhana*. In it, there is no external rite. The devotees sit together under the leadership of the principal person known as *Cakreśvara*, and repeat the *Haṃsa mantra* (so'ham). Vide *Mahānirvāṇa*, 8/204 onward).

TRIPĪṬHA

Collective name of Kāmarūpa, Pūrṇagiri and Jālandhara Pīṭhas.

TRIPURACAKRA

Same as *Śrīcakra* (q.v.).

UCCĀṬANA

Expulsion. One of the six Tāntric acts.

UTTARĀCĀRA

The way shown by Vedic injunction and the *guru* who is *jīvamukta.*

VĀGBHAVA

(i) A *Bīja* (q.v.).

(ii) Name of a triangle.

VAIKHARĪ

One of the four kinds of sound articulated in the throat. See *Śabdabrahma.*

VAJRA

(i) Name of a nerve within *Suṣumṇā.*

(ii) A weapon, thunderbolt, usually found in the hands of Buddhist deities.

VĀMĀCĀRA

Left-hand practices or doctrines, i.e. the worship of Śakti personified as Śiva's wife. Some explain it as a rite in which women, who are placed on the left of men, play an important part or which is a crooked way practised secretly.

Vāma is of two kinds—*Madhyama* in which all the five *Makāras* are resorted to, and *Uttama* in which *madya, maithuna* and *mudrā* are used.

VAŚĪKARAṆA

Bringing others under control. One of the six Tāntric acts.

VEDĀCĀRA

One of the seven kinds of Tāntric *Ācāra* (q.v.). The followers of this *Ācāra* attach importance to the Vedic mode.

VIDVEṢAṆA

Hatred, causing bad blood. One of the six Tāntric acts.

VIDYĀ

(i) Knowledge.

(ii) Aspect of Śakti, as Daśa Mahāvidyā.

(iii) *Mantra.*

(iv) Female partner of a Tāntric devotee.

(v) Certain forms of *Tattvas* and *Kalās.*

(vi) *Vimarśa-śakti* expressed with the idea of one-ness.

(vii) Name of a school or sect.

VĪRA

A Tāntric devotee of the second order. His mental power is highly developed. The conduct of such a person is called *Vīrācāra.* Vide *Kulārṇava* (17). *Prāṇatoṣiṇī* (7/1— p.495 onward).

VĪRĀCĀRA

See *Vīra.*

VIṢṆUKRĀNTĀ

A region of Tāntric culture, extending from the Vindhya range to Caṭṭala (Chittagong in Bangladesh).

VIŚUDDHA

A *Cakra* supposed to be in the throat. Seat of Sarasvatī, it is believed to be grey and like a lotus of sixteen petals.

YANTRA

Diagram, painted with minerals on something or on bare ground, at the time of worship. The worshipper imagines that the deity, being worshipped by him, for the time being resides in the diagram. Diagrams differ according to forms of the deities worshipped.

YOGINĪ

(i) A class of goddesses, generally numbering 64, supposed to be the proliferation of the eight *Mātṛkās.*

(ii) Female partner of the aspirant.

(iii) Goddesses presiding over nerve-plexuses

(iv) A class of female ascetics imparting Tāntric knowledge to the masses. It may also denote a medicine woman or a woman possessed by the goddess.

YONIMUDRĀ

A physical posture in which the person concerned fixes his anus on the left heel, tongue on the palate and eyes on the nose-tip. It is supposed to awaken Kuṇḍalinī (q.v.).

YONIPUṢPA

Black *Aparājitā* flower (*Clitoriaternatea*) as a symbol of sexual union. Vide *Paraśurāma-kalpasūtra*, 10/63.

YUGANADDHA

The condition of a man and woman in union. It is often found in Buddhist Tāntric art. Oneness, beyond duality, of *Śunyatā-Karuṇā.*

Select Bibliography

The following abbreviations have been used:

ABORI : *Annals of Bhandarkar Oriental Research Institute*
ASS : *Anandasrama Sanskrit Series*
CSS : *Calcutta Sanskrit Series*
GOS : *Gaekwad's Oriental Series*
IHQ : *Indian Historical Quarterly*
JASB : *Journal of Asiatic Society of Bengal*
JRAS : *Journal of Royal Asiatic Society*
SBH : *Sacred Books of the Hindus*
TSS : *Trivandrum Sanskrit Series*

Texts

(In Devanāgarī alphabetical order)
[Important texts have been published by A. Avalon in several volumes of his *Tāntrika Texts*. All of them are not listed here.]

Ahirbudhnya-saṃhitā — ed. Ramanujacarya, Madras, 1916.
Āgama-tattva-vilāsa (Raghunātha)—ed. P. Sastri, Calcutta, 1985.
Āryamañjuśrī-mūlakalpa — TSS.
Īśāna-gurudeva-paddhati (Īśānagurudeva Miśra) — TSS.
Uḍḍīśa-tantra—with Hindi exposition, Varanasi. Also pub. in Bengali *Sulabha-tantra-prakāśa*, Calcutta, 1887.
Ekākṣara-koṣa (Puruṣottama) — A. Avalon, *Tāntrika Texts*, I.
Kaṅkālamālinī-tantra, Calcutta.
Kāmakalā-vilāsa (Puṇyānandanātha) — with comm., Eng. translation and notes, ed. A. Avalon, Madras, 1961.
Kālīvilāsa-tantra — ed. P. Tarkatirtha, *Tāntrika Texts*, VI, 1917.
Kālyarcana-candrikā — Compiled by Nīlakamala Lāhiḍi, Berhampore (West Bengal), 1285 B.S.
Kubjikā-mata-tantra—ed. J. Schoterman. Also pub. in Calcutta.
Kulacūḍāmaṇi — ed. G.C. Vedantatirtha, *Tāntrika Texts*, Vol. IV, 1915.
Kulārṇava-tantra — ed. T. Vidyaratna, *Tāntrika Texts*, Vol. V, 1917.
Kaula-jñāna-nirṇaya—ed. P.C. Bagchi, Calcutta, 1934.
Kaulāvalī-nirṇaya—Tāntrika Texts, XIV.
Gaṇapati-tattva — Old Javanese text, ed., annotated and trs. into English by S. Singhal, New Delhi, 1958.

Gupta-sādhana-tantra, Calcutta.

Gurutantra — ed., trs. into Bengali by Jaganmohana Tarkalankāra, Calcutta, 1335 B.S.

Guhyasamāja-tantra, GOS, LIII, 1931.

Jñānārṇava-tantra — ASS. No. 69, 1912.

Tantra-samuccaya (Nārāyaṇa) — ed. G. Sastri, TSS, Nos. 67 and 71.

Tantrarāja-tantra — Pt. I, *Tāntrika Texts*, VII, 1918.

Tantrasāra (Abhinavagupta)—with notes, ed. Sastri, 1918.

Tantrasāra (Kṛṣṇānanda) — ed. Vasumati.

— with comm. and Bengali trs., Calcutta, 1927.

— ed. R.Chattopadhyaya (with Bengali trs.), Calcutta, 1282 B.S.

Tantrāloka (Abhinavagupta) - with Skt. exposition and Eng. Intro., ed. Dvivedi and Rastogi, 8 vols., Delhi, 1986.

Tāntrika Abhidhāna, Calcutta, 1910.

Tārābhakti-sudhārṇava—*Tāntrika Texts*, XXI, Calcutta, 1941.

—ed. Bhattacharya, Delhi, 1983.

Tārārahasya (Brahmānanda Giri) — ed. P.C. Pal and others, Calcutta, 1948 V.S.

J. Vidyasagara, Calcutta, 1896.

— ed. P. Sastri, Calcutta, 1313 B.S.

Tārārahasya-vṛtti (Gauḍīya Śaṃkara) — Varendra Research Museum, Rajshahi (Bangladesh), 1961.

Tripurā-rahasya—Jñānakāṇḍa, ed. G. Kaviraj.

—with Śrīnivāsa's *Tātparya* comm., Varanasi, 1965.

Tripurāsāra-samuccaya (Nāgabhaṭṭa)—with Skt. comm. of Govindācārya, Varanasi.

Nārada-pañcarātra — ed. K.M. Banerji, Calcutta, 1965; trs. into English in *SBH* , Vol. 23, 1921.

(Tantrokta) *Nityapūjā-paddhati*—Compiled by Jaganmohana Taralalamkara, Calcutta, 1378 B.S.

Nityāṣoḍaśī— part of *Vāmakeśvara-tantra (infra)*, *Kārṇava*, with comm., Varanasi, 1968.

Nīlatantra, ptd. in *Tantratara* by K. Bhattacharya, Calcutta, 1877-84.

Paraśurāma-kalpasūtra—with comm. of Rāmeśvara, ed. S.Y. Sastri Dave, Baroda, 1950.

Puraścaraṇa-bodhinī — compiled by H. Tagore, Calcutta, 1895.

Puraścaraṇa-ratnākara—compiled by M.K. Bhattacharya, Calcutta, 1360 B.S.

Prapañcasāra-tantra—ed. T. Vidyaratna, *Tāntrika Texts*, III, 1914.

Prāṇatoṣiṇī (or, *-tosinī*)—ed. Vasumati (with Intro.), Calcutta, 1335 B.S.

Bīja-nighaṇṭu (Bhairava)—ed. A. Avalon, *Tāntrika Texts*, I.
Bṛhad-brahma-saṃhitā—ASS, No. 68.
Bṛhannīla-tantra—ed. M. Kaul, 1984.
Mantramahodadhi (Mahīdhara) -with Skt. comm., Bombay, 1983.
—with *Naukā* comm. and Eng. Intro., ed. J.W. Dejong, Canberra, 3 vols. together.
Mantrābhidhāna (Part of *Rudrayāmala*, q.v.)—ed. Avalon, *Tāntrika Texts*, I.
Mahānirvāṇa-tantra — ed. Ādi Brāhma Samāja, Calcutta, 1876.
— Eng. trs. by M.N. Dutta, Calcutta.
— Eng. trs. by A.Avalon, London, 1913. (Tantra of the Great Liberation, with Intro. and Comm.).
Mātṛkā-nighaṇṭu (Mahīdhara and Mādhava) — ed. A. Avalon, *Tāntrika Texts*, I.
Mātṛkābheda-tantra—ed. R.K. Rai, Varanasi, 1983.
Mālinī-vijayottara-tantra—ed. M. Kaul, Delhi, 1981.
Mudrānighaṇṭu (from *Vāmakeśvara-tantra*) — ed. A. Avalon, *Tāntrika Texts*, I.
Yoginī-hrdaya (ch. 6-8 of Nityaṣoḍaśikārṇava)—with Amṛtānanda's *Dīpikā* and Bhāskara's *Setubandha*, ed. G. Kaviraj, Varanasi, 1963.
Yoginī-tantra—ed. B.N. Sastri, 1982; ed. B. Sastri (with Eng. intro.), ed. R. Chattopadhyay.
Rahasyapūjā-paddhati—compiled by Jñānendra Tantraratan, Calcutta, 1374 B.S.
Rādhātantra—ed. K. Mukhopadhyaya, Calcutta, 1383 B.S.
Rāghavadīpikā—Viśvadeva Ācārya.
Rudrayāmala-tantra—with Hindi exposition, Bombay, 1983.
—Uttaratantra, ed. J. Vidyasagar, Calcutta, 1937.
—ed. R.K. Rai, Varanasi, 1986.
Lalitā-sahasra-nāma—ed. V. Krishnamacharya, Adyar, 1959.
—with Bhāskara's exposition, Eng. trs. and notes, Adyar, (3rd. ed.), 1951.
Vāmakeśvara-tantra — ASS, 56, 1908.
Vijñānabhairava—with Eng. trs. J. Singh.
—with Kṣemarāja's comm. (up to V. 23) and Śivopādhyāya's comm. and notes, ed. M.R. Sastri, 1918.
—with Ānandabhairava's comm. and notes, ed. M.R. Sastri, Kashmir Skt. Series, No. 9, 1918.

Vināsikha-tantra (Śaiva Tantra of Left current)
—with Intro., Eng. trs., notes, index of verses and words, in Roman script, ed. T. Goudriaan, Delhi, 1985.
Śaktibhāṣya (on Brahmasūtra) by P. Tarkaratna, I, Calcutta, Śaka 1859; II, Calcutta,1861.
Śakti-saṃgama-tantra—ed. B. Bhattacharya, I, III, Baroda, 1932-47; Sundarīkhaṇḍa and Chinnamastā-khaṇḍa pub. separately, Summary by R.D. Shukla.
Śākta Upaniṣads, ed. A.G.K. Warri, Adyar, Madras.
Śāktānanda-taraṅgiṇī (Brahmānanda Giri)—ed. P. Sastri (with Bengali. trs.), 1349 B.S.
— ed. R. Chattopadhyaya, *Vividha-tantra-saṃgraha*, Calcutta, 1881-86.
Śāradātilaka (Lakṣmaṇa Deśika)—Contents analysed by A. Ewing, *JAOS*, 23, 1902, ed. with comm. by M.J. Bakshi, Varanasi, 1963.
— ed. Woodroffe, Adyar, 1937, with comm. and Eng. trs., Madras.
— ed. N. Brown, with Eng. trs., Harvard, 1958.
Śilācakrartha-bodhinī — compiled by H. Tagore, Calcutta,1298 B.S.
Śivasūtra (Vasugupta)—with five comms., ed. K. Sagar. Ed. J.C. Chatterji with Kallaṭa's comm. (included in Śivasūtra-vartika of Bhāskara).
Śyāmārahasya—ed. S. Tirthanath, Bengali, trs., Calcutta, 1389 B.S.
Śrītattva-cintāmaṇi (Pūrṇānanda)—CSS No. 19; tr. ed. by B.M. Samkhyatirtha and C. Bhattacharya, with intro. by R. C. Bagchi, Calcutta, 1936.
Ṣaṭcakra-nirūpaṇa (Part of *Śrītattva-cintāmaṇi*)—of the many eds., the most noteworthy is that by T. Vidyaratna (Avalon: *Tāntrika Texts*, II, Calcutta, 1913).
— Eng. trs. by A. Avalon, *The Serpent Power*, Madras, 1924.
Sarvānanda-taraṅgiṇī—several eds. pub. since 1882.
Sarvollāsa, ed. R.M. Chakravarti, Comilla (Bangladesh), 1941, with intro. by G. Kaviraj.
Sāttvata-saṃhita—with Skt. comm., ed. Trivedi, Varanasi—ed. Ananthachariyar, Conjeevaram,1902.
Sādhanamālā — GOS, Vols. I, II, Baroda, 1968.
Sulabha-tantra-prakāśa—Calcutta, 1887.
Saundarya-laharī (attributed to Śaṃkarācārya)—ed. (with comm. and Eng. trs., Woodroffe, Adyar, 1937).
— ed. N. Brown, with Eng. trs., Harvard, 1958.
Spandakārikā (Kallaṭa's *vṛtti* and Bhāskara's *Śivasūtra-vṛtti* ed. J.C. Chatterji, Varanasi, 1916.

Svacchanda-tantra—with Kṣemarāja's comm., Vols I-VI, 1921-25.

Haṭhayoga-pradīpikā (Svātmārāma)—with *Jyotsnā* comm. and Eng. trs., ed., S. Iyengar, new ed., Adyar. Eng. trs. by P. Singh, Delhi, 1881.

Haratattva-dīdhiti (H.K. Tagore), Calcutta, 1881.

Hevajra-tantra — ed. D.L. Snellgrove, with trs. 2 Pts. London, 1959.

BOOKS IN ENGLISH

Allan : *Catalogue of Gupta Coins*, LXXXIII.

Avalon, A. (John Woodroffe) : *Principles of Tantra*, Madras, 1960. (Eng. trs. of the *Tantra-tattva* by Shiv Chandra Vidyārṇava).

: Intro. to *Kaulajñāna-nirṇaya*, Calcutta, 1934.

: *Shakti* and *Shākta*, Madras, 8th ed. 1975.

: *The Great Liberation*, Madras, 1963.

: *The World as Power*, Madras, 1957.

: *The Garland of Letters*, Madras, 1955.

: Intro. to *Tantraśāstra*, Madras, 1952.

: *Serpent Power*, Madras, 1958.

: *Wave of Bliss* (Eng. trs. of *Ānanda-laharī*, first 49 verses of *Saundarya-laharī* and comments), 1917.

: *Wave of Beauty* (Eng. trs. of *Saundarya-laharī*, with text and comm.), Madras, 1957.

: *Mahāmāyā*, 1953.

Bagchi, P.C. : *Studies in Tantras*, Pt. I, Calcutta, 1939.

Bagchi, S. : *Eminent Indian Śākta Pīṭhas*, etc. in the background of the *Pīṭhas* of Kālighāṭ, Vakreśwar and Kāmākhyā, Calcutta, 1988.

Bajpai, I. : *The Philosophy of Tantrāloka* (Ahnika 1-3 with Eng. trs.), 1971.

Banerji, J.N. : *Purāṇic and Tāntric Religion*, Calcutta, 1966.

: *Development of Hindu Iconography*, Calcutta, 1956.

Banerji, S.C. : *A Brief History of Tantra Literature*, Calcutta, 1988.

Barth, A. : *The Religions of India*, London, 1889.

Basu, M. : *Tantras, a General Study*, Calcutta, 1976.

: *Fundamentals of the Philosophy of Tantras*, Calcutta, 1986.

Bernard, T. : *Haṭhayoga*, London, 1950.

Bhandarkar : *Collected Works*, Vol. IV.

Bharati, A : *Tāntric Tradition*, London, 1965.

Bhattacharya, B. : *Sādhanamālā*, Baroda, 1968.

: Intro. to *Buddhist Esoterism*, Oxford, 1932.

Bhattacharyya, N.N. : *History of Tāntric Religion*, New Delhi, 1987.
: *History of Śākta Religion*, New Delhi, 1974.
: *The Indian Mother Goddess*, 2nd ed., New Delhi, 1977.
Bhattashali, N.K. : *Iconography of the Buddhist and Brahmanical Sculptures in the Dacca Museum*, Dacca, 1929.
Bose and Haldar: *Tantras—their philosophy and occult secrets*, Calcutta, 1956.
Bose, N.K. : *Canons of Orissan Architecture.*
Brahma, N.K. : *Philosophy of Hindu Sādhana*, Calcutta, 1932.
Chakravarti, C.: *The Tantras — studies on their religion and literature*, Calcutta, 1963.
Chakravarti, P.C. : *Śakti in Indian Literature*, Calcutta.
Chatterji, K.K. : *The History of Dakṣineśvar Kālī Temple.*
Chattopadhyay, A. : *Atiśa and Tibet*, Calcutta, 1967.
Chen, C.M. : *Discrimination between Buddhist and Hindu Tantras.*
Chinmoy : *Kuṇḍalinī, the Mother Power*, 1974.
Colaabavala, F.D. : *Tantra, the Erotic Cult.*
Cunningham : *Archaeological Survey Report*, IX.
Dacca University : *History of Bengal*, I, p. 421 (P.C. Bagchi, *Religion of Bengal*).
Das Gupta, S.B. : *Obscure Religious Cults*, Calcutta, 1946.
: *Intro. to Tāntrik Buddhism*, Calcutta, 1950.
Das Gupta, S.N. : *A History of Indian Philosophy*, Vol. III, Indian ed., New Delhi, 1988.
Datta, A.K. : *Bhāratvarṣīya Upāsak Sampradāy.*
De, S.K. : *Bengali Literature in the Nineteenth Century*, Calcutta, 1962.
Desai, D. : *Erotic Sculptures of India*, New Delhi, 1975.
Douglas, N. : *Tantrayoga*, Delhi, 1971.
Eliot : *Hinduism and Buddhism*, in 3 Vols., Vol. II, London, 1957.
Farquhar, J.N.: *Outline of the Religious Literature of India*, London, 1968.
Filliozat, J. : *Classical Doctrine of Indian Medicine*, Delhi, 1964.
Frazer, J.G. : *Adonis Attis Osiris*, London, 1907.
Garrison, O. : *Tantra—The Yoga of Sex*, New York, 1964.
Ghosh, Aravinda: *The Life Divine*, 1939.
: *The Mother.*
Guenther, H.V.: *Yuganaddha, the Tāntrik view of life*, Benares, 1964.
: *The Tāntric view of life*, Berkeley and London, 1972.
Hastings : *Encyclopaedia of Religion and Ethics.*

Hazra, R.C. : *Studies in Purāṇic Records*, etc., Dacca, 1940.

Jacobs, H. : *Western psycho-therapy and Hindu sādhana*, London, 1961.

Kaviraj, G.N. : Śākta Philosophy, *History of Philosophy, Eastern & Western*, ed. Radhakrishnan, London, 1952-53.

: Some Aspects of the Philosophy of Śākta Tantra, Varanasi, 1967.

Khanna, M. : *Yantra*, London, 1979.

Krishna, G. : *Biological Basis of Religion and Genius.*

Leedbeater, C.W. : *The Cakras*, Adyar, 1927.

Lessing and Wayman : *Intro. to Buddhist Tāntric System*, Delhi, 1983.

Lhalungpa, L.P. (Trs.) :*The Life of Milarepa*, Boulder, Colorado, 1982.

Mookerji, A. : *Tantra Art*, Basel, 1966.

: *Tantra Āsana*, Basel, New York, 1971.

: *Kālī, the Feminine Force*, London, 1988.

: *Kuṇḍalinī*, Delhi, 1982.

Nath, R.G. : *The Yogīs of Bengal*, Calcutta, 1909.

Neumann, E. : *The Great Mother*, New York, 1961.

Pandit, M.P. : *Lights on the Tantra*, Madras, 1968.

: *Studies in the Tantras and the Veda*, Madras, 1967.

: *Gems from the Tantras*, Madras, 1967.

: *Aurobindo on the Tantra*, Madras.

: *Kuṇḍalinī-yoga*, Madras.

Payne, E.: *The Shāktas. An Introduction and Comparative Study*, Calcutta, 1938.

Pott, P. : *Yoga and Tantra*, Leiden, 1966.

Radhakrishnan, S. : *History of Philosophy, Eastern and Western*, Vol. I (Exposition of Śākta belief by G. Kaviraj), London, 1952.

Rao, T.A.G. : *Elements of Hindu Iconography*, Vol. I, Pt. ii, Madras, 1914 (For Kali image).

Rastogi, N. : *Kālī as a Metaphysical Concept in the Krama System of Kashmir*, 1986.

: *Introduction to the Tantrāloka*, Delhi, 1987.

R.K. Mission, Calcutta : *Cultural Heritage of India*, Vol. III (pt. 111 - Philosophy of Tantras); 1953 vol. IV (Pt. 1 - Evolution of Tantras, etc.), 1956.

Rele, V.G. : *Mysterious Kuṇḍalinī*, Bombay, 1921.

Rolland, R. : *Rāmkrishna.*

Sastri, H. : *Origin and Cult of Tārā*, Calcutta, 1925.

Sastry, K. : *The Veda and the Tantra*, Madras, 1951.

Saunders, E.D. : *Mudrā*, London, 1966.
Schrader, F.O. : *Intro. to the Pañcarātra and the Ahirbudhnya Saṃhitā*, Adyar, Madras, 1916.
Shah, P.R. : *Tantra, its therapeutic Aspect*, Calcutta, 1987.
Singh, L.P. : *Tantra, its mystic and scientific basis*, Delhi, 1976.
Sinha, A.K. : *Science and Tantrayoga*. Kuruksetra, 1981.
Sinha, J. : *Shākta Monism, Cult of Shakti.*
Sircar, D.C. : *The Shākta Pīṭhas*, Calcutta, 1960.
:*Shakti Cult and Tārā*, Calcutta, 1960.
Tagore, R.N. : *The Religion of Man*, 1930.
Thomas, E.J. : *History of Buddhist Thought*, 1953 (Reprint).
Thompson and Spencer: *Bengali Religious Lyrics* — Śākta (Heritage of India Series).
Tucci, G. : *Theory and Practice of Maṇḍala*, London, 1961.
Vira, R.V., Taki, S. : *A Dictionary of Secret Tāntric Syllabic Code*, Lahore, 1938.
Wall, O.A. : *Sex and Sex-worship*, London, 1919.
Wilson, H.H. : *Works*, II.
Winternitz, M. : *A History of Indian Literature*, Vol. I, Calcutta, 1927.
Woodroffe, J. : See A. Avalon.
Zimmer, H. : *Philosophy of India*, London, 1951.

PAPERS IN ENGLISH

ABORI, X, 1930 (article by B. Bhattacharya).
ABORI, IX, XV (articles by R.C. Hazra).
Do (Diamond Jubilee Vol.)—S.A. Dange's article—Sex in Stone etc.
Adyar Library Bulletin, XXI (article by C. Chakravarti).
Cultural Heritage of India, Vol. III, Calcutta, 1953 (article on Tantra by Pratyagatmananda). Vol. IV (article on Shākta Worship, etc., by C. Chakravarti), 1956.
IHQ, IX, 1933 (article by R.C. Hazra).
IHQ, VI, X, XXVII (articles by C. Chakravarti).
IHQ, Sep. 1951 (Śākta festivals of Bengal and their antiquity).
IHQ, XXXII, 1956 (article on Tantra by B. Bhattacharya).
JASB, Letters, XVIII.
Jha Comm. Vol. (articles on Tantra by C. Chakravarti).
Journal of Asiatic Society of Bangladesh, XVIII, No.1 (Baul Poets on Chāri Chandra by H.C. Paul).

JRAS, 1910 (On Tantras in Malabar).
K.B. Pathak Comm. Vol. (article by C. Chakravarti).
New Indian Antiquary, I (articles on Buddhist Tantra by S.K. De), 1938; VII, Nos. 5 and 6, 1944 (article on Gopāla Nyāyapañcānana by S.C. Banerji)

BOOKS IN BENGALI

[In English alphabetical order, Titles of works are written as they are pronounced.]

The *Bhāratakoṣa*, published by Vangiya Sahitya Parisat, Calcutta, and the *Sāhityika Varṣapañjī*, published by Pustak Vipani, Calcutta, may be consulted as reference books.
Basu, S.P. : *Niveditā Lokamātā*, Vol. I, Calcutta, 1971.
Bhattacharya, H. : *Hinduder Devdevī*, Calcutta, I, 2nd ed. 1982, II, 1978, III, 1980.
Bhattacharya, A. : *Vāṃlā Maṅgal Kāvyer Itihās*, Calcutta, 1964.
Bhaumik, H. : *Kālīkṣetra-dīpikā*, Calcutta.
Brahmachari, T.P. : *Tāntrik Sādhanā O Tantrakāhinī*, Calcutta, 1381 B.S.
Chakravarti, J. : *Śākta-padāvalī O Śakti-sādhanā*, Calcutta, 1382 B.S. (5th ed.).
Chakravarti, C. : *Tantrakathā*, Calcutta, 1362 B.S.
Chakravarti, N.: *Ūnaviṃśa Śatābdīr Kavioyālā O Bāṃlā Sāhitya*, Calcutta, 1880 Saka.
Chakravarti, S : *Mehārer Sarvānanda*, Calcutta.
Chakravarti, D. : Ed. *Ādyāpīṭher Ṭhākur Śrī Śrī Annodār Kathā O Gān*.
Chatterji, J.N. : Vāmākhyāpā.
Chattopadhyay, P. : *Tantrābhilāṣīr Sādhusaṅga*, Calcutta, 1983.
Das, U.K. : *Śāstramūlak Bhāratīya Śakti-sādhanā*, 2 vols., Birbhum, 1373 B.S.
Das Gupta, S.B. : *Bhārater Śakti-sādhanā O Śākta-Sāhitya*, Calcutta, 1365 B.S.
Das Gupta, Nalini : *Bāṅgalāy Bauddha-dharma*.
Gangopadhyay, B. : *Mahāpīṭh Tārāpīṭh*, Calcutta.
Ganguli, H.C. : *Śrī Vamalita I, II*, Calcutta, 1340 B.S.
Ghosh, B. : *Paścim Vaṅger Saṃskṛti*, Calcutta, 1957.
Gupta, Mahendra (Srīma): *Śrī Śrī Rāmakṛṣṇa-kathāmṛta*, 5 Vols. Calcutta, 1904-1932.

Kaviraj, G. : *Tantra O Āgamśāstrer Digdarśan*, Calcutta, 1963.
: *Tāntrik Vāṅmay men Śākta-dṛṣṭi*, Patna, 1963 (Hindi). *Tāntrik Sādhanā O Siddhānta*. vol. I, Burdwan, 1983 (2nd ed.), II (2nd ed.), 1983.
Lahidi, D. : ed. *Vāṅgālīr Gān*, Calcutta, 1312 B.S.
Majumdar, R.C.: *Vāṃlā Deśer Itihās*, Madhyayug (chs. 12, 13), Calcutta, 1373 B.S.
Mallik, K. : *Nātha Saṃpradāyer Itihas*, etc., Calcutta, 1950.
Mukherji, A.C.: *Ardhakālī*.
Mukhopadhyay, B.N.:*Śaktir Rūp, Bhārate O Madhya Eśiyāy*, Calcutta, 1990.
Mukhopadhyay, Sitanath: *Prācīn Kavioyālār Gān*, Calcutta.
Nag, K. : *Svadeś O Sabhyatā*.
Nandi, S. : *Kālī-rahasya*, Calcutta.
Nigudhananda : *Khuñje Phiri Kuṇḍalinī*, Calcutta.
: *Mahātīrtha Ekānnapīṭher Sandhāne*, Calcutta.
: *Ekānnapīṭher Sādhak*, Calcutta.
: *Śaktikṣetra Cavvis Upapīṭher Sandhāne*, Calcutta.
Nivedita : *Svāmijīke Yerūp Dekhiyāchi* (trs. by Svāmī Mādhavānanda), Calcutta, 1983.
Omkarnath, Sitaramdas: *Māṭṛgāthā*, 1372 B.S.
Prajñānānanda : *Bhāratīya Saṃgīter Itihās*, Calcutta, I, Calcutta, 1961 (2nd ed.) II, (1st half), Calcutta, 1978, (3rd ed.), II, (2nd half), 1979, (3rd ed.).
Rāmprasāder Granthāvalī—Basumati Sahitya Mandir, Calcutta.
Ray, Diptimay : *Paścim Vaṅger Kālī O Kālīkṣetra*, Calcutta.
: *Tantra-tattva-praveśikā*, Calcutta, 1395 B.S.
: *Tantra-tattva O Sādhanā*, Calcutta.
Ray, A. : *Śāktapadāvalī*, Calcutta.
(Svami) Saradananda : *Gītātattva O Bhārate Śaktipūjā*, Calcutta 1983.
Sarasvati, S. : *Pāl Yuger Citrakalā*, Calcutta, 1378 B.S.
Sarkar, M. : *Tantrer Ālo*, Calcutta, 1354 B.S.
Sastri, S. : *Tantraparicay*, Santiniketan, 1359 B.S.
: Saṃskṛtānuśilane Ravindranāth, Calcutta, 1984.
Satyadev : *Sādhan Samar*.
Sen, K.M. : *Bāṃlār Sādhanā*, 1352 B.S.
: *Bāṃlār Bāül*.
Sen, Sukumar : *Vaṅgabhūmikā*, Calcutta, 1974.
Sengupta, A. : *Paramapuruṣa Rāmakṛṣṇa*, Calcutta, 1358 B.S.

Siddhantabhushan : *Kaulamārgarahasya*, Calcutta, 1335 B.S.
Svami. S.N. : *Tāntrik Abhidhān*, Calcutta, 1910 B.S.
Vandyopadhyay, J.N.: *Pañcopasanā*, Calcutta, 1960.
Vandyopadhyaya, Sures Chandra : *Saṃgītaratnākara* (Bengali translation), 1379 B.S.
: *Smṛtiśāstra Vāṅgāli*, Calcutta, 1368 B.S.
: *Saṃskṛta Sāhitye Vāṅgāḷī Dan*, Calcutta, 1369 B.S.
: *Śaktiraṅga-vaṅgabhūmi*, Calcutta, 1398 B.S.
Vidyarnava, S.C. : *Tantratattva*, I, Calcutta, 1317 B.S.

PAPERS IN BENGALI

Ānandabājār Patrikā, Calcutta (Bengali daily), 13.9.81.
Ārati, Bengali journal, Vaiśākh, 1314 B.S.
Baṅgīya Sāhitya Pariṣat Patrikā, Calcutta, vols. 58, 59 (Article by C. Chakravarti), vol. 62, No. 3 (articles by R. Tarkatirtha).
Deś, Calcutta (Bengali weekly) , 27.2.82 (p. 9), 24.4.82 (p. 3), 8.5.82 (p. 3), 15.5.82 (p. 3), 10.7.82 (p. 6), 17.7.82 (p. 5),17.10.87 (Kālidevir Mūrtitattva by B.N. Mukherji).
Devayāna (Monthly journal), vol. vii. no. 4 (article by Dinesh Bhattacharya).
Sāhitya Pariṣat Patrikā, Calcutta, Vol. 45, pp. 222-231; Vol. 46, p. 80.
Viśvabhāratī Patrikā, Māgh-Caitra, 1362 B.S. (article by S.B. Dasgupta).

CATALOGUES OF MANUSCRIPTS

Bodleian Catalogue, I, by T. Aufrecht.
Catalogue of Palm-leaf and Selected Paper MSS. in Durbar Library, Nepal, by H.P. Sastri, Calcutta, 1905.
Catalogue of Skt. MSS in Asiatic Society, Calcutta, Vol. VIII.
Des. Cat of Skt. MSS. in Govt. Oriental MSS. Library, Madras, by M. Rangacharya, Vols. XII, XIII.
India Office Catalogue, IV, by Eggeling.
Notices of Sanskrit MSS., 2nd Series, by H.P. Sastri, Calcutta 1900.

BOOKS IN HINDI

Dvivedi, H.P. : Nātha Saṃpradāya, 1966.
Kaviraj, G : *Tāntrik Vāṅmay men Śākta=dṛṣṭi*, Patna, 1963.
: *Tantra Aur Āgamśāstra kā digdarśan* (Trs. by Tiwari), Varanasi.
: *Tāntrik Sādhanā Aur Siddhānta* (Trs. by Tiwari), Varanasi.
: *Tāntrik Sāhitya*, Varanasi.
: *Bhāratīya Saṃskṛti Aur Sādhanā*, Varanasi.

Index